# Closing the Golden Door

# Closing the Golden Door

Asian Migration and the Hidden History of
Exclusion at Ellis Island

· · · · · · · · · · · · · · · · · · · · · · · · · · · · · · · · · · · · · · · · · · · · · · · · · · · · · · ·

ANNA PEGLER-GORDON

The University of North Carolina Press  Chapel Hill

Set in Charis by Westchester Publishing Services
Manufactured in the United States of America

The University of North Carolina Press has been a member
of the Green Press Initiative since 2003.

Library of Congress Cataloging-in-Publication Data
Names: Pegler-Gordon, Anna, 1968– author.
Title: Closing the golden door : Asian migration and the hidden history
    of exclusion at Ellis Island / Anna Pegler-Gordon.
Other titles: Asian migration and the hidden history of exclusion
    at Ellis Island
Description: Chapel Hill : University of North Carolina Press, 2021. |
    Includes bibliographical references and index.
Identifiers: LCCN 2021041589 | ISBN 9781469665726 (cloth ; alk. paper) |
    ISBN 9781469665696 (pbk. ; alk. paper) | ISBN 9781469665733 (ebook)
Subjects: LCSH: Ellis Island Immigration Station (N.Y. and N.J.)—History. |
    Asians—Migrations—United States—History—20th century. |
    Immigrants—United States—History—20th century. | Alien detention
    centers—United States—History—20th century.
Classification: LCC JV6484 .P43 2021 | DDC 325.747/1—dc23
LC record available at https://lccn.loc.gov/2021041589

Cover illustration: East Coast of the United States labelled in Chinese. Detail
from Map NAID 4726132; Office for Emergency Management, Office of War
Information, Overseas Operations Branch; Posters, Pamphlets, Booklets, and
Publications, ca. 1942–ca. 1945; Records of the Office of War Information,
1926–1951, Record Group 208, Box 6, Entry 462A; National Archives at
College Park, College Park, MD.

Chapter 4 previously appeared in another form as "Shanghaied on the Streets
of Hoboken: Chinese Exclusion and Maritime Regulation," *Journal for
Maritime Research* 16, no. 2 (2014). Much of chapter 5 previously appeared as
"'New York has a Concentration Camp of its Own': Japanese Confinement on
Ellis Island during World War II," *Journal of Asian American Studies* 20, no. 3
(October 2017).

*For Maya and Naomi*

# Contents

# Illustrations, Map, Tables

## Illustrations

## Map

## Tables

# Acknowledgments

This project started in the Bob Hope Memorial Library at the Ellis Island National Museum of Immigration while I was working on my first book. In conversation, Barry Moreno commented on the lack of scholarship regarding Chinese at Ellis Island. It was an offhand observation, but it led me to years of research and rethinking. My deep thanks to Barry for all his work documenting the history of Ellis Island and to George Tselos and the late Jeffrey Dosik, also of the Bob Hope Memorial Library.

My research was not only sparked but also sustained by dedicated librarians and archivists. Most centrally, I appreciate the extraordinary work of the staff at the National Archives and Records Administration in New York City: Kelly McAnnaney, Bonnie Sauer, Matthew Aull, Katie Daniels, Kevin Reilly, Carol Savo, Angela Tudico, and Trina Yeckley. At the National Archives in Washington, D.C., my research was supported by George Briscoe and William Creech, along with others engaged in locating and screening files. And at Archives II in College Park, Maryland, by Lynne Goodsell, Holly Reed, and many others in the Textual Records and Still Photographs divisions. Closer to home, I have relied on librarians at Michigan State University for support in my research, teaching, and learning. In particular, I want to acknowledge Leslie Behm, Julia Ezzo, Kristen Mapes, and Emilia Marcyk. Thanks especially to Jeffrey Evans, Amanda Tickner, and Kasey Wilson, who created the map of Asian routes to Ellis Island, and Jingyi Zhang at the Center for Statistical Training and Consulting, who provided much-needed statistical assistance. At the Library of Congress, I was lucky to work with Remé-Antonia Grefalda, founding director of the library's Asian and Pacific Islander Collection. At the Museum of the Chinese in America, New York, my research was ably assisted by Samantha Chin Wolner. At the History Office and Library of U.S. Citizenship and Immigration Services, Marian Smith and Zack Wilske answered many, many questions. I was also assisted by other dedicated librarians and archivists, including at the Brooke Russell Astor Reading Room for Rare Books and Manuscripts, New York Public Library; the Columbia University Rare Book and Manuscript Library; and the Japanese American National Museum, Los Angeles.

Financially, my research was supported by Celia Vlasin, as part of the Vlasin Family Fellowship, the James Madison College Faculty Development Fund, and the Humanities and Arts Research Program, all at Michigan State University.

Washington, D.C., and New York City are expensive cities in which to conduct research. I am very lucky to have friends and family who were willing to accommodate me while I was visiting archives and libraries. Claudia Malloy and Chris Kleponis have been the most generous hosts and the best of friends as I spent weeks in D.C. over a period of years. My brother- and sister-in-law, Mark and Pat Gordon, were equally generous with their home in New York City. Mark passed away after I completed my research for this project. I am so grateful for the coffee, waffles, and company sitting in their kitchen, and so glad that I stayed to help complete the crossword when I should have been in the archives.

At Michigan State University, I have continued to find purpose in my work thanks to my students, colleagues, and friends. Teaching in the James Madison College, an undergraduate residential college of public affairs, and the Asian Pacific American Studies Program, I work with students who care about the past and the ways that we learn about the past today. But they care even more deeply about the future. I want to acknowledge all my students. Working with them in the classroom and outside the classroom has been the greatest joy of my scholarly life. In particular, my undergraduate research assistants spent hours poring over Annual Reports of the Commissioner General of Immigration, case files, newspaper articles, and passenger lists. Thank you to Lauren Abrahamson, Eleanor Bell, Daniel Davis, William Hack, Ian Hoopingarner, Courtney Heyse, Olivia Macy Rose, Cecilia Tang, and Salena Thompson. Special thanks to GlenEllen Lehmberg and Liz Witcher for their research work at the National Archives, to Jonathan Suan for his detailed newspaper research on both this and my next project, and to graduate student Scott Bullock for his insightful observations on the manuscript.

In the James Madison College and the Asian Pacific American Studies program, I have benefited from extraordinary colleagues who care for one another and for our students. Across and outside of Michigan State University, I have also played a small part in a band of survivors, supporters, students, and parents who have tried and tried and tried again—sometimes failing and sometimes succeeding—to make our institution more transparent, accountable, just, and safe for all. In this work, Andaluna Borcila has been a steadfast partner and brilliant collaborator. I owe a special measure of friendship and debt of gratitude to Kirsten Fermaglich, Andrea Louie, Terese Guinsatao Monberg, Mindy Morgan, and Naoko Wake. Terese deserves mention for first suggesting that the article I was writing about Asians at Ellis Island might, in fact, be a book. And Kirsten, in various tea shops and coffee shops throughout the years, read more versions of this work than anyone. I appreciate so much our working and writing together.

The longer I teach, the more I realize my intellectual debts to Robert G. Lee and George Sánchez, who helped me look away from Ellis Island as I explored my interests in Asian migration and immigration policy for my first book, only to have me turn my attention eastward again. Jack and Audrey Isbester are some of my oldest friends and best teachers about activism and ships. At conferences and presentations and in conversations, I have benefited from the generous insights, warmth, and thoughtfulness of many colleagues and friends, including Jason O. Chang, Roger Daniels, Manan Desai, Larry Hashima, Evelyn Hu-DeHart, Madeline Hsu, Richard Kim, Erika Lee, Josephine Lee, Beth Lew-Williams, Daryl Maeda, Mae Ngai, Ethan Segal, and K. Scott Wong. At the manuscript stage, I benefited enormously from the insights and guidance of my editor, Mark Simpson-Vos, as well as Grace Elizabeth Hale, Cate Hodorowicz, and Dominique Moore. Thank you also to Anita Mannur and the anonymous reviewers at the *Journal of Asian American Studies*, the *Journal for Maritime Research*, and the University of North Carolina Press. Sadly, Judy Yung passed away much too young in December 2020. I did not know her well, but benefited from her encouragement throughout my career and her pathbreaking scholarship on both Angel and Ellis Islands.

As always, my family is my safe harbor: Maggie Pegler; Lorna Pegler, Simon, Roma, and Rive Allix; Claire, Matilda, and Scout Pegler; Ellen Assad, Toby, David, Isaac, and Henry Pegler; Felice Gordon; Joel, Eli, and Talia Gordon; Pat, Bernard, Jen, and Dora Gordon; Rebecca and Bud Coulson. And friends as close as family: Deb Gordon-Gurfinkel and Elli Gurfinkel, Rebecca O'Connell, and Sarah Weatherall. This is where I choose to shelter, even through hard losses and changing tides.

After thirty years of marriage, Neil is still the person who supports me best and makes me laugh the most. By the time this book is in print, both of our daughters, who had not started high school when I began this project, will have left home on their own journeys. I am not sure if that is because of how slowly I write or how quickly they grow up. But I am looking forward to following their paths and forging a new path with Neil.

As I have settled into a secure place in middle age and middle America, I cannot turn away from the fact that so many people's lives have been upended. These are hard times for those who seek security, new opportunities, or to rejoin their families in the United States. My own experience of immigration was threaded through with my privilege as a white, college-educated, native English speaker with an opportunity to legally enter the United States. But it was still riven with uncertainty, inefficiency, and sometimes stunningly incompetent bureaucracy. As I lived in different locations while applying for permanent residence then citizenship status, the local office where I made these applications made a difference. These differences inform this book. I became a U.S. citizen in 1996, at another moment of significant anti-immigrant activism. As I talked with other new citizens after the ceremony, most of us agreed that a key motivation for becoming a citizen was never having to deal with the Immigration and Naturalization Service (INS) again. However, far too few immigrants have this option. They deal with the threat of one of the agencies carved out of the INS, Immigration and Customs Enforcement, every day. Each new anti-immigrant movement pushes the outside edges of extremism. As I teach my students, these are exceptional times in the history of immigration enforcement. They demand an extraordinary effort from all of us to make change.

Closing the Golden Door

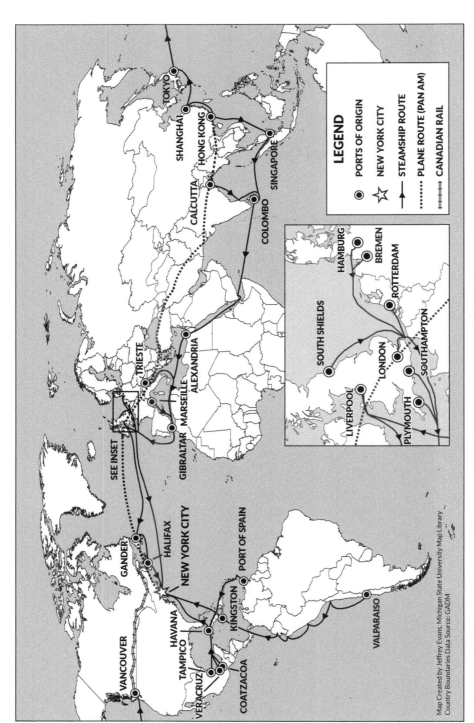

LEGEND

PORTS OF ORIGIN
NEW YORK CITY
STEAMSHIP ROUTE
PLANE ROUTE (PAN AM)
CANADIAN RAIL

TOKYO
SHANGHAI
HONG KONG
CALCUTTA
SINGAPORE
COLOMBO

SOUTH SHIELDS
HAMBURG
BREMEN
ROTTERDAM
LONDON
SOUTHAMPTON
LIVERPOOL
PLYMOUTH

TRIESTE
GIBRALTAR
MARSEILLE
ALEXANDRIA

SEE INSET

GANDER
HALIFAX
NEW YORK CITY
PORT OF SPAIN
KINGSTON
HAVANA
TAMPICO
VERACRUZ
COATZACOA
VALPARAISO
VANCOUVER

Map Created by Jeffrey Evans, Michigan State University Map Library
Country Boundaries Data Source: GADM

Asian immigrants' routes to Ellis Island.

# Introduction

## Locating Ellis Island in Asian American History

. . . . . . . . . . . . . . . . . . . . . . . . . . . . . . . . . . . . . . . . . . . . . . .

October 25, 1919. A sailor stood on the balcony of the Ellis Island immigration station and looked across New York's harbor at the Statue of Liberty. A subject of the Portuguese colony of Goa on the west coast of India, he was well educated and had read about New York and the United States. As he stood taking in the air with the immigration superintendent, he gestured toward the statue and asked what the word "liberty" really meant in America. His question was pointed. The statue had been gifted from France to the United States in 1884 as a symbol of shared republican ideals of liberty, but redefined by Emma Lazarus's poem as a "Mother of Exiles" who lifted her lamp in welcome "beside the golden door." The Goan sailor experienced neither liberty nor welcome. Along with thirty-four fellow Asian crew members, he was detained for ten days because he had been incorrectly listed in the ship's manifest as a passenger rather than a sailor. The white Britons who worked alongside him on the ship were not being held at Ellis Island as they were not subject to Asian exclusion laws. The Goan sailors were, according to their captain, "locked up in the ward assigned to undesirable aliens," given only three blankets and a bunk, and guarded by a police officer with a club. They had no pillows, no freedom to move about the island, and no word of when they would be released. One month later, they were still in detention.[1]

The Goan sailors, however, were not alone. They were part of a larger Asian presence at Ellis Island that has long been overlooked. Asians arrived in New York City from many points: China, Japan, Korea, India, the Philippines, Thailand, Singapore, Cuba, Trinidad, Mexico, Colombia, Peru, England, Germany, Canada, and from other regions of the United States. They traveled from east to east, from Asia to New York, often taking circuitous routes or engaging in secondary migration from the Caribbean, Latin America, Europe, and overland across Canada from western ports. They were immigrants, travelers, visiting dignitaries, elite students, ordinary laborers, U.S. citizens, sailors, and stowaways.

Edwin Levick, "View of the Immigration Station, Ellis Island (front side),"
Miriam and Ira D. Wallach Division of Art, Prints and Photographs, New York
Public Library (1902–1913).

Most Asians did not experience Ellis Island as a place of liberty, a "golden door" through which they quickly entered America. As they arrived in New York, they were subject to the same immigration laws that placed specific restrictions on immigrants of all races and nationalities. They were also inspected and interrogated under exclusion laws that prevented the entry of Asians, with limited exemptions. More than other immigrants, they were detained at the immigration station as their cases were reviewed, sometimes for days or weeks, occasionally for months or years. In addition to being detained upon their arrival, Asians were also held on the island as deportees, individuals who had lived in the United States but were being sent back to their countries of origin. During World War II, Japanese New Yorkers were held as "enemy aliens" at Ellis Island, along with German and other Axis nationals.

The experiences of Asians at Ellis Island reveal that Asian exclusion was both larger in scope and more limited in force than has previously been recognized. It was larger in scope as it reached into areas that have not traditionally been considered part of immigration policy. Historians such as

Roger Daniels and Erika Lee have demonstrated that exclusion was not incidental but central to the development of immigration policy, showing how Chinese exclusion laws shaped the implementation of racialized laws for all immigrants. Exclusion was, Daniels has argued, "the pivot on which all American immigration policy turned, the hinge on which Emma Lazarus' 'Golden Door' began to swing toward a closed position."[2] However, the policies, practices, and impacts of exclusion extended beyond immigrants and immigration policy. As this book argues, exclusion radiated beyond the regulation of immigrants to groups such as sailors, even if they never set foot in the United States, and into areas outside of immigration policy, such as Japanese internment.

At the same time, exclusion was sometimes limited in its force. Although Ellis Island was central to the immigration regulation of European arrivals, it was on the periphery of Asian exclusion. Since the 1990s, scholars of Asian American studies have realized the importance of attending to regions beyond California.[3] Mae Ngai has described this as the "de-centering of the field," as Asian Americanists look beyond histories of Chinese in San Francisco and Japanese in Los Angeles.[4] Historians have focused on the ways that exclusion was implemented on the United States' borders with Canada and Mexico, as well as at locations in the Pacific Northwest.[5] However, we know very little about how these restrictions were implemented at other ports, particularly in the eastern United States.

More recently, researchers have also considered the limits of exclusion. Historians Gordon Chang and Beth Lew-Williams have shown how early efforts to implement exclusion, pushed by U.S. representatives from California with popular support from their constituents, were constrained nationally by commercial and diplomatic concerns.[6] Lon Kurashige has explored the "two faces" of the debate around institutional anti-Asian racism, considering not only supporters of exclusion but also the "robust egalitarian opposition."[7] Madeline Hsu has considered elite Chinese migration to the United States during exclusion, emphasizing how immigration laws "not only erected *gates* barring entry to unwanted persons but also established *gateways* that permitted admission to peoples deemed assimilable but also strategic."[8] These studies focus on challenges to the passage of exclusion legislation and the ways in which this legislation was limited. *Closing the Golden Door* expands on this understanding by considering the ways such policies were also limited in their execution. At Ellis Island, as policies were implemented at the edges of exclusion, they became frayed.

## Locating Asian Exclusion

Histories of Asian exclusion have long focused on California, where anti-Chinese movements were concentrated from the beginning.[9] In 1848, the United States annexed Alta California and gold was discovered in the Sacramento Valley. White men newly arriving from the eastern United States during the Gold Rush confronted miners arriving from the coastal Guangdong region of China. Whites brought with them racist orientalist ideas about the Chinese as exotic others who did not fit traditional gender norms, were not fit for democratic self-government, and were potential vectors of Asiatic diseases. They also viewed Chinese as unfair labor competition. According to the *New York Tribune,* the common feeling among Californians was that "Chinamen swarmed in the cities, living in modes which repelled the whites from their neighborhoods and reduced rentals and values; they underbid European immigrants in many employments; and, whatever money they earned, instead of being spent, to the benefit of trade, was hoarded for a day of return to their native land."[10] As California became a state, lawmakers codified these racist understandings in the state's constitution and in statute. In debating the constitution adopted in 1849, lawmakers considered banning all Chinese migration to California but decided instead to restrict voting rights to white men. Starting in the 1850s, they also levied monthly taxes on nonwhite foreign miners and on ships bringing Chinese to California. And in 1854, the California Supreme Court ruled that Chinese, along with African Americans and Native Americans, could not testify in court.[11]

This early nativism was consolidated in the 1870s as Californians called for the complete exclusion of Chinese. At a time of economic depression, thousands of white working-class men gathered in San Francisco's vacant sandlots to protest the presence of Chinese. Demands to expel Chinese immigrants and end new immigration were captured and concentrated by Irish immigrant activist Dennis Kearney. Kearney led the loosely organized populist Workingmen's Party and ended every demonstration with the rallying cry "The Chinese Must Go!" According to one count, even if they didn't participate in rowdy protests, 99 percent of white Californians were "against Chinese immigration." As California adopted its second constitution in 1879, with more extreme anti-Chinese provisions limiting employment and confining Chinese to "prescribed portions" of towns and cities, the U.S. Congress considered national restrictions on Chinese immigration.[12]

Even before Chinese arrived in California in the 1850s, they had landed in New York. "The presence of Chinese in Atlantic world ports before the influx of Chinese in San Francisco should not be a surprise," historian Jack Tchen observes, as New York was a key trading port and China had a "centuries-long seafaring tradition."[13] Tchen estimates that by the mid-nineteenth century a small working-class community of maybe seventy Chinese men was centered in lower Manhattan, intermingling with African Americans and Irish and German immigrants. Most of the Chinese were probably sailors, some of whom were taking shore leave and others who had settled in the city. They worked as cooks, as peddlers, in boardinghouses, and as performers in Cantonese opera. Eleven were married, all to Irish women.[14] The first Japanese, mostly businessmen, settled in New York in the 1870s. In 1872, the Japanese government established a consulate in the city to protect its citizens' interests and promote trade.[15] Historian Vivek Bald has estimated that the first South Asians were Bengali peddlers who arrived in New York in the 1880s.[16] They were a small part of the increasing numbers of immigrants arriving and settling in New York City.

Before Ellis Island, immigration was dispersed and immigrants arrived through various ports. New York was the largest port of immigration, and its emigrant landing depot, called Castle Garden, was operated jointly by city and state officials. Opened in 1855, it was located in the Battery area at the southern tip of Manhattan close to the mixed immigrant neighborhoods in which Chinese lived. As U.S. lawmakers introduced the first federal restrictions on immigration and expanded them throughout the late nineteenth century, they decided that the federal government should take responsibility for implementing these restrictions. In 1875, the first federal immigration restriction barred the entry of criminals, prostitutes, and coolies (involuntarily imported subjects of "any Oriental country"). In 1882, encouraged by anti-Chinese activism in California, the U.S. Congress passed an act that stopped Chinese immigrants from naturalizing as U.S. citizens and prevented the immigration of Chinese laborers for ten years. This law subsequently became known as the Chinese Exclusion Act.[17]

In 1890, immigrant processing was transferred to the federal government, and Colonel John Weber took office as the first New York commissioner of immigration. Although this was a major shift in immigration enforcement, immigrants were processed at the Barge Office just a short distance from Castle Garden in the eastern Battery area. Commissioner Weber emphasized his fairness in dealing with immigrants as well as his professionalism in hiring only qualified staff and in firing those who demonstrated any dishonesty. Serving until 1893, Weber supervised the building of the Ellis Island immigration station.[18]

While serving as commissioner, Weber collected photographs of arriving immigrants and compiled them in a scrapbook. Although only a handful of South Asians arrived in New York in the 1890s, two men were photographed at the Barge Office in 1890. The men stood side by side behind a bench—one with his hands resting on the back of the bench, the other with his arms at his side. Two bundles laid on the floor in front of them. E. W. Austin, who operated the money exchange at the Barge Office, took the photograph and shared it with Commissioner Weber and news reporters. An illustration by Thure de Thulstrup based on Austin's photograph appeared in *Harper's Weekly* in 1891.[19] However, de Thulstrup framed a three-quarter-length portrait of just one of his subjects, the Sikh man wearing a turban. Cultural studies scholar Manan Desai has argued that the turban distinctively marked the "Hindoo," as *Harper's* labeled this image and as all South Asians were described by immigration authorities regardless of their ethnicity or religion.[20] Austin may have been intrigued by the turbaned man and de Thulstrup clearly focused his attention here. However, with the exception of his mislabeling, the visual representation of the Sikh man is respectful and similar to portraits of others arriving at the Barge Office: they are all marked by ethnic clothing and captioning as, for example, "A Hungarian," "Detained Polish Jew," and "A Group of Italians."[21] This image may presage the generally respectful treatment of immigrants, including some Asians, at Ellis Island.

In the 1880 census, 853 Chinese out of a total population of 106,465 were recorded living in New York City.[22] By 1890, New York's Chinese population was just over 2,500 and the U.S. Chinese population was recorded at 107,488.[23] However, activist Wong Chin Foo claimed that the number of U.S. Chinese was closer to 150,000, and, according to restrictionist W. H. Allen, "He ought to know better than the census officials, because the Chinese are stowed away in their dwellings in such manner that no correct count can be made of their numbers."[24] As Jack Tchen has noted, although it was relatively small, "the New York City Chinese quarter was the largest east of the Sierra Nevadas."[25] Japanese New Yorkers, whose numbers were also recorded by the census, totaled just 16 in 1880 and 125 in 1890, out of a continental U.S. population of roughly 2,000. Other Asian New Yorkers were only intermittently recorded in censuses by the U.S. government. Asians were a tiny fraction of the 1.5 million residents of New York City and 800,000

regular employment over here, the employer said, "Yes. Of course both were sent to one side, and ere this the contract laborer is doubtless on his backward way. "Ah," said the French American, "if I could spik Anglish—but, no. I spik well only as French to mek understand." "We understand perfectly," said the inspector. "Your English is good enough."

The baggage of the immigrants had all been examined, "for revenue only," on the steamer at her wharf. It was now removed to the ground-floor of the Barge Office. A stranger to the ways of those who seek our shores would never dream to look at half of it, that the stuff they bring is baggage. The dubious moiety of it consists of bags and pudding-shaped bundles, almost always done up in what once was white or light-colored cloth, but which has become stained and grimed with handling and with the soot of soft-coal smoke. The trunks, when they have them, are not like our trunks. Some are made of tin, others are clumsy chests, and still others are covered with cow-skin, "with the hairy side out," or are painted like an Indian on the war path. As a rule, the swelling bundles that look like overgrown puddings contain bedding, which the poor people have been obliged to buy, and do not want to lose.

As fast as a man or a woman left the boat, he or she went up to the top floor of the Barge Office, to pass down one of two runways, or aisles, between railings, and to be questioned again by the upstairs inspectors, who desired to know their names, nationalities, ages; whether they were married or single; the number in each family; whether they were travelling, and if they had money or tickets with which to travel; whether they were ever inmates of an asylum or prison; their condition of health, their occupation, and whether they were citizens or aliens.

Two women were suspected of being about to become mothers. If such a case were proven, and no husband was present or speedily forth-coming, the person would be returned to Europe. Women employed for the purpose were sent for to satisfy the authorities in these two cases—a task that should be most delicately undertaken. The officials insist that no complaint can be made upon the manner and spirit in which this feature of the work is treated. Not longago, in one of these cases, a fellow-passenger acknowledged an intention to wed the girl. "Then marry her now," said the official, and the wedding took place at once in the Barge Office.

After all the immigrants had passed their examinations (under the eyes of the doctors, who singled several out for further inspection and questioning), the people who meant to remain in New York were assembled in a great pen, and the others were led to the barge, which is kept for lack of other room, in which the railway travelers are held until evening, when the barge is taken to meet the emigrant trains that are always started at night. Those who were to be permitted to enter the country were set at liberty to ask questions at the information bureau; to wire their friends from the "telegraph center," or "telegraphen center," as it was variously called; or to have their money changed at the desk of Mr. E. W. Austin, the official broker, whose signs, announcing his business, read thus:

Cambio di Monete.
Argent de Change.
Pénzváltó Üzlet.
Zamin Pieniedzy.
Geld Wechsler.
Wexel Contor.
Money Exchange.

These terms are respectively Italian, French, Hungarian, Polish, German, Swedish or Scandinavian, and English. Current rates of exchange are posted and ordered to be paid. It is Mr. Austin's opinion that the money immigrants bring into this country is on an average between three dollars and five dollars per capita. It is the opinion of General O'Beirne that though such sums are all they may exhibit at the broker's counter, they actually bring in about fifty dollars per capita.

There is a lunch counter, also, in the Barge Office, and on it are to be seen bottles of beer, sandwiches made of junks of rye-bread, capped by great lengths of sausage, and pie, and crullers. When a prosperous looking Hollander was asked why he did not eat butter on his bread, he replied that he was not used to it; that he made a great deal of it every year, but sold it all and never dreamed of eating it.

Among the remarkable characters engaged to assist the government at the Barge Office is Mr. Najeeb J. Arbeely, ex-consul to Palestine, who is an Assyrian, and speaks fluently English, French, German, Italian, Greek, Swedish, Arabic, Hebrew, jargon, and several other tongues.

A GROUP OF ITALIANS.

A HUNGARIAN.

A HINDOO.

SWISS PEASANTS.

FRIESLAND BOY.

A MOTHERLESS ITALIAN CHILD.

DETAINED POLISH JEW.

MARRIAGE OF AUSTRIAN JEWS BY THE RABBI.

Thure de Thulstrup, "A Hindoo," in Julian Ralph, "Landing the Immigrant," *Harper's Weekly*, October 24, 1891.

residents of Brooklyn recorded in 1890.[26] However, immigrants as a whole formed a large proportion of the city, and nativists pushed for expanding restrictions on their entry.

In 1892, the year that Ellis Island opened, crowds gathered along the Manhattan and Brooklyn shorelines to watch a naval parade. "One heard English in every variety, with every accent known here or abroad," the *New York Times* commented. "One heard Italian in profusion, Spanish, French, German, the Russian Hebrew's patois, Chinese, and all those miscellaneous tongues which had overflowed in years past from Castle Garden."[27] Mentioned in passing, Chinese immigrants were part of the diverse mix of immigrants in New York City. In the same year that the station opened, Chinese exclusion was renewed and substantially expanded.

Ellis Island, designed as the U.S. government's central immigration station, was created as a space to implement federal restrictions on arrivals. When the station opened on January 1, 1892, these restrictions included bars on Chinese laborers along with criminals, prostitutes, polygamists, lunatics, idiots, paupers, "assisted immigrants" (whose passage was paid for them), those likely to become a public charge, contract laborers, immigrants suffering from "loathsome or contagious diseases," and those convicted of crimes or misdemeanors involving moral turpitude.[28] Although Emma Lazarus alluded to New York's harbor as a golden door to the United States, by the time her poem was engraved on the base of the Statue of Liberty in 1903, this door was already closing. Nonetheless, Ellis Island remained the United States' major immigration entry point through 1915, when immigration was curtailed first by World War I and then by the passage of racially restrictive quotas in the 1920s. Throughout the time that the immigration station was open, roughly 70 percent of all immigrants entered the United States through Ellis Island. Most of these arrivals were European; almost half settled in New York.[29]

The first immigration station was a massive pine building with a blue slate roof and imposing square towers at each corner. It was designed to facilitate careful vetting and efficient processing of arriving immigrants. Immigrants traveling in cabin class, including Asian arrivals, rarely stepped foot on Ellis Island. In deference to their elite class position, they were inspected on board the ship and transferred directly to shore. Steerage passengers, as well as cabin passengers who did not pass preliminary inspection, were transferred by ferry to Ellis Island. As arrivals entered, they piled their possessions in the ground floor baggage room, then climbed a double staircase to the vast registry hall on the second floor. As they climbed, they were separated into lines and inspected by public health officials. After the visual inspection, they were interviewed by registry clerks with questions about whether their passage was paid by another person, whether they were promised a work contract, and how much money they had in their possession. If they passed, immigrants entered one of two large wire pens depending on whether they planned to stay in the New York area or were traveling to another region. If they were not successful, they were detained for further inspection. There are no early records describing Asians' experiences during this inspection process, so it is not clear whether they were segregated based on race and immigration status or whether they were processed alongside other immigrants. About 20 percent of all Ellis Island arrivals were detained for additional inspection, sometimes overnight or longer. Asian immigrants were among those confined on the island. In total, only 1–3 percent of immigrants at Ellis Island were rejected. In contrast, on average, 15 percent of Chinese and Japanese immigrants in New York were denied entry (tables 1, 2, and 3).[30]

Early in the morning of June 16, 1897, as roughly 200 immigrants slept in locked rooms, a fire started in one of the station's wooden towers. As the fire spread, guards rushed to open the iron gates of the men's and women's detention rooms, rouse the detainees, and evacuate immigrants in the hospital building. Among the detainees were several South Asian men. All safely boarded a ferry that was regularly used to shuttle immigrants from their ships to the station and from the station to shore. On this night, as flames lit up the harbor and crowds gathered on the Manhattan, Brooklyn, and Jersey City waterfronts to watch the massive fire, the detainees were transported to the Barge Office and to hospitals around the city and, in some cases, were released to their families. Once again, the operations of the Immigration Bureau were temporarily housed in the Barge Office. During these years, under a new administration, the bureau was accused of inefficiency and indifference, as well as corruption.[31]

In December 1900, the second Ellis Island immigration station was opened. The station largely followed the arrangement of the earlier building but on a grander scale. It was and remains a stately French Renaissance-style structure built in fireproof redbrick and limestone topped with four elaborate towers. As arrivals disembarked from the ferry, they were greeted by the station's imposing facade, including three window arches that extended to the height of the building. According to architectural historian Robert Twombly, the station was designed not only to process arriving immigrants but also to project the strength of U.S. state power. Again, immigrants deposited their luggage on the ground floor and walked up the stairway to the massive registry hall, "two hundred feet long, one hundred feet wide, and topped by a fifty-six-foot vaulted ceiling." Here, with voices echoing throughout the hall, they were inspected and processed in the same way as at the Barge Office and the first immigration station. The physical organization of the hall changed from cages to benches in the early twentieth century. Starting in 1917, inspections were expanded to test immigrants' literacy in their home languages. However, the experience of being processed remained relatively consistent until the 1920s. At this point, as racially restrictive quotas were introduced, immigrants were inspected before embarking in Europe and brought to Ellis Island only if they required in-depth inspection.[32]

Although federal laws governed immigrants across the United States, Asians arriving in New York experienced exclusion differently from their counterparts in other immigration stations, especially those on the West Coast. Historians have shown how officials at Angel Island implemented exclusion strictly, often pushing beyond the boundaries of the law to introduce harsh additional regulations.[33] In contrast, New York case files suggest that interrogations of Chinese arrivals were more cursory than at other stations, detention times were shorter, and officials were more restrained in their application of exclusion laws. As Betty Lee Sung wrote in her 1967 Chinese American history, *Mountain of Gold*, "At Ellis Island in New York, at least, the conditions were sanitary and the detainees were not abused."[34] Sung was explicitly comparing Ellis Island with Angel Island.

Ellis Island officials were also relatively restrained in their handling of Japanese cases. After Japanese exclusion was introduced in 1907, national immigration officials wrote regularly to Ellis Island complaining about their lax regulation of Japanese arrivals and asking them to complete more accurate, detailed paperwork. The New York office responded by expressing concerns about how such enforcement might offend Japanese applicants.[35] This approach was likely shaped by the administration of immigration laws at Ellis Island, including an emphasis on professionalism and efficiency in processing mostly European arrivals. Immigration regulation was central to Ellis Island, but exclusion regulation was peripheral. The restrained implementation of exclusion may also have been influenced by the fact that Asian arrivals in New York were more elite and more likely to be temporary visitors than at other immigration stations.

The administration of exclusion was contested and constrained in New York, caused by disagreements among officials, successful advocacy by Chinese community members, and more substantial opposition to anti-Chinese laws among New Yorkers. Some New York inspectors were outspoken racists, while others worked closely with Chinese individuals and community organizations. Some inspectors completed their service with the bureau, then used their knowledge of the exclusion laws to represent Chinese immigrants in the immigration proceedings that they had previously enforced. This was common practice at many immigration stations, but New York was unusual as not only inspectors but also chief inspectors—the directors of the Chinese Bureau—followed this path. A broad range of New York Chinese community organizations protested exclusion, and, although their efforts were ultimately unsuccessful in preventing its expansion, they were relatively effective at influencing the implementation of exclusion in New York, including the hiring of interpreters. Especially as exclusion was being introduced in the 1880s and 1890s, New York organizations such as the Chinese Equal Rights League found non-Chinese allies in their early efforts.[36]

The contested implementation of exclusion led to the popular perception of Ellis Island as a relatively lenient site of immigration. This understanding existed among Chinese community members, newspaper reporters, and even immigration inspectors themselves.[37] Despite this perception, the percentage of Chinese immigrants rejected at Ellis Island was almost three times higher than in San Francisco (tables 1 and 2). Although the data are limited, Japanese immigrants were also rejected at substantially higher rates at Ellis Island than in San Francisco and many other ports (tables 3 and 4). Chapter 1, "Enforcing Asian Exclusion at Ellis Island," explores how and why the administration of exclusion was simultaneously contested, considerate, and strict in New York.

As exclusion was expanded in the 1890s, expulsion policies were introduced. Chinese civil rights leaders and community organizations fought against these new deportation laws that expanded the regulation of the Chinese beyond immigration stations and into their communities. Although resistance efforts were centered in California, Chinese New Yorkers formed almost all the test cases against the expansion of exclusion and expulsion. As the head of the New York Chinese Bureau noted in the 1890s, in contrast to San Francisco's sizable Chinatown, "The Chinese colonies in Boston, Philadelphia, and New York are not too large to be under strict police control."[38] Although the inspection of Asians arriving in New York was relatively restrained, officials were harsh in their regulation of Chinese New Yorkers and in their enforcement of deportation.

In the first decades of the twentieth century, Chinese, Japanese, and Bengali communities in New York became increasingly established. Between 1910 and 1920, the number of Chinese in New York doubled from 2,500 to about 5,000 out of a national population of roughly 60,000 Chinese. New York's proportion of the overall Chinese American population increased relatively steadily from 1 percent in 1880 to 16 percent by 1950.[39] The Japanese population of New York also doubled from around 1,000 in 1910 to more than 2,000 in 1920. However, it remained very small and stayed at this level until 1940, averaging less than 2 percent of the total Japanese American population.[40] Vivek Bald has described the presence of South Asian sailors in boardinghouses in lower Manhattan starting in the 1900s as likely transient but becoming more settled by the 1920s.[41]

The increasing size of Asian New York was driven by strong labor demand and limited discrimination. Working-class laborers and sailors who had jumped ship formed the core of these communities. However, proportionally, there were also more elite Chinese and Japanese living in New York City than in the western United States, including merchants, students, and diplomats. In his 1927 study of the impact of exclusion laws, sociologist Roderick Duncan McKenzie suggested that, as exclusion laws became stricter, the proportion of Chinese and Japanese living in New York became larger. McKenzie notes that the Chinese and Japanese communities were composed of merchants who were more able to secure entry to the United States than laborers and more likely to live in "centers of international trade."[42] In addition, more limited anti-Asian racism may have attracted westerners to New York. Although the state had licensing regulations preventing the entry of Asians into many professions, there was less formal discrimination toward Asians than in California. Not residentially segregated by law, Asian New Yorkers lived in locations across New York City and in the suburbs. Despite strong social prohibitions, Chinese, Japanese, and Asian Indians were not governed by antimiscegenation laws and were more likely to be intermarried with non-Asian women. Merchants were able to bring their Chinese wives to the United States, but Chinese laborers could not and some of them married non-Chinese women, often Irish immigrants. Japanese elites sometimes wedded socially prominent native-born white women. South Asian sailors and peddlers sometimes lived among and married African American and Puerto Rican women.[43] Commentators have attributed the eastward migration of Asians out of California to the relative lack of violence perpetrated against them in the eastern United States.[44] However, Asians throughout New York City remained vulnerable to everyday acts of harassment as well as personal and property violence.[45]

Threats and practices of deportation by Ellis Island officials not only criminalized unlawful entry but also policed the daily lives of Chinese New Yorkers and attempted to control the size of Chinatown.[46] In the 1920s, as the Chinese community in the city was becoming more established, it experienced a series of highly publicized conflicts among tongs, secret societies that engaged in both legitimate businesses and criminal enterprises. Chinese Bureau officials worked closely with New York police officers to conduct large-scale raids on Chinatown, using the tong wars as a pretext to round up and deport Chinese New Yorkers. However, according to members of the Chinese community, most of those whom they removed were jump-ship sailors and other unauthorized residents not involved in tong violence.[47] By this time, amid concerns about rising crime and the increasing population of Chinese New Yorkers, non-Chinese who had previously voiced concerns about the enforcement of exclusion lowered their opposition. The Chinese Bureau's efforts were supported by increasingly stringent deportation laws that enlarged the potential causes for deportation as well as the time period during which immigrants could be subject to deportation.[48]

As exclusion and expulsion laws were implemented at Ellis Island, they reshaped the immigration station into a deportation and detention center, turning the golden door into a revolving door. In 1917, twenty-five years after the immigration station opened, Ellis Island had sleeping and dining accommodations for up to 2,000 detainees.[49] When immigration official Henry Curran worked at Ellis Island in the 1920s, it was not uncommon for these facilities to be filled overnight with immigrants.[50] As early as the 1930s, Asian, white, and "colored" immigrants each had their own dormitories. Although most detainees were not Asian, Chinese arrivals held on Ellis Island during this time remember their dormitory being full.[51] The second chapter explores how Ellis Island became the United States' "chief deportation depot."[52]

New York was not only the largest port for legal immigration, it was also the largest seaport for clandestine immigration. As new immigration and exclusion laws were introduced, larger numbers of immigrants engaged in seaborne smuggling and stowing away to evade these restrictions. New laws preventing the entry of stowaways were introduced alongside deportation laws in the 1920s. However, popular perceptions and legal restrictions operated differently for unauthorized European and Asian immigrants. New

York officials expressed some sympathy for European stowaways. Stowing away was often romanticized as an alternative form of immigration for aspiring young men who were not wealthy enough to buy a ticket. In contrast, Asians involved in seaborne smuggling were typically viewed as "human freight" rather than as agents of their own unauthorized immigration. These popular perceptions were also enforced in law. If European stowaways met other requirements for immigration, they were allowed to enter the United States. However, under exclusion laws, all Chinese immigrants were deported if they were detected while stowing away or smuggling themselves into the United States.[53]

Asians who smuggled themselves into New York were helped by complex multiracial networks as well as the large number of Asian crew members who facilitated stowaways. Asian sailors who supplemented their income through smuggling were helped by their relegation to racially segregated positions in backrooms and below deck, where it was relatively easy to hide stowaways. Although all races were involved in smuggling, Asians were viewed with particular suspicion by government officials and by other crew members.[54]

As scholars have increasingly attended to Asian and Latin American migration as central to the history of immigration and exclusion, they have placed unauthorized immigration at the center of this history. However, most of the recent studies focus on smuggling across the United States' southern and northern land borders.[55] Very few address the ways in which Asian immigrants, or immigrants in general, attempted to enter the United States by stowing away or smuggling themselves on ships.[56] This is perhaps because land borders continue to be associated with unauthorized immigration in the present and because seaports, especially New York, are more commonly associated with legal immigration. Chapter 3, "Smugglers and Stowaways: The Dangerous Journeys of Human Freight," considers the ways that New York was a central location for seaborne smuggling along the Eastern Seaboard and how this impacted the implementation of exclusion at Ellis Island.

Immigration officials charged with enforcing exclusion and immigration laws viewed sailors, smuggled immigrants, and stowaways as part of the same problem. They were concerned that all seamen, but especially Asian seamen, would use their customary shore leave to jump ship and settle in the United States in defiance of exclusion laws. When six Chinese crewmen were brought to Ellis Island after surviving the sinking of their ship, RMS *Titanic*, in 1912, they were deported immediately.[57] Immigration officials were primarily concerned with New York, which had the largest number of sailors, the largest number of deserting sailors, and the largest number of deserting Asian sailors of any port in the United States. Thousands of sailors reportedly jumped ship each year in New York. Although the numbers of Asian sailors were smaller, hundreds deserted each year, joining coethnic and broader immigrant communities already established in the city.[58] "On the face of it you would think that a seaman belongs to his ship like a fish belongs in the water," one immigration official commented. "Unfortunately, however, a seaman is an amphibious animal: he can live on land as well as on water."[59] Like stowaways, European jump-ship sailors who were otherwise allowed to enter the United States could become legal immigrants, but all Asian jump-ship sailors were barred as laborers under exclusion laws.

As a result of their concerns, New York immigration officials placed increasingly tight controls on Asian sailors arriving in port. In contrast to the regulation of arriving Asian immigrants, where San Francisco officials pushed for harsh enforcement, Ellis Island placed the strictest restrictions on sailors and pushed for other stations to follow. These regulations and laws show how Asian exclusion was expansive, radiating beyond the control of immigrants to regulate laborers such as sailors. Inspections of sailors formed a significant proportion of immigration officials' work. In 1919, the bureau examined 800,000 alien seamen, with more than twice as many at New York as at the next largest port; by 1930, this had increased to almost 1.2 million inspections, with four times as many at New York as at the next largest port.[60] Asian seamen regularly challenged these restrictions on shore leave through legal efforts, through verbal and sometimes violent conflicts with their captains, and by jumping ship. Direct resistance to the officers of one's ship was defined as mutiny, and mutinous sailors were detained at Ellis Island prior to their removal from the United States.

Despite the Immigration Bureau's extensive role in regulating seamen, immigration historians have rarely paid attention to sailors because they explore immigration history through the prism of settlement. Although many sailors did settle in New York and other port cities, most were transient.[61] Historians have also focused mostly on those classified by the Immigration Bureau as immigrants. Sailors, like stowaways, were an "anomalous class" within immigration law.[62] They were neither immigrants nor nonimmigrants. Despite this lack of attention by historians, the regulation of sailors was centrally linked to immigration restriction and Asian exclusion. Chapter 4, "Asian Sailors: Shanghaied in Hoboken," explores the presence of Asian sailors in New York's harbor and the ways in which immigration officials attempted to prevent them from jumping ship and settling in the city.

Perhaps the clearest example of how exclusion extended into areas beyond immigration regulation came during World War II, when Ellis Island was repurposed as a detention center for interned Japanese and other Axis nationals. Most historians focus on the forced relocation and incarceration of 110,000 Nikkei residents of Japanese descent in the western United States.[63] However, immediately after the bombing of Pearl Harbor, officials arrested and imprisoned Japanese nationals across the United States. In total, during the course of the war, as many as 15,000 Japanese civilians were interned at Immigration and Naturalization Service (INS) camps, including at Ellis Island. The immigration agency used its investigations of arriving Chinese immigrants as a model for interrogating Japanese detainees and developed new parole practices. The INS's supervision of Japanese internment highlights not only the central role of detention within immigration policy but also the prison capabilities of the immigration agency.

Japanese immigrants living in New York were more elite, more residentially integrated, and much more likely to be intermarried than Japanese in larger communities in the western United States. But this did not protect them from internment or prevent them from being treated more harshly than German and Italian enemy aliens. Japanese New Yorkers suffered as they were separated from their families, confined in close quarters, and questioned about their loyalty. These experiences created a sense of unbelonging in America. Many internees felt complex conflicts of identity and loyalty, with some Japanese immigrants insisting on their Americanness and others seeking repatriation to Japan. Many internees' wives and children were U.S. citizens and therefore not subject to internment; nonetheless, they also struggled emotionally and financially during World War II. The internment of enemy aliens on Ellis Island, as explored in chapter 5, is central to Ellis Island's shifting role from a place of immigration to a site of confinement.

Ellis Island closed in 1954. It had long been the central office for Asian exclusion in the eastern United States as well as the region's main deportation and detention center. Chinese exclusion ended in 1943, and Asian exclusion ended in 1952. However, the establishment of the People's Republic of China in 1949 led to new laws and new fears of Chinese immigrants shaped by Cold War anticommunism. Chinese immigrants became especially vulnerable to raids, as immigration officials believed that most had entered illegally and Federal Bureau of Investigation (FBI) inspectors believed that many were communists. Nonetheless, as deportation was massively expanded in the 1950s, lower numbers of immigrants were detained at Ellis Island.[64] The use of parole, which had been developed to regulate Axis nationals during World War II, was used to underwrite the expansion of deportation during the Cold War. In addition, the expanded regulation of unauthorized Mexican immigration led to a redistribution of enforcement resources from the northeastern to the southwestern United States. And the advent of airplane travel led to a dispersal of entry control and deportation practices across the country. These events and their role in the shuttering of Ellis Island are explored in the conclusion.

## Rethinking the Ellis Island Model of Immigration and the Angel Island Model of Exclusion

The experiences of Asians at Ellis Island do not fit with—and, in fact, challenge—historical models of both immigration and exclusion. Many scholars have contested what is often known as the Ellis Island model of immigration. However, the experiences of Asians at Ellis Island also complicate what I call the Angel Island model of exclusion, which, in part, seeks to replace the Ellis Island model.

Ellis Island has long been viewed as a symbol of immigration to the United States, as a golden door. It was the largest port of immigration, received the largest number of European immigrants, and was designed as the visible representation of the Immigration Bureau's authority. As historian Vincent Cannato has shown, the station started being mythologized almost as soon as it opened.[65] "Ellis Island," muckraking journalist Jacob Riis declared in biblical language in 1903, "is the nation's gateway to the promised land."[66] Other commentators drew comparisons between Pilgrims and immigrants; immigrant writer Mary Antin stated in 1914 that "Ellis Island is another name for Plymouth Rock."[67] Although Ellis Island was built to regulate arriving immigrants in response to concerns about the potential dangers of large-scale European immigration, the station has become closely linked to idealized histories of past European immigration.

The central symbolism of Ellis Island within American understandings of immigration cannot be disentangled from the "Ellis Island model of immigration."[68] This model, sometimes known as the ethnic or assimilation paradigm of immigration, has shaped narratives of both Ellis Island and U.S. immigration. In terms of Ellis Island, most histories cover only the period until the 1920s, when the station was the nation's largest port of entry for European immigrants. Most historians do not focus on, and sometimes dismiss, the station's later history. "After 1924, immigration slowed to a trickle and Ellis Island fell into disuse," one popular history summarizes. Without mentioning the station's use during the following thirty years, the very next sentence states, "It was closed in 1954."[69] Some academic histories also share this formulation. "Closed by the government in 1954," historian Robert Fleegler writes in *Ellis Island Nation,* "the facility had fallen into disrepair."[70]

However, as this book argues, from the 1920s until it closed in 1954, the role of Ellis Island changed from an immigration station regulating the entry of arrivals to a detention and deportation center.[71] Although many historical studies obscure the station's importance after the 1920s, commentators at the time recognized Ellis Island's role in immigrant detention and deportation. The 1939 Works Progress Administration Guide to New York City stated that, "Long the wide-open door to the New World, Ellis Island is now barely ajar." The guide noted that "Most present-day immigrants do not go to Ellis Island; only those whose eligibility for admission is questioned are examined there."[72] During World War II, immigration officials routinely referred to "the Ellis Island Detention Station."[73] Other agencies shared this understanding. "Ellis Island, contrary to a popular idea, is not used as an immigration station by the US Immigration Service and it has not been so used for the last thirty years," the U.S. Coast Guard reported in 1949. "It is a detention center, where those few aliens (less than 1% of total) are kept temporarily whose papers are not in order or whose records do not allow immediate clearance."[74]

In addition to serving as a detention center for immigrants upon arrival, Ellis Island also became an important site for processing deportees. In 1934, a committee investigating conditions at the island concluded that "the problem of the alien at Ellis Island . . . is not only that of the immigrant but that of the outgoing alien."[75] Legal scholar Daniel Kanstroom has written of Ellis Island during the 1930s, noting that it was "ironically used as a receiving station for deportees from all over the United States."[76] Kanstroom is right, but this use is ironic only if we view the immigration station through the Ellis Island model, focusing on the period from 1892 through 1924 and overlooking its equally long history as a detention and deportation center.

As historians have reconsidered the history of immigration, they have reexamined the place of Ellis Island within this history. Some have shown how the station was built not only to process new entrants but also to regulate immigrants. Historian of science Amy Fairchild explores how Ellis Island's mechanized medical inspection procedure introduced arriving immigrants to U.S. practices of industrialization.[77] In *The Ellis Island Snow Globe*, cultural theorist Erica Rand considers how this inspection process attempted to limit entry to exclusively heterosexual, gender-normative immigrants and how the ongoing memorialization of Ellis Island presumes such immigrants.[78] In a documentary film and accompanying book, Lorie Conway turns her attention to the hospital building that sits across from the immigration station on Ellis Island, where arrivals were held in the hope that they would recover from their illness and gain entry to the United States. As she writes, this is a "forgotten chapter of Ellis Island's history."[79]

Other historians have emphasized that Ellis Island was only one of a number of arrival points for immigrants, drawing attention to immigration stations that operated in its historical shadow, such as El Paso, Detroit, and Angel Island. Although Ellis Island processed the largest number of immigrants (arrivals applying for U.S. residency), El Paso was a busier crossing point, with many more temporary arrivals, tourists, and daily border crossers. By 1921, travelers crossing daily between Juarez and El Paso numbered 15,000.[80] In contrast, Ellis Island processed about 5,000 immigrants per day during peak times, with the largest number—11,747—arriving on one day in 1911. Emphasizing the importance of the U.S. Southwest, historian George Sánchez critiques the ways in which "public mythology . . . still reveres Ellis Island and the Statue of Liberty and looks toward Europe."[81] Detroit was also a significant border port, although it has received less attention than El Paso largely because the Canadian and European immigrants who crossed into the United States at this point were rarely a concern for immigration authorities.[82] Other significant immigration stations that have received limited scholarly attention include Boston, Galveston, Miami, and New Orleans.[83]

Although it never rivaled Ellis Island in total numbers of immigrants, Angel Island in the San Francisco Bay has received more attention than other ports. From its opening in 1910 until it was destroyed by fire in 1940, the Angel Island immigration station was associated with Asian immigration. "We are all familiar with Ellis Island on the Atlantic coast," Lillian Soares wrote in 1917, "but many do not know of the existence of Angel Island on the Pacific where the incoming orientals are received."[84] Her words prefaced Mary Bamford's study, *Angel Island: The Ellis Island of the West*.

In contrast to the Ellis Island model, which assumes the relatively free immigration of racially unmarked Europeans as the main narrative of U.S.

immigration history, ethnic studies scholars have emphasized the centrality of race and exclusion in U.S. immigration policy. Within Asian American history, this approach could be called the Angel Island model of exclusion.[85] In part, this model focuses on the implementation of exclusion in San Francisco, the largest port of entry for Chinese immigrants. Scholars Him Mark Lai, Genny Lim, and Judy Yung first focused attention on the "ordeal of immigration and incarceration" at Angel Island in their pathbreaking 1980 study, *Island.* They emphasized how Chinese arrivals "viewed the interrogation process as unreasonable and harsh."[86] Even before the Angel Island immigration station was opened in 1910, as historian Erika Lee has shown, San Francisco was considered "the most difficult processing center for both newly arriving Chinese immigrants and departing Chinese residents." San Francisco officials were strongly anti-Chinese, and they were supported in this position by politicians and non-Chinese Californians. As a result, they implemented exclusion laws zealously and pushed national officials to adopt the "strictest interpretation possible."[87]

The Angel Island model importantly critiques the Ellis Island model and demonstrates that exclusion is a central paradigm, perhaps the central paradigm, for understanding U.S. immigration. In this approach, scholars have challenged the representation of Angel Island as the "Ellis Island of the West" and worked to displace the centrality of Ellis Island within immigration historiography. Roger Daniels, in a foundational 1997 essay, notes that if Ellis Island and the Statue of Liberty are "primarily icons of welcome, of acceptance, that other island, three thousand miles to the west, is an icon of suspicion, of rejection."[88] Erika Lee claims that "it is Angel Island—and not Ellis Island—that best personifies America's true relationship with immigration," an ambivalent relationship that both celebrates immigration and excludes immigrants.[89]

Although the Angel Island model is critically important to centering Chinese exclusion and racially based gatekeeping within immigration history, it has helped shape an approach that explores the presence of Asian immigrants at Angel Island and European immigrants at Ellis Island.[90] In their history of Angel Island, Erika Lee and Judy Yung note that "Ellis Island has become synonymous not only with America's immigrant heritage but also with its national identity in general." They go on to state that "in its celebration of how European immigrants were welcomed into and remade America, the popular Ellis Island mythology eclipses more complicated histories, like those from Angel Island."[91] However, this association of Ellis Island with European immigration not only eclipses more complex stories of immigrant struggle, detention, and deportation at Angel Island, but it also eclipses these difficult histories at Ellis Island itself. In these comparisons, Ellis Island is the big apple and Angel Island the bitter orange of immigration regulation. But historians are still comparing apples and oranges.

Chinese immigrants formed the majority of immigrants processed through Angel Island; however, Japanese and other Asians arrived in substantial numbers, while Europeans, Mexicans, and other immigrant groups also entered the United States via San Francisco. As Maria Sakovich has calculated, non-Asians represented about one-third of all applicants between 1915 and 1920, a number that dropped to about 15 percent after 1924.[92] Although Angel Island has long been associated only with Asian immigration, other groups are beginning to receive more scholarly attention. Most notably, Lee and Yung's comprehensive history of Angel Island explores Russian, Jewish, Mexican, and varied Asian migration through the immigration station.[93]

Just as non-Asian immigrants arrived in the United States at Angel Island, non-European immigrants arrived at Ellis Island. More than a thousand immigrants from the British Caribbean arrived in the United States each year starting in 1893; however, even though most settled in New York, there are limited data on arrivals through Ellis Island. Less than 1 percent of arrivals at Ellis Island are estimated to have been Afro-Caribbean. Immigrants from Syria, Lebanon, Armenia, North Africa, and, to a lesser extent, sub-Saharan Africa also entered the United States at Ellis Island. Mexicans mostly traveled north overland, but a few arrived in New York on ships traveling from Tampico. And Canadians also traveled by sea from Halifax to New York.[94]

In addition to Afro-Caribbean, Latin American, and Canadian entrants, Asians also arrived at Ellis Island from these locations and from Europe. In secondary sources, there are only a few scattered references to Asians at Ellis Island. Ellis Island librarian and historian Barry Moreno consistently attends to the presence of Asians in his reference works.[95] The 2014 revision of Lai, Lim, and Yung's *Island* incorporates important new research about Chinese detained at Ellis Island as well as translations of four of the poems carved into the station walls.[96] Vivek Bald details the experiences of Bengali peddlers and seamen in New York, including instances of being detained at and deported from Ellis Island.[97] And independent scholar Maria Elizabeth Del Valle Embry has developed an extensive website documenting Filipinos and other Asian arrivals at Ellis Island.[98] Other brief references to Asians at Ellis Island appear in histories of the immigration station by scholars such as Vincent Cannato and Ronald Bayor.[99] Given the large number of books published on Ellis Island, these are just a few brief acknowledgments of the existence of Asians at Ellis Island. As Moreno has noted, the presence of Chinese at Ellis Island "has been curiously overlooked by scholars."[100] The existence of other Asian groups is even less well researched.

This presence has been overlooked in part because only a small number of Asian immigrants entered the United States at Ellis Island, especially when compared with Asian immigrants on the West Coast and European immigrants at Ellis Island.[101] "An examination of the records of the New York Custom House," *Harper's Weekly* reported in 1898, shows "how few Chinamen attempt entry at that port."[102] And Ellis Island officials themselves noted in 1908 that "Japanese arrivals at New York are few."[103] It is clear that there were far fewer Asians than other immigrants at Ellis Island, but there were more than is suggested by the silence surrounding their stories.

Japanese formed the largest number of Asian immigrants through New York. As a percentage of national Japanese immigration until the 1920s, only 5 percent of all Japanese arrived via New York. During the 1910s, New York immigration officials reported that an average of 300 Japanese applied for entry through Ellis Island each year. By the 1920s, this had risen to about 500 Japanese applicants.[104] However, data on immigration of Japanese immigrants are less detailed and less consistent than data for Chinese immigrants, in part because of lax reporting by the Immigration Bureau in New York.[105]

Chinese were the second-largest group of Asian immigrants who traveled through New York in the early twentieth century. In the 1910s, about a hundred Chinese immigrants entered through Ellis Island each year. In the 1920s, more than 350 Chinese immigrants arrived on average. From 1901 to 1931, the percentage of Chinese applicants for entry in New York edged up from less than 1 percent of all Chinese applicants to more than 5 percent. Until the 1920s, San Francisco accounted for between 50 and 70 percent of all Chinese arrivals. However, this dropped to about 40 percent of all Chinese arrivals in the 1920s as Chinese immigration became more dispersed throughout the United States.[106]

Despite these relatively low numbers, Ellis Island was the largest port for Asian immigration on the Eastern Seaboard, and New York had the largest Chinese and Japanese communities outside of the western United States. "New York being the mecca of Chinese in the eastern part of the country," New York immigration commissioner Edward Corsi noted about his tenure in the 1930s, "it is natural that the Chinese Division at Ellis Island has its never-ending problem."[107] The problem, of course, was Chinese immigrants.

It is important to note that the presence of small numbers of Asian immigrants does not mean that there were small numbers of Asians. Immigrants, arrivals applying for the right to settle in the United States, were only a small percentage of total Asian arrivals. Nonimmigrant arrivals included temporary visitors such as passengers in transit across the United States, students, performers, tourists, and others. Immigration historians have long focused on Ellis Island because it processed the largest number of permanent immigrants; most historians of Asian exclusion have focused on Angel Island as it processed the largest number of Asian immigrants. However, nonimmigrant Asians traveled through New York in high numbers (tables 5 and 6). The circulation of Asians in and through New York requires us to understand exclusion and enforcement broadly, incorporating not only permanent settlers but also sailors, stowaways, and passengers transiting through the United States.

Although Japanese formed the largest number of immigrant arrivals through New York, more Chinese sought transit through the United States or came as nonimmigrant temporary residents. During the 1890s, an average of more than 500 Chinese were recorded in the manifests of ships traveling to New York, although this number dropped in the early 1900s. When immigration officials started to record the presence of sailors, as part of efforts to regulate them more closely under immigration and exclusion laws, the numbers were even more striking. Between 1916 and 1918, the first full year that crew members were recorded, the number of Chinese and Japanese recorded by immigration officials surged by 1,500 percent and the number of Asian Indians increased by more than 200 percent. Instead of hundreds of Asians, these data show that there were thousands of Asians, mostly sailors, circulating around New York's harbor every year (tables 5 and 6).

Ships were multiracial workplaces employing Chinese, Bengali, Filipino, and Japanese workers.[108] Some of these sailors jumped ship to stay in New York, either temporarily or long term. In particular, most of the Filipinos who settled in New York appear to have been crew members.[109] Between 1917 and 1954, the Immigration Bureau recorded an annual average of 8,000 Chinese, 3,500 Japanese, and 2,000 South Asian visits to and through New York. Filipinos averaged more than 1,600 each year, while other Pacific Islanders increased to more than 1,200 annually (although this likely included many Filipinos). Other groups, however, remained small. Data from manifests including immigrants and other arrivals show that between 1892 and 1954 averages of just thirty-five Hawaiians and six Koreans were recorded arriving on ships in New York each year. Asian sailors, including jump-ship sailors, had long been present in New York; after 1917, this presence was recorded (tables 5 and 6).[110]

Asian New Yorkers disrupt the traditional immigration model of being directly uprooted or transplanted from one's home to a new country.[111] Relatively few immigrants traveled directly from Asia to New York. Most appear to have traveled in a process of secondary migration, working and residing in the Caribbean, Latin America, or Europe before moving to the eastern United States. In addition, many Asians living in New York emigrated directly from Asia to California and later moved to the East Coast, a process of internal secondary migration.

Aside from Asian sailors who followed circuitous paths in their journeys to New York, most arrivals used one of three major routes to Ellis Island: from the Caribbean and Latin America, from Europe, or from Asia across Canada. These routes were paralleled by clandestine Asian immigration. Probably the largest number of Asian arrivals in New York came from the Caribbean, particularly Cuba and Trinidad.[112] There was a substantial Chinese and Asian Indian presence in the region as a result of indentured labor recruitment during the nineteenth century and labor migration in the twentieth century.[113] By 1917, South Asians formed 80 percent of all immigrant laborers in the British Colonial Caribbean, with the largest number in Trinidad.[114] Chinese also worked in the Anglophone Caribbean, especially Trinidad and Jamaica, and in Latin America, particularly Cuba, Peru, and Mexico.[115] Using an older English spelling of Toisan, the region from which most Chinese New Yorkers hailed, one immigrant noted that "before World War II more than half the heads of households in Tai-shan villages made their living in either Cuba or the United States."[116] Immigration officials were particularly concerned about unauthorized immigration from Cuba. On one occasion in 1922, fifteen Chinese Cuban citizens arrived in New York to meet with the Chinese delegation at a disarmament conference in Washington, D.C. As "respectable citizens" whose purpose was recognized by the Cuban legation, they were landed promptly. However, four days after their arrival, one of the supposed delegates was arrested at the Central Railroad Station in Detroit en route to Jackson, Michigan.[117] Upon further investigation in New York's Chinatown, inspectors learned that the other Cubans had never left the city and may have paid as much as $1,600 to secure their entry. Despite an extensive search, they were not located.[118] Some Chinese also arrived in New York on ships from Tampico and other ports in Mexico, although they typically traversed the land border between Mexico and the United States.[119] Japanese settled in Brazil, Peru, and elsewhere in Latin America in substantial numbers but do not appear to have traveled extensively from these countries to New York. Although there were very few Korean arrivals in New York in the early twentieth century, most arrived from ports in Cuba, Mexico, Trinidad, and Jamaica.[120]

The second major group of Asians at Ellis Island included those who had lived in, studied in, or traveled to European countries prior to arriving in the United States.[121] Many Asian arrivals from Europe used New York as a transit point.[122] Thirteen officers of the Japanese Army traveled through New York in 1895 on their way home to Japan after studying military tactics in Germany.[123] Tcheng Ka Ling lived five years in Vienna as part of a consortium of porcelain stone merchants with colleagues in Hamburg and Prague. He traveled through New York in 1915 en route to San Francisco.[124] Small numbers of Koreans also traveled from Liverpool, Southampton, and other ports in Europe.[125]

Third, Chinese immigrants also traveled to Vancouver, then crossed Canada overland to Halifax, Nova Scotia. From Halifax, they boarded a ship to Ellis Island. Chin Yuen Sing, for example, arrived in New York from Halifax in 1894. According to immigration authorities, even though he claimed to be a merchant and therefore exempt from exclusion, he was a laborer who had previously worked as a laundryman in Connecticut. He was refused entry.[126] Joseph Eng Young took this route by himself as a twelve-year-old child in 1922. He remembers feeling secure as he traveled this well-worn path, sleeping with other children in steerage and playing with them on the ship. He was detained for one week, meeting his father for the first time during his interrogation at Ellis Island, then joining him in his laundry in Newark.[127]

New York officials actively opposed the overland route. "The Bureau," according to its 1910 annual report, "can see no good reason for the adoption of the roundabout route of crossing Canada to Halifax."[128] Officials believed that Chinese used this route to smuggle themselves over the Canadian border. In 1910, Canadian border ports were closed to Chinese entrants, strengthening the enforcement of exclusion. After this date, Chinese arrivals in Vancouver were barred from entering the United States at any point on the Canadian border. They had to enter at either western or eastern U.S. seaports, such as Boston or New York.[129] Some Chinese New Yorkers entered the United States at San Francisco and then traveled east. However, most preferred to travel via Canada so that they could apply for entry—and possibly undergo detention—closer to their family and friends.[130]

Although this book addresses the presence and significance of Asians at Ellis Island, the island itself is a focal point rather than the only focus of this study. *Closing the Golden Door* considers Ellis Island as a key location within the New York harbor, the city, and the metropolitan area. The Chinese Bureau in New York City handled exclusion and immigration matters for the entire state. The city was also the central location from which many East Coast smuggling activities were organized and the destination for many hopeful stowaways. If smuggled immigrants or stowaways were discovered, they were detained at Ellis Island. Asian sailors rested at and reshipped around New York, sometimes through choice and sometimes coerced by their employers. Chinese immigrants and other New York City residents were in danger of deportation through the station if they violated the terms of their immigration. And, immediately after the attack on Pearl Harbor in December 1941, Japanese nationals were rounded up throughout the metropolitan area and detained on the island. New York was the central location, but not the only location, in a network of Asian communities on the East Coast. As the detained Goan sailor looked across New York's harbor at the Statue of Liberty in 1919, he was a part of larger currents of Asian sailors, stowaways, students, travelers, laborers, dignitaries, and U.S. citizens moving through New York. Many of these arrivals settled in the city, some were detained, and others were deported through Ellis Island.

Asian New Yorkers repeatedly questioned the promise of liberty that America claimed to represent. In 1885, when the Statue of Liberty first arrived in New York, Saum Song Bo received a request for contributions to help complete construction on the pedestal. The appeal was specially directed toward Chinese Americans such as himself. Writing to a missionary newspaper, he expressed his outrage that the French would donate such a statue to the United States after the passage of Chinese exclusion laws that prevented most Chinese from immigrating to the United States and all Chinese immigrants from becoming U.S. citizens. "The word liberty," Bo wrote, "makes me think of the fact that this country is the land of liberty for all nations except the Chinese." He was insulted that he would be asked to donate to such a statue when he and other Chinese did not have liberty in the United States.[131] Thirty years later in 1906, New York businessman Lee Chew argued that Americans made a show of "loving justice." "More than half the Chinese in this country would become citizens if allowed to do so, and would be patriotic Americans," Lee claimed. "But how can they make this country their home as matters are now?"[132] Radical novelist, poet, and New Yorker H. T. Tsiang, who was detained at Ellis Island in the 1930s, directly and succinctly addressed the ways that the United States and the Statue of Liberty turned their backs on immigrants. "Statue, turn your ass!" he wrote in a two-line poem, "Let us pass!"[133] His sentiments were echoed by many Asian New Yorkers.

# 1 Enforcing Asian Exclusion at Ellis Island

..................................................

September 4, 1939. William Fook Yee was, in his words, a "fourth generation" American when he arrived at Ellis Island in 1939. Three generations
of his family had worked in the United States. Yee's great-grandfather
worked on a sheep ranch in Wyoming in the nineteenth century as a ranch
hand who was "friendly with the Indians" and respected by his employer,
but chose to return to China when he had finished his working life. Yee's
grandfather immigrated to the United States shortly after the Civil War but
died of an unknown illness after just a couple of years in Walla Walla, Washington. Yee's father then emigrated, working as a laborer in various places
from Alaska to New York. Yee was born in 1924 and grew up in Toisan, a
farming district in Guangdong province in Southeast China. Almost all Chinese living in New York in the first half of the twentieth century came from
Guangdong, mostly from Toisan. In an interview with the Ellis Island Oral
History Project, Yee described himself as "one of the overseas children left
behind in China." He lived with his mother and older sister while his father
worked in the United States, returning to Toisan only three or four times.[1]

When Yee was sixteen, his father made arrangements for him to immigrate to the United States. His father's first concern was that Yee might be
conscripted by the Chinese Army to fight Japan, but he also felt that it was
time to continue the family tradition of working overseas. Yee traveled from
his home in Toisan to Hong Kong, where he boarded a massive modern liner,
the *Empress of Canada*. Along with twenty-three fellow passengers en route
to New York, Yee sailed to Vancouver, then took a train to Montreal, and
another to Nova Scotia. One month after he departed Hong Kong, Yee
boarded a smaller ship, the *Evangeline*, in Yarmouth, Nova Scotia. The following evening, he arrived in New York. "Looking at the Statue of Liberty,"
which he had learned about at school in China, he recalled, "I know I'm
there."[2]

Although he was a fourth-generation American, Yee could not immigrate
legally. As none of Yee's forefathers had been born in the United States, he
could not legitimately claim U.S. citizenship. Because his father was a

laborer, he could not immigrate under limited exemptions to Chinese exclusion that allowed the entry of diplomats, merchants, students, actors, and travelers temporarily visiting the United States. Instead, Yee claimed to be the son of a U.S. citizen, a man who was not his father and did not share his birth name. According to Yee, arriving as a paper son was the only way that Chinese could immigrate to the United States. Many Chinese would have agreed. Although there were some limited options for Chinese to immigrate legally, most appear to have entered through "indirect smuggling" schemes. Exact numbers are difficult to establish, but it is estimated that 90 percent of all Chinese immigrants arrived in the United States during exclusion using false documentation.[3]

When Yee's ship docked in New York, European and Chinese passengers were separated, with the latter ordered to the Chinese Division. Before they were detained, however, the Chinese arrivals were allowed to go into New York City. They chose to see "an American movie, a cowboy movie," and then returned to the island. Yee expected to be landed the next day. However, he was held for three weeks at Ellis Island—longer than the other Chinese on his ship—because immigration inspectors believed that he was a paper son. His papers said that he was sixteen, but he was taller than typical for his age. Inspectors knew that many paper sons tried to find papers that closely matched, but sometimes adopted identities that were not similar to their own backgrounds. Yee was in fact sixteen, although he was not who he claimed to be. Yee was interrogated: "How many neighbors did you have, what house, what direction your house facing, and, you know, how many relatives you have, and what gender are they, male or female, and so on and so forth." Anxious and unable to speak with his father, Yee kept a positive attitude while being detained. When he was finally told that he was free to go, he was ready in minutes, having already packed his bags.[4]

Ironically, given his reasons for emigrating from China, Yee was drafted into the U.S. Army four years after his arrival. He served in the all-Chinese Fourteenth Air Division. He hated serving in a segregated unit, comparing it to the discrimination faced by all-Black units. If he got shot, he pointed out, his blood was the same color as everyone else's. Yee was posted in China, where, in his words, he worked as a "buffer" between the American and Chinese forces because he understood both cultures and languages. While in service, he met his wife and they were married by an army chaplain in Shanghai. When asked whether he had to go through Ellis Island on his return from the war, Yee replied, "You kidding? The American army, with the stripes and everything won. You returned as a hero with the wife."[5]

· · · · · ·

Yee's experience reveals key aspects of Chinese migration to New York and the enforcement of exclusion at Ellis Island. Like many others, Yee traveled from Toisan as part of an established migration network with long-standing regional connections to join his father in New York. Although Yee followed the Canadian overland route, other Chinese arrived from the Caribbean, Latin America, and Europe. Despite this and in contrast to Europeans arriving at Ellis Island, exclusion laws prevented Yee from legally immigrating to the United States. European immigrants were processed quickly, and few were detained. All Chinese arrivals were subject to regulation by the Chinese Division, which interviewed them to ensure their identities and eligibility for entry under exclusion laws. New York officials emphasized that they treated Asian arrivals courteously; Yee's opportunity to travel into the city may support this. They also highlighted the speed with which they processed return certificates, verifying Chinese New Yorkers' residence and immigration status. Return certificates were required for Chinese planning to make a round trip to China, as Yee's father had done. However, many more Asian than European arrivals were detained and for longer periods.[6]

Nonetheless and not surprisingly, Yee found the experience of being detained and interrogated difficult. He described how many detainees were "depressed." Other oral histories mention that children were crying and completely shocked by being taken from families they had just met upon arrival in the United States. They describe how longer-term detainees became "tense and aggravated," creating an atmosphere of anxiety among all Chinese. These experiences, which show a disconnect between immigration officials and Asian detainees, are explored in more depth in chapter 2. Contrasting his arrival experience with his heroic return from World War II, Yee implied that passage through Ellis Island was demeaning. Like other travelers in New York, especially diplomatic representatives and other elites, Yee critiqued his treatment by immigration officials.[7]

Other aspects of the administration of exclusion at Ellis Island are not as clear in Yee's experience. As we will see in this chapter, exclusion laws were contested in New York. Across the United States, Chinese worked together to challenge exclusion and shape the enforcement of the laws. In California, most officials held anti-Chinese views and were strongly supported by the local white community. In New York and the eastern United States,

Chinese were more likely to secure the support of non-Chinese Americans who questioned or actively opposed exclusion laws. Exclusionary policies and practices were more contested, both by non-Chinese locals and among immigration officials. Some New York inspectors held clearly anti-Chinese views. Others, including senior officials, were more respectful of Chinese arrivals. Chinese community organizations had influence with the Chinese Division in New York, in particular in recommending Chinese interpreters; however, their involvement was challenged. Some reporters and restrictionists claimed that enforcement of exclusion was lax at Ellis Island. "It is evident," the *New York Times* editorialized in 1893, "that the enforcement of the law has for some time been perfunctory at the port of New York, and probably elsewhere."[8] Indeed, New York officials were critiqued by the national office for not rigorously enforcing, and sometimes resisting, restrictions against Chinese and Japanese arrivals.

These criticisms sometimes led to claims that Chinese were more likely to gain entry to the United States via New York.[9] However, these claims are not accurate. Asians arriving in New York did not have better chances of entry than those arriving in other ports. Although the data are limited, and are explored in more detail later in this chapter, Chinese arriving in New York were almost three times more likely to be rejected than those applying for entry in San Francisco. Japanese were seven times more likely to be rejected in New York, although their overall prospects for entry were better than those of Chinese arrivals in both San Francisco and New York. Rates of acceptance or rejection do not appear to be the key reason Chinese and Japanese arrivals chose this port, as applicants for admission through New York continued to rise even as larger numbers were rejected (tables 1, 2, 3 and 4).

Why, then, did Chinese, Japanese, and other Asians choose New York as a port of entry? The most obvious reason was convenience. As explored in the introduction, Ellis Island was the most direct entry point for most Asian arrivals traveling from Europe, Latin America, or the Caribbean. It was also the most convenient location for individuals who lived or were planning to live in New York or in the eastern United States. If they were detained at Ellis Island during an investigation, Ellis Island was closer to their homes and families, offering easier access to witnesses and visitors.

A more important reason may be that success rates were not the only consideration for arriving immigrants. Asian immigrants may have chosen to enter through New York in part because New York officials administered Asian exclusion with relative restraint and treated Asian immigrants with limited respect. Detainees carved poems in Chinese into the wooden walls of San Francisco's immigration station lamenting the "barbarians' cruelty" and their "hundreds of despotic acts." In contrast, the very limited number of poems from Ellis Island did not focus as extensively on immigration officials. Some writings were political statements about the 1930s Sino-Japanese war or references to erotic poems. Others criticized exclusion laws but expressed confidence.[10] One Ellis Island poem, for example, read as follows:

> Though imprisonment is bitter, my life will be long;
> When I landed from the ship, I feared bodily harm.
> I urge you: don't be afraid of immigration laws—
> It's certain we'll be freed to go home in peace.[11]

Chinese diplomats charged with representing their citizens' interests in the United States repeatedly emphasized that they did not necessarily oppose the exclusion of Chinese laborers. However, they took issue with disrespectful treatment by immigration officials, especially toward respectable merchants, students, and others who were entitled to enter.[12] At Ellis Island, Chinese arrivals remained subject to the law but received more respectful treatment.

The contested yet considerate enforcement of exclusion at Ellis Island was very different from the administration of exclusion in San Francisco. Since the publication of Him Mark Lai, Genny Lim, and Judy Yung's *Island* forty years ago, historians have understood the harsh ways that exclusion was enforced at Angel Island during the time that the station operated in San Francisco between 1910 and 1940.[13] Because San Francisco was the largest port for arriving Chinese, its officials played an outsize role in shaping exclusion enforcement and pushing the Immigration Bureau in Washington, D.C., to support stronger "gatekeeping" restrictions.[14] In her definitive study of exclusion, Erika Lee argues that exclusionists sought to make San Francisco's zealous enforcement of Chinese exclusion "a model for the nation."[15] This is the Angel Island model of exclusion. However, New York did not follow this model very well.

## Exclusion and Immigration Laws

During the exclusion era, Asians were increasingly prohibited from entering the United States. This process started with the very first federal immigration restriction, the 1875 Page Act, which prevented the entry of criminals, coolies, and immigrants imported involuntarily for "lewd and immoral purposes."[16] It was extended with the 1882 law that became known as the Chinese Exclusion Act. This law banned the admission of newly arriving Chinese laborers for ten years and barred all Chinese from admission to U.S. citizenship. Section four of the law entitled Chinese to receive return certificates prior to departing the United States, and section six required the issuance of certificates for "every Chinese person other than a laborer" allowed to enter the United States. In practice, the law exempted from exclusion Chinese nationals who were government officials, students, teachers, merchants, passengers in transit, and "travelers for curiosity or pleasure." As exclusion was expanded, more and more groups became defined as laborers. In 1898, the U.S. attorney general issued an opinion ruling that physicians, accountants, and other professionals were not exempt from the restriction on laborers. However, in a series of legal cases, Chinese members of the exempt classes secured immigration rights for their wives and minor children. U.S. citizens of Chinese descent also were allowed to travel freely; however, they had to prove their citizenship status, and, as paper son William Fook Yee's experience suggests, they were typically distrusted.[17]

The 1882 Chinese Exclusion Act has long been considered a definitive turning point in U.S. immigration law, marking the first racial and class restrictions on immigration as well as the beginnings of the United States' extensive immigration bureaucracy. However, the restriction law was constrained by commercial and diplomatic concerns, and it was repeatedly revised.[18] An 1884 amendment barred not only Chinese arriving directly from China but all people of Chinese descent, including those arriving from Cuba, Mexico, Canada, and Europe. These groups were more likely to arrive on the Eastern Seaboard, showing that exclusion laws recognized the varied routes that Chinese immigrants took to the United States. In 1888, the law was amended again to bar Chinese laborers from leaving and returning, unless they had substantial debts to repay or property in the United States.[19]

As Chinese exclusion was being introduced, other federal immigration laws were implemented and expanded. These general laws—sometimes called *immigration* laws to distinguish them from Asian *exclusion*—created specific restrictions on all immigrants. Alongside the 1882 Exclusion Act, a separate 1882 Immigration Law forbade the entry of lunatics, idiots, and those unable to take care of themselves without becoming a public charge. The 1885 Contract Labor Law barred assisted immigrants and contracted laborers, requiring all arrivals to pay for their own passage and secure work only after entry. And the 1891 Immigration Law continued these restrictions, adding individuals "suffering from a loathsome or contagious disease," paupers and people likely to become a public charge (a broader class than outlined in 1882), polygamists, and those convicted of crimes or misdemeanors involving moral turpitude.[20] The 1891 law also authorized the creation of a federal immigration bureaucracy and the building of the Ellis Island immigration station to administer immigration restrictions. As the federal government introduced these laws, it took over immigration enforcement from the New York state government in 1890 and from other state governments in 1892. Initially, the Customs Service managed Chinese exclusion, while the newly formed Immigration Bureau handled general immigration matters. In 1900, the enforcement of exclusion moved to the Immigration Bureau.[21]

Asian arrivals were regulated under both exclusion and general immigration laws. Even those Asian immigrants who were allowed entry under limited exemptions to exclusion could be rejected under immigration law. "Essentially, the entire question involved in the admission or exclusion of Chinese is not a distinct and independent subject," the commissioner-general of immigration wrote in 1908, "but in reality is merely part of the larger problem of immigration."[22]

After Chinese exclusion was consolidated, it was extended to other Asian immigrant groups. Japanese immigrants were restricted by a gentleman's agreement in 1907, in which the Japanese government agreed to stop issuing passports to laborers to avoid the indignity of exclusion by the U.S. government.[23] In 1917, a major law banned immigration from an "Asiatic barred zone," essentially extending exclusion to all of Asia, except for the U.S. colony of the Philippines.[24] As most Chinese and Japanese had already been excluded, Asian Indians were the major target of this law. The 1917 law also placed significant new restrictions on those likely to need public assistance, extended deportation provisions, and introduced monitoring of sailors. Each of these provisions disproportionately impacted Asians. In 1924, the bar on most Asian entry was consolidated with the Immigration Law, which banned all "aliens ineligible for citizenship"—namely, Asians and only Asians. As a result, the only groups of Asians allowed to enter the United States were those who were exempt from exclusion laws and Filipinos, who, as colonial subjects of the United States, were legally defined as U.S. nationals rather than aliens.[25] As each expansion of exclusion was introduced and implemented at Ellis Island, it was challenged by Asian and other New Yorkers and sometimes by immigration and exclusion officials themselves.

## Contesting Early Exclusion Laws
## and Enforcement in New York

Ellis Island officials, so the story goes, did not enforce exclusion laws as rigorously as officials at other ports. In 1893, a special inspector appointed in New York complained that this lax approach to enforcement "has admitted 409 Chinamen in one year, but has not debarred a single one."[26] Erika Lee's definitive study of Chinese exclusion focuses on Angel Island, suggesting that Chinese immigrants considered San Francisco to be the most difficult port through which to enter the United States. According to Lee, some immigrants may have chosen ports far from California, including those in upstate New York, because "they were known to have higher admission rates." As she notes, in 1898, 15 percent of all applicants were refused admission in San Francisco, while none were denied in the northeastern ports.[27]

However, the enforcement of exclusion in New York was not weak. Rather, it was contested and contingent upon officials in New York, including the customs collector, deputies, inspectors, and interpreters. It was also relatively restrained. Historian Arthur Bonner notes that "for the first ten years after the ban on the immigration of laborers, the Chinese in New York were spared the vindictive application of the law customary in California."[28] In contrast to the uniform support for exclusion in California, which opened up a space for harsh enforcement, attitudes toward Chinese immigrants and exclusion laws were contested in New York.[29] Together with different institutional practices and different types of Asian arrivals, this led to a more considerate immigration process at Ellis Island.

Anti-Chinese nativists complained that "people's indifference or open hostility" to exclusion laws in the eastern United States created problems for enforcement.[30] In 1904, the commissioner-general of immigration reported that in communities with smaller numbers of Chinese, "the Bureau found itself without the support of public sympathy or good will in its efforts to enforce the law."[31] A former immigration official suggested that this lack of support was due to the "utter indifference of our Eastern population to the 'yellow peril.'"[32] In these discussions, officials assumed that lack of opposition to Chinese immigration was based on a lack of contact with larger Chinese communities and, by extension, that contact would lead to support for exclusion. This racist perspective echoed restrictionists in the western United States who assumed that contact with Chinese automatically led to support for exclusion. In addition, as shown in the previous quotes, officials discussed "the public" and the "Eastern population" as though this included only white Americans. Such an approach marginalized and dehumanized Chinese members of the American public who routinely opposed exclusion.

Contrary to these claims, there was support for exclusion laws in New York, although it was less extensive than in California. New York newspapers had been favorable to Chinese migration starting in the mid-nineteenth century but gradually shifted to a more ambivalent position. In 1870, the *New York Herald*, with the largest circulation of any newspaper in New York or the nation, noted that Chinese immigrants were moving eastward, displacing "the ruddy daughters of the green island in New Jersey laundries," but that only time and experience will determine whether such migration "will prove a blessing or a curse to the country."[33] "A little experience with a degraded class of foreigners," the *New York Tribune* editorialized about Chinese in 1888, "is said to have brought the rest of the country more into sympathy with the efforts of the Pacific Coast to check a tide of undesirable immigration."[34] The *New York Times* was scornful of Californian support for exclusion through the 1880s but softened its editorial opposition to exclusion laws by the 1890s.[35] Half of New York's members of Congress supported the 1882 Exclusion Act.[36] And labor organizations in the city opposed Chinese and Asian immigration. In 1899, the Advance Labor Club of Brooklyn testified in favor of immigration restrictions and against the "hoards [*sic*] of other aliens from Europe and Asia," expressing concern about the increasing number of Japanese and "the steady expansion of the Chinese quarters in New York."[37]

In addition, especially during the early enforcement of exclusion, some New York officials expressed anti-Chinese views. J. Thomas Scharf, a special inspector appointed in New York in 1893 at the insistence of restrictionist senator Arthur Gorman, believed that almost all Chinese were unlawfully present in the United States and that weak enforcement made Chinese exclusion into a "farce."[38] He challenged the authority and questioned the integrity of his fellow officials. Only a few days after his transfer from Baltimore, Scharf's interactions with Customs Collector Francis Hendricks devolved into a series of rancorous exchanges.[39] Some of this tension may have been personal: Scharf was pompous and self-important, wondering why he, a gentleman with a legal doctorate and master's degree, "author of standard histories, and member of fifteen historical societies [was] going around Chinatown doing detective work."[40] Some of it was political: Scharf was a former Confederate and a Democrat among the mostly Republican employees of the New York Customs Administration.[41] However, most of the conflict was focused on the lax or corrupt enforcement of exclusion.[42]

Special Inspector Scharf and New York customs officials clashed over the implementation of Treasury Department rules, demonstrating the contested enforcement of exclusion. Customs officials argued that section six certificates of exempt status qualified their holders for entry without further investigation. Therefore, when inspectors at upstate border crossings detained Chinese arrivals and sent suspicious certificates for investigation, officials in New York City simply confirmed that the name on the certificate matched existing records and returned the document with their approval. In contrast, Scharf believed that collectors should conduct detailed investigations in such cases, should seek witnesses who were reputable U.S. citizens, and should "discard, as a rule, Chinese evidence." In essence, he wanted New York officials to follow the strict practices that were being developed and implemented in San Francisco.[43]

Based on his investigations across upstate New York, in New York City's Chinatown, and at Grand Central Station, Scharf maintained that hundreds of Chinese had been inappropriately admitted.[44] He also claimed that New York officials received bribes of up to $15,000 each year to facilitate the entry of ineligible Chinese immigrants, implicating the U.S. consul in Hong Kong and the former Chinese consul in New York, among others.[45] Although Scharf often overreached in his accusations, early officials *were* generous in their exemptions to exclusion. In 1893, a well-known gambler claimed merchant status and was landed. "Would the Exclusion act keep him out because he was a gambler?" the deputy collector asked. "The Exclusion act says that laborers must be kept out. Is a gambler more of a laborer than a merchant?"[46]

The enforcement of exclusion in New York was not only contested but also contingent upon local and national immigration officials. At first, Scharf received support from Treasury Secretary John G. Carlisle. However, he lost this backing as a new treasury secretary and a new customs collector were appointed. "It is an ascertained fact," Secretary Carlisle told Collector Hendricks in 1893, "that many hundreds of Chinese laborers have come into the country within the past year under the guise of merchants, students, actors, or other persons of the exempt class, aided in most cases by customs officers who were corrupt or indifferent to their duty."[47] Hendricks resigned and was replaced by former New York police official James Kilbreth.[48]

However, Customs Collector Kilbreth quickly came into conflict with Scharf when he determined that Scharf's evidence against some Chinese immigrants was weak and decided to admit them against Scharf's recommendation.[49] After Lyman Gage was appointed treasury secretary in 1897, he fired Scharf, claiming that he was "fertile in suspicion . . . but not very fruitful in evidence."[50] Special Inspector Scharf's zealous enforcement of the Geary Act in the 1890s was ultimately rejected as ineffective.[51]

Although Scharf was fired, his anti-Chinese attitude continued with the acting deputy collector in charge of exclusion, Francis Sterne Palmer. "At first sight," Palmer wrote in 1898, "it seems almost incomprehensible that any government should wish to exclude a race so peaceable and industrious— apparently such desirable material for future citizens." However, he proceeded to claim that Chinese refused to assimilate to American culture because they believed that they were already civilized. "The most debased coolie thinks himself fully civilized. Unhealthy and dwarfed in body and in morals, made foul by ancient vices, his blood often tainted by leprosy, the Chinese coolie is the natural product of an old, worn-out, rotten civilization."[52] Following Scharf, other New York inspectors assumed that almost all Chinese entered the United States illegally. Marcus Braun, for example, conducted a special investigation that claimed that all Chinese and Japanese migration across the Mexican-U.S. border was irregular. After this work was completed, he was transferred to Ellis Island.[53] Anti-Chinese attitudes were common throughout the Immigration Bureau, including in New York. However, complaints about the lax enforcement of exclusion should not be accepted as evidence of lower rates of rejection. They instead reflected the contested and contingent nature of enforcement, particularly in New York.

Despite support for Chinese and Asian exclusion among some New York politicians, unions, and immigration officials, these laws were challenged by Asian and other New Yorkers. Chinese New Yorkers contested exclusion laws, both formally and informally. They were more likely to secure non-Chinese support in New York than in the West, both among the public and within the Immigration Bureau. Japanese New Yorkers also challenged their exclusion in limited ways, relied on government officials for representation, and had allies within the Immigration Bureau.

Varied Chinese community organizations were engaged in protesting and influencing the enforcement of exclusion in New York. In San Francisco, opposition to exclusion was directed largely by *huiguan*, leading to a more top-down approach. *Huiguan* were merchant-led regional organizations that represented immigrants from different locales, collecting dues and providing social support. The huiguan federation, the Chinese Consolidated

Benevolent Association (CCBA), founded in the 1860s and based in San Francisco, took the lead nationally in opposing exclusion. The New York federation, established in 1883, addressed more local concerns. There is no record of the New York CCBA fighting directly against exclusion measures; however, the organization worked to ensure the fair enforcement of exclusion, including the hiring of competent interpreters drawn from its ranks.[54] When individual Chinese were denied entry, the CCBA hired lawyers on their behalf to appeal the Immigration Bureau's decisions. According to New York immigration commissioner Edward Corsi, the Chinese Chamber of Commerce was "the capital of the Celestials' Invisible Empire in the United States," ensuring "that no Chinaman is ever lacking in funds or witnesses to defend his case."[55] As explored in chapter 2, the Chinese Equal Rights League, founded in New York City in 1892 in response to the Geary Act, was also active in opposing the deportation laws that underpinned exclusion, and secured extensive non-Chinese support.

## The Chinese Division and the Immigration Bureau

As the administration of exclusion was expanded and transferred from the Customs Service to the Immigration Bureau in 1900, it continued to be contested in New York. Some tensions over the administration of exclusion were common to all immigration stations. However, New York officials questioned the exclusion law and cooperated with Chinese New Yorkers more extensively than in other locations. At the edges of exclusion enforcement, they also took a relatively restrained approach to Asian arrivals.

The contested, contingent treatment of Asians at Ellis Island was likely influenced by individual attitudes of officials as well as institutional practices at Ellis Island. As already explored, the Immigration Bureau reported that its enforcement efforts were hampered by lack of support for exclusion among "not only private citizens, but public officials and even judicial officers [who] occasionally resisted the attempts of the Bureau, going so far as to express their disapproval of the law."[56] These perspectives extended to some officials at Ellis Island. As the largest immigration station, it is possible that institutional practices concerning European arrivals influenced the ways that officials viewed Asian applicants. Ellis Island officials prided themselves on their efficiency and expertise. They worked hard to review the massive numbers of European arrivals promptly and professionally, inspecting them with the assumption that they deserved entry.[57] Starting in 1902, notices were posted throughout the immigration station stating that "immigrants must be treated with kindness and consideration" and delineating penalties for any violations.[58] As immigration and exclusion officials worked alongside each other, these perspectives may have shaped the implementation of exclusion at Ellis Island.

The treatment of Asians at Ellis Island may also have been shaped by the status of Asian arrivals and by Asian communities in New York. Chinese, Japanese, Koreans, Filipinos, and Asian Indians applying for admission in New York were more likely to be elite than Asians arriving at other immigration stations. New York officials noted this status approvingly and considered their cases accordingly. Officials expressed more favorable perspectives about Asians who arrived from Europe and via Canada compared with applicants from the Caribbean, where they were concerned about smuggling and weak enforcement of exclusion laws. They emphasized particularly the courtesy with which they treated elite arrivals. Of course, elites themselves did not always view their treatment by immigration officials in this way. In addition, the issue of corruption should not be overlooked in the relationship between Asian New Yorkers and Ellis Island officials. Scandals concerning the exploitation of immigrants and bribery of officials were not uncommon at Ellis Island. However, public revelations about fraudulent Chinese entries do not appear to have been more extensive in New York than at other stations, and corruption would not explain the lower numbers of admitted entrants in New York.[59]

Although Ellis Island has typically been associated with European immigration and Angel Island with Asian exclusion, New York officials were extensively involved in administering exclusion laws. At other ports, the commissioner handled both general immigration and Chinese exclusion. However, at Ellis Island there was "too much regular immigration business to permit of his being burdened with the enforcement of Chinese-exclusion laws."[60] Therefore, the New York commissioner focused mostly on European immigrants, as well as non-Chinese Asians, while the Chinese inspector in charge focused on administering Chinese exclusion.[61]

Immigration and exclusion officers had a hierarchical relationship: the New York commissioner was a powerful political position, appointed by the president, whereas the highest-ranking official in the New York Chinese Division was a civil servant. Commissioners reflected the immigration policies of the administrations for which they worked, but they also placed their own stamp on the administration of Ellis Island. Some, such as William Williams, who served two terms (1902–5, 1909–13), strictly enforced rules on European immigrants, going beyond the letter of the law. Others, such as Robert Watchorn (1905–9), Henry Curran (1923–26), and Edward Corsi (1931–34), were more sympathetic to arriving immigrants and instituted reforms to ease their time at Ellis Island.

Reflecting and reinforcing the institutional separation between immigration and exclusion enforcement, the offices were physically separate for many years: the Immigration Bureau was housed on Ellis Island and the Chinese Division moved repeatedly to different locations in lower Manhattan.[62] Although the Chinese Division offices were not located at the station, Chinese and other Asians were typically detained at Ellis Island. It was not until Ellis Island stopped being used as a major entry station in 1927, after massive reductions in European immigration, that the Chinese Division was transferred to the island.[63]

Upper-class Asians arriving in New York were processed similarly to European arrivals. Passengers traveling in first and second class were treated more respectfully and processed more quickly than others. In deference to wealthier individuals who could afford more expensive passage, public health service and immigration officials inspected cabin passengers in their quarters on board the ship and, if they were eligible to enter the United States, released them directly to shore. This process typically took a couple of hours, longer if there were not sufficient staff for all the arriving vessels. In contrast, travelers in third class or steerage were transferred by ferry to Ellis Island, where the immigration inspection process often took most of the day. Although Asian cabin passengers were inspected on board the ship along with Europeans, they were more likely to require further inspection under exclusion laws. Typically, only diplomats and dignatories were released immediately.[64]

At the immigration station, European and Chinese arrivals were separated from one another. Only about 20 percent of European steerage passengers were selected for additional medical inspection, and most of them were quickly approved. In contrast, almost all Chinese were subject to additional inspection under exclusion laws, and most were detained for at least a day before their hearing. Men and women were also separated from one another; however, unlike at Angel Island, where they remained separated for the duration of their detention, family members at Ellis Island were allowed to spend time together during the day. In addition, although San Francisco officials engaged in intrusive medical inspections based on their assumptions about Asians as dangerous vectors of disease and the annual reports of the surgeon general devote substantial space to detailing medical inspections in San Francisco, they do not identify medical inspections of Asians at Ellis Island beyond those that were required of all immigrants.[65]

Chinese who were not landed on primary inspection were typically assumed to be engaged in indirect smuggling schemes using fraudulent documentation, as this chapter will explore. Some, like William Fook Yee, were assumed to be paper sons falsely claiming U.S. citizenship. Others claimed that they were merchants. Members of the exempt classes carried section six certificates or other documentation that testified to their status. However, these were not accepted as prima facie evidence of their right to enter. On occasion, the secondary inspection involved an extensive investigation. More often, hearings were relatively short, constituting just one interview transcribed in a few pages rather than the extended interviews over multiple days common in California. Nevertheless, it is clear that the hearing process remained difficult for arriving Chinese.[66]

New York commissioner Corsi noted that the work of the Chinese Division was "the prevention of illegal entries by Chinese into New York Harbor and the metropolitan area and the apprehension, of course, of those found in New York City illegally."[67] However, the Chinese Division's work was much more extensive than this outline suggests. The Chinese inspector in charge of the port of New York handled all Chinese exclusion matters for the state, including the city and upstate ports close to the Canadian border.[68] The Chinese Division coordinated among different offices on the East Coast and throughout the country to investigate Chinese entrants and residents. In a particularly busy year, the New York Chinese Division conducted more than 500 investigations in the metropolitan area, involving an estimated 1,200 to 1,500 witnesses. "Our officers," the inspector in charge reported in a slower year, "are constantly visiting places where Chinese reside or are employed." Only a few of those investigations were for Chinese arriving or departing directly from New York; the vast majority supported investigations at other stations.[69]

### Inspectors and Interpreters

The staff within the Chinese Division was divided between inspectors and interpreters. This was a division of not only roles but also race. As a report on Ellis Island noted, the Chinese Division "staff consists of Americans, specially trained for work of this nature. The interpreters are Chinese."[70] Americans, in this understanding, meant white men. Inspectors were mostly formally appointed employees responsible for interviewing arriving passengers and investigating their cases. Most interpreters working on exclusion matters were ethnic Chinese employed on an ad hoc basis.[71] Ethnic Chinese interpreters were subordinate to white inspectors, and their salaries reflected this racial hierarchy: white inspectors and white interpreters earned about 20 percent more than Chinese interpreters.[72] Despite this racial discrimination, a position interpreting for the Immigration Bureau was respectable, paid more than other positions, and—at a time when twenty-six professions in New York were barred to Chinese—was a rare professional opportunity.[73]

Historian Mae Ngai has explored the interstitial position of interpreters brokering between Chinese and American government authorities, business interests, and communities.[74] Chinese interpreters were suspected of being biased toward Chinese applicants and susceptible to bribery. In San Francisco in particular, exclusion officials preferred white interpreters who had no affiliation with Chinese.[75]

In New York, interpreters typically had links to a range of Chinese community organizations, including respectable huiguan, criminally focused fraternal secret societies known as tongs, and the Christian Chinese Mission.[76] With smaller numbers of Chinese arrivals, many interpreters on the government payroll in New York worked as needed on a per-diem basis.[77] As a result, they translated both for immigration and for other cases. Worry Charles was employed as an interpreter in New York and other cities during the early 1890s, even though he also worked for a tong that he vigorously defended as a "patriotic" organization "and not an association of assassins."[78] In Boston during the same time period, Moy Loy interpreted for the federal government and the county court, represented Chinese obtaining leases, and also acted as a partner in one of the city's largest mercantile firms.[79] In the northern border crossing of Malone, New York, huiguan from New York City and Boston provided interpreters for various cases.[80]

These arrangements provoked concern among critics of exclusion enforcement in New York. Not surprisingly, given his zealous anti-Chinese attitude, inspector Scharf accused two interpreters of being "appointed by the Chinese" and being partners in a New York smuggling service. The accused men, Lee Foy and Yung Luck, were replaced by Dr. Joseph Singleton, "a Christian Chinaman who married an American girl and practices medicine in Brooklyn."[81] Scharf also claimed that ten associates of a Canadian Pacific Railroad interpreter had been admitted in New York without the required witnesses, because of collusion between railroad employees and U.S. officials.[82] A few years later in 1900, a customs collector in upstate Malone expressed concerns about the reliability of interpreters provided by Chinese organizations and implored officials in Washington, D.C., to hire an official interpreter for New York.[83] Perhaps in response to these concerns, the first Chinese interpreters formally hired by the Immigration Bureau were both hired in New York State: Charlie Kee in Brooklyn (around 1899), followed by Moy Shere Foo in Buffalo (in 1901).[84]

Interpreters were not only a flashpoint for nativist critics of exclusion enforcement in New York, but also a source of Chinese challenges to the administration of exclusion. In 1903, New York's CCBA opposed the choice of Chinese interpreters in the city. Claiming that the interpreters were not trustworthy and "not in any sense representative of the better elements of the Chinese communities," the association endorsed its president for the position of official interpreter. A "Chinese merchant of independent means," a contemporary commentator noted, he "agreed to accept in order to serve the Chinese community, though the salary was undoubtedly much smaller than the profits of his business."[85] Concerns about corruption were complex. Nativists expressed concerns that New York officials were compromised because they worked closely with Chinese organizations. Some immigration officials expressed concerns that Chinese interpreters were unreliable because they were selected by community organizations. And organizations such as the CCBA expressed concerns that some of their coethnic interpreters were untrustworthy and worked to have more control over the hiring process. Despite these complex concerns, New York officials worked closely and cooperatively with Chinese community members to secure interpretation services.

New York officials also quietly resisted efforts to use interpreters to enforce exclusion more assertively. In 1914, the commissioner-general of immigration proposed rotating interpreters. He claimed that this was due not to concerns about capability or corruption but to "avoid erroneous decisions" and to protect interpreters from community reprisals. As one of only five stations that had more than one interpreter, New York was included in this plan. During San Francisco's extensive interrogations, Chinese interpreters were rotated regularly because of assumptions that they could be bribed by their compatriots and would translate in a way that was favorable to applicants. The practice of rotation was designed to make such efforts to evade exclusion more difficult. The New York office did not openly oppose the introduction of interpreter rotation. However, as it had only two regularly employed interpreters and as most New York interviews were too cursory to require a change of interpreter, this practice was rarely enforced.[86]

At all immigration stations, inspectors and formally employed interpreters left the immigration service to become immigration brokers representing Chinese. For example, former Angel Island inspector Henry C. Kennah worked representing Chinese at a San Francisco law firm for about five years, until he was found guilty of operating a smuggling ring in 1917 and barred from representing immigrants.[87] In New York, however, the practice of inspectors moving from public to private service, from investigating to representing Chinese, appears to have been more extensive. Although records are limited, more former inspectors appear to have worked for longer periods as Chinese advisers. And, although there was typically only one regular employee working as an inspector in charge at Ellis Island, these individuals employed in more responsible positions also became Chinese advocates.

Harry R. Sisson started as a Chinese inspector in New York in 1905, became inspector in charge in 1907, and by 1914 was supervising at least twelve officers assigned to Ellis Island.[88] He took on additional responsibilities as a special representative in 1918, surveying enforcement of Chinese exclusion on the Pacific coast and making recommendations for more efficient and consistent administration of the law.[89] However, by 1922 he had moved on from the Immigration Bureau and until 1939 Sisson represented Chinese clients as an "adviser in Chinese procedure and immigration matters."[90] A. W. Brough, who served as Ellis Island's inspector in charge from at least 1924 to 1927, worked throughout the 1930s as a representative of Chinese arrivals.[91] It isn't clear why many New York inspectors worked on behalf of Chinese clients after leaving government service; however, their choice of work may have been influenced by more considerate implementation of Chinese exclusion in New York.

As an inspector at Ellis Island, Sisson dispatched his duties carefully, sometimes facing challenges and criticisms from Chinese and their supporters, at other times working with Chinese representatives. In 1907, Hoi Yin attempted to bring his wife and daughter into the country as the dependent of a merchant, one of the few groups of Chinese allowed to bring their families to the United States. However, Sisson's investigation determined that Hoi was not a merchant but a waiter at a Chinese restaurant just a few storefronts from his home on Mott Street in Chinatown. After Hoi's request to have his family join him was denied, his wife and daughter failed to appear at the upstate New York immigration station where they had originally planned to enter the United States. They did show up, however, a couple of weeks later, in Hoi's home. They were discovered by Sisson. "An attractive picture in their oriental robes," according to the *New York Times*, the woman and her daughter were arrested and transferred to detention at Ellis Island. However, the U.S. commissioner charged with reviewing their case sympathized with Hoi's desire to have his family join him. He turned upside down the assumption that Hoi, having illegally smuggled his family into the country, was an undesirable immigrant and suggested instead that Sisson was at fault. "Anyone who would bar either of these two women from the country," Commissioner Shields claimed, "is an undesirable citizen pure and simple."[92] Although the record does not show what happened to Hoi's family, the commissioner critiqued Sisson, his implementation of the exclusion laws, and his policing of family reunification.

A few years later, in 1913, Attorney Robert M. Moore brought an appeal on behalf of Chinese who had entered the United States from Canada, claiming that they had been born in the United States and were therefore U.S. citizens. Sisson disagreed with this claim and sought to have them deported to China. However, Moore successfully argued that, even if they were not born in the United States, this did not mean that they were born in and should be deported to China. The men were deported instead to Canada, presumably offering them an easier means of unauthorized entry back into the United States.[93]

In other ways, Sisson worked to alleviate the harsh treatment of Chinese under exclusion. In 1916 he negotiated with the national Immigration Bureau to allow Chinese performers to enter the United States under bond, helping to shape a key policy that facilitated immigration. In 1918, as special representative, he inaugurated changes to ensure all Chinese were "examined by a board of inquiry in the manner long in vogue in the cases of other aliens." Resulting from a successful court case brought by Quan Hing Sun against the San Francisco immigration commissioner, the introduction of the three-person board in Chinese cases was designed to increase fairness, reduce fraud, and limit detention times, as Chinese could be released immediately upon approval by the board. Sisson was selected to ensure the new policy's consistent implementation in West Coast ports, including San Francisco, San Diego, and Seattle.[94]

As a representative of the Immigration Bureau, Sisson worked to enforce exclusion law thoroughly but fairly. Later in his career, as a representative of the Chinese, Sisson worked similarly diligently to ensure that his clients had the best chance of entry through New York. From his spacious offices west of Chinatown, Sisson coordinated almost every aspect of the immigration application. He submitted forms and photographs to Ellis Island, sent letters informing officials when his clients were arriving in port, received notice of the dates and times of hearings and witness interviews, and acted as a witness on behalf of his clients. Sisson testified, for example, that Tom Yick was a "bona fide merchant," claiming to have called at his store weekly and passed by almost daily, with a clear view inside. Although other white witnesses were sometimes accused of being "professional witnesses" paid to lie on behalf of Chinese applicants, there is no evidence of these accusations against former New York officials. In the confrontational process that existed at Angel Island, Sisson might have been accused of switching sides. However, as he used his detailed knowledge of exclusion administration to guide Chinese clients, it is possible that Sisson considered his work part of the same process of efficiently and effectively complying with exclusion laws.[95]

Like inspectors, Chinese interpreters transitioned to work as immigration brokers. However, they were viewed with more suspicion than white immigration brokers, investigated more frequently, and convicted of violating exclusion laws.[96] Sing Kee, for example, moved from his home state of California to New York when he turned twenty-one in 1916.[97] Kee served in World War I, returning with a Distinguished Service Cross for not leaving his radio post despite being gassed and facing heavy fire.[98] Respected within both New York's Chinese and white communities, he worked as an interpreter for the Immigration Bureau between 1919 and 1928. Using his knowledge of the immigration process, he started the Chinese Overseas Travel Service, based in Manhattan's Chinatown. Throughout the 1930s and 1940s, he was a successful businessman. However, in the 1950s, as U.S. authorities became increasingly concerned about the national security implications of Chinese communists immigrating illegally to the United States, Kee was convicted of conspiracy to violate immigration laws.[99] Walter Eng had a similar trajectory in his career, working as a per diem interpreter at Ellis Island and then, in the 1950s, being convicted of conspiracy to violate immigration laws.[100] Frank Toy, who worked as an interpreter in New York in 1956, was twice tried by the U.S. government but was never convicted.[101]

Chinese arriving in New York experienced relatively considerate enforcement of exclusion that was different from the experiences of Chinese at other immigration stations. Exclusion officials worked cooperatively with local Chinese and, at the highest levels, engaged in a revolving door from immigration enforcement to immigrant advocacy. Their work was likely influenced by contested attitudes toward exclusion laws in New York, as well as institutional practices at Ellis Island. Chinese Division and Immigration Bureau officials prided themselves on the prompt, professional inspection of immigrants. However, they showed more respect to those they deemed respectable, higher-class Asian and European immigrants.

## Asian Arrivals in New York

The relatively restrained treatment of Asian arrivals at Ellis Island may have been shaped not only by different attitudes toward exclusion in New York and different institutional practices at the immigration station, but also by the higher-class status of Asian arrivals. Chinese, Japanese, Koreans, Filipinos, and Asian Indians arriving in New York were more likely to be educated elites than those entering through San Francisco and other ports. Immigration reports do not allow detailed analysis of different classes of arrivals at each port. Nonetheless, official and popular discussions of Asian migration and the Asian community in New York suggest that there were larger numbers of diplomats, merchants, students, and other members of the exempt classes who did not work as laborers. This status may have resulted in them being treated relatively respectfully and processed promptly.

New York officials emphasized that most Chinese arrivals at Ellis Island were "of the higher class."[102] They also noted that Japanese arrivals at Ellis Island were generally first-class passengers rather than laborers in steerage.[103] Although the number of Korean arrivals in New York was very small, between passage of a U.S. treaty in 1883 and Japanese annexation in 1910, the Korean government limited U.S. travel to diplomats, select professionals, students, and dependents. Early Korean arrivals at Ellis Island consisted almost exclusively of students and merchants, with the occasional representative of the Imperial Mission.[104] As U.S. nationals with rights of residence in the United States, Filipinos were not regulated under exclusion. However, writing in 1930, social worker and activist Bruno Lasker noted that Filipinos in New York were, compared with the West, "a small group of newcomers, with a relatively large proportion of students and other exceptional personalities."[105] Community historian Maria del Valle Embry has researched how "Filipinos who passed through Ellis Island were the Senators, provincial Governors, diplomats, jurists, writers, educators, students, and businessmen/women."[106]

Among the most elite arrivals at Ellis Island were royalty, diplomats, and other dignitaries on official business, including visits with presidents and members of Congress. Their arrival was covered broadly in the news. Pacific Islanders, including Hawaiians, are rarely represented in New York immigration records. However, Princess Victoria Ka'iulani of Hawaii traveled via Ellis Island to meet informally with President Grover Cleveland after American planters attempted to overthrow the Hawaiian monarchy in 1893. Princess Ka'iulani was months shy of completing her education in England, turning eighteen, and taking the Hawaiian throne. Her efforts to maintain Hawaii's independence were, ultimately, unsuccessful.[107] The Crown Prince of Siam, now Thailand, had a more spectacular welcome when he arrived in 1902 with a large entourage and seventy-seven items of luggage. Attended by a welcoming party of U.S. officials who had waited hours for his arrival, the Crown Prince spent time with U.S. reporters, then traveled to a specially assigned train in Jersey City that took him to Washington, D.C., to meet with President Theodore Roosevelt.[108]

Much more than at other ports, a significant percentage of Chinese entrants in New York were consular officials.[109] From 1913 to 1920, when these data were reported by port, between 21 and 42 percent of all New York Chinese entrants entered on diplomatic passports.[110] These figures include not only Chinese officials themselves but also family and other household members.[111] The Philippines did not have independent diplomats, but, as a colony of the United States, it was represented by nonvoting members of the U.S. Congress from 1907 through independence in 1946. These resident commissioners typically traveled to the United States via Ellis Island.[112] India had no diplomatic representation in the United States, because of its colonial status under Britain. However, Indian independence leaders frequently traveled via Europe to New York. For example, Indian revolutionary Har Dayal lived in India, England, France, and Algeria before traveling via Puerto Rico to New York en route to Cambridge, Massachusetts, in 1911. As historian Seema Sohi has argued, "By 1906, New York had emerged as a fulcrum in the global Indian anticolonial network that extended from East Asia to Europe to North America."[113] Korean independence leaders were not commonly recorded in New York immigration records. Most movements for Korean self-determination after the Japanese annexation of Korea in 1910 were based in Hawaii and the western United States, particularly San Francisco. And even when individuals were listed as racially "Korean" in New York immigration records, their nationality was recorded as Japanese, suggesting that their presence may only rarely have been recorded.

As elites accustomed to deference and as representatives of the Chinese government concerned with the administration of exclusion, diplomats registered both formal and informal complaints if U.S. officials did not admit them promptly or treat them with respect. Wu Ting Fang, Chinese minister to the United States, Mexico, Peru, and Cuba in the late 1890s and early 1900s, was perhaps the most vocal consular critic of U.S. exclusion enforcement. Consul Wu wrote to the U.S. State Department about the treatment of two Chinese diplomats en route to London via Vancouver, Montreal, and New York in 1899. Customs officials from Malone, New York, boarded the train on which the diplomats were traveling and, although the diplomats presented credentials from Chinese, British, and U.S. authorities, they were detained for twenty-four hours. Consul Wu formally complained that the men "on the business of the Imperial Government" were subjected to "great humiliation and indignity."[114] Wu himself experienced a shorter, four-hour delay upon his arrival in New York City that he described in his memoir. "We had first to wait for the doctor to come on board to make his inspection of all the passengers, then the Customs officials appeared and examined the luggage and boxes of all the passengers, and then, last but not the least, we had to wait for the immigration officers. All this necessarily took time, and it was not until all these inspections were completed that the steamer was allowed to enter the harbor, and to tie up alongside the dock." Wu negatively compared the United States with other nations, arguing that inspections should be completed more promptly. "I would be the last one to encourage smuggling," Wu wrote, "but would the national interests really suffer if the Custom House officers were to be a little more ready to accept a traveler's word, and if they were less ready to suspect everyone of making false declarations when entering the country?[115]

Ellis Island officials coordinated with consular officials and regularly emphasized their respectful treatment of diplomats, as well as elite arrivals more broadly. Consul Wu informed the U.S. secretary of state when diplomatic parties were traveling to New York and other U.S. ports, requesting that immigration authorities "extend the usual courtesies."[116] The New York Chinese inspector in charge reported that official classes were treated with "special attention and courtesy."[117] But the fact that they mentioned these courtesies only in relation to diplomats and other elites suggests that they were not common to all, and that they were not extended to laborers.

Asian students were among the elite groups that traveled to the United States via New York, either because they had previously been studying in Europe or because they were planning to study in the eastern United States.

Most Chinese students attended institutions in the East or the Midwest.[118] Information on Chinese student arrivals is limited, but existing records show that students were typically between 20 percent and 35 percent of all Chinese entrants in New York.[119] They came as beneficiaries of Boxer Indemnity Fellowships between 1909 and 1929, as recipients of scholarships from U.S. institutions such as Columbia University, and as self-supported elites.[120] Hundreds of Filipino students were sponsored by the U.S. government under the 1903 Pensionado Act, part of U.S. efforts to inculcate an Americanized elite within the newly colonized Philippines. Although most were men, some Filipina students attended the Teachers College at Columbia University sponsored by the U.S. government, the Red Cross, and the Rockefeller Foundation. Later, many Filipino students were supported by wealthy parents or funded their own education. As a result, substantial numbers of Filipinos studied in the United States, although most were based in the West.[121]

As students typically enrolled in college prior to their arrival, New York exclusion officials generally viewed such applicants favorably and treated them considerately. Upon students' arrival, inspectors checked enrollment letters and ensured that students had sufficient funding to complete their education. After six months ministering to Chinese in northern France for the Young Men's Christian Association (YMCA) in 1921, Andrew Chih Yi Cheng traveled via New York to resume his studies at Hartford Theological Seminary. He was landed promptly along with seven fellow Chinese students traveling to colleges in New York, New Jersey, Virginia, Illinois, and Iowa.[122] In contrast, after four years studying law at London's Inns of Court, Khem Singh traveled to study medicine in New York. Despite his elite status as the son of an Indian magistrate, Singh was denied entry, apparently owing to lack of funds.[123]

Students were required to maintain their educational status in order to keep their exempt status. Chinese students were allowed to work part time while they focused on their studies; however, if they dropped out of school, they were no longer considered legal residents. In one case, a Korean Chinese student left the college where he was studying in the southern United States and moved to New York, where he was detained by immigration authorities. After admitting that he ironed and pressed clothes "for fun sometimes," he was recommended for deportation and left the United States.[124] Filipino students did not have the same restrictions as Chinese students owing to their status as colonized subjects with rights to reside and work in the United States. Even if they dropped out, their status as nationals allowed them to legally stay in the United States.[125]

"Paper students," individuals who claimed student status when they intended to work, appear to have been rare, in part because there were more established and effective methods of gaming the exclusion system, such as claiming status as a merchant or paper son. In one exception in the early 1900s, a Japanese man attempted to gain entry for two Chinese laundrymen by having them pose as Japanese students. According to an inspector who discovered the fraud, the smuggler charged the men $750 to "land them safely in some laundry in New York."[126]

Nonetheless, the indeterminacy of student status seems to have allowed some Asians the opportunity to evade exclusion. Radical author H. T. Tsiang first arrived as a student around 1926. Thirteen years later, he was taken to Ellis Island and threatened with deportation for breaking his student residency requirements. There are at least two stories behind his detention, which lasted more than a year. The American Committee for the Protection of the Foreign Born, a civil rights organization that focused especially on representing leftist immigrants, claimed that Tsiang suffered poor health that prevented him from reenrolling in classes at Columbia University.[127] A fellow detainee at Ellis Island, however, recalls Tsiang describing how he registered for a class or two each spring "to keep up the fiction that he was studying," then failed to enroll in the fall, and was regularly taken to Ellis Island, where he received free room and board throughout the winter. Neither of these stories was likely entirely true. Although his case was eventually resolved and he was released, Tsiang continued to be harassed by the immigration authorities for his left-wing beliefs, which made him vulnerable to deportation.[128] The shifting status of students meant it was uncommon for them to come as paper arrivals, but also allowed some students, like Tsiang, to take advantage of their status.

As a major center of international commerce, New York attracted merchants trading in Chinese goods, Bengali crafts, and Japanese silk, lace, and pearls. Chinese merchants who arrived via Ellis Island were generally from the Caribbean, Latin America, and, occasionally, Europe. Bengali traders more often traveled from Calcutta to Southampton, then on to New York. Japanese importers arriving in New York also commonly traveled from Europe.[129]

More than the treatment of diplomats and students, the regulation of merchants in New York was contingent on race, class, and region. Merchants sometimes faced extensive and time-consuming investigations upon their arrival or return. At other times, interviews to determine merchant status appear to have been cursory. Some of this contingent regulation emerged

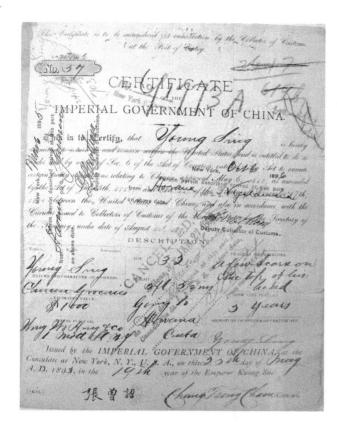

Young Sing, certificate of the Imperial Government of China, New York, New York, file 47/619, Chinese Files, 1921–1944, INS, NARA–New York (1893).

from class and racial biases, as officials assumed that Chinese were faking their merchant status, Bengalis were lower-class peddlers, and Japanese were legitimate merchants. Some variation in treatment was based on the regions in which merchants traded: merchants working in the Caribbean typically faced more scrutiny than those who traded in Europe or Japan. Young Sing, the owner of a grocery store on Mott Street in Chinatown, regularly traveled between New York and Cuba for work, although he was also regularly delayed for weeks by immigration authorities. His certificate bears numerous stamps detailing his journeys.[130] Groups such as the Cuban Asiatic Chamber of Commerce supported Chinese merchants in their dealings with the Immigration Bureau.[131] In general, regardless of where they were traveling or what they were trading, merchants arriving in New York were treated with more courtesy than those applying for admission in California.

Chinese exclusion laws drew a distinction between merchants and laborers, with merchants allowed to enter the United States and laborers barred. At the national level, immigration officials believed that many

Chinese laborers invested in shell companies to secure section six certificates and enter the United States as merchants. They dismissed "so-called 'mercantile firms,' located throughout this country and in Canada, Mexico, Jamaica, Cuba, and Hongkong," claiming that they were part of a global network of unauthorized Chinese migration. Although these firms recorded the investment of large numbers of Chinese merchants, exclusion officials claimed that their actual products were Chinese laborers, and their purpose was "to export and import the coolie and to amass fortunes in the business."[132] Like students, merchants not only had to prove their status upon arrival but also had to maintain this status to ensure their continued legal residence. In New York as in California, inspectors routinely traveled to Chinatown to check whether merchants were moving stock or performing other physical work, which might cause them to be classified as laborers and lose their exempt status.[133]

New York exclusion officials were particularly concerned that fraudulent merchants were entering the United States from the Caribbean and Latin America, because of both lax enforcement and active fraud. In Trinidad, the U.S. consul regularly issued section six merchant certificates even though his office was too busy to travel to the rural districts where applicants lived. In response to pressure from New York officials, who were concerned both by this lack of investigation and by the "personal appearance" of the applicants, the consul tightened the application process.[134] In Cuba, the U.S. consul also appears to have visaed certificates that did not have the required photographs and without any investigation into whether the firms in which applicants claimed partnerships even existed.[135] According to a 1922 report, many Trinidadian Chinese presented Cuban documents certifying their status as merchants in order to secure section six certificates. However, these Chinese had never traveled to Cuba. The same report also noted that the consul for Chile, Ecuador, and Costa Rica in Trinidad had approached the U.S. consul, requesting "secret and private" conferences and offering $200 bribes to issue section six certificates to various applicants who were not eligible.[136] Another report on Cuba expressed concern that a high-level U.S. immigration official made "irregular" decisions, suggesting that the official may have been corrupt.[137]

Exclusion officials in New York dealt extensively with Caribbean and Latin American arrivals. As explored in chapter 3, they were aware that these locations were sites where Chinese traveled to be smuggled into the United States; however, officials also understood that legitimate Chinese merchants traded across the Caribbean. Just as the national Immigration

Bureau sometimes pushed New York to be more careful in its enforcement of exclusion, New York officials asked the U.S. consul in Trinidad to investigate new cases more carefully. However, enforcement was rarely rigorous across the Caribbean.

New York officials enforced class distinctions between applicants whom they viewed as legitimate merchants and those whom they considered laborers. When Tcheng Ka Ling arrived at Ellis Island from Vienna in 1915, he was detained at Ellis Island for eleven days as officials attempted to determine whether he and his colleagues were, as they claimed, marble stone merchants or if they were, as officials derisively suggested, "soapstone peddlers."[138] Peddlers were considered manual laborers rather than merchants, as they lacked capital and carried their goods as they traveled to sell them.

These distinctions between merchants and laborers should have applied only to Chinese arrivals under exclusion law. However, in practice, this distinction appears to have been extended to other Asians. South Asians were not barred from entering the United States under exclusion laws until 1924. However, Bengali peddlers were prevented from entering the United States under general immigration laws because they were defined as contract laborers or assisted immigrants. In 1897, twelve Bengali men were denied admission in New York despite the fact that they appeared to have met all immigration requirements. Officials may have been suspicious because the men traveled in steerage rather than the cabin class expected of merchants. Upon their arrival, the men were listed in the ship's manifest as "merchants"; but upon their removal they were described as "laborers."[139] The merchant-laborer distinction was not part of immigration law and should not have been applied to South Asians. However, this case suggests that even before Chinese exclusion was formally extended to other Asian groups, officials were using this distinction to limit the entry of some Asians.

Despite their concerns about the difficulty of determining merchants' status, officials continued to allow the entry of most Chinese merchants. In 1920, only one section six merchant was rejected out of 230 applicants for admission in New York. Echoing earlier sentiments by customs officials in conflict with inspector Scharf, Chinese inspector in charge Harry Sisson acknowledged both "that the law is not being complied with" and that his office had no way to controvert statements made on section six certificates. When Tcheng Ka Ling applied for entry in New York, he was unable to prove almost anything related to his claims of being a marble stone merchant. Tcheng stated that he had $100 or $200 with him; however, he could produce only $23. He stated that he had ordered goods for the store, but he had no bill of lading. And he stated that his shop would be located in San Francisco, but he had no proposed address. Despite the weakness of his application, immigration officials in New York admitted him.[140]

Exclusion officials in New York typically conducted only brief interviews with Chinese merchants, which resembled the cursory interviews conducted with Europeans to ensure that they complied with immigration law. When merchant Dang Ham arrived in New York from Tampico, Mexico, in 1922, he was asked exactly six questions: his name, his age, a description of his wife, whether he had any children, his address (he answered only "a hotel"), and whether he knew anyone in the United States.[141] The brevity of this interview is striking when compared with the length of interrogations by inspectors in San Francisco during the same time, which commonly ran to hours over a period of days. Dang Ham was landed within two days.[142]

In addition to the relative speed and sometimes cursory nature of investigations in New York, Chinese merchants were often supported by colleagues who requested they be treated considerately. Consulates and business associates regularly wrote to New York informing Chinese Division officials when merchants would be arriving and, as they did with diplomats, requesting courteous treatment. The U.S. consul in Trinidad wrote to the Chinese inspector in New York when merchant Aldric Lee Lum was arriving at the port en route to visit his aging father in Hong Kong. Although the consul noted that it was typical for him to send dispatches both to Washington, D.C., and New York on the steamer *preceding* the Chinese passengers, an oversight meant that these communications would be arriving on the same steamer. The consul concluded that "Mr. Lee Lum and his party are very clearly exempt, and I commend them to your courtesy."[143] When Lawrence Joseph Akow, the owner of the Trinidad Auto and Cycle Company, planned a business trip in 1922, the export manager of the Federal Rubber Company wrote to New York authorities in advance of his arrival, assuring them of Akow's status as merchant and his work as a successful sales representative for the company. "We wish to make Mr. Akow's stay in New York," the export manager wrote, "one of pleasure and complete satisfaction."[144] Inspectors routinely agreed to process papers promptly and take care of arriving elites, even if they arrived after hours.[145] These accommodations were similar to those made for diplomats and students.

Chinese government officials, Chinese Americans, and their allies strongly opposed the introduction of exclusion. After it was enacted and upheld by U.S. courts, however, they focused on the administration of the law. Consul

Wu Ting Fang emphasized "the hardships entailed upon even the members of the exempt classes of Chinese by the harsh enforcement of the Exclusion Laws."[146] American publications also questioned the treatment of elites. The progressive *Outlook* magazine editorialized against Chinese exclusion in general, but took particular issue with the harsh enforcement of the laws against elite Chinese. "Some of the Chinese merchants, students, and travelers for pleasure, who are now treated [poorly] are graduates of Yale, Amherst, and other colleges and universities," the magazine noted. What would an American say if "he were kept overnight in a cage on a Chinese Ellis Island, stripped to the skin, measured, photographed, and cross-questioned by a lot of Chinese officials who neither desired nor endeavored to conceal their contempt for him? Such treatment of an American citizen would fill our newspapers with articles about Chinese barbarism."[147] In arguing for more equal treatment of Chinese, however, *Outlook* reinforced class distinctions between professionals and ordinary laborers.

Although they were not typically elite, travelers of all nationalities arrived in the United States temporarily. Immigration Bureau officials were concerned that many Chinese arrivals claiming transit or temporary working privileges were actually planning to end their journeys and settle permanently in the United States. As a result, they were frequently suspicious of Chinese passengers in transit. Although these groups are not traditionally considered within immigration histories, travelers in transit formed a large number of Chinese arriving in New York and inspected by Ellis Island exclusion officials.

In 1906, the New York commissioner noted that "the examination of tourists and transits, and some of the alleged American citizens, requires as much time and care as the examination of the immigrant alien."[148] In 1915, two Chinese brothers traveling in cabin class, twenty-two-year-old Tat Shue She and eleven-year-old Pui Shue She, docked in New York en route from Liverpool to Hong Kong, then waited four hours on board the ship for the Chinese immigration inspector. The *New York Times* reported their extended wait, drawing attention to their high-class status through reference to their father's position as a Hong Kong banker, their possession of a letter from the Chinese ambassador in London endorsed by the American ambassador, and the fact that, after being released, the brothers stayed at the Waldorf-Astoria Hotel.[149] In the same year, Terika Parahi, a Frenchwoman of Pacific Islander descent who worked as a servant in Paris, arrived in New York. She had sailed from Bordeaux with her mistress, and they were admitted to travel through the United States to visit family in Papa'ete, Tahiti. Both women had made the journey previously.[150]

As a cultural center, New York City was home to Cantonese theaters performing for the local Chinese community as well as Western entertainments featuring Sinhalese dancers, Filipino entertainers, Chinese acrobats, and other Asian circus workers.[151] Asian performers appear to have arrived in New York in relatively large numbers. In 1905, seven Japanese and two Koreans arrived as part of the Orrin Brothers circus en route from their home in Mexico City to Paris.[152] In 1914, twenty-nine Chinese theatrical performers arrived at Ellis Island; in 1915, this number was thirty-one. In terms of total numbers, only diplomats and students arrived in larger numbers during these years.[153]

In the early 1900s, the Immigration Bureau defined Chinese performers as laborers. However, New York inspector in charge Harry Sisson worked with national officials to introduce a bonding system that facilitated performers' entry. Such bonds were later expanded to other groups. "As you are doubtless aware," the national office wrote to Sisson in 1916 when seven Chinese Barnum & Bailey Circus performers applied for admission in New York, "Chinese persons coming to the United States in the capacity of acrobats or vaudeville performers are not admissible." However, Sisson worked to secure entry for the performers through the use of bonds. Five were approved with a $1,000 bond, and two were prevented from entering because they had trachoma, a contagious eye disease that was cause for rejection under immigration law. Chinese performers and sailors were among the first required to obtain bonds to ensure their departure. By 1929, bonds were required of all temporary Chinese visitors. Although they were intended to ensure temporary residence, some companies repeatedly renewed performers' permits, allowing them to stay for years. Travelers in transit and performers were not necessarily elite; however, limited New York records show them being landed promptly even though they were required to provide guarantees of their departure in the form of bonds.[154]

In 1911, Merwan Irani arrived at Ellis Island from Southampton, England, traveling to the Coliseum Circus in Chicago with a small entourage. Irani was listed in the ship's manifest as a "showman" born in Persia, his wife Khorseib was from Bombay, and four performers and an attendant were all from Madras. Upon their arrival, performers Perumall Sammy and Subramaino Pillay were certified by Public Health Service physicians as having physical deformities, while Gondia Ras and Lakshmi Bai were classified as

Augustus Sherman, "Perumall Sammy, Subramaino Pillay, Thumbu Sammy," Statue of Liberty National Monument, New York, National Park Service (1911).

idiots. Perumall was accompanied by his younger brother, Thumbu Sammy, who worked as his attendant. Among regular immigrants, such certifications would have led to rejection: the 1882 Immigration Law barred lunatics and idiots, while the 1907 Law prohibited entry to anyone judged "mentally or physically defective."[155] In addition to eugenic concerns, immigrants with mental or physical disabilities were assumed to be unemployable and likely to become a public charge. However, in the case of nonimmigrant circus performers, these disabilities were the source of their work.

All the arrivals, except for Irani and his wife, were photographed by Augustus Sherman, the chief clerk and an amateur photographer at Ellis Island.[156] Most of the photographs are respectful portraits. However, in one medicalized image Sherman links the processes of immigrant inspection and sideshow spectacle as Perumall Sammy is depicted with an open jacket and displaying his naked chest and deformity. By contrast, in a group portrait, Sammy stares confidently at the viewer, a shawl draped over his shoulder and a slight smile on his lips.[157] Despite Sammy's composure, it is not possible to know whether he and his colleagues were content or concerned about being photographed. Sherman depicted Europeans and Asians who may have worked in circuses in other photographs. In one, a "Russian giant" and a Burmese little person were depicted alongside inspectors for a sense of scale. A different Sherman portrait of three sideshow workers, titled "The Monkey-men from Ceylon," was also published.[158] Unlike sideshow work, the subjects of these photographs had no control over the circulation or representation of their bodies after the photograph was printed.

Travelers in transit were by definition not immigrants, arrivals who intended to reside permanently in the United States. As a result, they have often been overlooked by immigration historians. However, much of the Immigration Bureau's attention focused on nonimmigrants, particularly Chinese nonimmigrants, to ensure that they did not become permanent settlers. Typically, the number of temporary Chinese arrivals was ten times that of permanent arrivals in New York. And, increasingly, New York was an important port for travelers in transit. By 1922 and throughout the 1920s, similar numbers of Chinese passengers in transit arrived at both New York and San Francisco: between 1,000 and 1,500 travelers annually.[159] As with Chinese immigrants, the New York Bureau processed these arrivals relatively respectfully and promptly.

### Delayed Progress and Prompt Processing

At Ellis Island, as at other immigration stations, Chinese focused on detention as a particularly harsh aspect of the exclusion laws. In San Francisco, many poems expressed dismay at people's detention. "Over one hundred poems are on the walls," one man wrote. "Looking at them, they are all pining at the delayed progress." Similar feelings were expressed at Ellis Island. One Ellis Island poet wrote that

> I landed in the Flowery Flag
> Thinking I would be safe and free of sadness.
> Who knew that I'd be seized by immigration officials?
> They threw me in detention, ignoring my protests.
> How can I gain relief from these oppressive laws?

Only seven poems survived at Ellis Island; the small number is likely because of the small number of Chinese detainees.[160]

Chinese clearly experienced detention as a very trying time in which they were prevented, either temporarily or permanently, from entering the United States. These experiences of detention, both on arrival and prior to deportation, are explored in the following chapter. Across different categories, the process of reviewing Chinese arrivals appears to have been quicker and Chinese entrants seem to have been detained for shorter periods on Ellis Island than on Angel Island. As historians have focused on European immigration through Ellis Island, they have emphasized the speed with which European immigrants were moved through the immigration station compared with Asian arrivals at Angel Island. "Ellis Island was a way station, with most immigrants processed and released within hours," Iris Chang writes in her history of Chinese Americans, "whereas Angel Island was a long-term detention center, where many Chinese were imprisoned for months, even years."[161] However, although historians have compared Ellis Island and Angel Island, they have not considered whether the detention rates and times were the same for Chinese at both immigration stations.

Unfortunately, detention data are limited for both locations. As economists Robert Barde and Gustavo Bobonis comment, detailed detention data are lacking not only for Angel Island but also for "the better-known immigration portal on Ellis Island."[162] When the Angel Island station burned down in 1940, detailed immigration records were destroyed.[163] Similarly, samples from New York case files are not representative, as inactive files were destroyed by the New York office in the 1940s or 1950s. The New York office compiled monthly detention reports but was not required to forward these to the central Immigration Bureau. As a result, most of these reports also appear to have been destroyed.[164]

However, extant records provide some points of comparison. Pacific Mail Steamship Company records show that detention was common practice at Angel Island. Between 1913 and 1919, 70 percent of all arrivals, including Asians, were detained. Of these detainees, most were held for no more than three days and just 5 percent were held for more than a month. Chinese and Japanese were held longer than Europeans or other Asians. Almost one-fifth of detained Chinese, for example, were held on Angel Island for more than two weeks.[165] The length of Chinese detention increased over time. During the 1910s, the median detention period among all Chinese arrivals at Angel Island was thirteen days; in the 1920s, this had risen to twenty-four days; and throughout the 1930s, it was twenty-five days.[166]

At Ellis Island, only about 20 percent of all immigrants were detained for any period of time. New York records on Chinese arrivals are even more limited, primarily composed of individual accounts and case files. Betty Lee Sung is the only historian who compares Chinese detention lengths in New York and San Francisco. She suggests that Chinese immigrants in New York "were generally questioned within two to six weeks," which was, compared with other stations, "considered a speedy rate of processing."[167] In 1896, not long after the station opened, Yee Sing was detained on Ellis Island "for a few hours" while returning from London to San Francisco. He was asked to produce his papers and then released; however, because he worked as the editor of the Chinese-language *War Cry*, Salvation Army authorities noted that they were planning to make a formal complaint about his detention.[168] One surviving report from the Chinese inspector in charge for the month of October 1923 lists the status of thirty-six Chinese entry seekers. Eight applicants arrived on ships during October 1923: a diplomat with two female dependents, two students, one male and two female actors. All were admitted on the day of their arrival, although the actors had to provide a bond to ensure their departure. Despite the speed with which these applicants were processed, the report lists twelve entry seekers who had arrived in September and sixteen who had arrived in August or earlier. They remained part of this report because they continued to be detained at Ellis Island.[169] This limited evidence shows that, during this time period, most entrants were admitted with very limited inspection. However, those immigrants who weren't immediately admitted appear to have been detained for significant periods of time. Despite this, and likely because there were fewer Chinese arrivals and appeals, the backlog of cases that had not been resolved by the end of the fiscal year was consistently shorter at Ellis Island.[170]

New York officials emphasized the agency's promptness and fairness in administering other aspects of exclusion, such as conducting investigations of Chinese New Yorkers departing the United States. Chinese sought pre-investigation of their status as U.S. citizens or legitimate residents in order to secure a "return certificate" that would help them more successfully negotiate with officials upon their return. In 1920, the New York inspector in charge reported that, despite a threefold increase in applicants, "all cases were handled without delay or inconvenience to the applicants."[171] In 1933, the office claimed that it was "liberal in granting reentry permits," enumerating the ways in which an applicant could substantiate his or her claims to be able to return.[172] According to the newly formed Immigration and Naturalization Service (INS), 85 percent of claims were completed within ten days of the initial application. However, the same report cautioned that re-entry permits didn't automatically permit the holder to return to the United States and that "many aliens returning with permits are denied readmission for one reason or another."[173]

Return certificate cases were often time-consuming, involving significant work and detailed investigations by inspectors across the country. In one case, the family of four-year-old Tom Lee applied for a certificate to confirm that he was an American-born citizen and therefore entitled to return to the United States after a family trip to China in 1915. In cities such as New York, witnesses typically traveled to the main office to testify. However, Lee lived in rural upstate New York. Therefore, an immigration inspector and interpreter traveled about sixty miles from their district office in Ogdensburg to Lee's home in Watertown to conduct the investigation. Tom Lee himself was too young to testify, but his mother, father, and attending physician all testified to his birth in Watertown.[174] His case was approved, and his file, including his birth certificate, was then sent to the New York office and relayed to San Francisco, the port from which the Lees planned to depart.[175] In 1929, New York City native Tom Oy Ngan needed to depart for Europe en route to China, as she described, "almost immediately." The New York office promptly accommodated her request for a return certificate. Tom was scheduled for an interview and her application was approved in ten days. Perhaps officials were impressed by her eloquently phrased request, her elegantly monogrammed personal stationary, or her master's degree from Columbia University. Whatever the reason, they treated her courteously and ensured that she received her travel documents in time.[176]

Whether they were processing applicants upon arrival or applications for return certificates, New York officials emphasized their efficiency and their efforts not to inconvenience the Chinese with whom they engaged. Officials also highlighted the courtesy that they extended to elite Chinese. Although there is limited evidence to compare different stations' detention of arriving applicants and processing of other requests, New York officials' emphasis on their responsive treatment of Chinese applicants is itself more respectful than the ways in which officials spoke about Chinese at other stations.

Although Chinese and Japanese arrivals were regulated by different offices in New York—the Chinese Division and the Immigration Bureau—comparatively considerate inspection practices extended to both groups. Ellis Island officials expressed concern about offending Japanese arrivals and resisted the commissioner-general's efforts to make them enforce Japanese exclusion more strictly. In New York, both Chinese and Japanese exclusion were contested. In general, immigration officials favorably compared the effective administration of Japanese exclusion against the weaker enforcement of Chinese exclusion. With the cooperation of the Japanese government, they noted that the United States had "much more completely accomplished the exclusion of 'Japanese laborers.'"[177] However, such exclusion was not fully implemented at Ellis Island.

Immigration officials in Washington, D.C., pressed Ellis Island officials to be more rigorous in regulating and recording Japanese immigrants. In response, Ellis Island officials ignored or openly questioned national directives. After 1907, as the gentleman's agreement prevented the entry of Japanese laborers, the commissioner-general of immigration wrote to immigration officials across the country requesting that they send complete copies of the manifests of any arriving Japanese so that the bureau could determine their occupations.[178] Throughout the year, national officials wrote to Robert Watchorn, commissioner of Ellis Island, sending blank forms on which to record detailed information about Japanese arrivals and expressing concern that some Japanese admitted at Ellis Island may not be eligible for entry.[179] New York inspectors initially complied with these requests. However, when they ran out of Japanese forms, they stopped recording information about Japanese arrivals and didn't apply to Washington for more supplies. After the central office sent additional forms, Commissioner Watchorn responded that much of the required information was only relevant to Pacific coast ports or was not available from the ship's manifest. "If the Department deems it essential that the data called for in each of these reports is obtained," Watchorn continued, "it can be done only by the inspectors boarding vessels [and] procuring the facts from each individual Japanese who may arrive here." Watchorn was solicitous of the Japanese passengers' concerns, noting that such an approach "may lead to complaints of undue delay, as past experiences have shown that in a great number of instances, passports are in trunks, and for this reason inaccessible."[180] Rather than challenge Watchorn, the commissioner-general of Immigration, Daniel Keefe, agreed that the forms were more appropriate for Pacific coast ports. He requested that Ellis Island officials gather the information that they could easily obtain, but he accepted that since "Japanese arrivals at New York are few and do not belong in the laboring classes; the information called for by the said reports is therefore not important."[181]

As part of the 1907 gentleman's agreement, which prevented the entry of new laborers, Japanese were able to join family members resident in the

United States or to return to a residence or existing farming interest.[182] The Japanese government issued passports to professionals and returning laborers; however, even when newly arriving laborers were inadvertently issued passports, New York officials deferred to Japan and they were granted admission.[183]

However, as Japanese exclusion was expanded and enforced more stringently, Ellis Island officials were required to fall in line with other immigration stations. In 1909, Ellis Island officials were instructed to comply with the rules governing the examination and admission of Japanese. Despite the Immigration Bureau's insistence that Japanese exclusion be enforced uniformly across the country, Ellis Island officials may have continued to be more lax. Certainly, they continued to receive notices from the central office complaining that their record keeping was inadequate and inaccurate. Commissioner-General Keefe critiqued Watchorn for not correctly recording diplomats in the statistical records, resulting in curt exchanges between the officials.[184] Washington officials criticized Ellis Island inspectors for applying regulations too leniently when they allowed Japanese immigrants who listed their occupations as "valet" and "chauffeur"—occupations that defined them as laborers—to enter the United States. They corrected New York officials when they did not accurately record "Japanese without proper passports." And they chided Ellis Island staff for submitting a report late.[185] These problems may have been caused by the infrequency with which New York inspectors had to comply with Japanese exclusion regulations, or they may reflect that Ellis Island officials cared less than officials at other stations about completing such forms in detail. It is impossible to discern their motivations from the records. However, these records show an ongoing pattern of national officials instructing New York officials to provide more extensive and accurate information about Japanese arrivals, with New York officials consistently failing to respond.

Japanese in the New York area did not have the same organizational representation as Chinese in the East or as their Japanese counterparts in the western United States. The *Nihonjinkai*, or Japanese Associations, served a function similar to that of Chinese huiguan, both facilitating immigration and opposing exclusion. Founded after the implementation of the gentleman's agreement, these associations worked closely with the Japanese consulate to investigate applications for return certificates, record Japanese community activities, and sometimes facilitate picture brides' immigration to the United States. They also provided social support to and social control of Japanese in the United States.[186]

In 1924, a new law replaced the gentleman's agreement and barred all "aliens ineligible for citizenship." The 1924 Immigration Law incorporated Chinese, Japanese, South Asians, and other Asians under exclusion, although Filipinos continued to have rights of U.S. residence. The Japanese Association of America protested that the United States had agreed "not to subject the Japanese to the humiliation of an exclusion act" and lamented that the 1924 law "classified her people with the Chinese and low-caste Hindus."[187] After 1924, association branches became focused on local issues, including the education of the second generation.[188] The Japanese Association in New York was not especially active and, despite including the protection of members' rights in its charter, does not appear to have challenged the expansion of exclusion.[189]

Unlike their Chinese counterparts, Japanese immigrants and their local associations did not work with officials to shape the implementation of exclusion in New York. Partly this was because of the structure of Japanese Associations, but Japanese immigrants may also have decided such advocacy was not necessary because Ellis Island officials treated them considerately during the immigration inspection.

Strikingly, despite their relatively respectful treatment, Chinese and Japanese applicants for admission in New York were less likely to be approved than applicants in San Francisco or across the United States. These data are limited by the small numbers of applicants in New York, as well as uneven record keeping for Japanese applicants. Nonetheless, between 1905 and 1932, the number of Chinese applicants rejected at Ellis Island was, on average, almost three times (27 percent) the number rejected at Angel Island (10 percent). Despite Angel Island's reputation as the most difficult port of entry, a higher percentage of Chinese applicants were admitted upon their initial application in San Francisco. Although the rates of admission fluctuated, Chinese applicants in New York were more successful than in San Francisco (tables 1 and 2) in only nine years.

Japanese immigrants also seem to have been rejected in higher numbers on the East Coast, although they fared better than Chinese immigrants. As historians Erika Lee and Judy Yung have shown, Japanese arrivals at Angel Island were far more likely to have their applications approved than Chinese immigrants at the same station. From 1910 through 1932, less than 1 percent of Japanese applicants at Angel Island were excluded.[190] During the three years in which comparable data are available, 1910 to 1912, 2 percent of Japanese were excluded at Angel Island compared with 15 percent at Ellis Island (table 3). The numbers are lower when considering arrivals from

Europe who may have arrived at various ports on the East Coast, but 5 percent of Japanese were still rejected. Japanese arriving from Europe were five times more likely to be rejected than Japanese arriving directly from Japan (table 4).[191]

• • • • • •

Ellis Island officials were reputed to be lenient, even lax, in their regulation of Asian arrivals. This reputation likely started with inspector Scharf's criticisms of his colleagues in the 1890s and 1900s, then continued with other anti-Chinese restrictionists. If Scharf's accusations are true, the *New York Times* noted, they show "a very perfunctory compliance with the law."[192] This reputation was reinforced by Chinese complaints about the harsh treatment they received from Californian immigration officials. Leading merchant and CCBA representative Y. Y. Tang protested "the abhorrent, obnoxious, unfair attitude of exclusion and expulsion at the port of San Francisco which has virtually become to us a reign of terror."[193]

In contrast, Ellis Island officials regulated Asian arrivals with relative restraint. Chinese community members worked with some New York officials to seek more fair and considerate treatment during their immigration process. Exclusion officials may have been influenced by less hostile attitudes toward Chinese in New York, or they may have shared more moderate views. They may have also been affected by working alongside immigration officials who implemented laws governing European immigrants with courtesy and efficiency.

The Ellis Island approach to exclusion was contested and it was contingent: it was not followed by all inspectors and it was not extended to all classes of Asians. However, it helped shape Ellis Island's reputation for lenient enforcement. It is important, however, not to confuse the relatively professional, prompt implementation of exclusion with leniency, letting in larger numbers of arrivals. These are two separate matters.

When officials and organizations complained about lax enforcement in New York, their criticisms should be considered carefully. Restrictionists made these complaints to push New York to harden its enforcement of exclusion, making it closer to the exacting approach in San Francisco. Chinese emphasized the unfairness of exclusion administration in San Francisco to push against this approach. Instead of proving that New York enforcement of exclusion was perfunctory, these complaints demonstrate that exclusion was contested and contingent.

The reputation of Ellis Island as a relatively easy port of entry for Asians is not justified. Asians arriving at this port were not more likely to gain entry to the United States. Ellis Island officials implemented restrictions on Japanese arrivals more loosely, with national officials complaining about slipshod enforcement in New York. But lax implementation of the law does not appear to have led to leniency in terms of the numbers of Japanese allowed entry. Chinese and Japanese were not admitted in higher numbers than at other immigration stations, including San Francisco, but were treated respectfully and had their cases processed quickly. However, as explored in the next chapter, this considerate yet strict treatment of Asian arrivals in New York was challenged by the expansion of deportation within exclusion laws.

## 2 America's Chief Deportation Depot
### Expanding Expulsion across New York

· · · · · · · · · · · · · · · · · · · · · · · · · · · · · · · · · · · · · · · · · · · · · · ·

September 14, 1925. On a cool Monday evening, Chinese from across New York and surrounding towns gathered at the London Theater on the Bowery, a central thoroughfare that linked Chinatown with Manhattan's working-class entertainment district. The London was a large theater, seating 800, and it was reportedly packed. The Jock Ming On performers started at 6 P.M., as they had done nightly since their residency started one year earlier, singing the set pieces of Cantonese opera accompanied by a seven-piece musical ensemble of traditional strings, winds, and percussion. The opera was scheduled to end at 10 P.M. However, as the audience was socializing and enjoying the performance, U.S. immigration officials and New York City police officers created a cordon around Chinatown. They stopped Chinese walking in the neighborhood, along the Bowery, and across the city. They demanded to see their certificates of legal residence, and, although most people could produce documentation, they arrested those who could not. They raided every house on Mott, Doyer, and Pell Streets, three intersecting streets at the heart of Chinatown. Then they turned their attention to places of entertainment. They entered both Cantonese theaters: the London Theater and the Thalia Theater, a long-standing immigrant theater that Brooklyn entrepreneur and former immigration interpreter Philip Kee had recently converted to serve the Chinese community. Raising their voices above the Cantonese singing, immigration inspectors and police detectives instructed audience members to leave the London Theater. As the audience stood up and filed out of the theater, the Jock Ming On troupe continued. The theater managers offered to provide evidence of the actors' legal status, but they were not inspected and they completed their performance to an empty house. Adjusting their eyes from the bright interior of the theater to the dark night, audience members were told to produce their identity cards. They fumbled to find them. Those who could not produce their cards were bundled into patrol cars and driven to the U.S. Courthouse, just a few blocks away at Foley Square. Starting around midnight,

U.S. commissioner Garrett Cotter began hearings for the 450 Chinese who were unable to produce certification of their right to reside in the United States. By the end of the hearings, about one hundred individuals were held for further investigation and likely deportation. In total during the raid, an estimated 1,000 Chinese residents had been inspected, almost one-fifth of the Chinese population of New York.[1]

· · · · · ·

Chinese exclusion and immigration officials in New York were not only engaged in regulating the legal migration of Chinese and other Asians under exclusion but also extensively involved in the investigation, detention, and deportation of Asian New Yorkers. As the Immigration Bureau noted, exclusion depended on expulsion: "One can not be made effective without the other."[2] However, in contrast to their generally respectful treatment of Asian arrivals, New York officials had a reputation for harsh, even punitive, implementation of deportation. The small number of Chinese arrivals in New York may have facilitated more considerate treatment at Ellis Island, but the small Chinese community in New York also allowed for more forceful regulation after entry. A Chinese exclusion official noted that New York's modest Chinese colony, like those of other cities in the eastern United States, allowed for closer regulation than San Francisco's and "strict police control."[3] Threats and practices of deportation were used not only to enforce exclusion but also to regulate the everyday practices of the Chinese community in New York and to control its size.[4]

This chapter focuses on raids against Chinatown; however, other immigrants, including Asians, were raided. These incursions typically happened in social settings where immigrants gathered in large numbers, such as dance halls. In 1923, New York police raided an unlicensed Japanese dance hall on Riverside Drive, in which Chinese, Japanese, Senegalese, and white women worked as dancers. Everyone was arrested. The men were released because, as the magistrate stated, "there was no law in this state sanctioning race prejudice." The women were held on morality charges.[5]

Chinese New Yorkers played a significant role in resisting expulsion in the 1890s, protesting new laws and bringing a series of test cases challenging the legality of deportation.[6] They were unified in their opposition to expulsion laws and more likely to find non-Chinese allies in these efforts than Chinese in the western United States. Non-Chinese New Yorkers, including influential ministers and media sources, expressed profound concerns about deportation raids. They were more critical of expulsion laws than exclusion laws, although both were contested. However, during the 1920s, as the Chinese community in New York grew larger, non-Chinese New Yorkers largely dropped their opposition to deportation. As non-Chinese became more united in their indifference to expulsion, Chinese New Yorkers became more divided, with organizations and their members working against one another and sometimes with U.S. officials to target their rivals for deportation.

## Growing Chinese New York

New York's Chinese community became larger and more established in the 1920s. Although San Francisco remained the center of Chinese American economic, political, and community life, by 1920, half the Chinese population lived in midwestern, southern, and eastern states.[7] New York City's share of the U.S. Chinese population increased gradually from 2 percent in 1890 to 6 percent in 1910 to 11 percent in 1930.[8] During the 1920s, the percentage of Chinese immigrants taking up West Coast residence declined while the number in New York increased. Between 1923 and 1926, the number of Chinese living in New York state increased from 11 percent to 18 percent of the total number of Chinese in the United States. These patterns were similar for Japanese: during the same period, Japanese living in New York state increased from 5 percent to 27 percent of all Japanese. Between 1920 and 1930, the Chinese population in New York City grew by 50 percent from 5,000 to more than 8,000 residents, with an estimated 25,000 in metropolitan New York.[9]

The rise of Chinese New York was not primarily due to direct immigration to the city. Most of New York's population increase appears to be due to movement from the western United States. Historian Beth Lew-Williams has shown how anti-Chinese violence shaped the migration of Chinese communities in the western United States. Northern Californian counties where white vigilantes engaged in anti-Chinese violence saw precipitous declines in the Chinese population, while other counties with a demand for labor and limited violence saw a population increase. Chinese also moved east in search of a less hostile living environment in which they were one of many ethnic groups, not the focus of white discrimination and violence. Although there was discrimination and violence against Chinese in New York, there were no antimiscegenation laws or formally mandated segregation. These factors, combined with labor demand, contributed to the growing Chinese community.[10]

With increasing numbers of Chinese, New York City became the largest Chinese community in the eastern United States.[11] In addition to laundries and restaurants, where the vast majority of Chinese New Yorkers worked, there were more than fifty groceries, fruit stands, butchers, and bakeries serving Chinese in New York and across the surrounding area. All kinds of entertainment were available to Chinese residents, from small gambling rooms to nightly productions at the newly established Cantonese theaters.[12]

At the same time, the Chinese community was challenged by tong violence and upended by extensive deportation. During the 1920s, restrictions on immigration as well as alcohol and other drugs made new groups of immigrants illegal and many activities illicit. This strengthened tongs, fraternal secret societies whose members were often involved in illegal activities, including the unauthorized importation of immigrants. The 1920s "Tong Wars" in New York were sensationally publicized in mainstream newspapers to justify frequent raids on Chinatown.

Immigration officials and local police in New York invoked tong violence in order to conduct broad-based deportation raids. These raids impacted all Chinese residents but did little to control the tongs, as most of the deportees were not tong members. In some cities such as Washington, D.C., police challenged the rise of tongs by targeting specific tong members and charging them with crimes. In New York, officials used the tongs as a pretext to arrest and deport unauthorized immigrants generally. Although non-Chinese New Yorkers expressed concerns about deportation laws and deportation raids at the turn of the century, tong violence appears to have lessened their objections.

Chinese New Yorkers were concerned not only about clashes between tongs but also about confrontations between Chinese residents and U.S. authorities. Tong conflicts may have contributed to the expanding population of the city. Eng Ying Gong, a member of the Hip Sing tong, suggested that a six-month period of tong violence in the western United States during 1917 "did much to populate the East with Chinese."[13] Chinese New Yorkers recognized that immigration raids were designed to police their everyday activities and that, together with tong violence, they might destroy their thriving community.

Throughout the 1910s and 1920s, immigration officials expanded deportation laws and practices. They pushed for Chinese to be excluded under a broader range of restrictions, not limited to exclusion laws. And they developed national transportation systems to efficiently and economically deport larger and larger numbers of immigrants. These new strategies provided new means to expel Chinese when enforcement of exclusion laws became less reliable.

After exploring the expansion of deportation law and the impacts on Chinese New Yorkers, this chapter concludes with the everyday experiences of those detained at and deported through Ellis Island. Starting in the 1920s, as most arriving immigrants were no longer brought to Ellis Island, the immigration station was increasingly used for deportation and detention. "Now almost no immigrants go through Ellis Island in person; only their records are filed there," immigrant advocate Louis Adamic wrote in 1936. "The island is America's chief deportation depot."[14]

## Expanding Deportation Law

Deportation had multiple purposes: it was used to enforce exclusion laws, regulate the Chinese community, and prevent the Chinese population from becoming too large. First, deportation was a key mechanism for the enforcement of both exclusion and immigration restrictions. Immigration officials acknowledged that "the smuggling of Chinese will never be successfully prevented until there is put into operation a plan whereunder at least the majority of those who enter unlawfully can be promptly deported."[15] Second, deportation for crimes and minor offenses committed by immigrants in the United States was used to regulate the Chinese community. This regulation was implemented to not only control violent crime but also contain antisocial behaviors. In 1908, for example, New York City police officers made sixty-three arrests for disorderly conduct in the harbor precinct. As explored in chapter 4, Asians formed a large number of the sailors in New York. Not surprisingly, more than one-third of the people detained by the police around the harbor were Chinese. However, while non-Chinese arrestees received a substantial seventy-five-dollar fine for their behavior, Chinese were transferred to federal authorities for deportation.[16] Such practices are consistent with legal scholar Daniel Kanstroom's description of deportation as a means of "post-entry social control."[17] Finally, officials also appeared to view deportation as a means of population control, limiting the Chinese population of the United States. Annual immigration reports included charts showing how deportations of Chinese were increasingly overtaking legal admissions, suggesting that the role of deportations was not just to enforce the law but also to make sure that the Chinese American population didn't grow too large.[18]

As explored in the preceding chapter, exclusion policies were expanded in the late nineteenth and early twentieth centuries to ban more and more

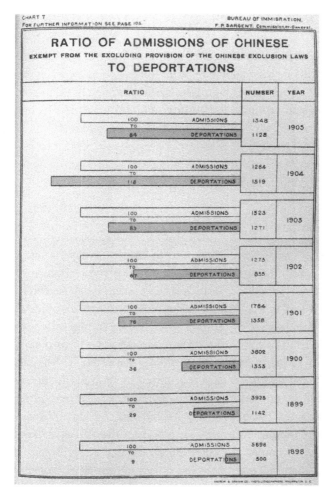

## RATIO OF ADMISSIONS OF CHINESE
EXEMPT FROM THE EXCLUDING PROVISION OF THE CHINESE EXCLUSION LAWS
## TO DEPORTATIONS

| RATIO | | NUMBER | YEAR |
|---|---|---|---|
| 100 TO 84 | ADMISSIONS / DEPORTATIONS | 1348 / 1128 | 1905 |
| 100 TO 118 | ADMISSIONS / DEPORTATIONS | 1284 / 1519 | 1904 |
| 100 TO 83 | ADMISSIONS / DEPORTATIONS | 1523 / 1271 | 1903 |
| 100 TO 67 | ADMISSIONS / DEPORTATIONS | 1273 / 855 | 1902 |
| 100 TO 76 | ADMISSIONS / DEPORTATIONS | 1784 / 1358 | 1901 |
| 100 TO 36 | ADMISSIONS / DEPORTATIONS | 3802 / 1353 | 1900 |
| 100 TO 29 | ADMISSIONS / DEPORTATIONS | 3925 / 1142 | 1899 |
| 100 TO 9 | ADMISSIONS / DEPORTATIONS | 5696 / 500 | 1898 |

"Ratio of Admissions of Chinese to Deportations," *Annual Report of the Commissioner-General of Immigration* (1905).

Asian nationals from immigrating to the United States. These laws started with Chinese groups, then were extended to Japanese, Koreans after Japan's annexation of Korea in 1910, and Asian Indians. Parallel to the expansion of exclusion and in order to enforce these new restrictions, the U.S. government introduced new deportation policies. Like immigration restrictions, the development of modern deportation policy started with Chinese exclusion. "Beginning with the Chinese Exclusion Act of 1882," a committee investigating conditions at Ellis Island noted, "subsequent acts have steadily added to the classes of aliens subject to deportation."[19] The 1882 Chinese Exclusion law was the first federal law to include formal deportation provisions. These were expanded in the 1891 Immigration Act, which provided that immigrants found inadmissible at the time of their entry were subject to deportation for one year after entry, a time period that was subsequently extended.[20] However, it was the 1892 reauthorization of Chinese exclusion, known as the Geary Act, and the 1893 McCreary Amendment to this act that most forcefully extended the reach of deportation. The Geary Act required that Chinese laborers register their presence in the United States, supported by a reputable white witness, and carry documentation certifying their registration and legal right of residence. Chinese who did not register would be deported. Deportation policy was, in Daniel Kanstroom's evocative phrase, "built on the backs of the Chinese."[21]

Chinese and other Asians opposed not only the exclusion laws preventing their entry into the United States but also the expulsion laws that underpinned exclusion. The Geary Act faced unified opposition from Chinese across the United States, led by the Chinese Consolidated Benevolent Association (CCBA). The San Francisco CCBA posted notices throughout Chinatowns across the country stating the Geary Act "is an unjust law and no Chinese should obey it."[22] The association vowed to provide legal support to those who refused to register and sought a one-dollar contribution from each member to mount a legal challenge. This was the same amount that Chinese were charged to register under the law.[23] Chinese were angry at the injustice of being targeted and the extension of exclusion regulation from the border to the interior, from Chinese arrivals to those who were long-standing residents.

Although the San Francisco CCBA directed opposition to the law, Chinese on the East Coast, especially those in New York, played a central role in protesting it. Immigration officials noted that the registration and deportation provisions of the 1892 Geary Act were "bitterly opposed, especially in the interior and eastern district of the United States."[24] Bostonian Charlie Wah Hong emphasized how the law was unjust and exposed American hypocrisy. "They talk about American liberty, and that this is a free country," Hong noted. "Why don't they pass laws of this kind against other nationalities? We can show that in comparison with our numbers there is less crime and less poverty among us than any other nationality which comes here."[25] Although New York newspapers had been ambivalent about Chinese exclusion, they routinely editorialized against the Geary law.[26]

A few months after the passage of the Geary Act, the Chinese Equal Rights League was founded by New York activist Wong Chin Foo and Philadelphia merchant Sam Ping Lee to organize opposition to the law. Membership was not limited to U.S. citizens, but the league required that its members be educated, Americanized, and committed to living permanently in the United States. In September 1892, the organization held a mass protest of 200 Chinese and many more non-Chinese supporters in the Great Hall of the Cooper Union, about a mile north of Manhattan's Chinatown. At the meeting, Chinese American speakers such as Wong Chin Foo and physician Joseph Thoms took to the podium, sharply dressed in Western suits, starched white shirts, and patent leather shoes that emphasized both their Americanness and their respectability. "We have been the victims of demagogues on the Pacific Coast," Dr. Thoms protested. "I have lived for many years under the despotism of the Chinese government, but I have never seen personal liberties interfered with as ours have been here." Wong Chin Foo argued that the Geary Act violated the promises made to mankind in the Declaration of Independence. The Chinese speakers were followed by white and African American ministers who similarly denounced the law. The meeting concluded with a unanimous resolution that the Geary Act was "monstrous, inhuman, and unconstitutional" and with a pledge of those present to protest.[27]

As legal historian Lucy Salyer notes, "Chinese did not simply complain about the new law; they refused to obey it."[28] Historian Kelly Lytle Hernández describes this as "the first massive civil disobedience campaign for immigrant rights."[29] Nationally, only 13,242 Chinese laborers registered, about 14 percent of those subject to the law.[30] In the eastern United States, resistance seems to have been even greater. In New York, it was estimated that maybe 1 percent of the city's roughly 3,000 Chinese residents registered.[31] Three individuals reportedly applied at the newly opened Federal Building in Brooklyn for certificates attesting to their legal residence, although only one completed his application. Among the applicants, laundryman G. Washington Chung attended his appointment and supplied a photograph as part of his documentation but did not bring the required witnesses. Ferdinand Gott, a former Navy steward who worked as a butler in Manhattan but lived and owned real estate in Brooklyn, also failed to complete his application. Only laundryman Sing Lee, a resident of Glen Gove, Long Island, complied fully with the law.[32] In Boston, just twenty individuals registered, from a population of approximately 1,000.[33] According to the Geary Act, all unregistered Chinese laborers were subject to deportation.

Chinese New Yorkers not only protested and defied the registration law; they were instrumental in challenging its legality. Chinese residents of Brooklyn worked with Chinese civil rights leaders such as Dr. Thoms to hire legal representation in early cases against the law.[34] As federal courts in different jurisdictions ruled in varied ways on the law, the CCBA brought a test case using three laborers from New York. Two of the men had refused to register, and one attempted to register but was refused because his witness was Chinese and was therefore found to be not reputable.[35]

In one of the most important decisions in immigration law, the U.S. Supreme Court upheld the Geary Act, ruling that the United States had "the right to exclude or expel all aliens, or any class of aliens, absolutely or upon certain conditions, in war or in peace."[36] It further determined that such a right was essential to the safety and security of every sovereign nation, and, as exclusion or expulsion was not a criminal punishment, it was not subject to constitutional protections.[37] Alluding to *Dred Scott*, white Civil War veteran General Horatio Collins King protested that under the decision Chinese have "no rights here that Americans are bound to respect."[38] The ruling was "a bombshell" according to Kanstroom: "Its repercussions are felt to this day."[39] As Salyer notes, "It removed all aliens, not just Chinese, from the protective shelter of the Constitution."[40]

Although Congress passed and secured expansive powers for deportation, it did not effectively fund these measures. Chinese New Yorkers pressed at this weakness in the law. After the Geary Act was ruled constitutional, the cost of arresting and deporting as many as 85,000 unregistered Chinese was estimated at between $7 and $10 million. However, Congress had authorized only $60,000 and failed to provide a mechanism for deportation.[41] Ny Look, a Chinese New Yorker who had long lived in the United States and served with the Union Army during the Civil War, was arrested in May 1893 for failure to register under the Geary Act. He was detained under the provision of the law requiring deportation "as hereinbefore provided." However, Judge Lacombe of the U.S. Circuit Court in the Southern District of New York noted that there were no such provisions in the law, and, because Look could not be detained indefinitely, he was released.[42]

In 1893, Congress passed a six-month extension to the registration deadline, designated the officials who could issue an arrest warrant, and developed deportation procedures. This became known as the McCreary Amendment.[43] It was during this time, between the Geary Act's May 1893 registration deadline and the November 1893 extension of this deadline, that special inspector J. Thomas Scharf arrived in New York.[44] As noted in chapter 1, Scharf undertook his own raids across the city and in upstate New York, and he was proud of his record of deporting "more Chinese than

"Chinatown, N.Y.C.—Police and Detectives Guarding Chinatown, July 6, 1909," George Grantham Bain Collection, Prints and Photographs Division, Library of Congress (1909).

all the other Inspectors together."[45] In this way, although he did not change the generally respectful treatment of arriving Chinese, he may have helped shape immigration officials' perspectives on deportation raids.

After the revised 1893 law went into effect, Chinese communities across the United States appear to have been increasingly raided. The first large-scale raid occurred in Denver in 1897 followed by raids in Portland throughout 1898.[46] According to protests from the Chinese legation, Chinese residential areas were surrounded by immigration officials, local police, and armed U.S. marshals who detained almost every Chinese person on the suspicion that some did not have certificates.[47] In the eastern United States, some of the earliest raids occurred in New York throughout 1902 and in Boston in 1902 and 1903.[48] Photographs depict the police presence in New York's Chinatown.

During this early period of deportation raids, many non-Chinese New Yorkers expressed concerns about expulsion. Immigration officials claimed that they were unable to enforce deportation law effectively in New York and the eastern United States because of a lack of public support. And they explained that this lack of enforcement had led to an increasing Chinese population in the East. "It has not been considered expedient to make arrests in the interior, and especially in the eastern section," U.S. officials noted in 1907. "Just so long as public sentiment is such in these sections as to interfere with active operations in the making of arrests, just so long will the number of unlawfully resident Chinese continue to increase."[49] Bureau officials lamented the "vigorous and extensive protest" against efforts to expel Chinese. They also asserted that protests were not due to Americans' genuine concerns about the surveillance, detention, and deportation of Chinese residents, but were the result of unauthorized Chinese immigrants cultivating friendships with white neighbors and influential citizens.[50]

Officials repeatedly sought to limit the legal protections available to Chinese in deportation proceedings, to expand the grounds for deportation, and to expedite the deportation process. For two decades after the passage of the Geary Act, there were separate expulsion processes under Chinese exclusion laws and under general immigration laws. Chinese initially had more legal protections as they were arrested under judicial warrants reviewed by the courts, whereas other immigrants were arrested under departmental warrants approved by a Board of Special Inquiry within the Immigration Bureau. Bureau officials explicitly addressed the "striking contrast" between these two processes, commenting on how the deportation of non-Chinese immigrants under departmental warrants was "effected with small expense and without invoking the tedious, elaborate, and expensive machinery of the courts," whereas the deportation of Chinese immigrants involved substantial costs. In 1905, the Immigration Bureau spent more than $67,000 deporting 621 Chinese laborers, not including court costs. Starting around this time, the bureau decided to arrest Chinese under immigration as well as exclusion laws.[51]

As with other key cases, the case that tested whether Chinese were deportable under general immigration law was brought in New York. In 1909, Wong You and three other immigrants were detained near the northern border of New York. They were charged with entering the United States without inspection and ordered deported under immigration law. Wong challenged this decision, claiming that his case should be processed under Chinese exclusion law. He had some success in the lower federal courts. However, in 1912 his claim was denied when the U.S. Supreme Court ruled that Chinese could be deported under either exclusion or immigration laws, judicial or departmental warrants.[52] As the *Annual Report of the Commissioner-General of Immigration* noted, the decision produced "most valuable results," making the deportation of Chinese immigrants quicker and more cost-effective.[53]

Form 595
U. S. DEPARTMENT OF LABOR
IMMIGRATION SERVICE

FILE COPY.

55/20

REPORT OF ALIENS COMPLETELY READY FOR DEPORTATION
IN NEW YORK CHINESE DISTRICT.

(Date) 11/13/33 , 192

55/20
(District file No.)

55331/427
(Bureau file No.)

WONG JU
(Name of alien)

NEW YORK CITY
(Town or city where located)

CHINA
(Country to be deported to)

GOVERNMENT
(Government or S. S. Co. expense)

SAN FRANCISCO
(Via what U. S. port)

Ellis Island – Government
(How detained and where)

Unnecessary
(Whether passport secured)

Ch.Excl.Law; L.P.C.; illegal entry
(Charge; same or insane, etc.)

GOVERNMENT PRINTING OFFICE          14—2014

Wong Ju, deportation card, file 55/20, Chinese Files, 1921–1944, INS,
NARA–New York (1923).

Taking advantage of the fact that Chinese could be deported under either immigration or exclusion rules, New York immigration officials typically listed multiple grounds for deportation. When Wong Ju (no known relation to Wong You) was deported in 1923, his deportation card noted that he had violated Chinese exclusion laws, entered illegally under immigration laws, *and* was liable to become a public charge (LPC) at the time of his entry.[54] Officials made the LPC claim despite the fact that Chinese deportees typically worked throughout their time in the United States. The LPC claim was entirely unrelated to the men's circumstances and intended simply to ensure that they were deported without the judicial review allowed under Chinese exclusion cases.

Ellis Island officials had a reputation of harshness in their implementation of deportation of Chinese and all immigrants. This was in strong contrast to their strict yet considerate execution of exclusion laws for arriving Asians. Officials may have equated the efficient administration of both admission and deportation. In 1902, the New York commissioner emphasized that "every effort" was being made to process arriving immigrants quickly and minimize their length of time in detention. Deportees, he added, "must also be taken back at the earliest possible opportunity."[55]

But others disagreed. In 1913, Marcus Braun requested an investigation on behalf of his employer, the German-American Steamship Line, into

New York officials' inhumane deportation practices. This criticism of deportation practices in New York was particularly striking as Braun was a former Ellis Island inspector who had previously advocated extensively for stricter restrictions on Chinese and Japanese immigrants.[56] After the Palmer Raids on radical immigrants in 1919 and 1920, Assistant Secretary of Labor Louis Post complained that Ellis Island was the only immigration station where officials "overlooked or disobeyed" the labor secretary's decision that radicals with families in the United States should not be deported. Post also protested that detainees at the island were given only a few hours' notice of their deportation, and so their families and lawyers were not aware of their departure until their ships were already at sea.[57] During the 1920s, Chinese sailors detained at Ellis Island were also shipped out without prior notice from Ellis Island officials, even as their cases were being investigated.[58] It is difficult to determine exactly how Ellis Island's enforcement of deportation compared with other stations. As the United States' "chief deportation depot," Ellis Island may have been the focus of immigration advocates. However, it is clear that deportation was strictly enforced at Ellis Island.[59]

Starting in the 1920s, new laws expedited the deportation process and expanded its reach. In 1920, the secretary of labor was identified as the final arbiter in deportation decisions, limiting immigrants' rights to appeal.[60] In the same year, reflecting the increasing centrality of deportation within immigration enforcement, a new position was created for an officer in charge of deportation.[61] As restrictions against immigrants became more stringent, the commissioner-general of immigration noted in 1924 that "the deportation problem becomes more difficult and exacting." "The deportation of aliens found to be unlawfully in the United States," he continued, "is rapidly becoming one of the most important functions of the immigration service."[62]

As deportation became increasingly important, it was also increasingly expensive and time-consuming. Despite the government's success in the *Wong You* Supreme Court case, officials remained concerned about the cost and efficiency of deporting large numbers of Chinese. Therefore, along with other deportees such as unauthorized Mexican immigrants, the Immigration Bureau allowed some Chinese deportees to "voluntarily depart."

The voluntary departure process started in the 1920s as an administrative procedure to reduce the cost and accelerate the process of deportation.[63] It allowed significant numbers of Asian jump-ship sailors to avoid formal deportation by working on foreign vessels shipping out of the United States, a practice known as reshipping foreign in lieu of deportation.[64] Smaller numbers of other unauthorized Asian immigrants also departed without being formally deported. Mabel Ng Fook and her husband were ordered deported to China in 1930. They were represented by Harry Sisson in their efforts to avoid formal deportation. As her parents lived in Barbados, Ng Fook argued that she should be allowed to return there at her own expense. She was arrested in November 1930 and was detained for three months at Ellis Island before the Immigration Bureau allowed her to depart for Barbados with her husband and American-born baby in February 1931.[65] Formally known as departure in lieu of deportation, voluntary departure was written into law in 1940.[66] However, it was hardly voluntary: immigrants who did not choose or were not eligible for this form of departure were deported.

### Tong Conflicts and Deportation Raids

As legal historians have explored, late nineteenth- and early twentieth-century deportation efforts were aimed at Chinese involved in criminal activities such as prostitution, gambling, and opium distribution.[67] This approach confirmed many white Americans' association of Chinese with criminality. Between 1925 and 1933 New York exclusion authorities, city police, and federal prosecutors took a broader approach, working together to conduct large-scale deportation raids against Chinese residents. Authorities claimed that these raids aimed to control tongs and their criminal activities, but raids became a convenient pretext to deport unauthorized Chinese residents and to threaten the expanding Chinese community. This was particularly true during the Great Depression. Although Chinese had been unified in opposition to the Geary Act and non-Chinese New Yorkers had been concerned about the harshness of laws, the rising power of tongs divided the Chinese community and unified non-Chinese in favor of deportation. Chinese Americans decried tong violence, but they were also concerned that massive and regular raids would destabilize the settlement and decimate the growing Chinese community in New York.

During the early twentieth century, the CCBA faced challenges to its preeminence in Chinatown, both as its prestige was lessened by legal failures to prevent the expansion of exclusion and as its authority was challenged by other organizations. The huiguan, or regional associations, that formed the CCBA were led by powerful merchants who collected dues from their members and provided limited social services in return. "Everyone is supposed to belong," a New York CCBA officer stated. "You are not Chinese if you don't belong." During this time, tongs became increasingly powerful because they were able to recruit members with a more open membership not based on regional affiliation and because they were more responsive to working-class members than the elite leadership of the CCBA. Many tong members were also members of huiguan. However, tong membership was available to those who did not have a common surname or were not from a well-represented district, and it was open to non-Chinese members. As with the CCBA, members paid dues.[68]

New York's two major tongs were the On Leong and Hip Sing. In San Francisco, which had a larger and more established Chinese community, there were many more tongs.[69] The On Leong tong was founded in Boston in 1894 and moved its headquarters to New York in 1904.[70] It was generally wealthier than the Hip Sing tong and counted more businessmen among its members. The Hip Sing, by contrast, was composed mostly of laborers from Toisan, including sailors, laundrymen, and restaurant workers.[71] It was established in New York at about the same time as the On Leong and, by 1925, had about 2,000 members in the city.[72]

Although these sworn brotherhoods engaged in criminal enterprises, they weren't defined exclusively by such activities. Tongs provided financial support and protection to their members, many of whom worked in legitimate business activities. If Chinese were detained by the police or immigration authorities, they could rely on their tong for interpretation and legal services.[73] Historian Michelle Chen shows that the Hip Sing provided a broad range of support during the 1930s: the organization not only funded the nationalist Chinese government in its resistance against Japan but also helped pay a member's rent in arrears, posted bail for another member, and invested pooled funds in a construction company.[74]

At the same time, tongs and their members were engaged in criminal pursuits and used violence to support these activities. Like other Chinese New Yorkers, most tong members lived and worked in various locations throughout the city.[75] However, the tongs controlled distinct areas of Chinatown, and if they worked in Chinatown, tong members worked only within the area claimed by their organization.[76] When power struggles over territory or criminal activities emerged between the tongs, these sometimes became violent turf battles popularly described as "tong wars." During these skirmishes, the tongs brought in professional fighters described by white Americans as "hatchet men" or, according to a coinage attributed to a New York City police officer, "highbinders."[77] In 1923, two Chinese sailors were arrested while unloading packages from a taxicab outside the Brooklyn

Seamen's Club. When the police opened the packages, they found German guns and ammunition inside. Although one of the men suggested that the guns were to be shipped to Chinese revolutionaries, the police suspected that they would actually be used by tong members closer to home.[78]

Such "wars" occurred intermittently from the 1890s through the 1930s, focused in different cities at different times but typically expanding to include tong members from other cities.[79] The secretive nature of the tongs and sensationalist mainstream accounts of their activities make it difficult to fully and accurately describe these conflicts. However, in New York, events leading to these battles varied from minor incidents such as a Hip Sing member picking up his mail from his cousin's shop in On Leong territory to the brutal 1909 murder and dismemberment of Bow Kim. Kim was a young woman at the center of a conflict between a member of the Four Brothers Guild, associated with the Hip Sings, and a man who joined the On Leong for protection. Her murder spurred a war between the tongs that resulted in fifty deaths.[80] These battles and their ongoing reprisals usually lasted a few days or weeks, with casualties mostly among the tongs' fighters but also including targeted leaders and occasional bystanders. At some point, a peace conference was convened with the assistance of the CCBA and the Chinese consul, after which the tongs returned to their less violent rivalry.[81]

Two intersecting developments helped foster the rise of tongs in New York and contribute to Ellis Island's ongoing transition from the United States' largest immigration station to a major deportation depot. First, starting in the 1920s, the U.S. government increasingly restricted immigration from Asia while also enforcing Prohibition. These policies strengthened tongs and other organizations involved in the illegal importation of people, alcohol, and other drugs. But they also led to increasing conflicts among tongs jostling for a larger share of this illicit business, as well as between tongs and the U.S. authorities trying to stop them.[82] Second, as the expansion of deportation policies accompanied the expansion of Asian exclusion and narcotics laws, U.S. authorities often used the efficient and inexpensive mechanism of deportation to regulate Chinese and other immigrant communities. Many of the supposed tong members deported during the 1920s had nothing to do with tongs. They were simply unauthorized immigrants caught up in the Immigration Bureau's dragnet. However, deportation was a powerful tool of "post-entry social control" that spread fear throughout the New York Chinese community.[83]

Attitudes toward tongs varied among Chinese New Yorkers.[84] The CCBA opposed the rising presence of tongs because they both challenged the

CCBA's preeminence and reinforced commonly held American ideas of Chinese criminality. Some ordinary Chinese blamed American police and courts for not controlling the tongs more effectively.[85] Across the country, they wrote letters to immigration officials in which they claimed that tongs were inherently violent, involved in illegal activities, and mostly composed of unauthorized immigrants. New Yorker Chin Ming wrote that "the Chinese Tong War will never be stop continued fight at any moment, very near sooner because too many bad men here, this bad men eighter percent haven't got certificate, if not search them out will make large trouble here."[86] At the same time, other Chinese did not want to invite government surveillance of the Chinese community. Their primary concern about tongs was that they brought U.S. authorities into Chinatown and made all residents subject to the threat of deportation.

Tong members themselves blamed the existence of tongs on the "abnormal environment of the Chinese in America," including the larger number of men than women owing to restrictions on women's immigration, the presence of prostitution, and the importance of gambling as a social activity. They also directly blamed the strength of tongs on the attitude of the white population, including violence and blackmail from which Chinese residents needed protection. In this way, they implied that U.S. immigration policies and anti-Chinese racism were fundamental reasons for tongs flourishing in the United States.[87]

Despite concerns among many Chinese New Yorkers about the ways that U.S. authorities used tongs as a pretext for deportation raids, the CCBA and tongs sometimes reported their rivals to these authorities. In contrast to its work of leading unified opposition to exclusion and expulsion laws, the CCBA supported the deportation of tong members and worked with the Immigration Bureau to achieve this goal. In San Francisco, the CCBA's lawyer shared lists of tong members with U.S. officials.[88] As explored in the conclusion, this pattern was repeated in the 1950s when the nationalist CCBA worked with immigration authorities to target Chinese radicals for deportation. At the same time, tongs and their supporters similarly worked with various New York institutions, including the Immigration Bureau, to bring down their rivals. On Leong members were suspected of working with the police to focus attention on criminal activities by the Hip Sings. Meanwhile, the Hip Sing worked with the moral reformers of the Parkhurst Society, providing information that the society used to raid On Leong gambling operations.[89]

In addition to these organizational attacks, individuals made reports to the New York Chinese Division against their neighbors and competitors.

According to one contemporary observer, perhaps as many as 90 percent of all deportation cases resulted from "a personal grudge."[90] In 1912, an anonymous tip claimed that laundryman Fong Yee Ying was in the United States illegally. "He has no certificate and is now at 52–54 Sand Street, Brooklyn," the informant wrote. "I hope you will send an investigator there and arrest him. . . . Don't delay or he will move some other place."[91] In another case, two informants provided a street address and directions to locate a man working illegally in a Brooklyn laundry, but the directions were inaccurate and the street numbers did not exist. When Chinese Division officials did not pursue the lead, the informants wrote a second letter, asking angrily, "You are a Customs Officer, why don't you make an arrest? What are you doing?"[92] In many cases, including the investigation of Fong Yee Ying, the targeted individuals were able to prove legal residence in the United States. Nevertheless, the individual investigations and larger raids contributed to an atmosphere in which the potential threat of deportation was always present.

Many Chinese suspected that the police were paid off not to investigate tong members' illicit activities. And, like the CCBA, tongs maintained connections with the New York Immigration Bureau. Worry Charles, who had worked for the Customs Service during the early 1890s as an immigration interpreter, also worked as a translator for the Hip Sing tong.[93] Three decades later, Sing Kee worked as an interpreter for the New York Immigration Bureau and was secretary of the On Leong tong, hiring lawyers to defend tong members.[94] These complex connections show that exclusion and deportation permeated Chinese people's lives in the United States. Even as they protested exclusion and expulsion, some Chinese organizations and individuals used U.S. laws, including deportation laws, to maintain their prominence in Chinese New York and challenge their rivals.

White nativists drew attention to tong violence as a way to bolster support for exclusion. In 1925, Frances DeNanny of the Immigration Restriction League (IRL) wrote to the Immigration Bureau noting that New York City "had been having a great deal of trouble with the Chinese residents owing to a Tong War." "As Chinese are not citizens, and as murder and assault are serious crimes," DeNanny inquired about "the rules necessary for the deportation of these people." Suggesting that IRL members wanted to take enforcement of the law into their own hands, she further asked, "Does the request for deportation have to come from a local official?" DeNanny received a cool official response that referenced the "tong situation as it is claimed to exist in New York City," emphasized that Chinese born in the

United States and their children were U.S. citizens not subject to deportation, and advised her to contact the Chinese inspector in charge if she had information about specific cases. DeNanny attached a sensationalist *New York Times* editorial about tongs to her letter, which was similar to many lurid media accounts of tong wars. However, the response from immigration officials was understated. It was, in fact, much more restrained than the aggressive tactics used by U.S. authorities to defuse tong violence and deport ordinary New Yorkers.[95]

Despite the vigorous expansion and implementation of deportation law, it is important to note that not all anti-tong efforts were successful. At least as early as the 1900s, congressional restrictionists favored a law focusing on the deportation of tong members.[96] In 1926, a bill introduced in the House Committee on Immigration described tong members as "undesirable" and provided for their deportation. The bill was extremely broad, claiming that going into hiding or hiring a bodyguard was evidence that an alien was a tong member. However, the bill did not make it out of committee and never became law, suggesting that there were limits to anti-tong activism.[97]

By the mid-1920s, New York was in the midst of an extended conflict between the On Leong and Hip Sing tongs. Caused in part by roughly 300 expelled New York On Leong members being accepted into the Hip Sing in Cleveland and Chicago, these New York conflicts were, according to one member, the "worst of all the tong wars."[98] During an outbreak in 1924, apparently directed from New York, there were nineteen murders and thirty-five additional attacks by tongmen.[99] In the spring of 1925, more than seventy people were killed in New York and many more were wounded.[100] Then, after six months of tenuous peace, fighting started again in September 1925.

In response to this fighting and as part of a broader concern about a "crime wave" in the 1920s, U.S. immigration officials and New York City police officers worked together to raid Chinatown.[101] Starting in 1925 and lasting until 1933, U.S. authorities regularly threatened New York's Chinatown residents with mass deportation.[102] Their raids were typically conducted throughout the night by a large force of about fifty U.S. officials and one hundred detectives and uniformed police officers. Three assistant U.S. attorneys conducted impromptu hearings on the sidewalk. All those who could not produce documentation were sent to the Federal Courthouse at Foley Square for hearings conducted throughout the night.[103]

The massive September 14, 1925, raid on Chinatown and the London Theater, mentioned in the opening of this chapter, was just one of a series of raids. Three days earlier, U.S. attorney for the Southern District of New York

Emory Buckner met with leaders of the On Leong and Hip Sing tongs to urge them to end their warfare. "He made it plain," according to the *New York Times*, "that the government intended to bring this about through wholesale deportations." Dissatisfied with their promises, Buckner launched his first major raid at 11 P.M. on Friday, September 11. By midnight, U.S. authorities had arrested sixty-eight men and discovered "two stills in a rookery in Chinatown, a small store of opium, and a miniature arsenal, including a rifle and several Chinese cleavers."[104] On September 14, the raid on the London Theater and across Chinatown resulted in one hundred detainees. Two days later, 600 were seized, and the number of men slated for deportation had risen to 191.[105] On September 18, another raid resulted in 500 men being detained, at least half of them again taken from the two Chinese theaters. The police also raided both the Hip Sing and On Leong halls, facing attacks, chasing fleeing tongmen, and taking some of the tong members into custody.[106] Although the arrested men did not admit to being members of a tong, some of them acknowledged that they had recently arrived in New York from Baltimore, Buffalo, Washington, D.C., and other cities with active tongs. By September 25, federal officials had investigated more than 1,200 Chinese in New York, as part of a "roundup of undesirables in Chinatown and environs."[107] Of these, 256 individuals were ordered deported and sent to Ellis Island.[108]

Although the 1920s raids were purportedly to control tong violence, such violence was largely a pretext for widespread exclusion enforcement and harassment of Chinese residents. U.S. attorney Buckner did not seem especially concerned about tong violence. "I have put the federal government in Chinatown," he stated, "and I am going to keep it there whether a tong war is in progress or not."[109] While Chinese without documentation were deported, even Chinese who produced their certificates were threatened. Without any basis in immigration law, the police warned legal residents that if they were discovered again in Chinatown at night, their residency rights would be revoked and they would be deported.[110]

Not surprisingly, because U.S. authorities did not target tong members, most deportees do not appear to have been engaged in tong violence. Instead, most of those arrested seem to have been Chinese without papers, including many jump-ship sailors, rounded up as part of a general dragnet. The police maintained that the deportees had been brought to the United States as crew members in order to participate in the tong war. However, one Hip Sing member claimed that only about 10 percent of those arrested were associated with tongs. And, despite their assertions that the jump-ship sailors were tong members, U.S. officials allowed the sailors to reship foreign, by shipping out on new vessels rather than go through formal deportation procedures. Sailors who reshipped were able to return to New York and could potentially jump ship again, suggesting that U.S. authorities did not view them as a serious threat.[111]

Some observers noted that the threat of deportation may have influenced tongs to limit their fighting. After a short outburst of tong violence in 1927, the U.S. attorney's hints of deportation may have encouraged Hip Sing and On Leong leaders to come together to reiterate their support for the 1925 peace treaty. Similar threats were made during each period of tong violence in New York. The *New York Times* noted that in 1930 "the raids were especially successful in this city" in bringing an end to tong violence. In 1933, in response to the possibility of conflict, the newspaper reported that similar "mop-up" operations were planned "whether or not there is actual warfare on between any of the tongs."[112] However, in 1936, journalist Gor Yun Leong suggested instead that the cost of fighting was significant and that lack of funds may have been partly responsible for the decline in tong violence during the Great Depression.[113]

The strategy of using exclusion laws and deportation provisions to regulate tongs was not implemented everywhere across the country. In Washington, D.C., for example, detectives developed a detailed case against the Hip Sings for weeks before raiding their headquarters and arresting sixty members on gambling charges.[114] Their careful police work and targeted actions show that there were other strategies for stopping tong wars, and that these methods were used outside of New York.

Although New York City's Chinatown had become a thriving ethnic community, Chinese residents expressed concern that the constant raids would lead to the end of the enclave.[115] Earlier tong violence in the West may have contributed to eastward migration and the rise of New York's Chinese communities. Now, restaurant owners and merchants fretted that the raids and deportations in New York would lead to a shortage of Chinese labor, crippling their businesses.[116] In addition to practical concerns, the raids contributed to many Chinese New Yorkers' feelings of unbelonging, despite having settled in the city. Later observers noted that the tong wars encouraged many Chinese families to move out of the city, settling in locations such as Newark and the Oranges.[117]

Immigration investigations and large-scale raids not only created opportunities for disgruntled individuals or rival tong members to provide tips about unauthorized immigrants but also created a situation that was ripe for extortion. In 1932, Louis Sing, a U.S. citizen who owned a laundry at Amsterdam Avenue on the west side of Manhattan, was visited by a white immigration inspector and a Chinese man. The inspector reviewed Sing's papers and stated that they were out of order owing to various technical problems but that they could be validated for $200. When Sing protested that he didn't have that kind of money, the Chinese interpreter responded that he would be arrested "on the spot." Searching his laundry in a panic, Sing was able to scrape together sixty dollars and agreed to pay the rest the following day. However, when the Chinese man returned alone to collect the remaining funds, Sing became suspicious and refused to pay. He learned from the CCBA that he was one of a number of Chinese New Yorkers tricked under this extortion scheme. The scheme worked because of the presence of immigration inspectors who conducted investigations and checked Chinese papers throughout the city, and who sometimes extorted immigrants. Sing reported his situation to the Ellis Island authorities, with a description of the Chinese man who had a noticeable and distinctive scar on his forehead.[118]

Officers of the Immigration Bureau's Chinese Division worked closely with New York City police detectives to investigate unauthorized Chinese immigrants, so it was not difficult for them to coordinate on Sing's case. Detectives quickly identified and arrested Harry Lee and brought him to Sing's laundry to confirm that they had the right man. But when their car pulled up in front of Sing's building at 8 A.M., during the height of New York City's rush hour, things did not run smoothly. For starters, Lee refused to get out of the car. The immigration inspector and police detective were able to force him into the laundry, where Sing recognized Lee and started to scream in Cantonese. Passersby thought that the laundry was being robbed and reported the hold-up to a police officer standing on a nearby corner. A few minutes later, more police officers arrived, aiming their guns at the white men detaining Lee until they could explain their situation and confirm their identities.[119]

Although this incident reflects some of the difficulties facing Chinese in New York—inspections by immigration officials, extortion from Chinese compatriots, and the ever-present threat of violence—the immigration official who recounted it described it as "an amusing happening." His attitude reveals the superior and slightly bemused perspective of many officials toward the Chinese people whom they regulated under exclusion. "I had many dealings with John Chinaman," the Ellis Island official recalled, but he "will always remain for me anthropology's greatest enigma."[120]

During the 1930s, as immigrants were blamed for the economic impacts of the Great Depression, the practice of raiding immigrant communities was revived and expanded from Chinese to other immigrant groups. In early 1931, the newly established Alien Bureau within the New York Police Department (NYPD) conducted extensive deportation raids. One inspector claimed that the raids would continue until the city was cleared of thousands of "illegal residents."[121] One of the most notorious raids, which echoed the raiding of the London Theater, occurred at the Finnish Workers' Educational Association in February 1931. As about 1,000 people gathered for a dance, thirty officers representing the Immigration Bureau and NYPD Alien Bureau ordered the band to stop and required each dancer to present proof of legal residence. Similar to the raids on Chinese New Yorkers, this was even less successful, with only eighteen individuals unable to prove their legal residence.[122]

The 1931–33 raids in New York led to a substantial expansion of detainees at Ellis Island: an average of 1,000 individuals were held at the station each day during these two years, compared with a daily average of 250 detainees throughout the rest of the 1930s.[123] After Daniel MacCormack was appointed as commissioner of immigration and naturalization in 1933 and New York police commissioner Edward Mulrooney stepped down in the same year, large-scale immigration raids and the practice of arresting potentially unauthorized immigrants without a warrant were discontinued.[124]

## Deportation Trains and the Expansion of Immigrant Removal

The expansion of deportation law was accompanied by increasingly efficient mechanisms for managing immigrant removal.[125] By 1919, deportation trains traversed the country, taking immigrants who had once arrived at Ellis Island, Angel Island, and other ports on a reverse journey to their ports of departure. These regularly scheduled trains show how deportation had become a central feature of immigration regulation. Throughout the 1920s and 1930s, both the frequency of the trains and the number of deportee passengers increased. In 1919, a deportation car departed about once a month, typically carrying European radicals on eastbound routes to Ellis Island and Chinese and other Asian deportees from New York westward to San Francisco.[126] By 1927, this had increased to roughly seven monthly journeys.[127] From the 1920s to the 1930s, the number of imprisoned passengers also rose from roughly 50 to 150 deportees on each journey, including about 90 Chinese on each westbound train and about 175 Europeans on the eastbound train. The largest train was twenty-two cars and carried 612 immigrants en route to Ellis Island.[128] The deportation parties typically started as a few coaches for men and sleepers for women and children coupled to regular passenger trains. However, as they added more deportees along the way, the trains were decoupled and one became a designated deportation train.[129] In 1920, Edwin Kline was placed in charge of these deportation "parties."[130] Twenty years later, he continued this line of work using the same trains to deliver Japanese enemy aliens from Ellis Island to other internment camps (see chapter 5).[131]

Westbound deportation parties revealed the increasing presence of Chinese in the eastern United States and their heavy representation among all deportees. Most deportees taken to San Francisco were Asian. The westbound trains typically started in New York, Hoboken, or Chicago, traveling via El Paso to San Francisco.[132] Although the records are fragmentary, a list from one 1919 transport to San Francisco shows that twenty-six individuals had Chinese names, while four had Japanese names. Thirty of the forty-four deportees on this train were Asian (from New York, Buffalo, Chicago, Carbondale, New Orleans, El Paso, San Antonio, Tucson, and Fresno). This particular journey took ten days, starting on May 24 in Washington, D.C., traveling north to Philadelphia, New York, and Buffalo, westward to Chicago and Carbondale, then due south to New Orleans and west along the Texas border, arriving in San Francisco on June 2, 1919.[133]

Eastbound trains typically started in Seattle or San Francisco and traveled to New York via the Great Northern or Southern Pacific railways.[134] On the return journey from San Francisco in June 1919, fifty-three deportees were delivered from San Francisco, Portland, Pocatello, Denver, Kansas City, Chicago, and Detroit to Ellis Island. As the last individuals were picked up in Detroit, an additional car had to be added to the train in order to accommodate the swelling number of deportees. All had European names and most were, according to the inspector in charge of transportation, "young, vigorous men, many of them having been in prison and many of them IWWs [Industrial Workers of the World] of the worst type."[135]

The containment of immigration prisoners created a mobile deportation station, extending the work of Ellis Island across the country. Windows on the trains were barred or fixed to open just a few inches; the deportees were under guard throughout their journey.[136] Despite these controls, a deportee, Leung Kai Main, escaped at some point during the journey. His body was later found in Ohio. The inspector in charge of transportation suggested that Leung realized he would be recaptured and committed suicide to avoid prosecution in San Francisco and, presumably, deportation.[137] By the 1930s, as deportation continued to expand, it appears that Chinese were increasingly deported out of Ellis Island. In one unfortunate event from the early 1930s, a Prince Line ship carrying more than 100 Chinese deportees from Ellis Island was lost at sea.[138] In 1941, of the 900 immigrants recorded on a list of Ellis Island deportees, more than 100 were Chinese.[139]

## "Ellis Island Is a Confined Place"

As deportation expanded, so did the number of immigrants detained at Ellis Island. "Ellis Island," William Fook Yee recalled when he was detained in 1939, "is a confined place."[140] By the 1920s, about 2,000 immigrants were detained overnight.[141] Throughout the 1930s, as immigrants were rounded up in deportation raids, detainees averaged about 1,000 per day.[142] It was, as journalist Gardner Jackson noted, "crowded to capacity."[143] However, in the period between Depression-era immigration raids and World War II, the numbers of detainees dropped to a daily average of between 150 and 250.[144] Although the majority of detainees were not Asian, in 1939 the Chinese dormitories were almost full.[145] The following year, out of 209 detainees, 47 were Chinese.[146] During the war, the detention of enemy aliens and stranded sailors pushed these numbers back up to roughly 1,000 detainees each day. By the 1950s, with about 1,000 individuals in detention at Ellis Island, as many as 200 were Chinese arrivals and deportees.[147] Chinese and other immigrants were detained both upon arrival and prior to deportation.

After passage of the 1924 Immigration Act, changing inspection practices meant that fewer immigrants were detained at immigration stations upon arrival. Most European immigrants were inspected in advance and no longer stepped foot on Ellis Island. Even though Chinese were also inspected in advance and issued visas by the U.S. consul, they were detained upon arrival in higher numbers and for longer periods.[148]

Chinese exclusion formally ended in 1943, after the United States allied with China to fight Japan during World War II. However, Chinese arriving at Ellis Island experienced the immigration process in ways that were not very different from those who arrived under exclusion rules. The repeal of exclusion ended racially based immigration restrictions, allowing a very limited number of 105 quota immigrants per year. The law also allowed Chinese immigrants to become U.S. citizens and provided for additional nonquota immigrants.[149] Thomas Louie and Gem Hoy (Harry) Lew arrived at New York–area airports in the early 1950s but were required to report to

Ellis Island for review of their immigration cases. Louie was not sure whether he was detained for two days or two weeks; Lew remembers being on Ellis Island for two months.[150]

Some Immigration Service concerns about Chinese arrivals in the 1950s may be related to the establishment of the communist People's Republic of China in 1949 and suspicions about Chinese communists in the United States. Other concerns are likely due to the recognition that, despite the end of exclusion, many Chinese continued to enter as paper sons. However, the tightened regulation of Chinese immigration started before 1949. In 1946, the New York–based *Xin Bao* (China Tribune) newspaper editorialized that "the immigration procedure is becoming increasingly difficult and, after entering the US, we have to endure racial discrimination."[151] Even if we account for the rhetorical emphasis of the editorial form, it is striking that three years after the end of exclusion, a Chinese American newspaper would claim that there were *increasing* difficulties in immigrating to the United States.

As noted in chapter 1, arriving Chinese were detained for shorter periods of time at Ellis Island than in San Francisco. Surviving records and detainee recollections suggest that the interviews undertaken by the Chinese Division in New York were shorter and enforcement of the exclusion law was more courteous. At the same time, Chinese were detained at Ellis Island for longer periods than other immigrants. Among all Ellis Island arrivals, most of whom were European, no more than 20 percent were typically detained, and these detentions were short. In 1907, for example, slightly less than 20 percent of all immigrants were detained, most of whom were waiting for a relative to meet them or for funds to facilitate their release; only 6 percent were held for additional investigation. In contrast, although the records are fragmentary and many arriving Chinese were released the day that they arrived, Chinese arrivals who didn't pass primary inspection appear to have been detained for weeks or months, much longer than other immigrants. Lew noted that some of his fellow detainees stayed at Ellis Island for six months or more. He, however, was finally released in February 1952, in time to celebrate Chinese New Year in New York's Chinatown, "just like in China." A few Chinese were imprisoned for as long as three years while they appealed their exclusion or deportation.[152]

Like arriving immigrants, Chinese deportees were also held at the detention center. They were brought to Ellis Island after being arrested in raids or after completing a jail sentence. Most deportees waited three to eight weeks for a deportation train to San Francisco. Jump-ship sailors were detained at Ellis Island while they waited to reship foreign. During the 1924–25 raids in New York, when 200 Chinese sailors chose to reship rather than be formally deported, it took a couple of months to find positions for all of them.[153] These extended detention times for Chinese upon arrival and prior to deportation from New York meant that, even though Chinese formed a small number of individuals at Ellis Island, they were a comparatively large number of the individuals in detention.

The time that immigrants spent on Ellis Island was undoubtedly difficult, owing to both the tedium and the tension surrounding their cases. The greatest ordeal, according to one detainee, was "the suspense and forced idleness."[154] "Argument always going on," Lew recalls, "just like in prison." Most of the time, detention was "boring." Even the guards, one detainee remembers, were "surly, bored, unfriendly." They did not mistreat the detainees, but stood in the corners of the Great Hall, at the doors of the dormitories, and around the island "watching us." In the dormitories, bunks were stacked on top of one another—mostly two high in the 1920s but growing taller as more immigrants were detained. The guards conducted counts five times a day, which unnerved some detainees. During his detention in 1940, Pierre Ferrand remembers the counts including men, women, children, and "others." He later learned that "others" referred to Asian detainees.[155]

Immigrants never knew when they might be called for questioning. They often had to wait weeks for their first interrogation.[156] Sometimes the interviews became contentious. At Wong Joe's deportation hearing, an inspector became frustrated that Wong claimed to have lived in the United States for thirteen years but could not speak English. He turned to two Chinese American men attending the hearing and demanded, "Why don't you, John and Lee, over here start a university and learn these fellows to talk English?" "We might teach them—can't 'learn' them," responded one of the men, correcting the inspector's English.[157] More often, immigrants attempted to comply with the process even if they questioned it. Although his detention occurred after the end of exclusion, Lew's session closely paralleled exclusion-era interrogations. "You know," he recalled in an oral history, "they ask you different kinds of questions like your sister's children, their names, their birthdays. I mean, how can people remember that?" Lew was not a paper son; however, he feared being sent home and wrote down all the details of his family's life to memorize them. Lew acknowledged that "it sounds ridiculous," but he knew that "you pick the wrong date, hey, you get sent back to China."[158]

One of the regular events that punctuated the monotony was mealtimes. Detainees were served "American" food. Lew recalls eating strange-looking new foods such as hamburgers and spaghetti. "Whoa!" he remembers thinking when he first saw meatloaf. "But you're hungry, you had to eat." Comparing his detention at Ellis Island to his experience of hiding in the mountains during the Japanese occupation of China, Lew recalled, "I got used to it. I ate all kinds of junk. In the mountains we ate all kind of junk." In part because he had little to do except eat, he gained fifteen pounds during his stay at Ellis Island.[159]

Although Lew questioned the necessity of his detention and criticized the conditions at Ellis Island, he acknowledged that he "had a good time there because we had nothing to do." In between meals, he played chess, cards, and ball games. He also made friends, some of whom remained close throughout his life.[160] Once a week all the detainees gathered together to watch English-language movies in the Great Hall, a huge vaulted room at the center of the building. Although Lew wasn't sure what was being said, he enjoyed the action and commented that "it's better than nothing to do."[161] Louie didn't remember any entertainment, but he described a small gift shop on the island where he bought a pack of cards to play with friends.[162]

Starting in 1923, the Daughters of the American Revolution (DAR) conducted craft projects with immigrants detained on the island, such as building model boats, carving soap, knitting scarves, and creating leather billfolds. The *New York Times* reported that "the newer ventures have been conducted mostly among Chinese boys, who seem to spend the longest periods on the island."[163] Detainees who stayed on the island over Christmas were treated to a party, regardless of their religion. Among the 500 partygoers in 1925, the *New York Times* listed "almond-eyed Chinese, ruddy-faced Irishmen, Jews from Bethlehem, Spanish senoritas, with high combs in their hair, and a group of pretty Japanese Geisha girls."[164] By 1931, 1,200 individuals were present for the party, including 800 detainees.[165] At other times, Chinese groups in New York planned celebrations for events such as Chinese New Year and offered to screen Chinese films for detainees.[166]

In the early years, Ellis Island did not follow practices of racial segregation used at other stations such as San Francisco. However, by 1934, Chinese were assigned segregated dormitories.[167] Although the Immigration and Naturalization Service (INS) did not publicly discuss the reason for the change, it may have been implemented to appease racist white immigrants held for secondary investigation. Mark Glanvill, a British national from South Africa, was detained with his family at Ellis Island in 1921. He

Times Wide World

A group of Chinese boys knitting on rakes and making model airplanes at the immigrant station on Ellis Island under supervision of Miss Elizabeth Estes, occupational therapist for the program of the Daughters of the American Revolution.

"A Group of Chinese Boys Knitting on Rakes and Making Model Airplanes at the Immigrant Station on Ellis Island," *New York Times* (1941).

expressed his revulsion that upon his arrival he had to walk through a corridor "completely blocked by a seething mass of humanity, filthy in the extreme—Europe's worst, negroes, Asiatics—dregs of humanity."[168] He protested not only the presence of Black and Asian immigrants in the space that he occupied, but also undesirable Europeans. British detainees requested segregation by nationality so that they would not be required to share accommodations with other racial and national groups, but the British ambassador agreed with immigration authorities that national segregation was not feasible.[169]

A plan of the island, developed in 1937 and revised in 1942, showed two dormitory rooms reserved for Chinese, two reserved for whites, and one room for "colored" immigration cases. Men's and women's sleeping quarters were located separately on either side of the main hall.[170] In their history of Angel Island, Erika Lee and Judy Yung point out that the racial segregation of immigrants was "similar to the Jim Crow laws that mandated de jure segregation in all public facilities in the American South."[171] However, whereas Jim Crow laws were state laws, segregation at Ellis Island was sanctioned by the federal government. Although the organization of the dormitories provided for the presence of "colored" immigrants, the main groups of nonwhite immigrants were Asians. Ellis Island operated a tripartite racial segregation system in which Asian-white separation was a central goal. By 1944, when large numbers of enemy aliens were being detained on the island, the "Chinese section" appears to have included Japanese and South Asians.[172] Racial segregation, along with complex segregations by immigration status, continued until Ellis Island closed in 1954.[173]

Outside of the dormitories, other areas were segregated more informally and less forcefully. William Fook Yee described how Chinese, eastern European, Mediterranean, and other detainees were kept apart during meals and exercise periods.[174] Asian detainees ate at separate tables but in the same dining room as Europeans.[175] Some aspects of informal segregation may have been based on language, with Chinese choosing to speak with others who shared their dialect. Yee notes that, because of this segregation, he didn't learn any English until he was released from the island.[176] Some may have self-segregated based on family ties. Although they slept in separate dormitories, Chinese men and women spent time together during the day lingering on the benches and at the limited number of tables scattered around the Great Hall.[177] Some children played together across families: Luisa Zichlinsky remembers playing ping-pong and doing puzzles with some Japanese boys in detention. Others were deterred by the lack of a common language.[178]

After decades of continuous use and somewhat clumsy repurposing as a detention center, Ellis Island was dilapidated. By the 1920s, the paint was worn and the roof required repair. "As a result of the chronic dirt," a 1923 report noted, "the buildings are pervaded by a flat, stale smell."[179] The doors between various rooms were locked, and the station was surrounded by wire fences. Officials and detainees alike recognized that the island was a prison.[180] "Often the object of unfavorable comment in former years," the *Annual Report of the Commissioner-General of Immigration* noted in 1926, "it is hoped that the term 'Ellis Island' may in time be freed from any unpleasant significance in the thought of our own people and the minds of the newcomers to our shores, and that the greatest immigration station in the United States may realize for itself and for the country its fullest possibilities."[181] By this time, however, the greatest immigration station had become the United States' chief deportation depot.

• • • • • •

Historians have long attended to immigration rather than deportation, particularly at Ellis Island. As Rachel Buff has argued, "Scholars of immigration have tended to focus on the 'golden door' without attending to exits, clearly marked or otherwise."[182] However, immigration researchers have increasingly shown that the twin mechanisms of restricting the entry of certain groups and deporting unauthorized immigrants were closely connected.[183] This was true at every immigration station, including Ellis Island.

Starting in the 1920s and continuing through the closing of Ellis Island in 1954, deportation was a central mechanism for the regulation of Chinese New Yorkers. Practices of deportation were complex and expansive, not limited to unlawful entry but reaching into every aspect of Chinese life. Deportation raids spread fear among Chinese New Yorkers and, as the city's Chinese population had become more established by the 1920s, raised concerns that the community would be decimated, even destroyed. Immigration officials and police raided Chinatown, claiming to be seeking criminal tong members but rounding up mostly unauthorized immigrants without any evidence of other illegal activity or tong membership. Immigration laws and policing practices not only criminalized unlawful entry but also criminalized the simple fact of being Chinese in America. Deportation was a powerful tool of "post-entry social control" used not only to implement exclusion and tamp down violent crime, but also to police everyday activities.

As detention and deportation became increasingly important, the number of Chinese and other Asians detained at and deported through Ellis Island also increased. As novelist Theodore Irwin suggested, Ellis Island was "the exit gate of the nation."[184] In addition to arriving immigrants and deportees, New York immigration officials were particularly concerned about Asian stowaways and jump-ship sailors. Their stories form the following two chapters.

# 3  Smugglers and Stowaways

## The Dangerous Journeys of Human Freight

· · · · · · · · · · · · · · · · · · · · · · · · · · · · · · · · · · · · · · · · · ·

June 1923. Dusk settled over the schooner *Mary Beatrice* as she nodded in the swells near Sandy Hook in the New York Bay, just fifteen miles south of Manhattan Island. It had been days since the ship's captain had gone ashore. According to the *New York Times,*

> After fortifying himself with liquor he had climbed over the side and gone off in a rum-running motorboat, with half of the $10,000 bribe promised by the twenty Chinese aboard his ship, if he succeeded in smuggling them into this country. The Chinese grew restless. Off on the horizon they could dimly make out the land, and they had been a month aboard the fifty-foot, weather-battered schooner. In the strictly Occidental clothing that they wore was the other half of the $10,000. Scattered about the cramped deck the Chinese discussed their situation. Heedless of the gutturals of the "cargo," the crew, a West Indian medley of two white seamen, a negro seaman and a negro cook, also discussed a situation. Their situation involved two rusty shotguns, two tarnished revolvers, the meat knife of the cook and the negro sailor's razor. Also the $5,000 ready money in the possession of the chattering freight.[1]

The four crew members demanded the Chinese passengers' money. The passengers shouted and charged, fighting the crew with their bare hands, two rusty axes, short knives, and sticks from the ship's woodpile. The crew responded with gunfire that ripped through one of the passenger's hands and sent him flying over the side of the ship. "Back and forth over the close quarters of the small deck, if the Chinese memory is correct, the battle was fought. One of the Chinese ran full onto the knife of the negro sailor; another went down before a full charge of buckshot. The negro cook, who wielded the razor, got a Chinese and then crashed down when he was struck a terrific blow over the head. Two more Chinese were knifed or shot to death, before the superior weight of their numbers began to tell." By now, five passengers and the cook had been killed. The crew members' ammunition had run out, and the passengers blocked the way to the storeroom, as they fought hand to hand with the crew. "With the Chinese swarming in ever closer, the two white sailors and the negro with the meat knife fought hard. Once a Chinese missed a blow aimed with a gnarled knot of firewood. He spun in within range of the negro's long, keen knife. The extended right arm of the Chinese caught the full lunge of the knife. Only a thin strand of flesh kept his hand in place. . . . Finally, and the Chinese could not tell how, for the fight became a wrestling tangle of humans, with the crew pulled down in a last rush of their adversaries, the crew was dispatched." As the *New York Times* concluded, the Chinese men had won. "The dusk had changed to night when the Chinese shoved over the side the bodies of the crew and the five of their dead countrymen."[2]

The *Times*'s coverage was both sensationalized and sympathetic. The newspaper described the fight in lurid detail for its readers, but also expressed concern for the Chinese passengers betrayed by the crew. Undercutting this sympathy was the suggestion that the story may have been untrustworthy. As the Chinese men were the only survivors, the conflict was described from their perspective. This was unusual. Most coverage of unauthorized immigration was told from the perspective of the officials who regulated such immigration. As with other Chinese immigrants undergoing secondary inspection and those facing deportation, the Chinese survivors were detained at Ellis Island and subjected to questioning. They were initially hesitant to talk. However, when forced to speak—under pressure from immigration inspectors who interrogated them throughout the night—their memory was questioned and they were described as unreliable narrators. The Chinese passengers maintained that they had departed from Havana, stayed two days off Sandy Hook, were attacked, and lost five of their number. However, the *Times* reporter and Ellis Island officials wondered why they had traveled to New York rather than take a more direct route to Florida; noticed a New York newspaper on board that was almost a week old, longer than the time the Chinese men claimed they had been stranded; and questioned whether they were attacked or had murdered the crew members.[3]

· · · · · ·

Seaborne smuggling was rampant in New York, the largest port in the United States. As early as 1898, New York special inspector J. Thomas Scharf complained that smuggling had made a farce of the exclusion laws. Although Scharf was an overzealous and unreliable inspector, he recognized that official statistics of Chinese entries into the United States ignored not only "carloads" of Chinese illegally crossing the United States' land borders but also "the vessel loads of Chinese smuggled into the country along the Gulf coast."[4] Scharf emphasized that Chinese attempted to enter the United States "from points on the coasts of both oceans, and New York is the great objective and distributing point for them."[5]

New York City was the central location through which seaborne smuggling activities were directed along the Eastern Seaboard, as well as the destination for many unauthorized immigrants. Chinese immigrants who smuggled themselves into New York used complex multiracial and transnational networks to facilitate their journeys. Many secret routes into the city shadowed legal immigration patterns. Like the legal immigrants outlined in chapter 1, most unauthorized Chinese immigrants appear to have smuggled themselves from the Caribbean, while others stowed away from Latin America and Europe. Also similar to legal immigration, more Asian stowaways appear to have arrived on the West Coast than on the East. However, as the major port for immigrant smuggling, New York provides important insights into practices of Asian stowaways and smugglers as well as enforcement efforts against such practices.

Starting with the 1917 Immigration Act and the U.S. entry into World War I in the same year, ports and shipping became heavily regulated. In the 1920s, laws governing immigration and exclusion were tightened for both European and Asian immigrants. These changes led to the expansion of seaborne smuggling to evade new restrictions as well as the closer regulation of such smuggling. New laws on stowaways paralleled the expansion of deportation laws and practices in the 1920s. The administration of legal Asian immigration was conducted with relative restraint at Ellis Island, while the implementation of deportation raids was often critiqued as excessive. The regulation of stowaways fell somewhere in between these approaches. New York immigration officials were ambivalent about European stowaways but consistent in their rejection of Chinese stowaways unless they could prove U.S. citizenship. Immigration officials aimed to prosecute stowaways but conflicted with federal prosecutors who wanted stowaways to serve as witnesses in larger cases against smuggling networks. This contested enforcement ultimately allowed some Chinese the opportunity to achieve their original goal of immigrating to New York without authorization.

As with exclusion and expulsion, race operated differently for Asians smuggling themselves into the United States than for European and other groups, sometimes providing them with greater security and sometimes putting them at greater risk. Ships were hierarchical, segregated spaces. Officers, including the captain, were typically white Europeans or Americans. At the same time, Chinese, Bengali, Filipino, and Japanese sailors worked on ethnically segregated teams stoking the engines below deck or in service behind the scenes. These hidden spaces provided some security for stowaways. However, Asian stowaways also faced greater risk of detection and danger upon detection. Asians discovered on board or disembarking the ship were typically assumed to be unauthorized. They were objectified by the smuggling agents whom they hired to secure their entry and by the immigration officials who attempted to stop them. Smuggling agents made significant profits from their work and were willing to sacrifice their customers if their profits were threatened.

Chinese who were discovered close to New York, either on board smuggling ships or as stowaways on larger vessels, were taken to Ellis Island to be interrogated and detained prior to their deportation. Once arrested, they faced laws that provided potential entry to European stowaways but rejected all Chinese stowaways under exclusion laws. In these situations, they relied on networks of defenders to support their cases, including former Ellis Island officials; however, they had very limited options and were typically deported. In some cases, they were able to ship out in lieu of formal deportation or, if their testimony was required in a smuggling case and they were bonded, to jump bond.

Chinese immigrants challenged their exclusion both through the indirect smuggling practices explored in chapter 1 and through direct smuggling and stowing away. Although some sources describe all unauthorized immigration as "smuggling," including the indirect smuggling schemes of paper sons and fraudulent merchants, this chapter focuses on those who directly smuggled themselves or stowed away on ships. Scholars have increasingly recognized the significance of unauthorized Chinese immigration during the exclusion era. They have focused especially on the ways that immigrants established false identities to enter the United States, sometimes described as indirect smuggling.[6] Historians have also considered direct smuggling of Chinese across the United States' borders with Mexico and Canada.[7] However, fewer historians have focused on the ways in which Chinese immigrants, and Asian immigrants generally, attempted to enter the United States by stowing away or smuggling themselves on ships.[8]

Not surprisingly, indirect and direct smuggling operations were interconnected. In the 1920s, Willie Fung operated a smuggling network out of his laundry in Key West, Florida, which provided clients with forged paper son documents and transported smuggled arrivals to various ports on the Eastern Seaboard, including New York City.[9] The presence of smuggling in New York reveals that Asian migration to the United States was far more varied than the archetypal journey directly from home country ports to San Francisco, creating complex networks throughout the Eastern Seaboard, across the Caribbean, and beyond. At the same time, attention to New York shows that the enforcement of exclusion extended into many areas that have not always been considered within histories of exclusion, including seaborne smuggling, shipping, and sailors.

The terms "smuggling" and "stowing away" help distinguish between two ways that immigrants landed secretly in the United States at secluded locations or near U.S. seaports. "Smuggling" is typically used to describe immigrants who hired smaller crews from locations closer to the United States, such as Cuba, Jamaica, Trinidad, and Caribbean ports in Mexico; "stowaways" is more often used to describe those who hid on larger ships over longer journeys from Asia, Europe, or Latin America.[10] At times, however, the terms were used interchangeably, as when crew members who helped immigrants stow away were described as smugglers.

### The Agency of Human Freight

Smuggling agents and newspapers viewed Chinese stowaways as "merchandise" or "freight." In contrast to the romantic image of European stowaways as resourceful, independent immigrants who yearned to come to America despite their financial inability to buy a ticket, many white Americans viewed Chinese stowaways as undesirable immigrants smuggled by others into the United States. Smuggling agents were racially diverse, but most who worked with Chinese clients were themselves Chinese. They did not critique Chinese immigration, but described their clients in dehumanizing ways.

Smuggling agents used coded terms to hide the true nature of their business. However, these codes describe their clients as objects, revealing the understanding that Chinese immigrants were the material goods on which their business was based. They described stowaways as merchandise, presents, or—in one case—as a piece of ginseng.[11] A smuggler in Cuba used the code "oval" to describe Chinese immigrants, stating in a telegram that a ship "left Friday with oval Stop Sullivan went to New York to arrange landing."[12] Historian Sarah Griffith has detailed the codes used in an Oregon drug smuggling ring, in which "flour" meant 250 pounds of opium had been delivered and "soda crackers" was a coded instruction to buy 100 pounds of opium (while "extra crackers" referred to 150 pounds).[13] Even when they were not concerned about speaking in code, Chinese smugglers often objectified stowaways, describing them as a "shipment" or acknowledging "receipt" of them.[14] White informants were also extremely dismissive of Chinese stowaways, stating, for example, that a ship was in harbor "to load Chinks."[15]

Unauthorized Chinese immigrants were routinely described in U.S. media in ways that implied they had little agency in their decision to immigrate to the United States. The *New York Times* referred to the Chinese passengers on board the *Mary Beatrice* as "chattering freight" and "contraband human freight," suggesting not only their inhumanity but also their illegality.[16] The *Times*'s use of quotation marks to describe the ship's "cargo" may indicate the crew's rather than the newspaper's perspective. However, like the common term "smuggled Chinese," such language located all the power over the smuggling process with the crew or "smugglers." As the *Mary Beatrice*'s passengers showed, however, this was not always or entirely the case.[17] Chinese and other immigrants were not smuggled by others but smuggled themselves. In the process, they challenged their exclusion. All immigrants—Asian or non-Asian, authorized or unauthorized, smuggled or stowed away—relied on themselves as well as others to enter the United States.

Often facing great dangers, immigrants were the active agents of their own unauthorized migration. They negotiated with crew members to stow away, or they hired a vessel to smuggle themselves into the United States, but they were deeply dependent on the crew and always faced the threat of discovery. The secrecy surrounding their journey was both essential to and potentially endangered their success, as crew members could harm them with impunity. And they had no legal protections because they were themselves illegal.

The description of "smuggled Chinese" as passively being smuggled rather than actively involved in smuggling was part of an expansive American discourse about Chinese immigrants as powerless agents of larger forces, accustomed to imperial subjection in China and domination by Chinese community organizations in the United States. Instead of viewing Chinese immigrants, whether authorized or unauthorized, as agents of their own migration, exclusionists described them as enslaved. Chinese immigrants were, as a California Senate address to the U.S. Congress claimed in 1878, "by the unalterable structure of their being, voluntary slaves."[18] This was, as Mary Coolidge described it in 1909, "the coolie fiction."[19]

The anti-Asian racism that was central to the implementation and expansion of exclusion policies also characterized officials' treatment of discovered stowaways. As with other developments in immigration policy, such as deportation, prohibitions on stowaways were first introduced in the 1882 Chinese exclusion law. These restrictions were not expanded to explicitly ban stowaways—including European stowaways—until 1917.[20] Some European stowaways were found to be eligible to enter the United States. However, unless they were U.S. citizens, all Asian stowaways were automatically barred. Although they had entirely different immigration statuses, stowaways and regular Chinese immigrants were considered similarly by immigration authorities; they were viewed as likely unauthorized entrants who required extensive inspection. One Boston immigration inspector boarding a large steamship in a driving winter storm on New Year's Day in the early 1900s asked, "Any stowaways or Chinese on board, Captain?"[21] Ellis Island officials were often sympathetic to European stowaways, even describing the denial of most stowaways as a "tragedy."[22] Such concerns were not expressed about the rejection of Asian arrivals, whether they attempted to enter as authorized immigrants, smuggled themselves, or stowed away to enter the United States.

Concerns about sailors and stowaways frequently overlapped, as sailors assisted stowaways, and stowaways sometimes illegally secured seamen's identification cards in order to land at U.S. ports.[23] As explored in chapter 4, crew members protested their own regulation as sailors under exclusion laws, but those involved in smuggling were probably more concerned about making extra money than challenging exclusion laws. Although all races were involved in smuggling, Asian sailors appear to have been viewed with particular suspicion by government officials and their fellow crew members.

By the early 1920s, U.S. officials were focusing increasingly on investigations of seaborne smuggling networks.[24] In the late nineteenth and early twentieth centuries, the Immigration Bureau investigated smuggling across the United States' land borders, including efforts by New York inspectors such as J. Thomas Scharf on the northern border in the 1890s and Marcus Braun on the southern border in 1906.[25] After the importation of opium was banned by federal law in 1909 and the sale of alcohol was banned by constitutional amendment in 1920, Ellis Island officials turned their attention more intently to seaborne smuggling. Smugglers first used sailboats such as schooners and sloops, later turning to motorized launches. After Prohibition, smugglers sometimes used larger ships anchored on rum rows just beyond U.S. waters, waiting for smaller, faster motorboats to transport illicit liquor and unauthorized immigrants to shore. The rum row south of New York City, where the *Mary Beatrice* moored in 1923, was one of the busiest in the nation. The rise in smuggling reflected not only the demand for alcohol and other drugs in New York but also the rise of the city as a destination for Chinese immigrants.[26]

Seaborne rum running, opium smuggling, and human smuggling operated on the same routes with the same handlers.[27] When Willie Fung's laundry in Key West was searched as part of a drug raid in 1922, a bundle of papers was taken from the premises; it included letters from Savannah, Georgia, Washington, D.C., Newark, N.J., and New York City related to smuggling Chinese immigrants.[28] U.S. officials found seamen's identification cards at the laundry, some of which appear to have been issued by the Chinese consul in New York and others that were plainly forgeries. In addition, they located materials for making forgeries, including "a Midget Acme stapler for fastening the photographs to the cards, a bottle of Higgins Vermillion waterproof ink, a stamp pad, a tube of glue, and a pair of cutting pliers."[29] With the passage of immigration restrictions in the 1920s, the commissioner-general noted that "bootlegging of aliens . . . has grown to be an industry second only to the bootlegging of liquor. In fact, the two frequently go hand in hand."[30] The dehumanizing characterization of immigrants as imported objects continued this understanding, with the suggestion that they were just another bootlegged import.

### New York, Capital of Seaborne Smuggling

New York was the epicenter of seaborne smuggling along the East Coast. During most of the nineteenth and twentieth centuries, the port of New York and New Jersey, which included docks in Manhattan, Brooklyn, and Staten Island as well as New Jersey, was not only the busiest port in the United States but the busiest in the world.[31] It was the largest U.S. port for trade, for legal immigrants, and for stowaways of all races. New York accounted for about half of all immigrant stowaways, dwarfing all other ports with a stowaway population that was typically at least three times bigger than the next port (table 7).[32] Although smuggling networks extended along the Gulf and Atlantic coasts, most smuggling agents appear to have brought immigrants to New York.

Smuggling into New York followed many of the same routes as legal Asian immigration and indirect smuggling through Ellis Island, with Asian stowaways arriving in New York from all points. However, Caribbean ports appear to have been the source of most Chinese smuggling and stowaways: Cuba, Trinidad, and Jamaica, as well as other Caribbean countries and the Atlantic coast of Mexico were key points of departure.[33] These voyages typically lasted about a week, with journeys from Jamaica taking roughly seven days, from Trinidad about eight days, and Tampico, Mexico, ten days. The shorter journey from Cuba typically took only about four days.[34] Stowaways also traveled from ports in Asia, such as Hong Kong, Shanghai, Singapore, and Calcutta, on journeys that lasted for months, often via Middle Eastern and then European ports.[35] Asian stowaways were similarly involved in active smuggling networks operating out of Valparaiso, Chile, and Marseilles, France.[36]

Seaborne smuggling was partly a response to increased enforcement of both immigration and exclusion laws, as the Immigration Bureau recognized. "The more rigid and successful the port inspections are made, the more persistent become the operations of the smugglers," the bureau reported in 1909; "draw the lines tight on the land borders, and it is soon found that the base of operations has been changed from Canada and Mexico to Jamaica and Cuba and that Chinese are being landed systematically at the seaports as sailors and stowaways."[37] Increased enforcement in ports also impacted stowing away. During World War I the New York inspector in charge of exclusion noted that "unusually strict wartime surveillance" of European docks contributed to a reduction in seaborne smuggling.[38] Starting in 1920, numbers of detained stowaways jumped up considerably.[39] Some of the postwar rise was likely due to increased enforcement and detection; however, it was sustained by strict racial immigration quotas on southern and eastern Europeans in the 1924 Immigration Law as well as the barring of almost all Asians as "aliens ineligible for citizenship."[40] Historian Libby Garland has shown how many Chinese smuggling practices were adopted by European Jews to enter the United States as part of multiracial smuggling networks, including between the Caribbean and the Eastern Seaboard. The expansion and consolidation of Asian exclusion appears to have contributed to the increased use of direct smuggling over indirect smuggling.[41]

The Immigration Bureau did not consistently report immigrant stowaways by race or nationality. In general, however, East Coast ports reported higher numbers of stowaways of all nationalities and lower numbers of Asian stowaways than ports in the West (table 7).[42] As the largest port, New York received about one-half of all stowaways. Until 1920, this number averaged 330 stowaways each year; after 1920, it was closer to 1,000.

In contrast, San Francisco had consistent numbers of around 60 stowaways annually. From 1914 through 1920, Chinese formed just 1 percent of all stowaways in New York but about 25 percent of all stowaways in San Francisco.[43] San Francisco officials reported about 15 percent of all stowaways in the port were Japanese.[44] However, there are almost no records concerning Japanese stowaways at Ellis Island, probably because Japanese were administered by the general immigration office in New York and were incorporated into general counts. South Asians also stowed themselves into the United States, but they were not recorded separately and their stories are difficult to trace.[45] In a later period, 1928 until 1931, almost 10 percent of all stowaways were Chinese or Japanese. However, these data are not broken down by port.[46] The higher number of Asian stowaways in San Francisco may partly result from institutional reporting practices, but it more likely reflects the larger number of Asians interested in immigrating to the western United States. It may also demonstrate that Chinese and South Asians had better alternatives to stowing away in New York, such as working as sailors and jumping ship.[47]

## Practices of Smuggling and Stowing Away

Unauthorized immigrants, whether they stowed away or smuggled themselves into the United States, were active participants in their own migration. They used extensive multiracial, transnational networks to secretly enter the United States via routes that paralleled legal immigration, and relied on the substantial number of Chinese and other Asian maritime workers. If they were discovered, they relied on legal networks, securing representation to challenge their detention through white immigration brokers and the Chinese Consolidated Benevolent Association (CCBA), the influential federation of Chinese ethnic regional associations.

Both Chinese stowaways and those chartering small vessels typically located a smuggling agent, who connected them to a sailor involved in assisting unauthorized immigrants. They would usually meet the sailor at a location away from the ship, such as a laundry in which the agent worked, at a saloon, or on the street. Sometimes they would meet for the first time on the dock immediately before boarding the ship.[48] The smuggling agents were almost always Chinese, and the crew members were frequently Chinese. In some cases, both the immigrants and crew members spoke Spanish.[49] However, if they didn't speak the same language, communication became limited after the Chinese smuggling agent was no longer available to interpret. Basic English phrases were the lingua franca of smuggling. Chin Sue told inspectors that a crew member "told me to go to New York with him." How did he do that, asked the suspicious inspectors, if the crew member didn't speak Chinese and the stowaway didn't speak Spanish? Chin replied directly: he said in English, "New York."[50] A Chinese man detected while attempting to swim to shore near 33rd Street in Brooklyn made an offer to the customs officer who detained him: "Two hundred and fifty bucks—Chinatown." "That," the *New York Herald Tribune* commented, "was all the English he could speak."[51]

These stowaway and smuggling arrangements were often part of extended networks facilitating unauthorized immigration.[52] Although most Chinese aimed to get to New York safely, not all stowaways came directly through New York.[53] Smuggling networks were not limited to the city but extended along the Gulf coast and East Coast from New Orleans to Tampa and Key West to Philadelphia.[54] Aided by a smuggling agent in Newark, Moy Lee and Wong Sieu undertook an unusually long journey. They traveled from China to Canada, overland to Montreal, then on to Kingston, Jamaica, and Savinilla, Colombia, before arriving in New York.[55] A common smuggling route from Caribbean countries took Asian immigrants on shorter journeys to ports such as Pensacola or isolated landing spots in Florida.[56] They also arrived at ports south of New York such as Baltimore and Philadelphia, often making their way to New York via train.[57] An informant in Key West described a "well-organized chain of smugglers operating throughout Florida, New York, Chicago, and California" to bring Chinese from Cuba to the United States.[58]

The East Asia Company was one such chain, founded in the early 1920s to smuggle Chinese immigrants to New York. The company had written policies that covered application forms and contractual obligations, as well as requirements for contacting both the main office—the location of which was not given—and the branch office in Havana. In order to conduct business, the company obtained a loan for a twenty-eight-foot gasoline-powered motorboat. And, as the passengers' "fare" included naturalization papers, the organizers of the company claimed that there would be "practically no difficulty in the way." However, if there was "any accident, the East Asia Company would bear all the responsibilities."[59] Another company, which operated a legitimate import-export business located at 936 Race Street in Philadelphia, was described by immigration officials as a "clearing house for smuggling Chinese." It brought unauthorized immigrants from Florida to New York's Chinatown.[60] Both the East Asia Company's bank loan and the presence of the import-export smuggling business in Philadelphia suggest the ways in which licit and illicit businesses were closely interlinked.

As the entire business model of smuggling was built on secrecy, the extent of unauthorized immigration through U.S. seaports is not always clear. Companies hid their practices, and immigration officials may have exaggerated the numbers of smuggled Asians.[61] In addition to difficulties estimating the scope of seaborne smuggling, it is hard to determine the success of smuggling networks or the effectiveness of the immigration authorities' work intercepting smugglers and stowaways. When immigration officials unearthed a smuggling organization, they often claimed that it revealed the potential for "fraud on a grand scale."[62] Officials believed, probably accurately, that these cases were the tip of an iceberg floating in the Atlantic just off the Eastern Seaboard.

Historical traces of business records seized by the Immigration Bureau and transcripts of immigration interrogations of smugglers, however, suggest that smuggling companies were not always effective and their security was sometimes weak. In one case, for example, a broker associated with the Henry Howkee Laundry in Tampa, Florida, asked the Balbin Stamp and Seal Company to engrave an impression stamp with details of the Chinese consul of New York. The broker also inquired about printing companies that would print certificates with the same information and asked whether the stamp maker knew of machines that could successfully attach photographs to such certificates. It was clear to the Florida stamp maker that these efforts were designed to manufacture fraudulent documents. He agreed to do the work, but instead reported his concerns to the immigration authorities. When Hen Lee returned to obtain the stamp, he was arrested.[63] Although the historical evidence is not conclusive, direct seaborne smuggling may have been less effective than indirect smuggling.

For some aspects of the smuggling enterprise, such as the cost of being smuggled into the United States, there is more consistent information. Discovered stowaways and smugglers provided this information to the Immigration Bureau. And discovered documents from smuggling raids reveal the amounts received and disbursed during the smuggling process. Not surprisingly, these costs appear to have increased over time and were larger for longer journeys. In the early 1900s, a journey from Asia or Europe to the eastern United States cost about $1,000. In 1909, the commissioner-general of immigration claimed that "A Chinaman apparently will undergo any hardship or torture, take any risk, or pay any sum of money up to $1,000 to enjoy the forbidden but much coveted privilege of living and working in the

United States."[64] During the preceding year, a case was brought in the Hong Kong courts attempting to secure payment for an outstanding $500 balance on the transportation of "a valuable thing" to the United States. As it turned out, according to immigration officials, the valuable thing was "nothing less than a Chinese coolie."[65] In 1921, Chinese passengers on board the SS *Helenus* paid $1,200 to stow away from China to New York.[66] In the same year, travel from France to New York had a similar cost: 1,000 francs was due two days before stowaways were landed, and if they successfully entered the United States, they were required to pay the balance of $1,000 once they had earned it.[67]

The cost of stowing away from Asia was lower than the cost of coming through indirect smuggling as a paper son or paper merchant. Immigrants themselves suggested that the going rate for a paper identity was $100 per year—for example, $1,800 for an eighteen-year-old. This higher cost was likely because the number of available fraudulent identities was more limited than the number of possible hiding spaces on a ship and because the process of creating a fraudulent identity was more complex—and if successful, one's legal status as a paper son or paper merchant was more secure.[68] Direct smuggling may also have been less expensive than indirect smuggling because it was less effective.

Smuggling costs from the Caribbean appear both less expensive and more varied. This may reflect more competition and more companies operating on these routes. Or it may simply reflect that more extensive information is available on smuggling into New York from this region, leading to more varied reported costs. In 1915, Charlie Low and Charlie Sing each promised to pay $100 and two cans of opium to be smuggled from Coatzacoalcos, Vera Cruz, Mexico, to New York.[69] In 1922, it cost roughly $600 to arrange being smuggled from Cuba to Key West and $850 from Cuba to New York.[70] The passengers on board the *Mary Beatrice* in 1923 may have thought they got a good price as they agreed to $500, including a down payment of $250 for transport from Havana and the balance of $250 upon their safe landing in New York. Other immigrants paid more. One agency charged $950 in silver for transportation between Havana and New York (including naturalization documents), while some Chinese were reported to pay up to $2,500.[71]

Like other smuggling businesses, the East Asia Company paid a small amount to a series of handlers to ensure that the immigrants were successfully landed.[72] Writing a letter to his accomplice who lived on Mott Street in New York's Chinatown, self-employed Jamaican smuggler Lee Ting provided a detailed accounting of these smuggling charges: $100 to "the

American" (in two installments of $50 cash), $10 to Chin Yee for taking care of the immigrant on board the ship and $10 for the use of the rowboat to get him to shore, $30 to Dung Fat for paying the American his second installment and assisting the immigrant once he arrived in Baltimore, and $5.30 for the train ticket to New York (to be paid by the immigrant himself). With payments totaling $150, Lee Ting estimated that he and his partner would make a total profit of $200, which amounted to $100 each.[73]

Immigration officials were well aware of these costs and the profits available to those organizing unauthorized immigration. "It requires no expert accountant," the bureau's annual report noted in 1909, to calculate that smugglers "can well afford to take extraordinary risks and can grow rich, even if a considerable number of their clients are captured and deported."[74] "The importation of Chinese has become a regular business, out of which a number of promoters, steerers, and attorneys make an enormous profit," the report noted in the following year. "Just so long as administrative methods are not made too difficult . . . profits are large."[75] Ignoring Chinese anger at the injustice of exclusion, immigration officials suggested that the only reason Chinese protested its harsh administration was because it cut into their smuggling profits.

Organizations such as the CCBA not only opposed the expansion of exclusion and worked with New York officials to help shape the administration of exclusion laws, but also contributed to practices of seaborne smuggling. CCBA members were merchants who may have been engaged in smuggling as part of their business. In addition, the organization monitored Chinese community members and worked to ensure they paid their debts. This may have contributed to smuggling, as immigrants could pay for their unauthorized passage over time and smuggling agents were relatively confident that they would be repaid. This was not fully understood by many Americans. According to New York immigration commissioner Edward Corsi, "The weird religion of the yellow man accounts for much present-day smuggling. He is a reliable liability. He pays his debts—because his religion paints a damning picture of the next world for those who leave unpaid debts behind."[76] This assessment, of course, overlooked cases such as the legal suit regarding nonpayment of smuggling costs that was tried in Hong Kong courts or the many financial conflicts and unpaid loans that were adjudicated by the CCBA in New York.[77]

What did immigrants attempting to stow away to New York receive in exchange for these smuggling fees? Successful landing was never guaranteed, but crew members who worked with stowaways guided them to board the ship, hide throughout the passage, and depart upon their arrival. Stowaways would typically be taken on board larger ships under cover of night. Some used a rowboat or other small boat to approach the ship.[78] Others simply walked up the gangplank with their contact on the crew, later claiming that they were not helped and that none of the crew had seen them.[79]

Occasionally, officials in the country of departure would prevent individuals from boarding ships because they suspected that they were not authorized to immigrate to the United States. In 1922, Cuban officials prevented eleven Chinese from boarding the American schooner *Mohawk*. However, they were unable to detain six additional Chinese or prevent the ship from sailing from Santiago del Norte. The American consul in Havana reported the ship to U.S. officials in the hopes that they would be able to intercept it and stop the Chinese immigrants from landing in Florida.[80] At other times, immigration officials in Washington, D.C., shared information with their Ellis Island counterparts about ships that had left Havana bound for New York with suspected stowaways on board.[81]

Sometimes it may have been possible for people to smuggle themselves on board without assistance. Although one merchant navy officer suspected that four crew members had assisted the Chinese stowaways discovered on his vessel, he acknowledged that it was possible that they smuggled themselves out of Jamaica without assistance. "It was an easy thing to get on board," he admitted, "as we were loading bananas all night and about one thousand people were working on the ship."[82]

Most often, stowaways received assistance. The Chinese firemen who stoked the ship's coal-powered engines were frequently the crew members accused of helping stowaways. As explored in the following chapter, firemen were paid less than other crew members and worked in the lowest, darkest, and most remote parts of the ship, allowing them to hide stowaways in places where they wouldn't be discovered.[83] Other seamen who worked with smugglers were storekeepers who had access to hidden storage areas, boatswains (bosuns) in charge of lifeboats and other deck equipment, and stewards with control over various areas of the ship as well as supplies such as food.[84] These men would provide stowaways with bread and water throughout the journey, sometimes twice a day, but more often just once in order to avoid detection.[85] In addition to supplies, crew members would provide other assistance as needed, such as ensuring that the stowaways were not in the cargo hold during fumigation.[86]

Ships were multiracial, multinational, and multiethnic workplaces, and many different groups were involved in smuggling. Ships were also

segregated and hierarchical. Typically, one ethnic group occupied a particular rank or role on board the ship. Service work (such as stewards' positions) and dirty, dangerous jobs (such as firemen's work) were often held
by exclusively Chinese, Filipino, or Bengali teams. This segregation, which
was developed in part to facilitate employers' exploitation of workers,
helped Asian crew members take part in smuggling without their super-
visors' knowledge. Asian crew members' difficult and demeaning work below decks or behind cabin doors on board the ship enabled them to carve
out a space to hide stowaways. Shipmates shared languages that were not
understood by officers, allowing them to communicate with limited oversight and helping them keep their stowaways secret. In addition, they often
shared community obligations, which constrained compatriots from reporting the presence of stowaways. However, despite the advantages of
coethnic smuggling, sailors of all backgrounds were involved in hiding
stowaways, including Chinese, Hawaiian, Spanish, French, Italian, Mexican,
Cuban, Puerto Rican, and Black sailors.[87]

Unauthorized passengers stowed away in varied places on board the ship,
some more common than others, many of them uncomfortable and even
dangerous. Stowaways often hid in storage rooms or cargo holds, where they
slept on the floor.[88] Smugglers made space among piles of cocoa sacks in
the hold "way down below" for Aldwin Chan to hide en route to New York
from Port of Spain, Trinidad.[89] In contrast, Eng Dow was crammed into a
small storage area as he traveled from Havana, Cuba, with six other Chinese stowaways. It was so crowded that he and the other men couldn't stretch
out but "lay against each other" to sleep.[90] Eng Ah Sing, who was discovered
in the refrigeration room with Eng Dow traveling from Havana, claimed
that they had to sleep standing up.[91] However, other stowaways on the same
journey acknowledged that they were transferred from a larger room to the
refrigeration room shortly before docking in New York.[92] Some stowaways
hid under bunks, where they had to remain for the duration of the journey,
never allowed to stretch their legs.[93] Some were battened down in lifeboats.[94]
One was discovered hidden in a barrel.[95] Others managed to arrange better accommodations. Jung Kie Ging and Jung Ching, for example, stayed
in the lazarette—a storage area at the rear of the ship—during the day, then
moved to a stateroom on the intermediate deck between steerage and the
upper decks at night.[96] Some stowaways were moved regularly to different
parts of the ship.[97]

On longer journeys from Asia, some stowaways stayed in the firemen's
quarters and hid only when the ship docked. After starting in Calcutta in

1921, for example, the MS *Dollar* docked briefly in Colombo, Sri Lanka; Port Said, Egypt; and Gibraltar, on the southern tip of Spain. At each port, the stowaways were hidden under canvas. In this case, all the Chinese members of the crew knew about the four stowaways. In addition to the No. 1 fireman, who provided direct assistance to the stowaways, all thirty-two firemen employed on board the ship were Chinese, as were a few other crew members. The Chinese crewmen and stowaways shared the same quarters.[98] At times, the ship's captain appears to have been aware of and paid to provide space for stowaways.[99] But in most cases, crew members hid stowaways without the captain's knowledge.[100] However, in transcripts of immigration investigations, it is never completely clear whether a crew member's response is true. In responding to interrogations by exclusion officials, crew members may have described the events as they accurately understood them, or they may have lied to suggest that they were not involved in transporting stowaways.

Smuggling by hiring a small vessel and crew was organized differently. In these schemes, the crew and unauthorized immigrants as a whole had to evade capture as they traveled to secluded points on the Atlantic or Gulf coasts, but the immigrants did not have to hide.[101] Nonetheless, their quarters were usually cramped. The *Mary Beatrice*, as noted, was only fifty feet long and carried twenty Chinese passengers as well as the captain and four crew members on its journey of more than 1,000 miles. The *New York Times* reported that the Chinese "must have been doubled up in knots in order to stay aboard the tiny craft." However, the paper maintained that they did not complain about the accommodations because they were "inured to the cramped quarters of junks plying their sluggish native rivers." This racialized evaluation was made despite the fact that the Chinese men were never identified as having worked on board junks in China.[102]

## Official Concerns about Smuggling from the Caribbean

U.S. officials were particularly concerned about smuggling from the Caribbean, especially from Cuba and Trinidad. Given the sizable presence of Chinese in Cuba, Chinese Cubans were part of both authorized immigration through Ellis Island and smuggling into New York's harbor.[103] During the 1920s, the Chinese Cuban population grew substantially from 10,000 to 25,000, compared with a Chinese American population that increased from around 60,000 to around 75,000.[104] Some unauthorized arrivals were longtime Cuban residents; others traveled to Cuba as a jumping-off point to reach New York. The passengers of the *Mary Beatrice* had worked on sugar cane plantations in the Caribbean and, like most immigrants, hoped to do better for themselves in the United States. As the *New York Times* reported, they intended "to exchange their arduous labors in the Cuban canebrakes for the easy money they heard was here."[105] State Department officials also believed that large numbers of Chinese traveled to Cuba in the 1920s as a convenient location from which to smuggle themselves into the United States. These Chinese typically traveled to Cuba through the Panama Canal or Vancouver overland via Atlantic Canadian ports.[106]

Immigration officials recognized that the smuggling of immigrants from Cuba was "not confined to any one race or nationality" and, at the same time, claimed that it was "principally" Chinese.[107] In 1922, an Immigration Bureau report estimated that 200 Bolshevik Russians and 200 Chinese were smuggled from Cuba into the United States each month.[108] Another 1922 estimate from the assistant secretary of state suggested that between three and five boats left Cuba weekly, each carrying between ten and thirty "contraband aliens." "While all of these boats do not carry Chinese aliens," the report acknowledged, "probably a majority of them do." These numbers gave a very wide range of between 30 and 150 immigrants smuggled from Cuba to the Eastern Seaboard each week, or roughly 120 to 600 each month.[109] Secretary of Labor James Davis reported in 1923 that "thirty thousand Chinese are waiting in Cuba today, watching for a chance to be smuggled into the United States."[110] These broad estimates suggest U.S. officials' uncertainty about the scope of seaborne smuggling. Immigration officials acknowledged that they had "no definite information" about Cuba. However, this did not lessen their attention. As one Detroit resident wrote to the immigration authorities after seeing a report on smuggling from Cuba: "That island has always been a menace and a nuisance."[111]

Immigration officials were also concerned about smuggling from other Caribbean islands, such as Trinidad. Although the Chinese immigrant population of Trinidad in 1921 was only about 1,300, the harbormaster reported that more than 14,000 Chinese arrived in the colony in 1921 and fewer than 12,000 officially departed. Despite this discrepancy, there was only a small net gain in the Chinese population, leading U.S. officials to believe that many Chinese were surreptitiously emigrating from Trinidad to the United States.[112]

Edward Chong Marsow was one such Chinese Trinidadian, discovered in one of the bureau's raids on Chinese living in Brooklyn. In August 1930, Marsow smuggled himself into New York, then worked to smuggle other

Chinese from Trinidad into the city. In the winter of 1933, Ellis Island inspectors conducted a raid on an apartment building in Brooklyn where many Chinese lived, but Marsow escaped. Inspectors found him two hours later standing on the snow-covered roof of the building, barefoot and in his pajamas. He claimed that he was not hiding from them; rather, he was a U.S. citizen who was simply sunning himself. When the inspectors expressed their incredulity as it was freezing cold, he replied calmly and simply, "It is my custom." About six months later, Marsow appeared before the U.S. commissioner to prove his U.S. citizenship, providing witnesses and information that supported his claim of being born in San Francisco before the 1906 earthquake.[113] The earthquake and subsequent fires destroyed records regarding Chinese immigration, and, in many similar cases, the government was unable to prove that an arrested man was an immigrant rather than a U.S.-born citizen. (This claim was often effective. However, it did not work for New Yorker Ho Chi Gong, who claimed to have had his papers destroyed in the San Francisco earthquake and fire even though he was born in 1907, a full year after the earthquake.[114]) Undermining Marsow's evidence, one of his neighbors sent inspectors a tip-off, explaining that Marsow had illegally emigrated from Trinidad. As a result, Ellis Island inspectors followed up with authorities in the British West Indies. They learned that Marsow had lived in Trinidad, unsuccessfully attempted to get a merchant's certificate from the U.S. consul to enter the United States, and had been convicted of opium possession. These revelations contradicted Marsow's statements and ended his citizenship claim.[115]

### The Threat of Detection and Other Dangers

Like the individuals on board the *Mary Beatrice*, stowaways and immigrants attempting to smuggle themselves into the United States often faced great dangers. These risks were different for those who hired a vessel and those who stowed away. Individuals who smuggled themselves faced the threat of detection from outside inspectors and upon landing, whereas stowaways also faced this threat on board the ship from other crew members and passengers. Conversely, in a potentially violent situation, stowaways gained protection from the presence of individuals not engaged in smuggling. The risk of detection was higher for Asians than non-Asians, as Asians were typically assumed to be unauthorized. In all cases, there was a threat of neglect, which sometimes endangered immigrants' lives. Stowaways and smuggled immigrants alike were heavily dependent on the trustworthiness of their smuggling agents and crew members.

Most smugglers appear to have made a good-faith effort to land their passengers. However, some crews intentionally tricked the immigrants that they transported. In 1923, Secretary of Labor James Davis reported that a group of Chinese traveling from Cuba to Florida were successfully landed without detection. However, the captain had left them on an island off the Florida coast rather than on the mainland. Secretary Davis believed that the captain made an honest mistake, but the immigrants had no means of getting off the island and were discovered. Despite Secretary Davis's faith in the smugglers' intentions, the Chinese immigrants had paid only $100. As in other industries, it appears that less competent or intentionally deceptive companies may have charged less for their services.[116]

Before it was common practice to pay half the smuggling fee upon safe arrival, some Chinese were reportedly taken out to sea and dumped "mercilessly into the ocean."[117] During the 1930s, there were rumors that "thirty smuggled Chinese were pitched overboard in the middle of the Atlantic" when the ship's captain heard of their presence and the smugglers chose to remove the evidence of their illegal activities in order to save themselves.[118] According to New York immigration commissioner Edward Corsi, unauthorized Chinese were sometimes thrown overboard when smugglers closer to shore were detected by immigration authorities. When an immigration cutter approached a boat attempting to smuggle Chinese into New York, for example, the smugglers began to throw the Chinese overboard "in a frantic effort to destroy the evidence." However, the Chinese fought back and threw the smugglers into the harbor instead.[119]

As a result of these practices, Corsi made a distinction between the "so-called 'honest' smuggler [who] actually tries to deliver his clients at an agreed location" and the "'dishonest' smuggler . . . an international racketeer who robs his victims and leaves them in the wilderness or dumps them in the ocean."[120] In 1927, the U.S. immigration commissioner drew a distinction between "the better organized and more reputable bootleggers" who charged a set fee and the unreliable "freebooters of the industry" who abandoned their charges a few miles inland or held them up at gunpoint.[121]

In addition to violence, stowaways faced the ever-present threat of discovery. European stowaways might be able to mingle unnoticed with hundreds of other immigrants in steerage; however, this was not possible for Chinese immigrants on ships with small Chinese crews or few Chinese

EIGHT YOUNG CHINESE STOWAWAYS LANDING AT THE BATTERY AND IMMEDIATELY
APPREHENDED FOR ILLEGAL ENTRY INTO THE UNITED STATES.

"Eight Young Chinese Stowaways Landing at the Battery and Immediately
Apprehended for Illegal Entry into the United States," from Edward Corsi,
*In the Shadow of Liberty: The Chronicle of Ellis Island* (1935).

passengers.[122] On the SS *Oruba*'s voyage from Jamaica to New York, for example, a woman remarked to the captain that she hadn't realized that there
were any Chinese passengers. As the captain knew that he had not boarded
any Chinese, he was immediately alerted to the stowaways' presence, had
the ship searched, and found four men hidden in lifeboats.[123]

Sometimes stowaways were discovered by a fellow crew member because
they were not well hidden. On board the SS *Norwich* in 1908, two stowaways
tried to hide in a cabin under the bunks of the two firemen who were assisting them. However, the Chinese firemen shared their cabin with the
ship's German carpenter. The stowaways were discovered shortly after they
boarded when the carpenter was searching for his tools. The firemen promised the carpenter "plenty of beer and everything" when they arrived in
New York, but the carpenter reported the men.[124]

Stowaways were also discovered by crew members during regular checks
of the vessel and by customs and immigration inspectors.[125] Officials would
investigate cargo that had an unusual appearance. And if they discovered

stowaways upon moving the cargo, they launched a more thorough search of the ship that often led to the discovery of additional stowaways.[126] Inspectors sometimes paid extra attention to particular ships, owing to previous experience with those shipping lines, concerns about specific captains, or tips from informants. A man who called himself "Captain Smith," for example, wrote to authorities in 1923: "Watch the SS Santa Veronica. She stow away two to three Chinamen from Cuba every trip acting by some of the sailors."[127]

Stowaways faced varied responses when they were discovered. If the ship was just two or three hours out, the captain sometimes returned the stowaways to the most recent port of departure. However, they were not always accepted, as they may not have originally boarded at that port. When four Chinese stowaways were discovered hidden in one of the SS *Oruba*'s lifeboats, for example, the ship was at least twenty hours from Jamaica, where the men were believed to have boarded. The captain returned to the ship's most recent port of call—Antilla, Cuba—to attempt to land the men. But the Cuban authorities refused to accept them. If landing was unsuccessful or impractical, the stowaways were typically locked up.[128] In one case on board the SS *Norwich*, a stowaway was put to work shoveling coal as a fireman for the remainder of his journey.[129]

If detected, stowaways often claimed that they had received no assistance, a response that immigration authorities believed was part of their agreement with the crew members who helped hide them.[130] They claimed they weren't provided with help or food even when they were discovered with food from the ship—and in the case of the four men hidden on the SS *Oruba*, one of the ship's napkins.[131] They sometimes stated that they had come from a different port than where they actually boarded. Jung Kie Ging and Jung Ching, for example, claimed to have come on board when the ship on which they had stowed away was docked in Havana, Cuba; however, the immigration authorities suspected that they had actually boarded at an earlier stop in Vera Cruz, Mexico.[132] If they were "returned" to Cuba, it would be easier and less expensive for them to once again try to smuggle themselves into New York.

Some stowaways were detected as they were attempting to leave the ship. Once they docked at one of the piers in Brooklyn, Manhattan, or Staten Island, the crew members who had assisted the stowaways during the voyage would often help them escape. Stowaways typically disembarked by boat or directly to the dock. Some stowaways would leave the ship via a lighter, a small unpowered barge that could move quietly through the water.

Another common approach was for the seamen who assisted them to disguise them as a fellow crew member. When Wong Kin Dock's ship arrived in New York, the men who had assisted him during his journey from France unlocked the door of the room where he was hiding and told him to walk ahead of them to the dock. He was arrested but reported to immigration officials that the South Asian stowaways with whom he had hidden were landed successfully as a separate group before him. Crew members loaned stowaways clothes such as sailors' overalls and peaked caps to hide their features and help them leave without attracting notice. Some crew members would cover the Asian stowaways with coal dust and then have them leave via the gangplank, hoping that watchmen guarding the piers would assume that they were firemen or Black workers.[133] These efforts suggest that all Asians, including many Asian seafarers, were viewed with suspicion. Black sailors were less regulated and assumed to be genuine, hence Chinese efforts to disguise themselves as Black to disembark without being noticed.[134]

Chinese attempting to smuggle themselves into the United States on smaller vessels were vulnerable throughout their journey, but they were at an increased risk of detection when they entered U.S. waters and any time that their journey paused—for example, while they waited on rum rows to be transported to shore. During Prohibition, Chinese smugglers were concerned not only about Coast Guard inspection but also about raids by other rum runners.[135] After they arrived near Sandy Hook, the Chinese on board the *Mary Beatrice* had to stay out of sight to avoid detection. As they waited at anchor "now and then a fast motor launch approached the vessel at night, but made off when Chinese instead of whisky were found to be aboard."[136] Other ships smuggling Chinese followed this same route. In 1924, a year after the events on board the *Mary Beatrice*, a small Nicaraguan bark, the *Gaviota*, was reported transporting Chinese immigrants from Havana to New Jersey's "so-called rum row, where these Chinese will be transferred to a swift launch to be landed at some house in Sandy Hook."[137] The *Florence*, a British motor yacht, followed the same approach.[138] However, the captain and the engineer enjoyed a night out in Havana before their journey, got drunk, and revealed their smuggling plan to one of the women companions they had brought back to their yacht. Their plan was foiled when it was shared with U.S. authorities.[139]

Violence and detection were not the only dangers faced by stowaways and other immigrants who attempted to smuggle themselves into the United States. At times, neglect was equally threatening. Stowaways were often poorly fed and kept in cramped and sometimes overheated quarters, conditions that were sometimes fatal. Of sixteen stowaways who boarded the SS *Helenus* in China, one died of disease and his body was thrown overboard while two suffered from beriberi, a severe vitamin D deficiency caused by poor diet, during the journey. The remaining men were "half-starved," and only a few of them were able to walk off the ship when they were discovered in New York.[140] Five years later in July 1926, ten Chinese stowaways boarded the freighter *Glendola* in Antilla, Cuba, expecting a three-day journey to New Orleans. However, the ship diverted to Brooklyn, leaving them trapped in "the thick hot air of a sugar-filled hold" for six days. Upon their discovery, one man died as he was taken to the ship's deck and the others were taken to Ellis Island.[141] In a later case, a "truck-load of teaboxes delivered to an address on Mott Street in New York's Chinatown proved to contain a score of dead Chinese, who had not survived their desperate effort to enter the country."[142]

If they were discovered with injuries, illnesses, or malnutrition, stowaways were treated at the hospital on Ellis Island before being interrogated by U.S. officials. In 1929, customs officers on a Coast Guard patrol boat rescued three Chinese men who had attempted to land by jumping overboard from a steamship in the New York harbor. They almost drowned in the strong ebb tide and were sent to the Ellis Island hospital for treatment prior to establishing their identities.[143] The two injured passengers discovered on board the *Mary Beatrice* were also sent to the hospital; the *New York Times* described the passengers as "slant-eyed bundles of bandages, one of them nursing a right hand nearly severed."[144] The hospital also received stowaways suffering from malnutrition.[145]

Severe illnesses and deaths spurred some sympathy for Chinese who attempted to stow away or smuggle themselves into the United States. However, this sympathy was often tempered with criticism. New York immigration commissioner Edward Corsi described stowing away as the "most hazardous of all methods of entry."[146] Although Corsi was sympathetic to the dangers involved in seaborne smuggling, he also questioned the stowaways' choices and used them to impugn China. "Why John Chinaman will risk death to get into the United States," Corsi wrote, "for the doubtful privilege of ironing shirts in a cellar laundry, or washing dishes in the cubby-hole kitchen of a chop suey restaurant is a mystery incapable of solution, unless the answer is that anything is an improvement on the unwholesome conditions in the Orient."[147]

If detected, smuggled immigrants and stowaways sought assistance from the people who organized their passage, from friends, and from the

Chinese community. When Fook Sim was detected upon his arrival in New York, he sent a message to Long Gim asking him to wire a colleague at the Wah Hing Company, where he had embarked in Marseilles. He wanted to inform the man who had organized his passage that all four men had been arrested and to seek his advice. He also requested Long Gim to wire Boston, to notify friends and cousins, and to seek help from them.[148] Although this letter was intercepted, it suggests a network of assistance available to stowaways if they were unsuccessful in their immigration efforts. Others were represented by lawyers, including the firm of former inspectors Storey and Sisson, who successfully requested stays of deportation and temporary bonds for stowaways and other unauthorized immigrants.[149] Immigration officials expressed their frustration at this network of support. "No matter how poor in body and purse," the bureau claimed about Chinese applicants in 1909, "if he has a clansman, or tongsman, or fellow 'company man' already in this country, the means will be found for his entry."[150] Chinese used complex networks not only to aid their unauthorized immigration but also to defend themselves if detected.

Immigration officials complained that they did not have enough money to fund investigations of smuggling and payments to informants, or enough manpower to investigate and arrest smugglers.[151] Making matters more difficult, officials investigating smuggling networks were sometimes concerned that smugglers were monitoring their investigations. One informant sent coded messages to immigration officials as he believed that workers at Western Union were paid by smugglers to monitor telegrams sent through the Havana office to report any planned immigration raids. When he wired the New Orleans immigration office about the SS *Chalmette* smuggling Chinese out of Cuba, the informant became suspicious as one of the Western Union employees inquired about the content of his message and questioned whether he represented the steamship company.[152] Corrupt immigration officials were involved in indirect smuggling schemes; however, there is not extensive evidence of their engagement in direct smuggling, perhaps because their role was not as important for these schemes.[153]

At times, Asians faced "wrongful discovery" and even arrest when they were assumed to be attempting to enter the United States illegally. A legal Japanese resident was taken to Ellis Island for questioning after he fell into the water in Hoboken, apparently trying to retrieve his cap. Although he was quickly released, others faced more difficulties.[154] In 1924, Mohammed Ali was sentenced to three years in federal prison in Atlanta and fined $1,000 for his role in a smuggling ring. Two Bengalis who were with him when he was arrested were also detained. The young men, identified as Mali and Radi in the *New York Times*, claimed they were traveling around the world when their ship docked in New York and just happened to be talking to Ali on the pier when they were seized by immigration officials as Ali's accomplices. They spent two weeks in a Brooklyn jail before the charges against them were dropped, and an additional six weeks in New York before they were taken to Ellis Island for deportation. It is not clear why the men were deported if there were no charges against them.[155] These cases suggest how all Asians fell under the suspicion of illegal immigration, but also the difficulties of determining legal status in the context of substantial seaborne smuggling.

The dangers of seaborne smuggling were significant as unauthorized Chinese passengers were trapped between crew members and immigration officials, attempting to avoid violence, detection, and neglect. Secrecy and seclusion were key to a successful journey, but also posed potential threats. As Ellis Island and other officials increasingly turned their attention to seaborne smuggling in the 1920s, these dangers increased. However, even when Chinese faced detection, they worked through networks in the United States to challenge their detention and deportation. Seaborne smuggling expands our understanding of the scope of Chinese evasion of exclusion.

## Enforcing Laws against Seaborne Smuggling and Stowing Away

The fact of stowing away did not necessarily preclude immigrants, especially Europeans, from entry to the United States. "I must confess we did not always know what to do with stowaways," wrote Boston immigration inspector Feri Felix Weiss. "Their status was at times puzzling to say the least."[156] The Immigration Bureau acknowledged in 1906 that "the stowaway is an anomaly in immigration work and statistics."[157] Initially, stowaways were treated as "derelicts" and were automatically deported. Weiss describes a story of a British stowaway who was discovered and immediately placed on a return ship. Only after Weiss had successfully dealt with the stowaway, he returned to his office to discover a new rule on stowaways that might have allowed him to stay.[158]

When the first secretary of commerce and labor, George Cortelyou, came into office in 1903, he ordered that stowaways be treated "just like any ordinary passenger, and either landed by the inspector as American citizens . . . or brought before a board of special inquiry." They were allowed to apply for admission, and if they met the criteria for entry, they would be landed. For some stowaways, however, these criteria were difficult to meet. Even the most cursory interviews checked stowaways' nationality, ability to read or write, and means to support themselves. If they did not have sufficient money—which was common, as they had typically been unable to pay their fare—stowaways were considered "public charges from the very start."[159] While European stowaways might be admitted, Asian stowaways found it almost impossible to gain entry because they were subject to both general immigration and Asian exclusion laws.[160] In these cases, the hearing chairman typically concluded that stowaways were denied under both acts.[161] Even if Asians met all the requirements for admission under immigration law, they could still be excluded because they were Asian.

There were very few exemptions under the Chinese exclusion acts that allowed entry only to U.S. citizens, merchants, students, and a few other limited groups. Some Chinese stowaways claimed rights to admission as merchants. Upon his discovery as a stowaway on board the MS *Dollar* in New York in 1921, Leong Ah Tong claimed that he had previously been admitted as a merchant through San Francisco and, although his return certificate was destroyed in a fire in Hong Kong, he was returning to take care of business with the Wing Tan Company in Los Angeles. However, after San Francisco officials could not locate any record of his presence in the United States, application for a return certificate, or membership in a firm, Leong admitted that he was not a merchant but just a store clerk attempting to enter the United States for the first time in order to join his father in Canada. He was denied admittance.[162]

There were rare cases, however, in which Chinese stowaways were landed, specifically when they satisfactorily proved U.S. citizenship. In 1921, for example, Leong Hor stowed away from Marseilles to New York. When he was discovered, he claimed to have been born in New York and, despite his limited recollection regarding his experiences, was admitted as a U.S. citizen.[163] In 1948, Ng Yue Thung arrived as a stowaway in Honolulu. He claimed that he had been admitted as a U.S. citizen through Ellis Island ten years earlier, and, after the New York office shared the relevant files and photograph with immigration officials in Honolulu, he was also admitted.[164]

In the early 1900s, almost all Asian stowaways were debarred, while many Europeans were admitted.[165] However, the 1917 Immigration Law made almost all alien stowaways inadmissible. As a result, the rejection of stowaways increased substantially.[166] In 1917, before the new law was introduced, more than half of all stowaways arriving in New York were admitted.[167] No Chinese stowaways were among those allowed to enter.[168] After 1917, stowaways formed a substantial number of arrivals who were rejected. In 1920, stowaways were the third largest group of rejected arrivals, after immigrants liable to become a public charge and those who failed the literacy test.[169] Nationwide numbers of stowaways were reported starting in 1928, revealing that less than 1 percent of all stowaways were admitted, but not one alien Chinese or Japanese stowaway was allowed to enter the United States.[170]

The administrative regulation and documentation of discovered stowaways expanded during the 1920s. This expansion paralleled new immigration restrictions, Asian exclusion and deportation laws, and increased attention to seaborne smuggling during Prohibition. Starting around this time, photographs were taken of stowaways, typically a set of four photographs with the stowaway's name hanging around his neck for identification and the file number stamped on the image.[171] The photographic documentation of Chinese smuggled across land borders had been introduced years earlier, although it was not enforced consistently on the U.S.-Mexico border.[172] The New York office was more efficient about regulation of unauthorized Chinese entrants on the Canadian border. "You should have these Chinese photographed immediately," the Chinese inspector in charge wrote about one group in 1915, "in order that we may send copies to the Inspector in Charge at Buffalo for the purposes of attempting to show that they recently entered the United States from Canada."[173] However, the New York office didn't implement the photographic identification of stowaways until about a decade later.

Crew members faced a range of responses if they were found to be involved in smuggling. Before smugglers were regularly charged with criminal activity, crew members suspected of assisting stowaways were typically discharged from the ship's service.[174] After being discharged they might simply ship out in another captain's employment, allowing them to continue to smuggle people into the United States. By the 1920s, when prosecution was more common, immigration officials made greater efforts to get stowaways to cooperate with investigations and help convict crew members. On one ship from Marseilles, the entire crew was mustered for a lineup so that the Chinese stowaways could identify those that helped them. They were able to locate one person who assisted them, but not the man that they paid. Upon further investigation, it was determined that he had jumped ship and escaped.[175]

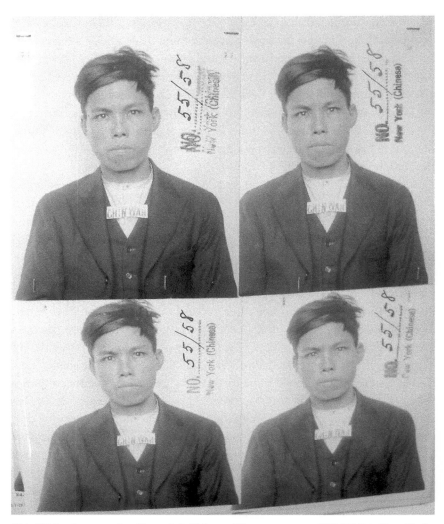

Chin Wah, photographs, file 55/58, Chinese Files, 1921–1944, INS, NARA–New York.

The Immigration Bureau worked with the U.S. Attorney's office to attempt to prosecute individuals involved in organizing stowaways' passage. Immigration officials were sometimes at odds with federal prosecutors because they believed that stowaways should be prosecuted, whereas prosecutors wanted to use stowaways as witnesses in their cases against smugglers.[176] The U.S. Attorney's office faced a range of difficulties in seeking to convict smugglers, many of which deterred them from pursuing such cases. Some courts ruled that any conspiracy occurred when the parties first made their arrangements and boarded the stowaways. As the conspiracy occurred abroad, these rulings suggested that it was "impracticable to prosecute on the conspiracy charge in the United States."[177] Others noted that if the stowaways were intercepted at sea, there was no crime committed in the United States, as there was no illegal effort to land stowaways. In the 1908 case of the SS *Norwich*, two firemen were widely known to have assisted stowaways, but this couldn't be proved in court because they were not discovered in the act of helping the stowaways to land.[178] Prosecutors also faced delays as the ship's captain or other officers were needed to testify but they typically shipped out shortly after the stowaways were discovered. Therefore, prosecutors had to wait until officers returned to New York to present their cases.[179]

U.S. prosecutors, frustrated by the difficulty of convicting smugglers, would sometimes keep former stowaways in the United States as material witnesses in cases against smugglers.[180] These officials paid Chinese stowaways a witness fee of one dollar for each day that they were detained.[181] Stowaways were initially detained at Ellis Island, and their detention costs were paid by the shipping line on which they stowed away; however, after the ship left port, the U.S. government paid the costs for their detention until trial.[182] After the trial's conclusion, the stowaways were deported.[183] When stowaways were discovered on board the SS *Java*, a tramp steamer with irregular routes, Boston immigration officials suggested that it would be better to deport the stowaways immediately rather than pursue prosecution, as the SS *Java* only made occasional stops at Atlantic ports and the Immigration Bureau might be financially responsible for deporting the stowaways after any trial.[184] The infrequent routes of tramp steamers meant that sometimes as many as one hundred stowaways were detained at Ellis Island waiting to be returned to their ports of origin.[185] As just one example, Aldwin Chan, who stowed away from Trinidad in 1925, was detained at Ellis Island for two months.[186]

With the assistance of stowaways, prosecutors were sometimes able to secure convictions of crew members involved in smuggling. In 1921, two Chinese firemen on board the SS *Helenus* were sentenced to two years for attempting to smuggle Chinese immigrants into New York, and a Chinese crew member on the SS *Atreus* was sentenced to one year.[187] In the same year, prosecutors successfully convicted a Chinese boatswain and a fireman who worked on the SS *Bowes Castle*, although they believed that more crew members were involved in assisting (or had knowledge of) the forty stowaways on board. Upon completion of their sentences in a federal penitentiary, the smugglers were released to immigration officials and deported.[188] Chinese Division officials closely monitored prisoners toward the end of their sentences, communicating with prison officials to ensure that smugglers would not be released to the general population. The prisoners were guarded carefully, then transferred from jail to Ellis Island, where they were detained until they could be deported. Immigration officials certified that deportees were on the ship as it departed. In the case of the *Bowes Castle*, they also followed up with a letter to their counterparts in the Hawaii Bureau asking officials to make sure that these individuals were still on board when their ship docked in Honolulu.[189]

Although immigration officials and U.S. prosecutors increasingly undertook enforcement actions against smuggling in the 1920s, this expansion was sometimes in tension with rigorous enforcement of exclusion. Prosecutors typically needed to rely on stowaways to make their case against smuggling agents; however, stowaways were often unreliable witnesses. By the 1920s, immigration officials had introduced a new policy of allowing stowaways temporary admittance on bond while waiting to testify in smuggling cases. In 1921, four stowaways from the MS *Dollar* were admitted for ninety days on a $1,000 bond from the National Surety Company, a typical arrangement.[190] Although the New York inspector in charge noted that these were the same terms as those granted to other stowaways, the bond was issued only after the stowaways had given "damaging testimony against the No. 1 fireman" and only one day before the witnesses were to appear to give preliminary testimony before a grand jury. The bond issuance was clearly part of "an effort to secure an indictment against the No. 1 fireman."[191] Bonds were also requested by immigration brokers such as Storey and Sisson in the case against fireman Lee Gee, who assisted with smuggling four Chinese on board the SS *Knight Templar* from Singapore. Storey and Sisson requested bonds for both the stowaways and the fireman, even though the fireman pled guilty and witness testimony was not required. Storey and Sisson claimed "it would unquestionably be a hardship and possibly place their lives in jeopardy to deport them on the vessel on which they arrived."[192] Their requests were granted. It is not clear, however, why deportation would be such a danger or why the bonds were approved. In some cases, corrupt immigration officials may have been paid to support bonds, as they were paid to approve entering applicants. However, there is no clear evidence of this practice at Ellis Island.

Although the bonding of former stowaways helped secure witnesses, it was not without problems. Most often, witnesses breached their bonds and entered the United States without authorization.[193] This is not surprising, as unauthorized entry had been their original intention in stowing away.[194] Of the five witnesses in the *Bowes Castle* case, for example, two were denied entry after their testimonies while three breached their bonds.[195] In at least one case, witnesses who agreed to testify in support of the government's case turned hostile and provided little assistance. Immigration officials believed that the witnesses had "evidently been 'reached' during their stay on Ellis Island" and pressured to change their testimony.[196] In some cases, bonded Chinese stowaways turned out to be imposters.[197] In 1922, a man presented himself before Ellis Island authorities for deportation as a bonded stowaway. However, upon investigation, he admitted that he was a jump-ship sailor who had had little luck finding work in New York. He was approached by a Chinatown acquaintance who gave him the name of a returning stowaway and told him when to present himself at Ellis Island so that he could secure free passage to China. In other cases, U.S. officials were paid to substitute immigrants facing deportation with those seeking to travel to China.[198] In this way, Chinese who desired to return home could secure transportation at the government's expense, while the immigrant who desired to stay in the United States could remain. These actions used the enforcement of exclusion against itself.

New York officials coordinated with other immigration stations to deport stowaways, as they did with other aspects of immigration enforcement. When a Chinese stowaway discovered in Philadelphia was unable to be promptly deported to Jamaica because there were few United Fruit Company ships sailing from Philadelphia to Jamaica, he was transported to New York and held at Ellis Island for about two weeks until he was deported.[199]

Sometimes stowaways who had previously worked on ships were offered the opportunity to ship out to a new port instead of being deported. This practice, explored in detail in chapter 2 and used extensively with jump-ship sailors, was known as reshipping foreign in lieu of deportation.[200] In May 1925, May Chan wrote a plaintive letter to the immigration authorities at Ellis Island inquiring about her husband, Aldwin Chan. He had been detained at Ellis Island and let her know that he would "be coming back home" to Port of Spain, Trinidad. "I look for him by every boat," she wrote. "I am grived [sic] for him." The Chinese inspector responded curtly that Chan had been discovered as a stowaway on board the SS *Voltaire* and had reshipped foreign to Asia one month earlier.[201]

Although ships remained the primary means for smuggling from the Caribbean to the United States, small planes also came into use in later years.

"At nightfall in Matanzas [Cuba] it is not unusual to see a tri-motored plane roll out of its hangar, pick up two muffled figures who scramble quickly into the cabin, and immediately take off into the clouds," one Ellis Island official reported in 1933. "Morning finds the same plane landed in a deserted New Jersey cow pasture." According to a specific incident in this account, the young Chinese boys then jumped into the back of a furniture van and were delivered to a warehouse in Philadelphia. The owner of the warehouse paid the smugglers $1,500 for their part in the scheme and provided an advance to the Chinese boys to help take care of their living expenses until they found work. They walked out of the front office of the warehouse as if they were U.S. citizens.[202] In 1950, the Immigration Service reported that it had broken up a smuggling ring that flew Chinese and European aliens from Cuba to Miami under cover of night. The report concluded that "smugglers are resorting to new techniques in plying their trade" and that "the airplane has now joined the ship and the automobile as a vehicle for illicit traffic."[203]

. . . . . .

On February 28, 1909, Moy Lee and Wong Sieu arrived at Ellis Island after stowing away on a Hamburg American liner, *Prinz Sigismund*, from Jamaica via Colombia to New York. This was their second attempt to land in the city. However, at 4:45 A.M. as they walked down a Brooklyn gangplank with the Italian storekeeper who had hidden them in the ship's storeroom, they were discovered by Edward Seabrooke, an African American inspector with the U.S. Customs Service. Instead of being taken into town, as their Chinese smuggling agents in Newark and Kingston had planned, they were taken into detention at Ellis Island. The next day, they were interviewed by Harry Sisson, the inspector in charge of the New York Chinese Bureau. Like all the immigrants whose stories are outlined in this chapter, Moy and Wong were discovered as they attempted to enter the United States. Their discovery revealed "the first threads of the web of evidence against a well-organized system for smuggling."[204] However, many immigrants successfully smuggled themselves into New York.

In the 1920s, as exclusion laws were expanded and Prohibition was introduced, U.S. officials became increasingly concerned about seaborne smuggling of Asians, especially from Caribbean countries. In 1922, when the Immigration Bureau launched investigations into smuggling from Cuba and Trinidad, immigration broker Harry Sisson represented Chinese stowaways in their immigration cases.[205] The Immigration Bureau's efforts to enforce Asian exclusion and smugglers' efforts to evade such regulation created additional difficulties for unauthorized immigrants. New York officials worked hard to detect seaborne smuggling and aimed to strictly enforce laws against stowaways, as they did with deportation. However, they were constrained by federal prosecutors' concerns not to deport individual immigrants but to investigate complex smuggling networks, a goal that sometimes allowed bonded immigrants to smuggle themselves into the United States. Despite being described as "human freight," Asian immigrants exerted agency in their journeys. They were aided by the large number of Asian sailors whose work offered opportunities for smuggling and stowing away. If they were detected, Chinese immigrants used the resources of Chinese community organizations and representatives such as Storey and Sisson to fight their cases. Their journeys were difficult and sometimes dangerous. These journeys led them to New York, the largest port in the world and "the great objective" for many Chinese immigrants.[206]

# 4 Asian Sailors

## Shanghaied in Hoboken

. . . . . . . . . . . . . . . . . . . . . . . . . . . . . . . . . . . . . . . .

June 28, 1927. As the Holland-America liner the *Rotterdam* sat moored in Hoboken, New Jersey, on a warm, breezy evening, eighty-four Chinese crew members attempted to leave the ship. They had been denied customary shore leave and told to remain on board. They refused. The Chinese crew signed on to the ship in the Netherlands, but en route to the United States they discovered that they were hired in the place of striking seamen. The strikers had earned thirty-eight dollars a month, but the Chinese men were being paid only fifteen dollars. When the men tried to rush ashore in New Jersey, the Hoboken police beat them back with clubs and black jacks. Many of the sailors were severely beaten, including ten who were treated for head wounds, but a number forced their way ashore.[1]

The police arrested fifty-four of the escaping sailors and transferred them to Ellis Island. Immigration officials ruled that the men would be detained at the island and returned to the Netherlands. The prisoners were held incommunicado, not allowed to speak to even their legal representatives from the Chinese Seamen's Institute, an organization representing Chinese sailors. "Anybody who can show us proof that he has been retained as their attorney will be allowed to see them," Police Inspector Daniel Kelly confirmed with reporters. However, he did not permit lawyers to meet with the seamen because they had not specifically requested an attorney. The Chinese were accused of mutiny, but their supporters claimed that they were being illegally held under immigration laws when they were entitled to shore leave.[2]

Many groups protested the treatment of the sailors and called for an investigation. The Chinese Seamen's Institute sent a formal complaint to President Coolidge.[3] The Chinese consul requested a report from the Hoboken police commissioner. The American Civil Liberties Union launched its own investigation in New Jersey.[4] And New York congressman Fiorello La Guardia, who had himself worked at Ellis Island twenty years earlier, called on the secretary of labor to investigate, criticizing the "shanghai methods used upon the unfortunate Chinese in the streets of Hoboken."[5]

However, as dawn broke on Saturday, July 16, the detainees were secretly taken by tugboat to the *Volendam,* and by nightfall they were on their way back to the Netherlands. When the sailors' lawyer contacted the deputy commissioner of immigration to ask whether the government's position had changed so that he would be allowed to communicate with his clients, he was informed that "the only change had been the removal of the men." La Guardia was furious, describing the removal as "kidnapping" and arguing that federal Immigration Bureau officials were being used as "marionettes" to do the bidding of private steamship companies.[6]

. . . . . .

This incident was unusual: the Immigration Bureau's regulation of sailors rarely became a matter of public protest. Nevertheless, it demonstrates the interconnections of Chinese exclusion and maritime law, the ways in which immigration officials used exclusion laws to regulate Asian seamen, and the ways in which these seamen resisted their regulation. It also suggests how, as part of the global maritime industry, Asian sailors were deeply integrated into transnational social and labor networks that spanned ports and communities in Asia, Europe, and the Americas. In the late nineteenth and early twentieth centuries, Asians both worked as sailors and were transported by ships as legal passengers and as stowaways. At the same time, many governments increasingly asserted control over their territorial boundaries and the people who attempted to cross these boundaries, including sailors and immigrants.[7] Motivated by nativist concerns about labor competition, as well as racist beliefs that many groups of immigrants were culturally inassimilable and virulent vectors of disease, federal immigration and exclusion restrictions were introduced in 1875 and expanded over the next fifty years. As explored in chapter 1, restrictionists viewed Asians as economically threatening, culturally different, and likely bearers of dangerous diseases. Although these views were held more forcefully by Californians than New Yorkers, Asians were subject to harsh exclusion laws that eventually prevented almost all lawful Asian immigration to the United States.

Asian exclusion was expansive, radiating beyond immigrants to incorporate groups such as sailors. When immigration and exclusion laws were introduced and consolidated, they were accompanied by restrictions on Chinese and then all Asian sailors. Immigration officials, charged with enforcing immigration and Asian exclusion laws, were concerned that these statutes did not effectively address maritime workers. They complained that sailors held a "preferred status" or "privileged position" in immigration policy and were allowed to "come and go largely at will" because of governmental concerns not to hamper international trade.[8] This relatively free movement allowed many seamen, including Asian seamen, to enter the country without authorization.

In matters of Asian exclusion, New York was at the edge of enforcement. In other matters, such as the regulation of sailors, New York City, its port, and its immigration station were at the center of enforcement. As the largest port in both the United States and the world, New York was a central location for the U.S. entry of seamen, and Ellis Island officials were centrally involved in trying to stop them. Efforts to incorporate Chinese sailors under exclusion statutes were not initially successful. However, in contrast to their relatively restrained implementation of exclusion laws against arriving immigrants, particularly elites exempt from exclusion, Ellis Island officials pushed for the strict regulation of sailors under existing laws. Their approach was adopted and codified as administrative rules by the national Immigration Bureau. These rules distinguished between Chinese and other sailors, treating Chinese sailors more harshly than their European or other Asian counterparts. But officials in stations such as San Francisco, with a reputation for the harsh enforcement of exclusion laws against immigrants, did not adopt the strict rules regulating Asian sailors.

Concerned about competition with an expanding Asian workforce, white maritime unions in the United States supported the expansion of exclusion to regulate Asian seamen. These unions pushed for the 1915 La Follette Act, which granted increased freedoms to most sailors but placed new restrictions on Asian crews. In response to and somewhat in tension with these freedoms, Congress incorporated the registration and inspection of all seamen into immigration law in 1917 and extended exclusion to almost all Asian groups. Five years later, Japanese and Asian Indians were made subject to exclusion rules governing sailors that had previously covered only Chinese seamen.[9] The exploitation of Asian labor was underpinned by U.S. immigration restrictions, which were a frequent target of seamen's resistance.

Chinese and other Asian sailors did not passively accept the restrictions placed on them. They challenged their unequal treatment through unions, through legal strategies, through verbal and violent conflicts, and by jumping ship.[10] If they defied officers, they could be accused of mutiny. If they jumped ship, they were deserters. If they were arrested by U.S. authorities, these mutinous and deserting sailors were detained on Ellis Island prior to their removal from the United States.

Ellis Island had a reputation among Asian sailors as an awful place to be detained. Ellis Island officials were also known to strictly enforce and consistently expand the regulation of sailors. *New York Globe* reporter Alfred W. McCann noted that Asian Indian seamen, sometimes known as lascars, were "panic stricken" when it was suggested that they might be detained at Ellis Island. "Through an interpreter they said they all knew about this terrible place, and would not go there." A colonial Indian official agreed that "properly treated lascars would never desert in New York with the threat of Ellis Island hanging on them."[11]

Although the Immigration Bureau was extensively involved in regulating alien sailors, immigration historians have paid limited attention to maritime workers, and maritime historians have rarely focused on immigration policies.[12] Even though immigrants traveled by sea, immigration historians typically take a terracentric approach, assuming that "history is made exclusively on land."[13] As early as 1979, Peter Kwong explained that "there is very little about seamen in the literature of Chinese in the United States," both because seamen were mobile and because settlers were often unauthorized.[14] As historian Lars Amenda noted more than thirty years later, the relationship between "Chinese seaman and Chinese migrants . . . is an essential, but still poorly investigated aspect of Chinese migration and migration in general."[15] Immigration historians generally focus on settlement, and while many sailors did settle in New York, most were transient. Some historians such as Jack Tchen have paid attention to sailors as the leading edge of Asian diasporic settlement in New York.[16] However, historians of Asian and other immigration have mostly focused on individuals classified as immigrants. Sailors were legally defined as neither immigrants nor nonimmigrants, a term that encompasses temporary visitors such as tourists and students.[17] Like the stowaways with whom they were grouped in the immigration commissioner's *Annual Reports*, they were an "anomalous class" within immigration law.[18] Finally, the oversight of Asian sailors is shaped by the fact that scholars of Asian immigration generally attend to the western United States. While most Asian *immigrants* arrived in the western United States, most Asian *sailors* arrived in the east. Although it has been largely overlooked in immigration history, the regulation of sailors has long been linked to both immigration restriction and Asian exclusion.

## Early Chinese Exclusion and Maritime Regulation

As early as the passage of the Chinese Exclusion Act of 1882, officials attempted to ensure that Chinese sailors were included in the law's description of Chinese laborers. A few days after exclusion went into effect, a U.S. ship arrived in San Francisco's harbor. On board were Ah Sing, a cabin waiter, as well as fourteen additional Chinese crew members who had originally shipped out of San Francisco. Customs officials tried to prevent the crew from landing, but U.S. Circuit Court judge Stephen Field overruled them, noting that the prohibition against bringing Chinese laborers from foreign ports did not apply to sailors who had originally boarded in the United States.[19] As exclusion laws were being expanded, a ban on Chinese seamen continued to be debated. When Chinese exclusion was made permanent in 1902, a preliminary version of the law prohibited Chinese sailors from working on American ships. Although this provision was removed from the bill, many restrictionists continued to express concerns about Asians competing with white sailors at sea.[20] These concerns were explicitly racial; ships had international workforces, and, as explored later, very few of the crew on U.S. vessels were U.S. citizens.

Immigration officials had two key concerns about deserting seamen. First, they were concerned about genuine sailors jumping ship and staying in the United States in violation of exclusion laws. Second, they were concerned about smuggled immigrants and stowaways who were landed as seamen to evade exclusion. Regarding the first concern about jumping ship, as immigration and exclusion laws were expanded, long-standing concerns about how sailors might use customary freedoms to stay in the United States in violation of immigration and exclusion laws were increasingly foregrounded. In 1912, the Immigration Bureau's *Annual Report* noted that deserting seamen were "the most serious defect" in both immigration and exclusion laws.[21] In 1922, the official in charge of regulating sailors acknowledged that "the seaman's occupation is a wide open door through which unlawful entries can be effected."[22]

Officials recognized that the expanding exclusion of Chinese laborers led to increased unauthorized immigration, including settlement by jump-ship sailors. The commissioner of immigration opened his 1930 *Annual Report* stating, "When, in 1882, laws were placed on the statute books absolutely excluding Chinese laborers, it was like damming up a more or less placidly flowing stream. At every point the flow sought to escape its bounds.

Immigration officers were for many years kept busy day and night stopping the leaks. This flow now, after nearly half a century, has fairly subsided. Some of it, however, . . . has formed new channels, and is entering by way of the so-called deserting-seaman route."[23] Although their use of hydraulic metaphors suggested a natural process, officials understood that this was not natural. They recognized the central role that immigration laws played in shaping both authorized and unauthorized immigration patterns.[24]

The problem of jump-ship sailors was not limited to Asians. Immigration officials recognized that many seamen, including European seamen, violated immigration laws to enter the United States.[25] Nonetheless, the bureau's *Annual Reports* discussed the problem of Chinese seamen separately and focused on deserting Chinese seamen extensively. In 1907, in regard to Chinese sailors, the commissioner-general of immigration noted that "the situation concerning this class of persons is even more serious than that affecting alien seamen in general."[26] He claimed that during the preceding year, "it has been necessary for the immigration officials to guard against the landing in this country of over 21,000 Chinese seamen."[27] The following year's report added that "both the immigration and the exclusion laws are violated by seamen of the Chinese race."[28]

Second, immigration officials were concerned that the borders between bona fide seamen and smuggled immigrants were as fluid as the seas that brought them both to the United States. They viewed sailors, stowaways, and smuggled immigrants as part of the same problem. Smugglers operating around New York were often either sailors who used small boats to help immigrants enter the United States illegally or crew members on larger ships who helped hide stowaways. Although most of the deserting seamen were likely genuine sailors who simply decided to stay in the United States, some Chinese used the limited regulation of sailors to smuggle themselves into the country in spite of immigration restrictions and exclusion.

In addition to the smuggling and stowing away explored in chapter 3, in some sophisticated smuggling schemes, ships' officers would register immigrants as crew members with the agreement that the fake crew members would desert once they arrived in the United States.[29] In addition, some sailors, it was suspected, paid for the privilege of working on the ship because this status allowed them "a chance for freedom in America."[30] Some individuals listed as crew members worked only one journey, paying the captain for the opportunity to jump ship and smuggle themselves into the United States. "It takes but a few hours," commented New York commissioner

Edward Corsi, "to teach a Chinaman how to replace another Chinaman on a ship's crew."[31] Others were passengers who did not work on board the ship but were listed as crew to allow them to enter the United States without inspection. In a twist on the practice of sailors assisting stowaways, seventy-three Chinese stowaways were discovered when a ship docked in San Francisco in 1921. On closer investigation, inspectors learned that the men were not stowaways but crew members who had worked throughout the journey and hid themselves upon arriving in port. In their place, seventy-three individuals claimed to be the crew in order to land in the United States.[32] "The crux of the problem," according to officials, was "to prevent aliens gaining a foothold in this country in the guise of seamen."[33]

Immigration officials were less concerned about European sailors leaving their employment in New York because they were only subject to lenient immigration laws and rules, not to Asian exclusion. Starting in 1903, sailors could formally become immigrants by passing the medical examination and meeting other requirements for immigrants. In official terms, they were "brought to Ellis Island for inspection under the immigration laws."[34] Or, in the words of one shipping company representative: "We sent them to Ellis Island and they were let off."[35] Like European stowaways who were allowed to adjust their status and enter the United States as immigrants before 1917, European seamen legally applying for admission were almost always approved. And European maritime workers were granted even greater latitude than stowaways. They were allowed to adjust their status even after the passage of racially restrictive quotas in the 1920s that limited southern and eastern European immigration and throughout the Great Depression. In 1931, for example, only 19 out of 776 applications for legalization were denied because the seamen did not meet the criteria.[36] Of course, as Chinese and other Asian seamen were excluded by law, legalization of admission was not an option for them.

Immigration Bureau officials acknowledged that their efforts to prevent unauthorized entry had limited success. "Despite all that is said and all that is done," Commissioner-General of Immigration Daniel Keefe noted, Chinese "have smuggled themselves or been smuggled ashore in seaports as sailors or stowaways, or have by fraud and perjury managed to land in an apparently regular manner."[37] Direct smuggling, jump-ship sailors, and indirect smuggling of paper sons and other Chinese were, in this estimation, part of the same intractable problem.

## Mapping the Presence of Asian Sailors in New York

Most concerns about unauthorized Asian immigration were focused on San Francisco because it had larger numbers of arriving Asian *passengers* than any other U.S. port. However, concerns about deserting *sailors* were focused on New York because this port had larger numbers of seamen. In 1919, New York reported ten times as many alien seamen as San Francisco: 285,000 individual inspections to San Francisco's 25,000 inspections. By 1930, as the Immigration and Naturalization Service conducted almost 1.2 million seamen inspections, close to half of these occurred in New York (568,359) compared with only 17,000 in San Francisco.[38]

Just as New York was the port with the largest number of arriving seamen, it was also the port with the largest number of deserters. If, as immigration inspector Feri Felix Weiss claimed, deserting sailors were "the leak in the sieve" of U.S. immigration policy, New York was the largest hole in this sieve.[39] As reported deserters ranged from 1,000 to 35,000 annually, New York remained the port with the highest percentage of deserting seamen, averaging 43 percent of total desertions (table 8). Although these numbers were high, they were self-reported by steamship companies, and officials believed that the real number of deserters was probably higher.[40]

It is not clear whether the pattern of larger numbers of seamen in New York was also true for Asians, as the Immigration Bureau did not consistently report the number of Chinese and other Asian seamen. In 1913, the bureau estimated as many as 40,000 Chinese seamen in all U.S. ports, with 4,277 recorded in New York.[41] Between 1914 and 1920, there were between 4,000 and 8,000 examinations of Chinese seamen in New York each year.[42] Historian Vivek Bald reports somewhat smaller numbers of South Asian seamen, estimating that a total of 20,000 to 25,000 "moved in and out of New York's docklands" between 1914 and 1924.[43]

The numbers of reported Chinese and Japanese jump-ship sailors in New York were larger than at other immigration stations, but still relatively small (table 8). This may have been because Chinese successfully used their kinship networks in the city to avoid detection. Certainly, immigration officials believed that the numbers of deserting Chinese sailors were much higher than those arrested. Before the 1920s, the bureau estimated that there were between 3,000 and 5,000 Chinese seamen who had left ships in New York and remained in the port, "idle and (in many instances) destitute."[44] By 1922, some of these men had shipped out and the bureau estimated that the numbers had dropped to between 2,000 and 3,000 Chinese deserters.[45] Japanese were also singled out, although the bureau was not unduly concerned as reports noted that "the number who have thus deserted and remained in the United States has not been large."[46] Filipino seamen settled in New York, but they were not separated out in records of jump-ship sailors. Between 1927 and 1932, even as the numbers of deserters were decreasing, there were about five times as many Chinese and Japanese jump-ship sailors in New York as in San Francisco (table 8).

Although Immigration Bureau estimates of deserting sailors were high, they were not exact. Immigration officials strongly suspected that sailors settled in New York and other cities, but they were not sure if this was permanent. Many reported deserters worked for short periods of time or were listed as jump-ship sailors but had shipped out on other vessels. Officials had no clear information about the numbers of sailors who might still live in the United States, and this lack of information caused them concern. In 1930, the commissioner-general of immigration acknowledged, "We can not keep such seamen under surveillance and we do not know, as a matter of fact, how many leave and how many remain."[47]

As a result of these practices of jumping ship, sailors formed a substantial number of New York's Chinese residents. Through the 1890s, a majority of Chinese residents of New York were sailors.[48] In 1889, activist and founder of the Chinese Equal Rights League Wong Chin Foo reported about 350 sailors and cooks in New York and 100 in Boston, with only a handful in other ports.[49] Like other Chinese in New York, sailors typically came from the Guangdong region of China, although they were more likely to hail from Dapeng than Taishan. As historian Heather Lee has shown, jump-ship sailors could seek assistance from their regional huiguan, the Tai Pun Benevolent Association, or from a fellow Dapengese, quickly locating work and a place to stay in New York.[50]

However they arrived in New York, Chinese lived throughout the city, especially if they worked as laundrymen and were required to set up shop close to their customers. In addition to Manhattan's Chinatown, many sailors and other Chinese resided in the area south of the Brooklyn Navy Yard. The area was lively but run down, described by the 1939 Works Progress Administration guide to New York City as having grimy cobblestone streets, "while beyond the dull waters of the East River looms the New York sky line, like the backdrop of a stage set." Serving the Chinese community, the area included Chinese agents such as Low San, who hired crews for shipping lines as well as Chinese restaurants that both employed and served jump-ship sailors.[51]

South Asian sailors, mostly Bengali, also settled in New York. In 1892, *Harper's Weekly* reported that "Lascars take up their quarters in some one of the foreign seamen's boarding-houses, usually on the east side, near Chatham Square." Like early Chinese sailors, they stayed close to Manhattan Chinatown restaurants, "where they can feast upon queer dishes" and gamble.[52] As historian Vivek Bald has shown, these early residents were typically temporary. Yet, they developed networks throughout the Eastern Seaboard and inland to upstate New York and the upper Midwest. Bald explores how, by the 1910s and 1920s, former lascars had translated their hard work in the industrialized boiler rooms of steamships to better-paid work in steel mills and automobile factories from Bethlehem, Pennsylvania, to Detroit, Michigan.[53]

Records of arrivals through Ellis Island show that Filipino seamen settled alongside Chinese south of the Brooklyn Navy Yard. This neighborhood included Filipino lunchrooms, shops, bars, boardinghouses, and the Manila Karihan Filipino restaurant that served "native food, extremely rare in the eastern part of the United States."[54] When he arrived in New York in 1917, Astanialas Bantog gave his address as the "Philippino Boarding House" on Sun Street in Brooklyn. Many other sailors gave nearby addresses on Sands Street, a major thoroughfare that ran from the Navy Yard to the Brooklyn Bridge.[55] Some had worked in the merchant marine, but others formerly served with the navy as part of the U.S. military. During the 1920s, past experience in the U.S. Navy and status as U.S. nationals allowed Filipinos to secure service positions with the federal government: about 300 Filipinos worked in the Chicago post office, with much smaller numbers working at post offices in New York, San Francisco, and Los Angeles.[56] Several hundred men also secured positions in navy yards around the mainland, including in Brooklyn.[57] However, during the Depression, anti-Asian measures in the merchant marine displaced many Filipino sailors. "The employment agencies do not want to give them jobs, and the relief agencies refuse to give them aid, with very few exceptions," Maximo Manzon reported in 1938. According to Manzon, former sailors were crowded into rooms in Brooklyn boardinghouses, some sleeping on billiard tables in their day or working clothes.[58] Another smaller community of Filipino sailors formed on South Street near Chinatown and the Manhattan docks.[59]

## Asian Sailors in the Maritime Workforce

The substantial population of Asian sailors in New York was due to the large number of Asian sailors employed in shipping. Most of the ships arriving in the port of New York and trading with the United States from the late nineteenth through the mid-twentieth centuries were British merchant marine vessels.[60] In the 1930s, roughly 40,000 South Asians were employed on British ships, about one-quarter of all British seamen. Approximately 5,000 Chinese worked as British seamen during the same time period. These numbers had been higher before the Depression and rose again during World War II. As merchant seamen were increasingly in demand and Chinese seamen were registered on British vessels, as many as 60,000 South Asians and 10,000 Chinese sailors worked for the British merchant marine.[61] The U.S. merchant marine was similarly dependent on noncitizens, who formed more than 90 percent of crew members, although it was less dependent on Asian labor.[62]

From its earliest development, the expansion of merchant navies had been closely intertwined with the expansion of global capital and colonialism in Asia.[63] As a result, the Pacific trade had a long history of Asian mariners, with Filipino and Chinese sailors working in the colonial Spanish galleon trade since the late sixteenth century.[64] Chinese were often employed through shipping agents who controlled many aspects of their employment. If hired through an agent, they earned half of what white sailors earned and less than what Chinese could earn if they jumped ship in New York. South Asians were typically employed through British colonial labor contracts known as Asiatic or "lascar" articles. These contracts paid colonial workers less than a quarter of standard European labor rates, provided smaller living quarters on the ship, and restricted the geographic regions in which they could work. Both Chinese and South Asians relied on coethnic petty officers, known in India as *serangs*, who translated for their crews but also enforced these contracts on board the ship.[65]

As outlined in chapter 3, ships had long been hierarchical, multiracial workplaces. As steamships replaced sailing ships in the latter half of the nineteenth century, more and more Asians were recruited to do the dirty work associated with steam engines, and the feminized service of cooks and caretakers. Large steamships, the kind that typically docked in New York, had as many as twenty boilers with one fireman responsible for breaking and feeding coal to each boiler, in conditions of extraordinary heat with no fresh air or light.[66] Immigrant advocate Bruno Lasker noted that employers believed that "white workers could not stand the heat."[67] As oil-powered ships became more common in the early twentieth century, the work of the fireman changed from hard labor to supervision of the engine room, and whites increasingly replaced Asian firemen.[68] The Goan seamen who protested their detention at Ellis Island in the introduction of this book worked as stewards and cooks on liners trading between England, the East Indies, and the United States.[69] Immigration officer Feri Felix Weiss noted about one ship he inspected, the *Aspinet*, that "the officers were white, the crew were yellow (Malay), and the stowaways were black—there was certainly a color chart of races on board."[70]

In addition to being employed in harsh or service work, Asian crew members were frequently mistreated and had limited options if they were abused.[71] Sometimes, immigration officials expressed sympathy with abused seamen, but their policies supported the shipping companies' harsh working conditions and even forced labor. As a result, desertion was one of the few ways that sailors could change their treatment, better their working conditions, or earn higher wages. Mistreatment was not limited to Asian sailors; many seamen's unions complained about harsh working conditions and limited rights. However, Asians appear to have been especially abused and had limited recourse owing to their status under exclusion laws. In 1908, the entire Chinese crew of a British steamer jumped overboard in an escape attempt in New York's harbor. Since shipping out of Shanghai, they had been overworked, fed rotten food, charged exorbitant prices for their work clothes, and beaten and fined if they didn't work for any reason, including severe illness. Immigration authorities were sympathetic to the crew, describing them as "poor fellows." Ham Ching Ta, the ship's steward, explained that the firemen had been "worked like beasts" and that all the crew had been "kicked around like dogs." "We would all rather die than go back on that ship."[72] In fact, two of the crew had drowned in their escape attempt. The remaining crew members were rescued and detained. After discussions between New York's chief inspector Harry R. Sisson, Immigration Commissioner-General Robert Watchorn, and the Chinese and British consuls, most of the survivors were provided steerage accommodations on the luxury liner *Lusitania*, returning to China via Liverpool. Three remained at Ellis Island to testify in the coroner's inquest concerning their colleagues' deaths.[73]

Other crew members "subjected to cruel treatment" were forced to continue their work, with the support of the Immigration Bureau. In 1909, twenty Chinese seamen deserted a Norwegian steamship in Staten Island, were captured, and were taken to Ellis Island. Because the crew was barred from landing in New York, the Norwegian consul determined that they should continue to work on the same ship en route to Sydney. The crew disagreed. As they were removed from Ellis Island, Moy Sing and his coworkers refused to board the tugboat to return to the ship. The immigration inspectors were unable to force them, so they marched the crew back to the station, broke them into two groups of ten men, and secured reinforcements. Then fifteen Ellis Island employees surrounded each group of ten men and dragged them onto the tug despite the Chinese seamen's physical and audible protests.[74] In 1921, a group of Punjabi, Goan, and Malaysian lascars were maltreated while working from Calcutta across the North Atlantic to New York, including the denial of sufficient rations and warm clothing that were required under their contract. Once they docked in Brooklyn, two men jumped ship and thirty-three Punjabi sailors went ashore to register their complaints with the British vice consul. The captain, meanwhile, listed them all as deserters and shipped out with a new crew. When their case came before the U.S. Circuit Court of Appeals, the judges agreed that they had deserted and sentenced them to imprisonment.[75] As in the case of the shanghaied crew of the *Rotterdam*, U.S. authorities actively enforced the interests and decisions of shipping companies and the countries under whose flags they sailed, even to the point of forced labor and incarceration.

### U.S. Maritime Union Support for Asian Exclusion

While immigration officials were primarily concerned about regulating Asian sailors to ensure they did not violate exclusion laws, maritime unions viewed such regulation as a way to limit labor competition. Despite working alongside one another and sharing common concerns about working conditions and wages, members of the International Seamen's Union (ISU) typically viewed Chinese and other Asian sailors as competitors rather than allies.[76] Historians have long identified the central role of working-class whites and labor organizations in supporting early exclusion laws.[77] However, the influence of seamen and maritime unions has not been extensively acknowledged.

Throughout the early twentieth century, the ISU was at the forefront of efforts to expand exclusion, including using immigration laws to restrict labor competition from Asian sailors. The union played a critical role in protecting American sailors through legislation and strikes for better working conditions, wages, and treatment; however, it also saw racist labor laws as a key part of its role to protect white sailors.[78] Andrew Furuseth, president of the ISU, was a founding member of the Asiatic Exclusion League formed in San Francisco in 1905.[79] The union testified on the problem of Asian seamen before the House Immigration and Naturalization Committee.[80] Union officials, including Furuseth, introduced a resolution in support of expanding Asian exclusion to Filipinos.[81] Influenced by the ISU, politicians complained that Asian sailors were "the cheapest labor in all the world." In 1915, Jacob Gallinger, a Republican senator representing New Hampshire, expressed his disbelief that "we exclude Asiatic labor from the United States in order to preserve the standards of our own labor, but we allow foreign ships owned in Europe or Japan to come freely into the ports of the United States manned with this same Asiatic labor and steal the carrying trade of the United States away from American citizens."[82] The high number and low wages of Asian sailors was linked to broad concerns about labor competition in the United States and helped foster calls not only for the increased regulation of sailors but also for the expansion of exclusion itself.

Maritime union members' and immigration officials' concerns were different but interlinked. Asian sailors' low pay and shoddy working conditions increased the likelihood that they would desert their posts upon arrival in New York, leading to unauthorized entry and increased labor competition. Although all seamen faced difficult working conditions and mistreatment, these problems were particularly acute for Asians employed on unequal colonial lascar contracts. Even among seamen who did not work on lascar articles, employment contracts were highly restrictive and discriminatory.[83] As late as 1937, a judge ruled that the employment articles on which the Dollar Lines employed Chinese seamen violated U.S. law and "amount to peonage."[84]

While some unions continued their policies of racial exclusion, others worked to organize sailors across industries regardless of race. As outlined later in this chapter, the National Maritime Union (NMU) and the New York Lien Yi Society successfully worked together in the 1930s, offering a new model of unionism that crossed racial lines and brought substantial changes for a broad range of maritime workers.[85]

### Asian Sailors' Bona Fides and Bonds

Seamen had long engaged in conflicts with their captains about their working conditions and contracts, including their right to leave the ship when in port.[86] Before 1901, there was no U.S. legislation protecting or restricting sailors' rights to shore leave. Seamen had not been included in exclusion or immigration laws, and they were generally allowed to go ashore without immigration inspection. In addition, there was no requirement to report jump-ship sailors to immigration authorities.[87]

In 1901 the attorney general ruled that while seamen were not expressly subject to immigration laws, this exemption only applied to genuine seamen.[88] Aliens who became seamen for the purpose of entering the United States illegally were immigrants. Therefore, the Immigration Bureau had the right to detain and examine crew members to distinguish between bona fide seamen and immigrants.[89] Following this ruling, immigration officials argued that immigration laws that applied to ships' passengers should also apply to crews, and that captains could be held liable if any of their crew members escaped in violation of these laws.[90] This was the beginning of the contested, changing status of seamen. Especially for Asian sailors, the traditional "freedom of the seas" became increasingly constrained.[91]

Working at the largest immigration station in the largest port for both arriving and deserting seamen, Ellis Island officials were centrally involved in developing the practices to prevent seamen's illegal entry into the United States. Enforcement practices developed at Ellis Island were frequently extended to other ports. Ellis Island officials were generally restrained in their treatment of Chinese immigrant arrivals, particularly elite arrivals. However, this restraint didn't extend to seamen. New York immigration officials argued for, and implemented, the strict regulation of Asian seamen. In contrast, San Francisco officials were more lenient with Chinese and Japanese deserting seamen. They declined to take any action on Asian jump-ship sailors, stating that "as a rule, they reship within a short time." In 1916, they noted that "the attention of the United States attorneys invariably is called to the matter but thus far no prosecutions have been attempted."[92]

New York officials were strict in their enforcement of laws against jump-ship sailors. They pursued court cases as early as the 1900s but had little enforcement success: courts were reluctant to interfere, ships had frequently not returned to port when the court was in session, and officials had to prove the captain's "negligence or connivance."[93] In 1904, three Chinese seamen escaped from the S.S. *Hudson*. A Brooklyn grand jury indicted the captain, but when the case finally came to trial more than two years later, he received a suspended sentence.[94] In 1909, New York inspector in charge Harry Sisson noted that the bureau had gained convictions in only two cases against captains (including the captain of the *Hudson*), and in each case the judge suspended the sentence.[95]

Asian seamen were not only treated more harshly at Ellis Island than at other immigration stations, but were also treated more harshly than other seamen at Ellis Island. Although there were initially no regulations requiring the Immigration Bureau to monitor Chinese sailors more closely than other sailors, it was common practice for Ellis Island officials to place guards on ships with Chinese crew members to prevent them from entering the United States in violation of exclusion laws.[96] The New York Immigration Bureau employed twelve watchmen for this purpose in New York until 1904, when the commissioner-general reduced the number to five, arguing that the bureau's guarding of Chinese crew members encouraged captains to shirk their responsibilities.[97] In place of watchmen, who were often ineffective, the commissioner-general suggested a system in which an official would board each ship, inform the captain of his liability for escaped Chinese, and "take a list—perhaps including personal description and photograph—of the Chinamen on board." The official would then return to confirm that the same men departed with the ship or, if they had escaped, refer the matter to the U.S. attorney general for prosecution.[98] Although these controls do not appear to have been implemented at the time, they were very similar to early photographic documentation requirements for other Chinese arrivals. Such measures were implemented by statute in 1917, in the form of seamen's cards for all sailors.[99]

Following Ellis Island practices, Immigration Bureau rules soon distinguished between Chinese, Asian, and other sailors. And each time new regulations were implemented, Chinese and other Asian sailors resisted them. In 1907, the Immigration Bureau implemented a rule that required a $500 bond for every Chinese seaman granted shore leave to ensure his departure from the United States within thirty days.[100] Regulations for non-Chinese arrivals were also promulgated in 1907; however, they did not require bonds.[101] The new bond rule transferred the regulation of Chinese crew members from immigration officials to the ship's officers. Although Chinese seamen should have been allowed shore leave like other sailors, in practice captains viewed the bond as a potential fine and Chinese sailors were prevented from leaving their ships in New York and at other U.S. ports.[102]

Asian seamen resisted their captains' orders to remain on board, both because of their expectations of customary shore leave and because of their anger at the unfairness that others were allowed to leave while they were detained. Shore leave was a central flashpoint for conflict between Asian sailors and their officers. Seamen who had been cooped up for months on board the ship not only wanted the opportunity to explore New York but also often needed to stock up on basic supplies.[103] In 1907, twenty-two Chinese crew members deserted an oil tanker in New York while waiting for their cargo to be loaded for Singapore. According to the captain, they were dissatisfied with the food available on board. Although the captain would have received substantial fines had the men not been caught, every crew member was rounded up by the police and charged with violating immigration law.[104] In 1910, twenty Chinese seamen had been forced to remain on board a British steamship for three weeks, while twenty other crew members, "all Englishmen, got liberal shore leave." On the morning that they were leaving for New Zealand, one of the Chinese seamen asked the first mate for a few hours ashore. When the officer refused, the seaman drew a knife and chased him around the ship until he was tripped by a white crew member and an all-out fight ensued between the Chinese and white crew. Seven of the Chinese crew members jumped overboard in an attempt at freedom, and four of them drowned. The three survivors were arrested and held in police custody while the remaining Chinese crew members were held in irons on board the ship.[105] In 1909, four Japanese crew members were discovered on Brooklyn's Pier Seven as they attempted to leave their ship. Customs officials stopped them, shouted to the pier watchman to make sure that nobody escaped, and, after a struggle, detained them in order to send them to Ellis Island as "discharged sailors not reshipping."[106] South Asian seamen also challenged being detained on board the ship. In 1930, about 40 lascars attacked the officers of the S.S. *Irisbank* shortly before it was to leave New York. As in earlier years, the men were unhappy about their treatment, "chiefly the restriction on shore leave." The *Times* reported that the lascars shrieked and howled and "brandished anything they could pick up" as they attacked. However, the large number of men in the close quarters of the engine room inhibited their movement and the officers fought back. By the end of the melee, three officers and three lascars had been injured. And although one officer remained in the hospital in New York with scalp lacerations, no arrests were made and the ship sailed later that afternoon.[107]

Anger about detention on board the ship was not only a matter of comfort, customary rights, and the ways that these rights were constrained by racist exclusion laws. Sometimes, the limitations on Asian sailors' shore leave raised fundamental safety concerns. When a fire broke out early in the morning of January 31, 1929, on a Dollar Line ship awaiting passengers for a round-the-world cruise starting in Jersey City, a Chinese crew member made the initial discovery and alerted the crew. However, although

Chinese formed 103 members of the 206-strong crew, the *New York Times* reported that a night guard "tried to prevent their escape to the streets of Jersey City." When the police arrived, the Chinese alone were detained on the pier, even though the fire injured four crew members and killed two.[108] The following year, seventy-one Chinese stewards were detained under watch when another Dollar liner caught fire, then were returned to the ship before the fire was fully extinguished.[109]

In maritime law, resistance to the captain's orders was "mutiny," and the term was frequently invoked in reference to Asian sailors' resistance to being denied shore leave.[110] In some cases, the crew did not even have to defy the captain to be accused of mutiny. In 1914, twenty-one Chinese crew members were removed from a British freighter in dock at Staten Island and taken to Ellis Island by immigration authorities because the captain believed that they were "acting strangely and showed signs of mutiny." The Chinese men were "sent home" to Hong Kong and the ship sailed for Buenos Aires with a white crew.[111] When Chinese sailors left ships in defiance of their captains' orders, it was not always clear whether they were simply attempting to secure shore leave or whether they were deserting seamen planning to settle in the United States. They entered the liminal legal area between shore leave and desertion. Regardless, if they were captured, they were detained at Ellis Island.

## The 1915 La Follette Act and the 1917 Immigration Act

Two acts passed within two years of one another manifested the tensions between the freedom of sailors to seek work and the control of seamen to ensure that they didn't violate exclusion and immigration laws. The La Follette Act of 1915, commonly known as the Seamen's Act, improved safety and working conditions while also codifying the freedom of seamen to seek employment on new ships by decriminalizing desertion.[112] The 1917 Immigration Act implemented controls on these same workers to ensure that they did not immigrate illegally.[113] Key to the tension between the laws was the question of whether crew members were bona fide seamen or simply immigrants seeking to use maritime freedoms to enter the United States. Immigration officials argued that they needed to determine sailors' bona fides to see whether they were entitled to the freedoms that they claimed. Maritime unions argued that such restrictions impacted all seamen, most of whom were genuine, and placed restrictions on their freedoms. Both were right. These tensions were resolved on the backs of Asian sailors. Immigration officials assumed that Chinese and other Asian seamen were particularly likely to be unauthorized and therefore should be subject to extensive regulation, while other alien seamen maintained their freedoms.

The ISU and its president, Andrew Furuseth, were central in developing and implementing the La Follette Act. However, union members imagined the new freedoms and benefits that the law provided as freedoms for white seamen. The law required that at least three-quarters of a ship's crew be able "to understand any order given by the officers."[114] Supporters emphasized this as a safety measure, but it also aimed to end the long-standing practice of hiring Asian crews who understood basic English commands and relied on Asian petty officers to translate more complex instructions.

Although unions claimed that the law would create more work for American sailors, shipping companies argued that the law made U.S. merchant marine ships less competitive with British and Japanese ships that employed extensive and less expensive Asian labor, damaging the industry and putting U.S. sailors out of work.[115] American merchants in Manila protested the bill, claiming that it paralyzed the Pacific trade. In highly paternalistic language, they claimed that "our wards, the Filipinos, at whose door no fault can be laid, must suffer greatly because of this untoward bill."[116]

At the same time that members of Congress were debating the Seamen's Act, they were also debating immigration provisions that became the 1917 Immigration Act.[117] Seriously addressing the problem of alien seamen for the first time within immigration law, the 1917 act gave immigration officials more power to inspect and control arriving crews.[118] Most significantly in terms of enforcement, the 1917 law required manifests of alien seamen, not just passengers.[119] It addressed public health concerns about seamen by implementing a small fifty-dollar penalty for each crew member who had a "loathsome or dangerous contagious disease," required treatment, and restricted their shore leave.[120] The law also imposed a substantial $5,000 penalty for knowingly signing a crewman with the intent to land him in the United States.[121] Although this provision signaled the seriousness of such smuggling, it was very difficult to prosecute.[122]

In debating the 1917 Immigration Law, members of Congress "found much difficulty in incorporating provisions which would not conflict with the latitude granted seamen under the La Follette Act."[123] However, they were *also* concerned to make sure that the freedoms guaranteed to sailors did not undermine the newly implemented immigration restrictions.[124] The La Follette Act was followed by a Treasury Department regulation that required seamen to carry photographic identification cards that certified each inspected man's right to disembark, similar to the plan suggested earlier by the commissioner-general of immigration.[125] Under this provision, each sailor was examined on board, and if he didn't have any disease that prevented his entry to the United States, two cards were created with his photograph. The original was given to the seaman and the duplicate was kept by the Immigration Bureau.[126]

The law raised concerns among seamen. Some protested that their captains intentionally did not have photographs available as a way to prevent them from leaving the ship.[127] A more substantial problem was that the implementation of seamen's identification cards didn't prevent sailors from jumping ship; instead, it created a new market for the cards themselves. One report noted that the El Pobre Diablo (the poor devil) boardinghouse near the Custom House in Valparaiso, Chile, was a known place for the illegal exchange of seamen's identification cards. Down-and-out sailors sold their identification cards to stowaways, who replaced the sailors' photographs with their own photographs, allowing them to disembark at U.S. ports.[128]

Asian sailors and their unions claimed that the restrictions in the 1915 La Follette Seamen's Act and 1917 Immigration Law were designed more to prevent them from working than to ensure legal immigration. However, despite these concerns, they used the 1915 act to strengthen their working situation. In 1920, a newly formed union described by immigration officials as the "Oriental Seamen's Union" boarded ships docked at New York's piers to inform maritime workers of their rights under the law. Many Asian seamen, who were hired at low wages in international ports, could earn better wages and secure better working conditions if they joined new crews in New York.[129]

As a result of the 1917 Immigration Act, the regulation of sailors became a substantial part of the Immigration Bureau's responsibilities at Ellis Island and other immigration stations. In 1918, immigration officials conducted about 8,000 inspections of Chinese seamen.[130] In 1919, as ocean trade resumed following World War I, immigration officials conducted more than 800,000 inspections, issued more than 260,000 seamen's identification cards, and certified more than 4,000 seamen as having "loathsome or contagious diseases."[131] The regulation of seamen was, according to the Immigration Bureau's *Annual Report* in both 1919 and 1920, "perhaps the largest single item of work performed by the bureau's field officers."[132] As the special representative for Seamen's Work noted, decreased immigration during this time was offset by increases in the inspection of arriving seamen. In fact, the issuance of identification cards to sailors was more time-consuming than immigrant inspection.[133] The numbers of seamen examined by immigration officials increased steadily, and by 1930, almost 1.2 million alien seamen had been examined. This is considerably higher than the typical number of immigrants inspected annually and comparable to the peak years of immigration in 1907 and 1914, when more than 1.2 million immigrants entered the United States. Immigration officials themselves drew attention to this comparison.[134] These figures suggest the expansive reach of immigration law and the Immigration Bureau's extensive work regulating groups not legally considered immigrants.

## Expanding Asian Exclusion and Maritime Regulation

The expansion of regulations concerning seamen was closely connected to the expansion of Asian exclusion. In addition to recording and monitoring seamen, the 1917 Immigration Act established a "barred zone" from which Asians could not migrate to the United States. Before 1917, only Chinese and Japanese had been excluded from the United States. This was now expanded to prevent the entry of immigrants from a broad area, stretching from Arabia through South Asia to the Malay archipelago.[135] Although the Philippines fell within this zone, Filipino workers and seamen were U.S. colonial subjects who were entitled to reside in the United States. The barred zone addressed concerns voiced by the chair of the House Immigration and Naturalization Committee in 1912 that, although Chinese laws prevented Chinese sailors from landing, there were no laws to keep out other Asian sailors.[136] However, in replacing the Chinese exclusion laws with a comprehensive new regional Asian exclusion policy, the 1917 law also removed the legal basis for requiring bonds of Chinese seamen. Although all seamen were required to carry photographic documentation starting in 1918, between 1917 and 1922, there were no specific bonding requirements for Chinese or other Asian seamen.[137]

Immigration authorities were not content to let this stand. In June 1922, regulations to ensure that Chinese merchant seamen did not illegally enter the United States were expanded to include almost all Asian seamen. The Immigration Bureau required all Asian barred zone seamen who shipped from foreign ports to provide a $500 bond, a full personal description, and a photograph to indemnify against their staying in the United States longer than sixty days.[138] The extension of bonds for Asian sailors was a significant expansion of the Immigration Bureau's regulation of sailors.

As they had done with earlier restrictions, Asian sailors and their supporters resisted these new rules. Commercial and governmental organizations representing South Asian and Japanese seamen were concerned that these groups would be treated like excluded Chinese. They feared that their nationals would be associated with the Chinese and treated poorly by U.S. authorities, threatening the livelihood of non-Chinese seamen. The Bengal Chamber of Commerce, for example, protested that the U.S. government was considering applying "the provisions of the Chinese Immigration Act to the Asiatic crews of steamers plying between India and the United States." The chamber expressed concern that this would lead to shipping lines dispensing with their Indian crews. Worried about the impact on South Asian sailors, the British government also contacted the U.S. government about the status of these regulations.[139] And a Japanese shipping line wrote to the U.S. Department of Labor questioning the expansion of the "special rule and measure governing Chinese immigrants and seamen to which Japanese seamen are not subjected."[140] Although Asian sailors of all nationalities occupied the lowest rungs of maritime employment, they rarely competed with one another for work. However, they fought not to be pushed further down the U.S. racial hierarchy by being subject to the racist restrictions that had previously applied only to the Chinese. Despite these expressions of concern, the regulations were implemented.

Chinese also fought against these restrictions. However, they expressed their resistance through appeals to elevated American ideals, fundamental freedoms and rights to shore leave. Although similar rules had been implemented for Chinese seamen in 1907, they resented the reimposition of bonding requirements and increasingly strict regulations that now required a full personal description and photograph.[141] Officers of the Brooklyn King Jay Association wrote an open letter to President Harding, noting Chinese sailors' dedicated service transporting troops and munitions during World War I. "Claiming to champion the cause of liberty," they wrote, "this country cannot do it more successfully by infringing upon the liberty of the war time Chinese seamen." The authors pointedly referenced the recent dedication of the Lincoln Memorial in Washington, D.C., describing Lincoln as the father of equality and stating "we cannot believe [the memorial] is to serve only as a mask."[142]

Such resistance was not limited to New York. According to officials in Seattle, the new bonding policy was countereffective, causing more desertions.[143] "Having enjoyed shore leave for a time, the Chinese resent bitterly the fact that they are not allowed shore leave as are the citizens of other countries."[144] Although the sailors were not U.S. citizens or permanent U.S. residents, their opposition to the new rules was framed in terms of rights and citizenship, urging U.S. officials to meet their own promises of liberty and claiming that Chinese deserved rights equal to those of U.S. citizens.

Chinese seamen also challenged the new regulations by refusing to be photographed, taking shore leave, and deserting in violation of their bonds. Shortly after the rules were introduced, the S.S. *Albert Watts* docked in New York. Chinese crew members on board the ship refused to have their photograph taken or otherwise comply with the new rules before they disembarked.[145] If they deserted, many found jobs and destroyed or sold their seamen's identification cards, which were issued to them starting in 1918 in an attempt to regulate their movement.[146] If arrested, they claimed to be U.S. citizens. In 1923, the *New York Times* reported that "immigration inspectors are busy in New York and elsewhere rounding up aliens who cannot produce papers to show that they came by the regular method."[147] A "respectable proportion" of such deportation cases were former sailors.[148]

The Chinese protests were a sign of an increasingly settled and organized community in New York. The New York Chinese Seamen's Institute was incorporated in 1922, in part because of concerns about changing U.S. regulations. The institute provided legal assistance to Chinese sailors, such as the imprisoned Hoboken crew.[149] However, its efforts were not limited to the United States. The institute was linked to the Chinese Seamen's Union (CSU) and its successful 1922 strike that earned wage increases of 15–30 percent as well as union recognition.[150] The New York Chinese Seamen's Institute held a mass meeting at Mott Street in the heart of Chinatown, appealing to British and American labor and arguing that the CSU strike "goes to the very root of the labor movement of the world."[151] South Asian maritime unions engaged in successful labor actions in Calcutta in 1919 and Bombay in 1920, earning substantial wage increases. However, the Indian Seamen's Association, formed by Indian radicals in Britain in 1922, was less effective, mostly because of British colonial government controls.[152] There was more than one seamen's institute in New York in the 1920s, including a club and residential home close to the community of Filipino sailors living around Sands Street, Brooklyn.[153]

Not only were Chinese seamen successful in these labor actions, but they also effectively challenged restrictive U.S. rules in the courts. Courts sometimes upheld and sometimes overruled Immigration Bureau regulations attempting to control the entry of Chinese and other Asian seamen. Chinese seamen's representatives challenged their detention on board the ship, both on habeas corpus grounds and on the basis that they were not laborers within the meaning of the exclusion acts. In response to the new 1922 bonding rules, Judge Julius Mayer of the U.S. District Court in the Southern District of New York ruled that Chinese sailors were entitled to shore leave on the same basis as other sailors, without furnishing a $500 bond.[154] However, the Immigration Bureau initially claimed that this ruling was specific only to the single case that came before the court, concerning Ho Chung. The bureau refused to make any changes to its bonding rules.[155] Immigration officials accepted the legal ruling that Ho Chung was a bona fide seaman but claimed this did not apply to any other sailor as it was not known whether they were legitimate. New York officials continued to take a strict approach to deserting seamen. San Francisco and other West Coast ports allowed shipping companies to issue blanket bonds because of the difficulty and time required to issue individual bonds.[156] However, New York required individual bonds. By 1923, rather than risk the desertion of bonded seamen in New York, many shipping companies employed day and night watchmen to prevent Chinese sailors from leaving their ships.[157]

Officials in New York noted that the new regulations had improved "the seaman situation," with shipping agents more carefully monitoring their Chinese crews. Although immigration authorities never claimed that their goal was to reduce the use of Asian sailors or prevent labor competition with white maritime workers, the inspector in charge of Chinese exclusion in New York noted with satisfaction that some shipping companies had "given up altogether the use of Chinese on their vessels."[158]

The 1924 Immigration Act, sometimes known as the Johnson-Reed Act, followed fast after the 1922 expansion of rules placing controls on Asian sailors. The law has long been notorious for limiting overall immigration and implementing racial quotas that heavily favored northern and western European immigrants over southern and eastern Europeans. It is also widely known for consolidating Asian exclusion laws. However, the 1924 act also codified restrictions on Asian sailors.[159] Recognizing that the implementation of racial quotas would increase the incentives for illegal immigration, the law clearly defined the difference between bona fide seamen and others, allowed a period of sixty days for seamen to ship out on a foreign vessel, and made them deportable if they stayed any longer.[160] The 1924 law applied to immigrants and seamen of all races.[161] However, unlike Asian jump-ship sailors who were barred from permanently entering the United States, European seamen were able to legalize their status as immigrants by passing the requisite medical examination and meeting other requirements for immigrants.[162]

Although the 1924 law consolidated various Asian exclusion laws, it had a mixed impact on Chinese sailors. In some ways, it was fairer. The law required all sailors to be detained on board before their medical examination, and it ended the practice of detaining Chinese seamen until they were bonded. At the same time, it continued practices of discriminating against Asian seamen by giving immigration officials discretion to deny shore leave and determine who was a genuine sailor.[163] Officials acknowledged that they were "guided by intuition" whether an individual was a bona fide seaman or someone who signed on as part of the ship's crew to gain unlawful entry to the United States. In many cases, this "intuition" worked against Chinese and other Asian seamen.[164]

After the implementation of the 1924 law, restrictionists continued to express concerns about the "deserting seamen route." However, the actual number of deserting seamen declined. In 1927, the ISU claimed that "bootlegging" immigrants earned people in the shipping industry between $3 million and $4 million.[165] Nevertheless, between 1924 and 1932, the number of reported deserters dropped from a high of more than 35,000 to less than 1,500 jump-ship sailors. Although the records are scattered, the number of Chinese, Japanese, and other Asian jump-ship sailors also declined during this period. The Great Depression may have accounted for much, but not all, of this reduction, which started in the 1920s and plummeted after 1930 (table 8).

### Changing Alliances during the Depression and World War II

During the 1930s, sailors often struggled to find work. As a global industry, shipping was deeply affected by the global economic crisis. Limited employment opportunities "on land as well as at sea" meant that desertions were reduced.[166] Some unions such as the ISU expanded their campaigns against Asian sailors, describing Chinese sailors as "coolies" to suggest that they were not free workers and that their low wages undercut white sailors.[167] Other newly established unions such as the NMU, founded in 1935 under the auspices of the Congress of Industrial Organizations, allied with the CSU to organize all workers in a given industry regardless of their rank or race.[168]

Depression-era concerns about labor competition led to new restrictions on Asian sailors, as well as new alliances to resist such restrictions. The 1936

Merchant Marine Act introduced a requirement that 90 percent of crew members on U.S. merchant ships hold U.S. citizenship. As a result, even though it is not clear that these quotas were met, as many as 4,000 Filipino merchant mariners were discharged from their positions in 1937.[169] According to historian Peter Kwong, "Chinese workers were systematically laid off by the shipping companies—fired with no warning, dropped off at any convenient port, and left to make their way home."[170] Many of these discharged sailors settled, some temporarily and others longer term, in the Navy Yard area of Brooklyn and in lower Manhattan.

In the same years, 3,000 Chinese seamen joined the NMU's 1936–37 seamen's strike for better working conditions, an equal wage scale, and equal rights to shore leave for Chinese seamen. Although the NMU's demands for working conditions were met, the labor action did not end the discriminatory denial of shore leave. One year later, the CSU led a strike to protest Dollar Lines' layoffs as a result of the Merchant Marine Act. Gaining the support of the NMU, the strike was successfully resolved with the company agreeing to pay six months' compensation to laid-off workers.[171] These successes were part of a gradual shift as more Americans started to see Chinese as potential allies.

Wartime conditions led to new restrictions on sailors, but also accelerated changing understandings of Chinese nationals, including Chinese seamen. In 1942, immigration officials noted that the "control of alien seamen has continued to be one of the Service's most difficult problems."[172] However, the control of *Asian* alien seamen was no longer the Immigration Service's primary problem. Officials were now focused on *enemy* alien seamen, particularly Germans and Italians. As early as 1939, two years before the United States entered the war, German and Italian seamen became stranded in New York because of war in Europe. These "distressed seamen" were the first individuals to be detained at Immigration and Naturalization Service (INS) internment camps that were later used to house Japanese and other enemy aliens. At the height of the internment program, the INS held a total of 1,285 Italian seamen as well as German and other enemy seamen.[173]

As attitudes against America's enemies hardened, allies were viewed more favorably. Chinese and South Asian seamen formed a large portion of the British merchant navy, with shipping recognized as both essential to the war effort and exceptionally dangerous work. In 1938, nearly one-third of the British merchant marine were nonwhite seamen, with approximately 10,000 Chinese and 40,000 South Asian seamen working on British ships. These numbers grew during the war.[174] Filipino sailors working in the U.S.

merchant marine were also viewed with increasing respect, especially after Japan attacked the Philippines in 1941 and the United States entered the war. Many Americans, who had previously seen Chinese as unauthorized immigrants who threatened their livelihood, increasingly viewed them as heroic fighters against the Japanese threat in Asia.[175] Although South Asian sailors supported the Allied war effort through their work, they were also colonial subjects seeking independence from Britain. As a result, their work did not always fit neatly with the rhetoric of the United Nations fighting fascism at sea.[176]

Chinese seamen continued to receive lower pay than white seamen and also endured worse employment conditions, including denial of shore leave. After Japan occupied Chinese seaports, where Chinese seamen had been able to secure shore leave, this denial became increasingly untenable. As they had done before, Chinese seamen both fought directly with white officers and challenged immigration regulation through legal means.[177]

In 1942, emboldened by their service in support of the war and without the option of shore leave in their home ports, several Chinese crews in New York were involved in different attempts to force their way ashore.[178] On April 11, thirty-seven Chinese sailors on board a ship at Staten Island challenged their denial of shore leave after four months at sea. They pushed their way off the ship and made it as far as the pier "but were rounded up with nothing worse than fisticuffs," transferred to immigration custody, and taken to Ellis Island.[179] On the same day, twelve Chinese seamen docked in Brooklyn confronted Captain Hilton Rowe in his quarters and angrily complained about their ongoing detention on board a United Nations freighter. Although officials had not required that they remain on board, the captain claimed that he was forbidden by U.S. immigration regulations to allow them to land. In response, Ling Young Chai attacked one of the ship's officers with a marlinspike. In the ensuing struggle, the captain shot and killed Ling, and an all-out fight ensued between white and Chinese crew members. One hundred police officers equipped with riot gear such as high-powered rifles and tear gas rushed to the area, and a large crowd gathered to watch the events. Varied authorities, including the New York INS office, were involved in the investigation of the Chinese seamen and the captain, who was acquitted of manslaughter charges.[180] Almost two months later, as twenty-five Chinese seamen attempted to leave their ship in Staten Island, two were shot and seriously wounded by a watchman.[181] Concerned about the impact of large numbers of desertions on the war effort, the British government pushed for an Alien Seaman program in May 1942. The program

Edward Gruber, "East Meets West. First Chinese Seamen to Get Shore Leave," Farm Security Administration-Office of War Information Photograph Collection, Library of Congress, Prints and Photographs (c. 1942).

reinforced policies of controlling sailors' contracts and detaining deserting seamen, with Ellis Island designating ten inspectors for its enforcement.[182]

Chinese seamen used their alliance with Britain and the United States—as well as the sympathy extended after Ling Young Chai's death—as an opening to press for changes in racist work practices.[183] Chu Hsueh-fan, president of the Chinese Association of Labor headquartered in New York, emphasized that "racial discrimination directed against the Chinese seriously impairs the war effort."[184] In June 1942, Chinese seamen secured new benefits from the British merchant marine, including an increase in wages, war bonuses, and the right to live in Britain temporarily "on the same basis as a British seaman." The agreement promised "equality of treatment," but—in raising wages from one-fifth to more than two-thirds of wages paid to white seamen—it did not grant full equality. In addition, shipping companies failed to provide many of the newly won benefits. Changing attitudes toward Allied merchant mariners helped Chinese seamen achieve more equal status with the British government.[185] Yet, they were still prevented from taking shore leave in the United States.

In August 1942, Chinese seamen finally secured their longtime goal of "free gangway" when the War Shipping Administration and the INS developed new regulations granting Chinese the right to shore leave on the same basis as other seamen.[186] These new practices brought Chinese seamen the freedom for which they had long fought, ending the central point of conflict between Chinese seamen, ships' officers, and immigration officials.[187] Photographs taken by the Office of War Information capture this moment as the "first Chinese seamen granted shore leave in wartime

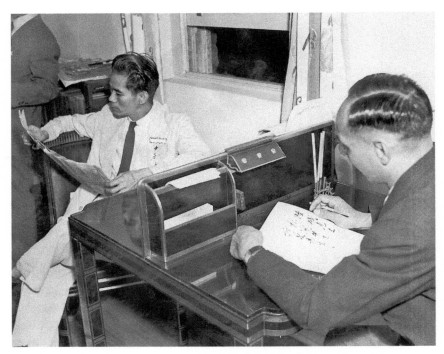

"Rendezvous for Chinese Seamen Opened Here. In the library and reading room of the clubhouse for those sailing on British and Dutch merchantmen," *New York Times*/Redux (1943).

America."[188] When a new seamen's club opened in the heart of Manhattan's Chinatown in 1943, public officials recognized the courageous contributions of Chinese sailors. Fiorello La Guardia, who had worked his way from Ellis Island inspector to congressman to mayor of New York City, and who had criticized immigration officials' summary deportation of Chinese seamen in 1927, noted that the club was "a step toward giving Chinese seamen the same rights as those enjoyed by seamen of other nations."[189]

Alongside this recognition of Chinese rights to shore leave, Chinese also secured the end of exclusion laws in 1943. Support for repeal was framed largely in terms of recognizing China as an ally and challenging Japanese propaganda against the United States in China. President Roosevelt urged repeal as "important in the cause of winning the war and of establishing a secure peace." However, liberals recognized that other Asian exclusion laws continued to stand.[190]

Asian seamen emphasized their common cause with Britain, the United States, and other Allied nations but did not hesitate to critique the racism that they experienced. "We left our families behind to serve on Allied ships because we wanted to do our share to gain final victory," one Chinese seaman wrote, "but British and Dutch ships distinguish between the white race and the yellow race and are prejudiced against us." The seaman concluded that Allied actions of discrimination and incarceration "do not differ from Axis dictatorial brutality."[191] In 1944, a Filipino merchant seaman went to court in a case against two Italian American soldiers who had broken into his Brooklyn home and stolen from him before they were shipped out to the Pacific theater. Peter Villanova noted that he shared a common cause with the men. "I am fighting for my country in bringing food and ammunition to the fighting fronts. Those two boys are out fighting for their country and they are avenging my people in the Philippines—my father, my sisters, my brothers." Villanova declined to press charges, saying, "Let those boys stay and fight."[192] Although merchant seamen played a supporting role to the military, they faced the highest casualty rates among all branches of service during World War II.[193] As allies, Villanova emphasized their shared dangers and shared work.

After the war's end, New York's maritime ports were increasingly eclipsed by the region's airports. Chinese, South Asian, and Filipino sailors continued to jump ship. And they were routinely detained by the immigration authorities.[194] Nonetheless, by the 1950s, Los Angeles and seaports outside the Northeast rose in relative significance as places of immigration and crew inspection, while New York declined.[195]

· · · · · ·

As workers who, by the very nature of their work, necessarily crossed national borders and docked in multiple ports around the world, sailors had established customary rights to shore leave and to choose the vessels on which they worked. However, in the late nineteenth and early twentieth centuries, as the proportion of Asians in the maritime workforce increased, so did the concerns about them voiced by restrictionist congressional representatives and white labor organizers. Asians were subject to new exclusion laws concerning their migration and new maritime laws attempting to control their work on board ships. These laws revealed U.S. concerns about the increasing number of Asian sailors in the maritime workforce and labor competition with white sailors, as well as the ways in which sailors used their status to illegally enter the United States in violation of exclusion and immigration laws. White maritime unions were concerned about labor competition and saw Chinese exclusion as a means to limit such competition.

Although Asian sailors did not have a different status under maritime laws, they were barred from U.S. residence by exclusion laws and were therefore treated more harshly than Europeans working on the same ships.

Asian sailors' experiences reveal the interconnections between racialized exclusion and maritime labor regimes at the beginning of the twentieth century. As a result, Asian sailors came under the Immigration Bureau's scrutiny through extra-statutory practices that attempted to prevent them from taking shore leave in U.S. ports. After the passage of the Seamen's Act in 1915, restrictionists in Congress incorporated sailors under the provisions of the 1917 Immigration Law. Subject to immigration inspection to ensure that they were bona fide sailors, medical inspection to ensure that they did not enter port with contagious diseases, and photographic identity card requirements to prove their right to shore leave, Asian sailors contested these new controls at every turn. They successfully challenged aspects of the law's implementation in Congress and in court.[196] They fought their detention on board the ship through their union representatives, through challenges to the ship's officers, and, in some cases, with their fists. They were suspected of selling their seamen's cards to unauthorized immigrants. And sometimes they simply destroyed their seamen's cards and settled in the United States in spite of exclusion and immigration laws.

As the major shipping port in the United States during this time, New York was at the center of these conflicts. As the detention and deportation center for New York, Ellis Island was the location at which sailors who violated immigration and exclusion restrictions were held. However, as the United States entered into World War II, the Immigration Service turned its attention to a new group of aliens and Ellis Island became a detention center for Japanese, German, and Italian enemy aliens.

# 5 Japanese Internees

New York Has a Concentration Camp of Its Own

. . . . . . . . . . . . . . . . . . . . . . . . . . . . . . . . . . . . . . . . . . . . . .

December 7, 1941. The city of New York prepared for war. Rear Admiral Adolphus Andrews made clear that "every possible step has been taken to protect [the] New York area from such an attack as surprised Pearl Harbor." "One of the first steps," the *New York Times* reported, was a roundup of Japanese residents. Just hours after the attack, more than one hundred armed Federal Bureau of Investigation (FBI) agents supported by squads of local police officers swept across the city detaining Japanese New Yorkers through the evening and into the night. The Japanese consulate at Rockefeller Center received the earliest attention. The consul general and staff members were taken to their homes by police officers and instructed not to leave without a police escort. The Nippon Club, an elite social center on Manhattan's Upper West Side, was also closed. Twelve Japanese club members were escorted home by police officers, with crowds silently watching them depart. Detectives next turned their attention to Japanese businesses across the five boroughs, monitoring restaurants while people finished their meals, then taking Japanese restaurant workers to their homes under police escort. By eight o'clock in the evening, special agents and local police had started their raids on private homes. By the end of the night, more than one hundred people had been arrested and taken to detention on Ellis Island, almost all of them Japanese men.[1]

One of the individuals caught up in these raids was Dr. Kinichi Iwamoto. Just before midnight, FBI agents and New York City police officers arrived at his home. Quickly gathering up a few travel essentials in a suitcase, Iwamoto was taken to the local precinct station. He and other detainees were booked as "prisoners of the Federal authorities," loaded into squad cars, and taken to the heavily guarded U.S. Courthouse in downtown Manhattan. As Iwamoto remembers, "We were arraigned, fingerprinted, and photographed with a number hanging from our neck." Detainees were interviewed and their responses were checked against FBI case histories that had been prepared months earlier. Most, like Iwamoto, were taken to the Barge Office at the Battery. Iwamoto was loaded onto a small government boat with about twenty other detainees and transported to Ellis Island. As he made this short journey, he noticed the silhouette of a soldier standing outside the cabin

"Japanese residents of New York on way to Ellis Island,"
*New York Times*/Redux (1942).

door and watched "his rifle and bayonet through the darkness." In the space
of a few hours, Iwamoto had been reduced from a medical doctor, husband,
and father of two young children to an "enemy alien."[2]

Another physician, Dr. Saburo Emy, had been detained earlier in the evening. Although he had immigrated to the United States at age fifteen, gradu-
ated from New York University, lived in the country for thirty-five years, and
had not returned to Japan for twenty-four years, Emy was considered suspect. "This," he remarked stoically as he was whisked onto the ferry to Ellis
Island, "is an unfortunate situation." A photo of two Japanese men en route
to Ellis Island on December 7 is captioned in part, "Note their grim expressions as they are shown a newspaper, showing headlines on the attack." The
raids continued for days, as carloads of Japanese prisoners were unloaded at
the courthouse. "Some of the Japanese were crestfallen," the *New York
Times* reported, "some were smiling, but none offered resistance."[3]

· · · · · ·

The arrest and detention of Japanese New Yorkers shows the ways in which
wartime actions against Japanese nationals were part of a broad array of

Two Japanese men aboard the ferry to Ellis Island after being taken into custody by federal agents on December 7 in a roundup in New York City. Bettman Collection via Getty Images (1941).

controls on Asians and other immigrants. By the 1940s, these controls had been consolidated. Immigration and Naturalization Service (INS) enemy alien confinement shows both the expansive reach of Asian exclusion and the ways in which exclusion became frayed at its edges, particularly at Ellis Island. Similar to Chinese exclusion, Japanese wartime confinement spread beyond its center in California. And, as it extended to New York, it was contested. The incorporation of Asian exclusion practices into wartime Japanese confinement was not limited to New York: Japanese nationals were rounded up and detained by the INS across the United States and were monitored by the immigration agency throughout the war. However, the linkages between enemy alien internment, Asian exclusion, and immigrant detention are particularly apparent at Ellis Island and at the moment that the United States' most famed immigration station became an enemy alien confinement site.

Japanese New Yorkers were quickly rounded up, detained at Ellis Island, and interned in INS camps because immigration officials were well trained in the work of alien detention. INS officials had longstanding experience interacting with aliens, interrogating arrivals to ensure they were entitled to enter the United States, and supervising detainees and deportees. Although Ellis Island officials did not participate in the FBI raids rounding up Japanese civilians, they had extensive experience raiding locations in Chinatown to enforce Chinese exclusion laws.[4] The Foley Square courthouse where Japanese were arraigned was the same office where Chinese were charged after being rounded up in raids; the Barge Office was the same location where the New York Chinese Division had previously been housed and Chinese deportees had once been taken for investigations before being transferred to Ellis Island. Immigration Commissioner Earl Harrison noted that many individuals appointed to run internment camps had "years of experience in dealing with non-citizens, singly and in groups."[5] Although INS officials sometimes wrestled with how best to undertake their varied responsibilities, their extensive experience with detention created a relatively seamless transition from general alien detention to enemy alien internment.

Immigration stations were well prepared to serve as internment camps because immigrant detention was already one of their central purposes: Ellis Island had dormitories segregated by gender, race, and immigration status, which readily allowed for the incorporation of new groups of alien detainees. INS officials noted their success in using existing detention centers such as Ellis Island and in acquiring outside facilities, so that "the Service was able to receive, secure, and care for all enemy aliens as rapidly as they were apprehended." Within two days, 1,000 people had been arrested; within one week, the number was more than 2,200; and, at points during 1942, nearly 7,000 enemy aliens were in INS detention.[6]

Ellis Island officials also had experience in interrogating aliens to determine whether they should be released. INS officials developed and administered the twenty-one-page enemy alien questionnaire, including questions related to immigration status.[7] Interrogations conducted by the civilian hearing boards to determine enemy alien loyalty shared similarities with immigration board hearings to prevent the entry of Chinese barred by exclusion laws. When internees were paroled, U.S. officials used practices developed to investigate Chinese immigrants to ensure that enemy aliens were complying with the terms of their parole.[8] When internees were transferred among internment camps or repatriated, the INS used the same trains that it had used for the past twenty years to deport immigrants, supervised by the same deportation officer, Edwin Kline.[9] The U.S. Border Patrol also assisted with expanded border enforcement, registering and paroling enemy aliens, and administering INS internment camps in the U.S. Southwest, North Dakota, and Montana.[10] Immigration enforcement practices were quickly deployed for the purposes of wartime confinement.

INS officials used their experience with immigration regulation to imprison, interrogate, and monitor enemy aliens on parole in New York. However, it was not only immigration practices that were extended to the regulation of enemy alien detainees. After the war ended, new practices developed to regulate enemy aliens, such as parole, were extended to the regulation of all immigrants. The INS's supervision of enemy alien internment highlights the central role of detention within immigration policy as well as the continuities between Asian exclusion and wartime confinement.

The use of Ellis Island as an internment camp shows that wartime Japanese confinement was not limited to the western United States but affected almost all Nikkei, people of Japanese descent with different citizenship statuses. Many aspects of the wartime confinement experience were similar for first-generation immigrant Issei arrested immediately after the attack on Pearl Harbor and for Nisei, U.S. citizens of Japanese descent who formed the majority of those forcibly relocated in the U.S. West. People's loyalties were questioned and their livelihoods were destroyed, communities were torn apart, and families were subject to severe financial hardship and emotional distress. However, Japanese in New York, where enemy alien internment was more contested, experienced a different environment. Some Nikkei New Yorkers believed they faced less racism than in the western United States; others disagreed. In New York, there were fewer discriminatory legal restrictions on Japanese, and there was more social integration. Nonetheless, Japanese nationals living in the city were rounded up in the same way as they were across the United States. Civilian hearing boards at Ellis Island attempted to consider the complexity of people's loyalties; however, these efforts sometimes led to arbitrary decisions. And families were separated as Issei men were arrested, but the possibility of parole allowed for family reunions and the ongoing presence of a Japanese community in New York. Despite this more contested enforcement, as with all forms of Asian exclusion, Japanese civilian confinement was not only about physical prevention of entry or separation from others in the United States but also about the enforcement of Asian unbelonging, the refusal to accept that Asian residents belonged in America.

## The Invisibility of Wartime Confinement on Ellis Island

The role of Ellis Island as a confinement site was widely known during World War II. "For the time being," the *Times* wrote in early 1942, "New York has a concentration camp of its own." ("Concentration camp" was one of many terms used in U.S. government and media sources to describe U.S. confinement sites before this term became primarily associated with Nazi camps.[11]) "It lies out in the harbor, in the upper bay, beneath the green pepper-pot domes of the big Kremlin on Ellis Island. On clear afternoons, if you turn a pair of binoculars on it from the Battery or Staten Island ferries, you can see some of its 600 enemy aliens marching round and round inside the wire of their bleak and treeless exercise ground."[12] Despite this recognition, the presence of Japanese and other enemy aliens at the immigration station has been largely ignored by historians of Ellis Island who view the station through the prism of arriving immigrants, as well as by historians of Japanese American wartime confinement who focus on the western United States.[13]

Historians of Japanese Americans during World War II have focused mostly on the forced relocation and incarceration of roughly 110,000 ethnic Japanese from the western United States after President Franklin Delano Roosevelt's Executive Order 9066 in February 1942.[14] The War Relocation Authority (WRA) was established one month later, hastily building a bureaucracy and constructing permanent prison camps. In addition to WRA confinement of ethnic Japanese, as many as 15,000 Japanese nationals were arrested by the FBI and interned by the Department of Justice under the INS Enemy Alien Program.[15] Many memoirs and histories mention the FBI's arrests of Issei fathers before WRA incarceration in the western United States.[16] However, INS enemy alien internment was not simply a precursor to WRA efforts: it was implemented across the country and throughout the war. This history is less well known.[17]

There are three key reasons that historians of wartime confinement have not focused on the INS Enemy Alien Program. First, most historians of Japanese Americans focus on larger communities in the West. When they turn their attention to wartime confinement, the defining event in Japanese American history, historians are more likely to attend to the ways in which substantial communities in California and Washington were affected.[18] Second, the numbers of Japanese nationals in INS custody were relatively small: they formed only about 12 percent of all ethnic Japanese incarcerated during World War II. Japanese nationals were also incarcerated by the

WRA, forming about one-third of all WRA prisoners.[19] Finally and most importantly, there was an established legal basis for Japanese enemy alien internment.[20] The individuals detained at Ellis Island from 1941 through 1948 were enemy aliens, citizens of a nation that was at war with the United States.[21] In contrast, two-thirds of those incarcerated by the WRA were Nisei, U.S. citizens who had not previously been subject to wartime incarceration. Scholars have largely focused on the forced removal and imprisonment of U.S. citizens because it was a new development in U.S. law that has since been rejected as a massive violation of civil rights motivated by racism, economic competition, and wartime fears.[22]

Although wartime confinement has commonly been referred to as Japanese American internment, many scholars draw a distinction between "internment," which refers to legally established practices of imprisoning enemy aliens, and "incarceration," which more accurately describes the forced relocation and imprisonment of U.S. citizens. This chapter follows such an approach, using "internment" to refer to enemy aliens who were interned, "incarceration" to describe the WRA imprisonment of western Nikkei, including U.S. citizens, and "confinement" to include all forms of wartime detention.[23]

In recent years, historians have paid more attention to the internment of German, Italian, Japanese, and other enemy aliens by the INS, as well as Latin American Axis nationals in the United States.[24] Yet, even within these histories, the role of Ellis Island as an internment camp is rarely mentioned. With the exception of the Densho Encyclopedia's online map, Ellis Island does not appear in any published map of confinement sites.[25] Written coverage is just as scant: Jeffery Burton and his coauthors' comprehensive overview of Japanese American confinement sites has one paragraph on Ellis Island, and Tetsuden Kashima's in-depth history of Japanese American imprisonment addresses Ellis Island just a few times. Paul Clark emphasizes the ways that Japanese enemy alien camps have been thought of as "the other camps" but describes "all of the major Japanese internment facilities" without mentioning Ellis Island.[26] When it is recognized, Ellis Island is understood as a temporary detention center for individuals awaiting determination on their cases. However, enemy aliens were interned at Ellis Island for extended periods of time, and the INS described it, along with other internment camps, as one of its "permanent detention stations."[27]

Ellis Island's role as an internment camp was most publicly acknowledged in 1998 when the Japanese American National Museum (JANM) brought an exhibition, *America's Concentration Camps: Remembering the*

*Japanese-American Experience,* to the Ellis Island Immigration Museum. The exhibition, which had previously been displayed at the JANM in Los Angeles, was adapted to include recognition of Ellis Island's role in wartime confinement. However, despite broad media attention to the exhibition, most articles focused on controversies about describing U.S. camps as concentration camps.[28] Only one mainstream media article mentioned the presence of Japanese internees on Ellis Island.[29] Again, the role of Ellis Island as a confinement site was overlooked.

At the same time that historians of Japanese Americans focus mostly on forced relocation and incarceration in the western United States, historians of Ellis Island pay almost no attention to enemy alien internment for one central reason: they view Ellis Island primarily as an immigration station. Histories typically focus on the period between 1892 and 1924, when Ellis Island was the central entry point for immigrants to the United States, particularly European immigrants. This approach obscures the station's related roles as a detention, deportation, and internment camp.[30]

### The Impacts of Enemy Alien Internment in Nikkei New York

Most of the individuals detained at Ellis Island were residents of the New York metropolitan area. Although smaller than many communities in the western United States in 1940, New York's 2,000 Japanese residents made it the largest Japanese community on the East Coast. During the war, with the forced relocation and incarceration of Japanese Americans in the West, the city grew in significance.[31]

Nikkei New Yorkers were more integrated into the city but also more dispersed and divided than in larger communities in the western United States. They were relatively few in number, relatively elite, and legally allowed to marry across racial lines; therefore, Japanese New Yorkers were more likely to be residentially and economically integrated as well as intermarried. Japanese lived throughout the city and in many suburbs.[32] In 1940, approximately one-third of the members of the New York Japanese Association had spouses who were not Japanese.[33]

Despite this integration, Japanese New Yorkers' immigrant and elite status also made them suspect. In New York, the Japanese community was composed of more first-generation residents as well as higher numbers of professionals than Japanese Americans as a whole. In 1940, 70 percent of Japanese living in New York City were foreign-born compared with

43 percent in San Francisco.[34] In addition, about one-third of Japanese New Yorkers were Kaishain, employees of Japanese companies and banks who worked in the United States for roughly five years before returning to Japan. U.S. authorities were particularly concerned about Issei with extensive professional connections in Japan. Even though the community was relatively elite, it included class divisions. About one-third of Japanese New Yorkers worked in domestic service. Others owned restaurants, tearooms, boardinghouses, and groceries or worked in these Japanese-owned establishments.[35]

Some New Yorkers believed that they faced less racism and "were treated better than some of the Japanese elsewhere."[36] Others emphasized that they still faced discrimination. Of his thirty years in the United States, New York Buddhist leader and journalist Yeita Sokei-An Sasaki wrote, "I have been subjected to daily humiliation, as regularly as I have eaten my three meals a day."[37] The evening after the bombing of Pearl Harbor, a middle-aged man, Teddy Hara, was standing in front of the boardinghouse where he lived in Midtown Manhattan when he was attacked by three white men and hit repeatedly with the butt of a gun until he was unconscious. Hara's injuries were so severe that he lost his sight in one eye. That same night, the windows of the Taijo Trading Company at 121 Fifth Avenue were smashed.[38]

Just as Japanese New Yorkers' integration did not shield them from discrimination, violence, or internment, it also did not protect them from being treated more harshly than German and Italian enemy aliens. Even though all enemy aliens had the same legal status, they were not treated the same. Whether they were short-term visitors or long-term residents, Japanese nationals were more likely to be investigated, arrested, and detained than other enemy aliens. Buddhist priest Hozen Seki was arrested and taken to Ellis Island in September 1942. His biographer noted that the FBI "seemed to show respect" for Reverend Seki and treated him "in a gentlemanly manner without any high-handed attitude."[39] But this respectful treatment was shaded with suspicion.

Despite assurances that raids were targeted at specific individuals, every Japanese person was considered suspect. "Most, if not all, of the estimated 2,000 to 2,5000 Japanese nationals living in New York," according to the *Times*, "were to be taken into custody." Every one of the 134 Japanese nationals living in New Jersey was investigated by the FBI. "After the outbreak of the war," one Japanese New Yorker noted, "every Issei in the metropolitan area had been visited and investigated by the FBI."[40]

Initially, raids focused heavily on Japanese. Nationwide, there were 600,000 registered Italian nationals, 300,000 Germans, and 90,000 Japanese; however, Japanese nationals formed about half of those arrested at both the national level and in New York.[41] The numbers of Japanese immigrants arrested in New York were especially high compared with the small Japanese community. Index cards in the Department of Justice Records at the National Archives in College Park may not be complete, but they identify at least 440 Japanese enemy aliens detained at Ellis Island.[42] Throughout 1942, New York arrests increasingly focused on Germans, who became the majority of internees on Ellis Island. In total, between 22,000 and 32,000 foreign nationals were imprisoned under the Enemy Alien Program. Of these, as many as 15,000 were Japanese nationals.[43] These proportions reflect Americans' special concerns about Japanese residents, both because of Japan's attack on the United States and because of long-standing discrimination against Asians.

The *New York Times* reported plans to take almost all Japanese nationals in the city into custody but acknowledged that some of these detainees were "Japanese who were born in the United States."[44] In other words, they were U.S. citizens. As this confusion suggests, some U.S. citizens of Japanese descent were picked up during FBI investigations and held at Ellis Island. An INS memo about arrested aliens noted that the "first task should be to clear those who are citizens."[45] Typically, if U.S. citizen Nisei were brought in for questioning, they were released immediately.[46] However, in some cases Nisei were not recognized as U.S. citizens.

U.S. citizens Naoye Suzuki and Nori Sato were both interned at Ellis Island, each on two separate occasions, and later ordered to leave the Eastern Defense Command. When Suzuki was apprehended in January 1942, he was immediately transferred to Ellis Island. Seven months later, after he realized through his own research that he could not legally be held as a U.S. citizen, he was released. Yet, officials continued to question his citizenship and his loyalty because he had registered with the Japanese consulate, worked for a Japanese company, and was a Kibei, born in the United States but educated in Japan. In November 1942, three months after his release, Suzuki was again interned at Ellis Island. He was finally released in March 1943 and was excluded from the Eastern Defense Command for security reasons. Nori Sato was held twice at Ellis Island for periods of eight and five months, punctuated by "a brief interlude of freedom." Like Suzuki, Sato was a Kibei whose U.S. citizenship was challenged because he worked for the Japanese government and the Mitsubishi Company and, according to a report from the Friends' Service Committee, had "contacts with enemy alien Japanese before Pearl Harbor." This formulation ignored the fact that Japanese nationals were not enemy aliens until the United States entered the war after the bombing of Pearl Harbor. Japanese Americans were frequently assumed to be Japanese aliens in citizenship, culture, and loyalty. These assumptions contributed to U.S. citizens' feelings of alienation and unbelonging. Suzuki commented that "he wants to be loyal to America, but his experiences to date have brought him into [contact with] few Caucasian Americans who either believe him or want him to be loyal to America."[47]

With the onset of war, many Nikkei experienced wrenching conflicts about their identity and loyalty. Some were unequivocally supportive of the United States. Organizations such as the Japanese American Citizens League and the New York–based Japanese American Committee for Democracy (JACD) sent telegrams to government officials affirming their members' loyalty to the United States.[48] In one of the more unusual expressions of loyalty, a doctor in suburban White Plains, New York, attempted to commit hara-kiri with a pocket knife because he believed that "my country has done wrong in attacking the United States."[49] Some, including diplomats and militant nationalists, strongly supported Japan.[50] Ordinary Japanese New Yorkers also expressed their belief that Japan was justified in the Sino-Japanese war and that the United States had been pressured by Great Britain to enter the war.[51] However, many others were not sure of their allegiances or had none. Yuki Kijima candidly acknowledged that she didn't know where her sympathies lay: she felt loyalty to Japan but had lived in the United States for many years.[52] Kyuzaburo Saito fought for the United States in World War I but did not want to take up arms against Japan. He expressed his hope that neither country would win but that "both would tire out and quit."[53] These complex responses did not fit neatly into many Americans' understanding of mutually exclusive loyalty to either the United States or Japan.

Questions of loyalty were compounded by U.S. laws that forbade Asian naturalization. Japanese immigrants were enemy aliens not only because Japan was at war with the United States but also because Asian immigrants were barred from naturalizing based on racist assumptions that they were inassimilable and unfit for U.S. citizenship. Although Germans and Italians had the option of becoming U.S. citizens, Japanese immigrants did not.[54] For Issei who wanted to become U.S. citizens, exclusion and racism created feelings of alienation and unbelonging. Kinichi Iwamoto, for example, felt like a "man without a country."[55] Other New Yorkers negotiated exclusion by drawing a distinction between legal and emotional citizenship, emphasizing that emotional citizenship was more meaningful. The pastor of Shozo Hamada's church wrote to U.S. authorities stating that "although he cannot become an American citizen in name, he is a true American at heart."[56] U.S. citizenship did not prevent the incarceration of Japanese Americans in the West, but it was still valued by many Issei New Yorkers.

Japanese internment not only created conflicts within individuals but also disrupted the home lives of Nikkei families on the East Coast. In the West, families experienced extreme dislocation as entire communities were forced to relocate. Although parents often faced difficulties maintaining their parental roles in the camp environment, families were generally allowed to stay together. However, almost all enemy aliens interned by the INS in New York and across the United States were men. In the East, families were more likely to be separated because spouses had different citizenship statuses. Kinichi Iwamoto's wife was a U.S. citizen of German descent and his two children were American-born citizens, but Iwamoto was subject to arrest and detention because he was a Japanese national.[57]

Women formed just one-fifth of the Issei population of New York City, but they were far fewer of those detained. According to existing records, only four Japanese women were held at Ellis Island, and they were held for less time than was typical for Issei men.[58] Issei women were less likely to be investigated, because they did not have religious or community leadership roles, or professional contacts with other Japanese, all positions that marked them as potentially disloyal and dangerous in the eyes of the FBI. However, the very low numbers of women interned by the INS also emphasizes that WRA incarceration was extraordinary, not only because it confined U.S. citizens but also because it imprisoned entire families, including women and children.

Families in New York struggled financially and emotionally during internment. Japanese Americans in the West had their financial livelihoods destroyed by incarceration and lived at near-poverty levels in WRA camps. Outside of the West, the internment of only one family member, typically the wage earner, created different financial problems. Although enemy aliens' assets were frozen while they were detained, family members were allowed to receive some funding from these accounts. Kinichi Iwamoto's wife, daughter, and son received a monthly allowance of one hundred dollars while he was on Ellis Island.[59] Other families faced major hardships if they did not have sufficient savings. The Federal Council of Churches of Christ in America provided assistance to Japanese including, according to one of its officers, "food and housing for families which have been left behind when their men had been taken over to Ellis Island." Ten months after Toru Matsumoto was first picked up and detained at Ellis Island, his parole case was expedited because his wife and son had no financial support and were being cared for by friends. Matsuhei Matsuo's wife was reported by U.S. officials as "seriously ill," "unable to speak English," "destitute," "helpless," and "alone"; nonetheless, her husband was repatriated to Japan. These difficulties were even worse for families in which the spouses were not legally married, as husbands were only allowed to withdraw funds from frozen accounts to support "legitimate families." Although they did little to help, immigration officials advised women to go to state agencies for assistance, expressed their sympathy, and referred to "many tragic situations which arose due to the internment of the heads of families."[60]

The emotional difficulties, even shame, of internment may have been greater than the financial struggles. While Kinichi Iwamoto was detained at Ellis Island, a neighbor reported to the immigration authorities that his wife kept her apartment shades drawn. The neighbor suggested Mrs. Iwamoto might have thought she was "under observation of some sort and was possibly a little nervous because of her husband's apprehension."[61] The neighbor's comment reveals that Mrs. Iwamoto *was* being observed; however, the drawn shades could have meant many things, including embarrassment, isolation, or fears for the safety of her family. When Saburo Emy was arrested, his mixed-race Nisei wife had an eleven-month-old child and was heavily pregnant with her second. Describing herself as a "patriotic American citizen," she begged the attorney general to expedite her husband's hearing date, explaining, "I need him so much, especially now." Emy was not released immediately, but he was allowed to leave Ellis Island on parole two months later, after his wife had given birth.[62]

Some families faced such difficulties that they sought to be together even if this meant family internment. Satomi Seki, wife of Buddhist minister Hozen Seki, asked for her seven-year-old son to join his father at Ellis Island because he was being insulted by his friends and attacked by strangers. Several white children had beaten the boy, calling him a "Jap" and threatening to kill him, even though he emphasized that he was "American same as you are." As Hozen Seki was awaiting transfer away from Ellis Island, he begged for special consideration to be reunited in a family camp. "As you know," he wrote to U.S. officials, "the child's tender heart under these circumstances in his young age will affect his character. If he becomes anti-American through these circumstances, I can not tell how sad and sorry

I shall be." His American-born wife was concerned about being interned and worked instead for her husband's parole. Hozen Seki, however, remained interned and alone throughout the war.[63]

Toru Matsumoto, a Christian community leader detained at Ellis Island, explained that common-law and interracial marriages were particularly vulnerable to the pressures of internment. A few women left their Japanese common-law husbands, while some Japanese men denied these relationships to protect their common-law wives from accusations of disloyalty. Matsumoto wrote of marriages between Japanese and U.S. citizens that "some such marriages were broken up, but others were more firmly established."[64] Although they were rarely detained at Ellis Island, women, in different ways and with varying degrees of success, struggled to keep their families together during their husbands' internment.

While Japanese New York was being torn apart by arrests, most Americans found these raids justified and even reassuring. Immediately after the bombing of Pearl Harbor, New Yorkers swamped FBI and police station switchboards with descriptions of suspicious activities by potential enemies. There were so many calls that the telephone operators couldn't handle the volume and additional operators had to be called in. Although these unfounded suspicions were investigated, they didn't yield any useful information.[65] Nevertheless, the FBI raids helped assuage many Americans' concerns. A 1949 report compared the ethnic tensions during World War I to the common bonds of World War II, explaining that "the remarkable unanimity brought about in this country by the attack on Pearl Harbor and the efficient work of the Federal Bureau of Investigation in rounding up suspicious aliens together produced a remarkably calm internal situation."[66] Without any irony, the authors acknowledged how Japanese and other aliens were excluded from this "remarkable unanimity" and how, in fact, it was built on their arrests.

### The Evaluation of Japanese Loyalty in Ellis Island Hearings

During the war, the INS operated twenty-five facilities at which Japanese and other enemy aliens were housed.[67] These existed in addition to the larger and better-known WRA camps. Although the vast majority of internees were men, four INS camps, including Ellis Island, had special facilities for the internment of women, and one additional camp, Crystal City, could accommodate families.[68] Diplomatic personnel were detained at luxury resorts such as White Sulphur Springs, West Virginia, and Hot Springs,

Virginia.[69] Wartime responsibilities led the immigration agency to expand its personnel from 6,885 to 8,500 during the 1942 fiscal year, enlarge its permanent facilities, and increase space at two specially purposed "large detention camps used for aliens awaiting deportation."[70] Although a significant expansion, these figures also show that the INS already had substantial capacity to regulate aliens.

As an INS detention center, Ellis Island housed many groups of detainees with different legal statuses. These varied forms of detention were in contrast to WRA camps, where almost every individual was a person of Japanese descent forcibly relocated from the Western Defense Command.[71] Different groups of INS detainees were housed in separate areas, although there was some interaction and communication between them. Men were segregated from women and children. Enemy aliens were segregated from immigrants and sailors. And, among enemy aliens, Japanese, Germans, and Italians were segregated from one another.[72]

The types of detainees housed at Ellis Island changed during the course of the war. Immediately after the raids, most of the detainees appear to have been Japanese. As the war progressed, larger numbers of Germans were interned. On June 30, 1943, Ellis Island held 340 German prisoners, some of whom were U.S.-born children and about 66 of whom were women, many with the same family names. In contrast, there were only 18 Japanese, 10 Italians, 2 Polish Brazilians, and 1 Romanian, all of whom were men.[73] Earlier in the war, there were many more enemy aliens than other detainees. However, by 1945 there were about twice as many immigrants awaiting deportation as enemy aliens.[74] Although Ellis Island was well equipped for the detention of aliens, the segregation of these varied groups created additional complexity for immigration officials.

Despite the war, there was still limited immigration, and some arrivals were held at Ellis Island for investigation before being admitted. In addition, wartime exigencies meant that stowaways and many unauthorized immigrants could not be deported but were detained at the station. In 1942, more than 200 unauthorized immigrants—most of them sailors—were detained at Ellis Island. In 1943, 200 Indonesian sailors were detained at Ellis Island after they had left their vessels to seek wages equal to those of white maritime workers. A similar number were held at the station in 1945 when they jumped ship after the war's end to avoid transporting munitions to Dutch colonists fighting against Indonesian independence.[75]

Within the Enemy Alien Program, individuals were detained until they received a hearing from the Civilian Hearing Board under the authority of the U.S. attorney. In this way, enemy aliens were afforded more due process than those imprisoned by the WRA. The board made one of three recommendations: release with minimal oversight, parole with regular supervision, or internment. Detainees were also asked whether they requested repatriation to their home countries. Although detention was described as temporary, enemy aliens were detained for much longer than the few days that European immigrants arriving at Ellis Island were typically held for secondary inspection or the weeks of detention experienced by Chinese arrivals. Most aliens received a hearing on their case within thirty days but had to wait several months more for a decision. Case reviews were based on extensive FBI reports and a twenty-one-page questionnaire completed by detainees.[76]

Asian American studies scholar Bob Kumamoto has explored the ways that the FBI assessed Nikkei loyalty in the decade preceding the United States' entry into World War II. Historian Eric Muller has detailed the "loyalty bureaucracy" implemented in WRA camps after 1942, and Mae Ngai has shown how this bureaucracy fostered complex responses, including Japanese American renunciation of U.S. citizenship. As these scholars show, different branches of the federal government, such as the War Department, the FBI, and the WRA, varied and even clashed in their understandings of Nikkei loyalty.[77] Muller emphasizes that these various agencies failed to establish a satisfactory definition of loyalty, either collectively or individually. "Each agency's conclusions about Japanese American loyalty," Muller argues, "ultimately reflected much more about the agency and the context in which it was operating than about the American citizens whose cases it was judging."[78] However, none of these historians focuses on INS enemy alien hearings.

Most New York hearings were conducted at Ellis Island, but some were held at the U.S. Courthouse in Manhattan.[79] In New York, as a result of these hearings, half of all recorded Japanese detainees were interned, one-quarter were paroled, and almost one-fifth were released without parole. The remaining number do not have complete information recorded. On average, Japanese who were viewed as no security risk were detained at Ellis Island for forty-seven days while the determination that they could be released without parole was being made. Japanese who were viewed as potentially dangerous stayed on Ellis Island for about three months (104 days) until they were transferred to another internment camp. Those who spent the longest time on Ellis Island were Japanese who were seen as lower risk but required supervision: they were detained for an average of almost five months (142 days) before they were paroled. A limited number were released from parole during the war; most were monitored through November 1945 and others until 1946. The average time that Japanese New Yorkers spent under parole restrictions was 961 days, more than two and a half years.[80]

Although all hearing boards varied in their efforts to evaluate Issei loyalty, Japanese at Ellis Island appear to have received fairer hearings than those at other stations. Like all enemy aliens, Ellis Island detainees were not entitled to counsel; however, unlike Issei apprehended in the western United States, they were detained closer to their families and were allowed to call character witnesses.[81] U.S. officials generally viewed American and Japanese cultural identities as mutually exclusive and assumed that Japanese cultural identity was a sign of potential disloyalty to the United States. But authorities in New York were often more understanding of the complexities of Japanese loyalty, with many factors influencing their decisions.[82] Despite these differences, loyalty hearings at Ellis Island, like loyalty hearings at other stations, were often arbitrary and exposed the fragility of integration.[83]

Ellis Island hearing boards considered varied factors in deciding whether a detainee was loyal and received parole. However, examples of U.S. acculturation—such as Christian beliefs, membership in interracial groups, or connections to the U.S. Armed Forces—were the central consideration. Boards viewed family members in the United States, especially white or American wives, as a sign of American affiliation, while they considered family members in Japan as potential evidence of disloyalty. Saburo Emy's professed loyalty to the United States and his devotion to his American family were factors cited in the decision to grant him parole.[84] Takashi Katsuki was paroled after four months' detention at Ellis Island, even though his father was a retired Japanese naval officer, because his marriage to a white American Christian woman had caused him to become estranged from his Japanese family.[85] Kayao Kawano was confined for about a year and a half at Ellis Island, Fort Meade, and Fort Missoula before he was paroled. U.S. authorities eventually determined it was "doubtful if he would be dangerous to internal security, especially with an Irish wife who seems to influence him decidedly."[86] Yet, such decisions were not always consistent. Despite his white American wife and U.S.-born daughter, Iwajiro Noda was viewed with suspicion. His hearing board claimed that he had "no ties in America not easily removable" and ordered him interned. In 1943 he was repatriated.[87]

In their efforts to avoid detention or secure release from parole, some detainees emphasized family members serving in, or their own work for, the U.S. Armed Forces. Nobuji Ashikaga's wife asked for her husband to be released from parole, noting their three sons serving in the U.S. Army. Toshio Kono was considered for deportation after the war, but his role as an instructor teaching Japanese to U.S. Army officers at Yale contributed to an immigration decision allowing him to stay in the United States.[88] The fact that Issei were threatened with detention and deportation despite family and personal military service also suggests the arbitrary quality of these hearings.

Aspects of the enemy alien hearings paralleled Chinese immigration interrogations that were developed and expanded starting in the 1880s to prevent the entry of Chinese barred by exclusion laws. In both cases, U.S. officials were concerned about Asian duplicity. Similar to Chinese who were required to provide two credible white witnesses during immigration investigations, Japanese detainees sought white witnesses of "high social standing" to bolster their cases during loyalty hearings. In some cases, in the words of the hearing board, witnesses of "a very high order" contributed to less restrictive decisions. Buddhist priest Yeita Sokei-An Sasaki, for example, was ordered interned in 1942, but after a rehearing featuring "impressive" and "influential" witnesses, he was paroled. This was despite evidence of "anti-American" writings.[89]

If they were recommended for parole, Japanese detainees also needed a "reputable citizen" to supervise their behavior. Most, but not all, New Yorkers were able to secure parole sponsors. In contrast to the western United States, Japanese detained on Ellis Island were more likely to have lived among white neighbors and friends who supported their release. Elite status, which could be used against detainees if their links to Japanese diplomatic or business circles made them suspect, could also be helpful to detainees if they had connections to white Americans. In February 1942, Fred (Seiki) Naito, a worker in domestic service, was approved for parole. However, because his potential sponsors were joining the armed forces, traveling for business, or already supervising other Japanese parolees, the board refused to approve a sponsor. In June 1942, six months after he was first brought to Ellis Island and four months after he should have been paroled, Naito was interned. He was not released until January 1946.[90]

In the western United States, WRA administrators generally evaluated membership in U.S.-based organizations as signs of U.S. loyalty and involvement in Japanese social clubs or associations as potential indicators of disloyalty.[91] However, in New York, these distinctions were less clear. New York hearing boards viewed membership in the New York–based JACD favorably, in part because the interracial organization adopted the paradoxical position of both promoting adherence to American democratic values and supporting WRA incarceration.[92] As noted in chapter 1, *Nihonjinkai* or Japanese Associations represented the Japanese community in the United States, working with the Japanese government to facilitate immigration and to oppose anti-Japanese restrictions. Membership in the Japanese Association was viewed as a sign of potential disloyalty because the association received funding from the Japanese consulate; however, involvement in the New York Japanese Association was judged less harshly than membership in the larger branches on the West Coast.[93] More surprisingly, a New York hearing board initially recommended a form of parole for Kuro Murase despite his leadership role in the ultranationalist Hokoku Dan, although this decision was overturned by U.S. attorney general Francis Biddle.[94] These rulings suggest that Issei New Yorkers were treated somewhat leniently in regard to organizational memberships. However, while the New York hearing boards attempted to understand the complexity of Issei loyalty through their consideration of family, friends, and organizational memberships, these efforts were inconsistent.

The enemy alien hearings were based on extensive FBI reports and a twenty-one-page questionnaire completed by detainees. Unlike the relatively brief Chinese exclusion interviews conducted at Ellis Island, these were typically very detailed. Kinichi Iwamoto's experience was fairly typical. Iwamoto recalled that during his hearing, "my family background in Japan and my whole life history in Japan and the USA was thoroughly scrutinized." Iwamoto was a doctor, and his largely Japanese patient base, including many consular officials, initially raised FBI inspectors' suspicions that he might be dangerous and disloyal to the United States. But Iwamoto gave more mundane reasons for preferring Japanese patients: "He had difficulty making English speaking patients understand him." Iwamoto had two witnesses attest to his character: a doctor and a U.S. Air Force major. He also received support from colleagues at the hospitals where he worked, carefully noting that "all those who signed letters were of non-German and non-Italian descent."[95]

Despite these recommendations, Iwamoto was not paroled until March 27, 1942, almost four months after he was first imprisoned. His detention, however, was shorter than the average five months for Ellis Island parolees. While on parole, Iwamoto was free to practice medicine again. He was required to report regularly to his sponsor, a fellow doctor at the Lutheran Hospital, and was not allowed to associate with other Japanese. An FBI agent visited his office every two weeks for about five months, after which Iwamoto "was finally freed from his vigilance."[96] In a different case, Suki Ports remembered her mother calling her father for permission each time that she planned to leave the house. "My sister and I thought, 'What an obedient wife,'" she recalled. "We only learned later she was calling the FBI."[97]

In December 1943, Iwamoto was released from parole, earlier than most Issei. His case file repeatedly mentions his lack of resistance to parole restrictions, suggesting that Iwamoto's model compliance was important to his release.[98] During their hearings, some detainees challenged the ways in which Japanese were viewed as potentially disloyal. However, they needed to be very careful about how they expressed any criticisms of the arrest and detention process. For Iwamoto and others, compliance was equated with loyalty, and loyalty was key to avoiding internment.

Some individuals who were paroled were required to resettle outside New York. The two U.S. citizens held at Ellis Island were forced to settle in Chicago. Naoye Suzuki found employment at the University of Chicago, while Nori Sato worked in a low-wage job at the Lanzit Corrugated Box Company.[99] In New York, Sato had an active social life mingling with elite Japanese and attending shows "almost every day." However, after he was forced out of the city, he struggled to find a good job and make friends. "My health is very bad now," he reported. "I lost so much weight in detention [at Ellis Island], and I am run down very much." He was desperately lonely, unable to make connections with white Americans who viewed him with suspicion, and unable to associate with Japanese as he had been warned that he would be imprisoned if he was "seen hanging around with suspicious Japanese."[100]

New York's Japanese community was small yet important, integrated into the life of the city and surrounding suburbs. Japanese New Yorkers were allowed to include witnesses in their hearings and better able than Japanese on the West Coast to secure witnesses, as well as reputable citizens to supervise them if they were paroled. Established residents were more likely to be acculturated and even intermarried, but elite Issei were also viewed with suspicion because of their connections to important Japanese officials and businessmen. New York INS officials attempted to understand the complex situations of Japanese civilians during their hearings. However, the impacts of wartime confinement on Japanese New Yorkers were substantial and painful, reinforcing a sense of exclusion and unbelonging.

## The Administration of Enemy Alien Confinement at Ellis Island

Although enemy alien and immigration detainees had varied legal statuses and were physically separated from one another, they shared common routines and experiences of boredom. They also shared the anxiety of waiting for their hearings, then for the outcomes. By January 1942, a daily routine was established at Ellis Island. The day began early with a clanging bell. One internee remembers the day starting at 5:30 A.M. and another recalled the bell at 6:20 A.M. "I don't know why," Naoye Suzuki commented later, "there was nothing to do."[101] After detainees got ready, they were marched to the dining room by guards. Breakfast was served at 7:30 A.M.[102]

Replicating the racial segregation of Europeans and Asians that existed on the island before the war, Germans, Italians, and Japanese were housed in separate dormitories. However, enemy aliens used the dining room at the same time, with Germans and Italians eating in one area while Japanese dined in another. Lunch was served at noon and dinner at 5:15 P.M.[103] Kinichi Iwamoto described the food as "adequate" and the rooms as "comfortably heated."[104] Others were more critical. "The food was terrible," Yae Aihara recalled. "The only good food I remember was a shriveled up orange."[105] Suzuki also commented that Japanese were not served rice, but "the Germans liked it because we didn't eat the pig knuckles and sauerkraut." When the guards were not looking, they shared their plates with the Germans.[106]

Both immigrant and enemy alien detainees had few responsibilities on the island, and time passed slowly. They occupied the hours by playing cards, chess, or other games. They were allowed to read newspapers and to access the Ellis Island library, which offered books in thirty languages. Internees took care of their own laundry, sticking their wet shirts to the white tiled walls to press them and catching them before the dried garments fell to the floor. Church services interrupted the monotony for Christians, including visits from the Japanese Methodist Church in Manhattan. In later years, volunteers from the American Friends Service Committee worked on the island, assisting in various ways, including providing Christmas packages and fruitcakes to detainees. As the war progressed, detainees were required to work in areas such as the kitchen, cooking food for their INS guards as well as other prisoners.[107]

INS officials met the internees' basic needs but also implemented restrictions on enemy aliens that were not required for other immigrant detainees. On alternating Wednesdays, short personal visits were allowed. Iwajiro Noda's daughter was able to visit her father twice in the month after he was arrested, but each visit lasted only about ten minutes. In the interim, detainees were allowed to write letters and even to telephone. However, the letters were censored and the telephone conversations were carefully supervised. Internees were provided with basic necessities, such as toothpaste and laundry detergent.[108] And if they had their own funds, they were allowed to buy noncontraband personal items such as stamps, stationery, and tobacco.[109] Iwamoto recalled that an American woman volunteered to run errands for some of the men, purchasing various items.[110]

Internees clearly experienced hardships and recognized that they were being imprisoned. Guards were posted in the corners of the Great Hall and around the station and were, as one detainee remembers, "surly, bored, unfriendly."[111] At Ellis Island, one of the most significant problems was overcrowding. Military bunks "were squeezed into an immensely large hall where 150 to 200 people were confined."[112] The average number of individuals detained each day increased from 236 in 1940, to 347 in 1941, 666 in 1942, and 828 in 1943. These numbers stayed steady at 829 in 1944, dropping to 786 by 1945.[113] In 1942, the INS requested quick movement on Ichio Kushihashi's case because of overcrowding at Ellis Island. However, Kushihashi remained on Ellis Island for five months before he was paroled to his father's farm in Nebraska.[114]

Amid this overcrowding, detainees were initially allowed outside to get some fresh air and exercise for just two to three hours each week.[115] By 1942, prisoners were allowed to exercise daily after 3 P.M.[116] Behind the fencing originally built for detained immigrants, the prisoners walked in circles around the windy exercise yard, "their overcoats flapping about their legs and their collars turned up about their ears." According to the *New York Times*, "that endless circle of tramping men is the trade-mark of a concentration camp."[117] When it was especially crowded, men had to play cards or other games on their bunk beds. At night, they slept on the same bed where they had spent most of the day.[118] Lights were turned out at 10 P.M.[119]

Immigration and other government officials understood that their work was not simply detention but also imprisonment. Detention can be defined as restraining people's movements temporarily, often while awaiting the outcome of a legal ruling such as a decision to admit or deport an immigrant or to parole an enemy alien. Imprisonment or incarceration suggests a longer-term detention, often after such a legal decision has been made. As early as July 1941, plans were drawn up to house enemy aliens in "incarceration quarters regularly used for federal prisoners."[120]

Officials explicitly compared their work to that of U.S. prisons. Nick Collaer, chief of the Detention and Deportation Service, noted concerns that Ellis Island had a lower staff-to-prisoner ratio than that recommended by the Federal Bureau of Prisons. He also acknowledged that the INS's work at Ellis Island was more complex because, as already noted, the station housed different types of detainees, with each group requiring segregation from one another. In addition, because Ellis Island housed enemy aliens, the detention center needed to meet the standards of the Geneva Convention. At the same time, Collaer acknowledged that most INS prisoners had not committed crimes but were law-abiding people who had been caught up in larger political events. Therefore, although guards surveilled their prisoners to ensure that they were not engaged in disloyal activities, they were not especially concerned about violence or crime.[121]

The work of imprisonment was apparent at Ellis Island. In 1944, the INS employed 157 people at Ellis Island, 111 of whom were guards.[122] In contrast to the period before 1924, when most staff had been employed in processing immigrants, the high ratio of guards to other staff shows how much the immigration station had become a prison. Although the vast majority of Ellis Island staff were employed as guards, INS officials remained concerned that the guard force was understaffed.

Historian Paul Clark has argued that INS internment camps had less conflict than WRA camps because they were managed by experienced immigration officials and housed only aliens, leading to fewer generational conflicts. Nevertheless, there were significant problems at INS camps, including strikes, beatings, and the shooting deaths of three internees at Lordsburg and Fort Sill.[123]

At Ellis Island, Japanese and other inmates sometimes challenged the everyday indignities of their confinement, and these challenges occasionally rose to the level of formal meetings and strikes. In August 1942, four Japanese bridged their segregation to attend a mass meeting of almost 400 detainees in the German dormitory. Although there were few recorded interactions between different groups of detainees, the Japanese nationalists shared common cause with the Nazi supporters who eulogized recently executed German saboteurs, gave Nazi salutes, and sang the "Nazi marching song."[124] In September 1942, a small number of Japanese detainees went on a hunger strike to protest new restrictions on their activities.[125] There was no public mention of these events because of a news blackout on such acts of resistance.[126]

These conflicts continued even after the war. By July 1944, almost all kitchen work was done by Germans who had been permitted internment at Ellis Island so that they could be close to their families in New York. However, after the war ended in Europe in May 1945, they became increasingly upset about their ongoing detention. In July, forty German kitchen workers went on strike, arguing that they were paid too little and that they should not have to cook for all the Ellis Island detainees as well as INS employees. The Germans' strike was quashed after INS officials threatened them with guardhouse confinement and transfers to another internment camp.[127] As late as 1948, 169 German internees who were fighting against their repatriation remained at Ellis Island.[128]

## The Implementation of Repatriation from Ellis Island

Among all Issei detained at Ellis Island, about 40 percent were repatriated.[129] This figure was higher than national averages, reflecting the significant number of Japanese diplomats, businessmen, and temporary residents in New York. As New York was the only U.S. port from which ships departed as part of a prisoner repatriation and exchange program, repatriates from other regions of the country were also brought to Ellis Island briefly before their departure. During the war, two repatriation voyages were facilitated on the neutral Swedish liner, the *Gripsholm*. The first left the city in June 1942 and the second in September 1943. New York was selected for the program because more potential repatriates lived on the East Coast and because officials needed an intermediate location at which to make the prisoner exchanges: the first was conducted in Maputo, Mozambique, and the second in Goa, India. Although operating ships in wartime waters was dangerous, Japanese and U.S. officials were both keen to facilitate exchanges in order to ensure that their diplomats were employed during a time of crisis and that their citizens were returned home safely.[130]

U.S. prisoners of war from Japanese-occupied territories in Asia arrived in New York on the *Gripsholm* in August 1942 and in December 1943. After the liner docked at the American Export Line pier in Jersey City in 1942, almost 1,500 passengers from the United States and Allied nations were investigated on board and released directly from the ship over a period of days. In 1943, although most of the more than 1,200 American repatriates were released directly, 30 were taken to Ellis Island for further investigation.[131] In both 1942 and 1943, these arrivals included almost 100 U.S. citizens of Japanese descent.[132]

Decisions about repatriation were complex choices based not only on national loyalty but also on political considerations and family obligations. Although most Japanese consular representatives were repatriated on the first *Gripsholm* voyage, Yuji Kawamoto, a clerk at the Japanese embassy, successfully fought against forced return to Japan. He didn't present himself to U.S. State Department officials as required, and after his arrest, he sought support from JACD members who wrote telegrams emphasizing that he was "actively pro-democratic" and should not be punished with repatriation.[133] When the *Gripsholm* arrived in New York for the second exchange, Kinichi Iwamoto was called from his shift at the Lutheran Hospital to Ellis Island, where U.S. officials told him that Japan had requested his repatriation. Iwamoto declined, emphasizing his settled life in America.[134] "The reasons were obvious," he recalled before members of the Commission on Wartime Relocation and Civilian Internment in the 1980s. "I had an office to practice in New York City. I had a duty to support my wife and two children. That's all."[135]

Similarly, Japanese nationals who decided to seek repatriation had varied reasons. In addition to loyalty to Japan, some expressed concern about their ability to support themselves during the war, and others hoped to avoid internment. Aizo Hayasaka emphasized that he was loyal to Japan and would do anything that the Japanese emperor asked of him. He chose repatriation because, as he told U.S. officials, "he is getting old, cannot secure work and is afraid he may have to go on relief." Toyaji Ina did not want to return to Japan but also sought repatriation because he was out of work. After he got a job, he withdrew his request. Some requested repatriation "whether or not I am ordered interned"; others requested it only if they were interned. Many were torn. Yuki Kijima felt allegiance to both Japan and the United States but was clear on her loyalty to her family: if her husband was repatriated "she must go with him." Hiroji Baba initially petitioned for repatriation but then withdrew his request when he was informed that his decision would not get him released any earlier. Shigero Mori also applied for and then withdrew his request for repatriation: a summary of his case noted that "this was at Ellis Island," and he thought it would be better to be repatriated "than be confined in an internment camp."[136]

These changes of heart suggest that a key reason some people requested repatriation was to shorten their imprisonment. Unfortunately, requests for repatriation essentially ensured that detainees would be recommended for internment instead of parole. Although hearing boards denied it, they consistently considered such requests in their evaluations of detainees. Tomito

Hirano, for example, had an order for parole signed and ready to be enacted. However, when he expressed a desire to return to Japan, the hearing board reconsidered his case and reversed their decision. Hirano was interned.[137]

In most cases, people who requested repatriation were returned to Japan. Some of the repatriates formed the Ellis Club in Tokyo, an organization of individuals who had been detained at Ellis Island. And some time after the war, they invited one of the American women volunteers who had assisted them while they were detained at Ellis Island to visit them in Japan.[138] But in other cases, people were denied repatriation because of suspicions of espionage or because of lack of space on the second *Gripsholm* voyage.[139] And finally, there were those Japanese nationals who were repatriated against their will.[140]

The Kanogawa family sought repatriation but were unsuccessful. Their story reveals the interconnections between those detained in INS and WRA camps, as well as the humiliating ways in which Japanese detainees were treated. Sho Kanogawa, an Issei leader from Seattle, was detained by authorities on December 7, 1941, and interned at the INS camp in Fort Missoula, Montana. Kanogawa's wife and four children were rounded up in early 1942, detained first at the Puyallup Assembly Center south of Seattle and then at the WRA Minidoka Camp in Idaho. The Kanogawas saw no hope in their situation and agreed to be repatriated to Japan. However, their nineteen-year-old daughter decided to stay in Minidoka with her fiancé. In the fall of 1943, Sho Kanogawa traveled from Montana and his wife and younger children traveled from Idaho to Ellis Island. On a train originally designed to hold detainees being taken to immigration stations for deportation, Mrs. Kanogawa and her children traveled for four days, guarded and with the shades drawn for the entire time. Yae Aihara, the youngest daughter, recalled "we couldn't see anything."[141]

When the Kanogawas arrived at Ellis Island, it was "a dark, miserable place" with peeling paint on the walls of huge dormitories. Women and men were housed separately, so the family was not reunited until they were in the dining room. As they rushed to hug one another after a two-year separation, their reconciliation may have looked similar to the immigrants being greeted by family members at Ellis Island. However, in this case, they were being reunited before their repatriation. Despite their intentions, the Kanogawa family couldn't travel to Japan because there were not enough berths on the ship. Aihara describes being angry about this turn of events, but also that their inability to repatriate was "a stroke of luck." In order to stay together, the Kanogawas requested internment at Crystal City, Texas.[142]

Immigration authorities often described internees in dispassionate and dehumanizing language, just as they had earlier described "contraband" Chinese and shipments of Asian deportees. The Kanogawa family stayed at Ellis Island for about four days waiting for transportation to Crystal City. They were then taken to Grand Central station, where Aihara remembers that their group of twenty-one prisoners was "paraded . . . all through that whole big station" by military police with rifles.[143] Their humiliation was similar to that felt by Japanese nationals in the early raids in which they were rounded up by FBI officials in public, even spectacular, displays of authority.[144] INS officials routinely described these moments of movement in ways that reduced their prisoners to objects. A December 19, 1941, memo described how an employee had "delivered 364 Japanese and 25 Italians" to Fort Missoula at 2:45 P.M. and that "he had 110 Germans on the train who he expected to deliver at Fort Lincoln at about 3:00pm tomorrow."[145] The INS's treatment of many Nikkei internees, as well as its rhetoric about them, dehumanized them and reduced them to inanimate objects. After being released from U.S. incarceration in 1946, the Kanogawa family did not return to Seattle but moved instead to Boyle Heights near downtown Los Angeles.[146]

## Japanese American Resettlement in New York

At the same time that the Kanogawa family was leaving New York in 1943, longtime residents were joined by Japanese Americans released from WRA incarceration. Despite opposition from elected officials, by September 1, 1944, more than 1,000 Japanese Americans had resettled in New York State. Many more arrived in 1945 and 1946.[147] Although resettlement for Japanese Americans and parole for Japanese nationals offered relief from imprisonment, it did not offer freedom from discrimination, suspicion, or shame. Even without forced relocation, the social and economic impacts of the war on New York's Japanese American community were substantial. Both parolees and resettled Japanese Americans had their social lives regulated. Parolees were required to avoid other Japanese at risk of rearrest, and Nikkei who left WRA camps were discouraged from associating with their friends and compatriots. Parole officers and sponsors also monitored and reported on parolees' social lives.[148] The Suzukis, for example, were described as "an ideal couple" in part because they "very seldom had any visitors" and left their house only to go to work or church.[149] Many former enemy alien internees expressed difficulties obtaining work because Japanese businesses were shut down during the war and they faced discrimination from other employers. Yasuo Matsui, an architect who had worked on the Empire State Building, requested release from parole as he believed his status made it difficult for him to secure employment. His request was denied, but due to his poor health and finances, he was allowed to report to his parole officer and his sponsor less frequently.[150] After Kinicho Iwamoto was released on parole, he typically left the house only to go to work. Iwamoto's medical practice was severely decreased because most of his patients were Japanese and many had been repatriated or interned. In accordance with the conditions of his parole, Iwamoto avoided all contact with other Japanese.[151] Although most forcibly relocated, confined, and paroled Nikkei worked hard to return to a form of normalcy after World War II, their communities, families, and lives had been upended.

· · · · · ·

Ellis Island's use as an internment camp has long been obscured by the iconic image of the island as the United States' immigration station. Similarly, Ellis Island's role as an enemy alien detention center has long been overlooked in histories of Japanese American wartime confinement. However, histories of enemy alien internment, Asian exclusion, and immigrant detention are critically important and closely interconnected. These connections come into focus at Ellis Island.

The INS administration of Japanese enemy alien internment relied on existing practices of interrogating, investigating, and detaining Chinese and other Asian immigrants under exclusion laws. Ellis Island officials were experienced in detention, and the Ellis Island station had long been organized as an immigration prison with segregated facilities for different types of detainees. Enemy alien hearings paralleled exclusion and deportation hearings conducted by INS officials. If Japanese detainees were paroled, these same officials investigated parole compliance using practices they had developed to investigate Chinese immigrants. If detainees were interned, they were typically transferred from Ellis Island to another internment camp; if they were repatriated, they were transported to Ellis Island. In both cases, the INS used its existing deportation bureaucracy, including the same chief deportation officer supervising the same trains that were previously used to deport Chinese and other Asian immigrants.

Internment had a profound and lasting impact on New York City. Japanese New Yorkers may have faced less discrimination and, as a result, were more likely to be intermarried or residentially integrated than Japanese living in the western United States. Nevertheless, they were still raided, interned, and treated more harshly than German or Italian nationals. They were not subject to wholesale forced removal and incarceration, but their loyalties were strained and their families were torn apart. Ellis Island officials attempted to understand the complex loyalties of Japanese civilians, but their efforts often resulted in arbitrary rulings. Almost half of all Japanese New Yorkers were repatriated to Japan. Yet, the Japanese population of the East Coast increased, largely because of resettlement and the uprooting of long-established Japanese communities in the West.

World War II enemy alien internment affected every Japanese person in New York. Although historians have increasingly paid attention to enemy alien internment, the importance of New York and the role of Ellis Island have been largely overlooked. The iconic image of the island as the United States' largest immigration station during times of peak European immigration from the 1890s through the 1920s has obscured its equally important role as an alien detention center.

Wartime confinement was not only built upon existing practices of exclusion, detention, and deportation but also contributed to their expansion in the postwar period as parole procedures developed to monitor enemy aliens were extended to all aliens. In 1946, more than 116,000 unauthorized immigrants were removed from the United States, almost 50 percent more than the previous year. The INS proudly noted that "never in the recorded history of the Service have so many illegal entrants been expelled." Even though the INS had expanded its detention facilities during the war and accelerated deportation proceedings as the war ended, this massive expansion of deportation was costly and time-consuming. In order to address these concerns, the INS extended "the basic principles of the parole system, as applied to alien enemies, to aliens under immigration proceedings generally." Immigration officials acknowledged that "prior to the administration by this Service of the alien enemy parole program there was no formalized uniform system in effect on parole supervision over aliens under deportation proceedings."[152] After the war, the implementation of a new immigrant parole system based on the paroling of enemy aliens allowed for the massive expansion of Cold War deportation. As explored in the conclusion, these expanded deportation practices rebounded to impact Chinese New Yorkers and ultimately led to the closure of Ellis Island.

# Conclusion

## The End of Detention at Ellis Island

• • • • • • • • • • • • • • • • • • • • • • • • • • • • • • • • • • • • • • • • • • • • • • •

November 1952. Chan Fo was working in his New York City laundry when two Federal Bureau of Investigation (FBI) agents arrived. "Without giving any reason," Chan recalls, they told him to pack his belongings "within three minutes." Chan quickly phoned relatives to take care of his laundry while he was gone, then the FBI agents took him to Ellis Island and charged him with unauthorized entry into the United States. Chan had, in fact, stowed away on a ship to Boston. However, when the agents interrogated him, it was clear that his unauthorized status was a pretext for his arrest. They were actually concerned about his activities in the United States on behalf of the Chinese Hand Laundry Alliance (CHLA) and its newspaper, the *China Daily News*. Their questions were political: "Do you know what kind of organization is the CHLA?" "What kind of newspaper is the *China Daily News*?" "Do you know that it propagandizes for the Communist Party?" Chan had served on the CHLA Executive Committee and subscribed to the *China Daily News*. He answered the questions directly, even the one asking whether he preferred the Chinese Communist Party (CCP), which had established a government in China in 1949, or the Kuomintang party (KMT), which had set up a nationalist government in Taiwan. "Of course the Communist Party is better!" he replied. "I don't know what's good about the KMT!" Chan was detained at Ellis Island for one year. He was eventually released on parole but had to report to officers at Ellis Island once each week and any additional times that they instructed. A few months later, FBI agents arrested him again. In May 1954, Chan was deported. FBI officials escorted him from New York to San Francisco, where he was placed on a ship to Hong Kong. He sold his laundry for the paltry sum of $400, so he had very limited finances. One month later, he arrived in Hong Kong and was immediately sent to the Chinese mainland. In November 1954, just six months after Chan left Ellis Island, the detention center was closed.[1]

• • • • • •

The Chinese exclusion laws were formally repealed in 1943. After more than sixty years of restrictions, Chinese immigrants earned U.S. naturalization rights, a limited quota of 105 immigrants per year, and the opportunity for wives and others to immigrate outside of the quotas. Recognizing the Chinese diaspora, the law provided that up to 75 percent of the quota be reserved for Chinese born and resident in China.[2] However, Chinese immigrants continued to enter as paper sons and their applications continued to be challenged. Even after they received approval from the U.S. consulate in Hong Kong, many arrivals were detained at Ellis Island. Chinese immigrants continued to be interrogated upon arrival by the New York Chinese Division in ways that were established under exclusion.[3]

Despite the repeal of exclusion, Chinese immigrants in New York and across the country remained particularly vulnerable to the threat of deportation. In the 1950s, U.S. officials' long-standing concerns about unauthorized Chinese entry were compounded with fears of communism. Chinese New Yorkers were threatened not only by anti-Chinese racism and anticommunist policies but also by conflicts between nationalists and communists within the Chinese community. These threats fostered anxieties about Chinese people's loyalties and place within the United States.[4]

As historian Jane Hong has explored, the end of Chinese exclusion was only part of the process of ending Asian exclusion. Although historians have focused on Chinese exclusion, the end of Asian Indian, Filipino and Japanese exclusion were also contested. Indian independence organizations centered in New York worked to end the exclusion of Indians and all Asians, but their work was riven by religious and class divisions. The India Welfare League, a New York–based community organization, was formed by Muslim jump-ship sailors, whereas the India League of America (ILA) was an elite lobby of high-caste Hindus and their white allies. Many of the Indian ILA leaders had immigrated to New York and other eastern states to attend or teach at universities. Each organization took different approaches in pushing for naturalization and immigration rights. But they were aided by U.S. Cold War concerns that independent Asian nations might ally with communists. In 1946, two days before Filipino Independence and a year before Indian Independence, the United States passed the Luce-Celler Act. The law ended Filipino and South Asian exclusion by granting U.S. naturalization rights along with limited annual immigration quotas of one hundred persons for each country, although most migration happened outside of the quotas. In 1952, following pressure by the Japanese American Citizens League, all naturalization restrictions on Asians were ended by the McCarran-Walter Act. However, the law was widely criticized for maintaining racist immigration quotas.[5]

Divisions between nationalists and communists in Chinese New York had existed since the split between the KMT and the CCP in 1927 as well as the founding of the leftist CHLA in New York in 1933 and the publication of the *China Daily News* in 1940.[6] The nationalist Chinese Consolidated Benevolent Association (CCBA) often represented elite merchants and their interests, whereas the CHLA represented working people and challenged the CCBA's political dominance. As explored in chapter 1, throughout the late nineteenth and early twentieth centuries, the San Francisco CCBA federation brought major test cases on repressive exclusion laws, often involving Chinese New Yorkers. The New York CCBA also assisted immigrants and worked with immigration officials to ensure relatively considerate treatment of Chinese arrivals, especially exempt elites. However, the federation's failure in these legal challenges, lack of attention toward the interests of poorer Chinese Americans, and unrelenting support of the KMT caused some Chinese to question the CCBA's dominance in Chinatown. The CCBA's centralized power was challenged by fraternal secret societies known as tongs in the 1920s and by leftist unions and organizations in the 1930s.[7]

By 1949, New York was the second-largest Chinese community in the United States, rivaling San Francisco in size. The U.S. Census claimed roughly 13,000 Chinese residents in New York compared with roughly 18,000 in San Francisco; however, Chinese community estimates suggested 30,000 residents in New York and 25,000 in San Francisco. New York's community was more heavily first-generation immigrants and probably had larger numbers of unauthorized immigrants, including jump-ship sailors, which could explain the discrepancy between the official and estimated figures.[8] As a large community, it was a focus of U.S. concerns about Chinese communism.

Working with U.S. agencies such as the FBI and the Immigration and Naturalization Service (INS), Chinese nationalists exploited many Chinese residents' unauthorized immigration to pursue their anticommunist agenda. The history of anticommunist harassment is not the entire history of Chinese immigrants during the Cold War. As historian Madeline Hsu has shown, educated postwar refugees were often viewed sympathetically as "the best type of Chinese," and these perspectives helped foster ideas about Chinese as a model minority.[9] Nonetheless, Chinese arrivals were routinely detained at Ellis Island, and progressive Chinese New Yorkers feared deportation through the detention center.

In his memoir, *Paper Son*, Tung Pok Chin gives a detailed account of the ways in which he was harassed by FBI agents and the impacts of this harassment on him and his family. Chin was a Brooklyn laundryman and an interpreter at the True Light Lutheran Church in Manhattan's China-town who had served in the U.S. Navy during World War II; he was also a paper son, a member of the CHLA, and a writer who published his poems in the *China Daily News*. Like other Chinese with complex loyalties, Chin sympathized with many of the CCP's goals but did not consider himself a communist; he believed that communism had benefited ordinary Chinese people but would not be appropriate for the United States. FBI agents regularly surveilled Chin's laundry and monitored his trips to Chinatown; they interrogated him in his laundry on three occasions, interviewed his children at school, tapped his phone, and intercepted his mail from China and Hong Kong. Chin expressed how an us-and-them perspective de-veloped in the Chinese community in response to this harassment. "This ubiquitous 'they' in any general conversation gradually came to mean the entire category of FBI men, Immigration and Naturalization officials, and any other interrogators lumped into one."[10]

In response to his fears both about being investigated by the FBI and about not being accepted as American, Chin carefully monitored his behav-ior. He subscribed to both Chinese and American publications but dis-carded the Chinese papers every day and kept a copy of *Life* and the *New York Times* "for display." He hung a photograph of his enlistment in the navy and his military discharge papers over the bell that his laundry cus-tomers rang for service. "Basically," Chin wrote, "we tried to make the place look as American as possible." In describing the accusations of com-munism made against him, Chin explained, "I was hurt. In my heart I felt like an American; America had been my home for over two decades; my children were born here; I served in the US Navy; and I was as patriotic as anyone. Now, because of a few poems and articles, they wanted to deport me." His greater fear, however, was that his U.S.-born children would never be accepted as Americans.[11]

The coordinated U.S. surveillance and harassment of Chinese New York-ers created feelings of forced unbelonging, just as internment and enemy alien status had done for Nikkei New Yorkers. Chin addressed the racism with which Chinese were viewed, comparing his situation in the 1950s to that of Japanese during World War II. As he noted, the United States had declared war on Germany, Italy, and Japan, "yet no German or Italian Amer-icans were rounded up and sent to internment camps." He feared that Chinese Americans were similarly targeted under McCarthyism. "Although many European nations had also turned to communism," he noted, "we

"Chinese Aliens Who Were Arrested Here Yesterday: The men in the Day Room at
Ellis Island with Security Officers George Prelli, left, and James McMahon,"
*New York Times*, Bettman Collection via Getty Images (1951).

Chinese could be set apart by our appearances and our names, and so, the
theory went, one had to be wary of all Chinese."[12]

The Kang Jai Association (KJA), a regional association of seamen and
others from Hainan Island, was one of the organizations that experienced
expulsion from the CCBA, harassment by the FBI, and raids by the INS. In
1951, during a period of "stepped-up apprehensions," at least one hundred
KJA members were deported to China. On Sunday, January 28, riven by divisions among its members about whether to support a CCBA loyalty statement, the New York KJA "voted to disband rather than engage in political
controversies." Three days later, just before Chinese New Year, seventy-four
INS officials and New York City police officers conducted a midnight raid
on the KJA's main offices and two dormitories in Brooklyn. After a three-
hour investigation, INS officials took eighty-three Chinese to Ellis Island.
Combining concerns about unauthorized entry and subversive activity, the
director of the INS's New York District claimed that the group contained
"many active Communists, deserting seamen and other aliens illegally in

the United States."[13] Forty-two of the men were subject to deportation, and, in total, it is estimated that 127 members of New York's KJA were deported during this time.[14]

Former KJA president and suspected communist Kwong Hai (Harry) Chew was working on a U.S. merchant ship when the association was raided. Upon his return, he was denied entry and detained at Ellis Island. At first, he was held without any information about the charges against him. After he won his case to learn the charges, he was accused of being a member of the Communist Party and lying about his membership. Kwong refused to acknowledge membership or accept deportation. He remained on Ellis Island for more than two years fighting his case, which was finally resolved when he gained U.S. citizenship in 1967.[15] After his Ellis Island detention, Kwong was paroled. However, like weekly parole requirements for enemy aliens during the war, these requirements made it difficult for him to retain his job. In New York, even though most INS administrative offices were located in Manhattan, parolees were required to report to Ellis Island, a round trip that took as long as four hours. Kwong had to give up his career as a merchant seaman and work instead at Lindy's Delicatessen on Broadway.[16]

During the Cold War, as Chinese exclusion ended, the INS emphasized the connections between unauthorized immigration, criminality, and radicalism. Immigration officials expressed political concerns about "illegal entrants," claiming in 1951 that many "have been found to be professional criminals. Others are subversives. Many are susceptible to communist influence because of their exploited and depressed economic situation in their home countries and, in many instances, in the United States after their arrival."[17] Mexican and Filipino labor organizers in the western United States were also targeted by the INS as potential communists.[18] As in the 1920s and 1930s, the immigration agency linked unauthorized migration to apparently threatening criminal and radical behavior as a means to justify widespread deportation, even though deportees were rarely a threat. They were simply unauthorized.

## Expanding Deportation and Contracting Detention

Throughout the postwar period, shifts in exclusion and deportation policies affected Chinese and other Asians at Ellis Island, as well as the fate of the detention center itself. The INS engaged in a massive expansion of deportation across the United States with the goal of ensuring the "maximum number of deportees with a minimum of deportation expense."[19] From 1946 through 1954, the INS proudly reported that it had broken previous deportation records.[20] During this time, the annual number of formally deported immigrants rose from more than 14,000 to almost 27,000 individuals.[21] Although anticommunism was a key reason for expanded immigrant regulation, the number of individuals deported as "subversive or anarchistic" was typically very small. Successful deportations of subversives increased from just four in 1949 to sixty-one in 1954.[22] In total, between 1946 and 1966, only 253 immigrants were deported as subversives. These low numbers did not reflect lack of attention: in 1956 alone, more than 8,000 individuals were investigated as subversives.[23] However, there were many easier routes through which the INS could target and deport suspected communists. This was especially true for Chinese leftists, who were typically targeted as unauthorized immigrants rather than radicals. Although the number of subversives detained and deported during the Cold War was limited, the impact of anticommunist harassment was profound: it decimated leftist organizations and terrorized the Chinese American community.

The INS worked toward its goal of national mass expulsion through four intersecting practices that expanded, accelerated, and dispersed immigration regulation. These practices were: voluntary departure procedures, parole practices, locally contracted detention centers, and the extension of inspection and deportation to airports throughout the United States. All of these practices dispersed immigration regulation throughout the country and away from traditional stations such as Ellis Island.

First, the INS massively expanded informal voluntary removals. As outlined in chapter 2, "departure in lieu of deportation" started as an administrative procedure in the 1920s to reduce the cost and accelerate the process of deporting unauthorized immigrants, especially Chinese jump-ship sailors and Mexican border crossers.[24] Immigrants who chose not to depart through this process were still deported, but voluntary removal allowed deportees limited control over their expulsion. Voluntary departure procedures were codified into law with the Alien Registration Act of 1940, known as the Smith Act, which also required the registration and fingerprinting of all foreign nationals over the age of fourteen and criminalized membership in and affiliation with subversive organizations. The registration provisions enabled the rounding up of Japanese enemy aliens in the 1940s, while the criminalization of affiliation facilitated the harassment of Chinese leftists.[25] Between 1946 and 1954, the number of immigrants removed through voluntary departure procedures without formal deportation hearings exploded from more than 100,000 (in 1946) to more than 1 million (in 1954).[26] As deportation was expanded it was also expedited.

Second, the INS used parole, a practice first developed to regulate enemy aliens during World War II, to expand deportation without increasing detention. Chinese and other individuals were paroled while appealing their denial of entry or while in formal deportation proceedings.[27] From 1947 to 1954, the number of deportable immigrants under parole supervision increased from almost 7,000 to almost 35,000. As during World War II, the INS regularly reviewed detainees at Ellis Island and provided parole to "so-called 'hardship' cases." These practices led to fewer immigrants being detained, although Chinese remained a large number of Ellis Island detainees and remained in detention for longer periods than other detainees.[28]

Third, detention increasingly shifted from permanent centers at immigration stations such as Ellis Island to contractual prisons, primarily in the U.S. Southwest.[29] Despite the construction of new federal detention centers in Texas and California, substantial numbers of potential deportees were detained in local prisons. In 1954, 83,000 detainees were held in state, county, and city jails out of a total of more than 500,000 immigration prisoners, "the highest in the history of the service." As the INS admitted, although prison officials attempted to comply with regulations requiring immigrants' segregation from convicted criminals and other prisoners, this was not always possible owing to overcrowding, inadequate accommodations, and aging buildings.[30] In contrast to the careful monitoring and separation of prisoners by status at Ellis Island, this contracted detention led to poor oversight and illegal imprisonment conditions.

Finally, the "post-war swelling of air transportation" led to the dispersion of immigration regulation throughout the country. As they had in the mid-nineteenth century before the establishment of Ellis Island, immigrants in the mid-twentieth century arrived at multiple ports of entry. In 1948, the INS recognized 450 ports of entry, including interior airports.[31] Deportation was also facilitated by air as it was less expensive and required less detention time, with small groups of deportees removed frequently on regularly scheduled flights. When CHLA member Chan Fo was transported from New York to San Francisco, the INS no longer used specially scheduled deportation trains. Deportation, like other aspects of exclusion regulation, had become dispersed.[32]

Although these practices were largely described as cost-saving changes, they led to significant new developments in immigration administration. On

"Chinese Immigrants at Ellis Island Waiting for Authorization to Enter the United States," Keystone—France, Gamma-Keystone Collection via Getty Images (c. 1940–50).

the one hand, they helped accelerate a long-standing INS goal of removing immigrants with maximum speed and minimal oversight. On the other, control of migration was no longer confined to a few central immigration stations, one of the goals when the federal government took control of immigration regulation from state governments in 1890 and opened Ellis Island in 1892. Instead, a flexible immigration force was assigned throughout the country, extending enforcement practices from urban centers such as New York to all immigrant communities. These changes led to reconsideration of the role of Ellis Island.

### Declining Detention at Ellis Island

The end of Ellis Island was facilitated by the end of large-scale detention. In 1942, the *New York Times* wrote that "thirty years ago, when Ellis Island was the safety valve of Europe and the feed-pipe of the melting pot, visitors used to fill the galleries of the inspection room to watch the twenty-

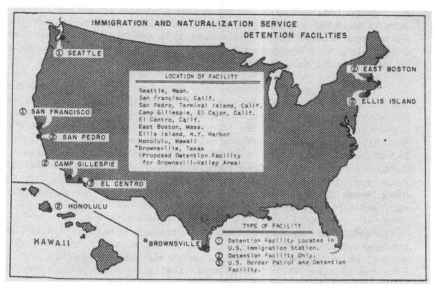

"Immigration and Naturalization Service Detention Facilities," *Annual Report of the Immigration and Naturalization Service* (1951).

one long lines of new immigrants filing past the inspectors down on the floor. Today the floor of the big room is occupied by a few family parties playing cards at the tables, a few children romping, a sprinkling of individuals reading alone, one or two tapping portable typewriters. The old Ellis Island still exists, but the flood of immigration has dried up to the merest trickle."[33] After 1943, when INS administrative responsibilities were transferred to the Columbus Circle office in Manhattan, Ellis Island became a full-time detention center. By 1951, unlike San Francisco and Seattle, which included detention facilities located inside immigration stations, Ellis Island was a "Detention Facility Only."[34]

Questions about Ellis Island's future had been raised as early as 1947.[35] Ellis Island received new detainees by train or airplane and transferred them to different facilities or to airports for deportation every day.[36] However, the postwar period saw significant decreases in detention. The number of detainees at Ellis Island dropped from a daily average of more than 800 between 1943 and 1945 to about 300 in 1949 and 1950.[37] There were spikes in the number of Chinese detainees in the early 1950s because of both rising postwar arrivals and anticommunist deportations, including the raid and roundup of KJA members.[38] The INS reported that "stepped-up apprehensions" during this time briefly raised the number of detainees to an average

Erika Stone, "Young Chinese Man Reading Newspaper at Ellis Island" (c. 1951), Museum of the City of New York, 96.173.6. Courtesy Howard Greenberg Gallery, New York.

of 840 each day.[39] One Chinese man detained at Ellis Island in 1951 suggested that there were at least 200 other Chinese detainees, although he could not estimate the number of white detainees because they were housed separately.[40] INS officials reported that as many as 125 children were detained on the island in May 1951, when a new school opened on the island, compared with 35 children on average throughout the year.[41] By 1954, the daily average was between 200 and 300 detainees at Ellis Island, in a space designed with dormitories and facilities for 1,500.[42]

Throughout the early 1950s, as detention and deportation expanded, it also shifted westward. In addition to extensive investigations of suspected Chinese leftists, most of this expansion was focused on unauthorized

Mexican immigrants in the U.S. Southwest and in Chicago. "In all other districts," the INS reported in 1954, "detentions either decreased substantially or remained the same."[43] These shifts allowed the reallocation of personnel from Ellis Island to Texas and California.[44] Extensive new detention facilities were built during this time at Hidalgo, Texas, and Chula Vista, California, while the existing El Centro and San Francisco detention facilities were updated and improved.[45]

Although the numbers of people being detained and deported were increasing, the average length of time spent in detention was reduced. From 1948 through 1954, the average length of immigrant detention dropped from almost eleven days to just two and a half days.[46] These lower numbers were largely due to the "rapid expulsion of Mexicans after apprehension" and the implementation of parole for many detainees. The INS was also engaged in an ongoing review of detention "particularly at Ellis Island, San Francisco, and along the Mexican border."[47] At Ellis Island, detention times appear to have been longer than the national average. In 1954, the *Christian Science Monitor* reported that most detainees stayed at Ellis Island no more than seventeen days.[48]

Both in New York and nationally, Chinese immigrants were subject to the longest periods of detention. "The care with which suspected subversive aliens had to be examined when they sought admission, and the extensive research into the backgrounds of Chinese claiming United States citizenship," according to the INS, "all contributed to an increase in detentions."[49] In addition to the time taken to review their cases upon admission, Chinese spent more time in detention because, if they were denied entry, they typically appealed. At Ellis Island, the *Christian Science Monitor* noted in 1954, "there is a group of Chinese that has been here for three years, appealing its case from court to court."[50]

### Closing the Golden Door

The closing of Ellis Island in 1954 did not lessen the persistence with which the FBI and INS harassed Chinese New Yorkers suspected of being procommunist. In December 1955, the U.S. consul in Hong Kong, Everett Drumright, issued a report claiming that almost all Chinese immigration was fraudulent and that Chinese communists were entering the United States under a passport and visa "racket." Released to the media in 1956, the evidence regarding the paper son system was not new: the INS had long complained publicly about the use of fake documentation to facilitate unauthorized immigration. However, Drumright's connection of fraudulent immigration to communist infiltration was alarming to many Americans.[51]

The Department of Justice responded to concerns about the intersections of unauthorized and subversive Chinese immigration by introducing the Chinese Confession Program. The program offered the possibility of legalization in exchange for confession of prior unauthorized immigration. However, many Chinese were concerned about revealing their paper status to the INS, both because they did not trust the U.S. government and because one person's confession would invariably implicate others. As concerns about confessions spread during New Year's celebrations in February 1956, Betty Lee Sung described how many Chinese stayed away from Chinatown, banquets were canceled, and New York City businesses lost $100,000 in one week.[52] New York laundryman Tung Pok Chin recognized the value of the confession program for some people: after his brother-in-law was legalized, he expressed a newfound confidence and sense of belonging in the United States. But Chin chose not to confess, in part because of the impact of implicating others but also because many individuals associated with leftwing organizations were denied and deported. In all, more than 11,000 Chinese admitted entering the United States under false citizenship claims, and 19,000 additional individuals were incriminated through these confessions.[53] Although it was intended to end illegal Chinese immigration, the Confession Program had a limited impact on ongoing unauthorized entry.

In discussions about the closing of Ellis Island, officials considered the station's deteriorating physical condition. In the immigration agency's own words, detainees were housed in areas where the "walls and floors were in bad shape" and provided with "uncomfortable, inadequate, and inappropriate furniture."[54] One detainee described the huge windows in the massive Registry Hall being covered in "accumulated grime." Yet, when he cleaned a pane, he recalled the "finest sight of the New York skyline that you could imagine."[55] During the 1950s, the INS planned renovations. The agency consolidated the offices of security personnel and installed a public address system that allowed "contact at all times between security personnel and every post inside and outside the station."[56] However, only the first phase of the renovation plan was completed; proposed updates to the family quarters and other living areas were never implemented.[57]

Despite its shoddy state, officials praised the public image of the former immigration station.[58] The 1954 *Annual Report of the INS* praised Ellis Island as especially effective in maintaining good public relations through public visits to the detention center. Annually, the service reported that "approximately 1,500 persons, including high school and college students, foreign consuls, members of the press, women's and men's civic organizations, and study clubs are granted permission to visit Ellis Island." The INS also reported "upwards of 50,000 persons visit aliens who are detained at the Island."[59] New York district director Edward Shaugnessy pointed out that diplomats also "watched" Ellis Island, monitoring the immigration cases of their nationals. He was concerned that new facilities being considered at the Brooklyn Naval Depot would "never even commence to compare in appearance and comfort with the present Ellis Island facilities." He noted that "Ellis Island is known the world over and in recent years has become a showplace, even to the point of being listed in tourist guides."[60]

Although numbers at Ellis Island had been lower in the years immediately preceding the move, immigration officials looked for a facility capable of holding about 400 to 600 detainees.[61] Even as they searched for replacement facilities in the New York area, including possible conversions of military camps to detention centers, immigration officials developed a plan showing their ideal station.[62] Modeled on a panopticon, their plan featured a central staircase enclosed with a protective grille and circular viewing platforms. These platforms would allow "one Detention Officer to observe all Warrant Day rooms, Night Rooms, Baggage room in basement, and roof area, without physically entering these areas, and, even without being under observation by those areas."[63] It was a dream of detention and surveillance that would not be realized.

When Joseph Swing assumed the duties of commissioner of the Immigration Service in June 1954, he determined that Ellis Island's old age, large size, and inconvenient island location made it too costly to maintain.[64] On November 11, Attorney General Herbert Brownell Jr. announced immigration procedures that would reduce the need for detention, including expanded immigration inspection on board ships combined with conditional parole or bonded release for most immigrants as their cases were being reviewed. Of course, arrivals who potentially posed a national security threat would continue to be detained. Although he did not state it explicitly, this included arrivals from communist China. These were reported as new procedures, but they more accurately represented the expansion of existing approaches. At the same time, the attorney general announced the closing of detention centers at Ellis Island, Boston, Seattle, San Francisco, San Pedro, and Honolulu. On the day of the announcement, Ellis Island detainees were transferred to other federal detention facilities in the New

York area, and the last ferry to Ellis Island was scheduled for the following week.[65] Ellis Island was closed in 1954.

· · · · · ·

Within the Ellis Island model of immigration, the station has long been viewed as central to narratives of U.S. immigration. Both at the time of its operation and since, "Ellis Island" has become shorthand for any immigration entry point. When a witness in 1911 hearings before the House Immigration Committee was asked whether he believed that a policy he proposed for Ellis Island should be extended to other ports, he agreed: "When I said Ellis Island, I meant the immigration authorities."[66] Among many others, Republican senator S. I. Hayakawa and Chairman of the Angel Island Immigration Station Historical Advisory Committee Paul Chow have described Angel Island as "the West Coast's Ellis Island."[67] Journalists and scholars also refer to emerging immigrant enclaves in Miami, Memphis, and communities across the South and the Midwest as "new Ellis Islands."[68] When Vietnamese refugees arrived in Los Angeles in the 1970s, the *New York Times* reported that the city "has become the Ellis Island of the 1970s, the portal through which most of the Asian refugees pass . . . on their way to new homes in all 50 states."[69] These references have the effect of emphasizing Ellis Island's centrality even as they seek to displace it.

The Ellis Island model also shapes histories of the station itself. Most books about Ellis Island, whether popular or scholarly, focus on the period from its opening in 1892 to the end of large-scale immigration during the 1920s.[70] In this way, Ellis Island's role as a site of exclusion and a detention and deportation center is obscured. However, Ellis Island was the central office for Asian exclusion in the eastern United States, as well as the region's main detention and deportation center. The INS long recognized Ellis Island as a detention center. When Angel Island opened in 1910, immigration officials praised its location, saying that "the ideal arrangement for detention purposes [is] one under which applicants can actually be isolated, such as that existing at Ellis Island."[71]

The importance of Ellis Island in facilitating the detention and deportation of immigrant Americans, including Chinese and other Asian Americans, challenges the Ellis Island model of immigration. At the same time, the work of New York officials implementing Chinese and Japanese exclusion in ways that were both strict and considerate complicates the Angel Island model of exclusion, the historical approach that focuses on the stringent implementation of Asian exclusion laws at Angel Island.

The passage of racial quotas in 1924 has typically been the end point of most histories of the island. However, Ellis Island did not close because of the end of large-scale European migration. It remained open for thirty of its sixty years as a detention and deportation center. The closing of Ellis Island was not caused by the end of immigration, but precipitated by the end of enemy alien detention in 1948 and changing practices of detention and deportation in the 1950s.

In May 1965, President Lyndon B. Johnson signed a proclamation that made Ellis Island part of the Statue of Liberty National Monument under the authority of the National Park Service. The proclamation noted that "Ellis Island was a temporary shelter for those who sought refuge, freedom, and opportunity in our country," a suitable complement to the Statue of Liberty. Five months later, when President Johnson signed the 1965 Immigration Act, which ended racial quotas on immigration, he stood in the shadow of the Statue of Liberty and gestured toward Ellis Island. The work of the station enforcing immigration, exclusion, and deportation laws was done. The detention center was shuttered.[72]

# Appendix of Tables

TABLE 1 Chinese Admitted and Rejected by Port of Arrival, 1905–12

| | New York total applicants | | Other eastern ports total applicants | | San Francisco total applicants | |
|---|---|---|---|---|---|---|
| | Chinese admitted | Chinese rejected | Chinese admitted | Chinese rejected | Chinese admitted | Chinese rejected |
| Year | % admitted | % admitted | % admitted | % admitted | % admitted | % admitted |
| 1905 | **9** | | **1** | | **2,202** | |
| | 8 | 1 | 1 | 0 | 1,838 | 364 |
| | 89% | 11% | 100% | 0% | 83% | 17% |
| 1906 | **24** | | **33** | | **1,966** | |
| | 21 | 3 | 25 | 8 | 1,847 | 119 |
| | 88% | 13% | 76% | 24% | 94% | 6% |
| 1907 | **23** | | **5** | | **2,302** | |
| | 21 | 2 | 2 | 3 | 2,150 | 152 |
| | 91% | 9% | 40% | 60% | 93% | 7% |
| 1908 | **44** | | **3** | | **3,310** | |
| | 38 | 6 | 3 | 0 | 3,055 | 255 |
| | 86% | 14% | 100% | 0% | 92% | 8% |
| 1909 | **42** | | **2** | | **4,937** | |
| | 38 | 4 | 2 | 0 | 4,539 | 398 |
| | 90% | 10% | 100% | 0% | 92% | 8% |
| 1910 | **73** | | **143** | | **4,744** | |
| | 62 | 11 | 138 | 5 | 3,976 | 768 |
| | 85% | 15% | 97% | 3% | 84% | 16% |
| 1911 | **90** | | **625** | | **3,437** | |
| | 76 | 14 | 569 | 56 | 2,963 | 474 |
| | 84% | 16% | 91% | 9% | 86% | 14% |
| 1912 | **42** | | **32** | | **3,535** | |
| | 40 | 2 | 22 | 10 | 3,300 | 235 |
| | 95% | 5% | 69% | 31% | 93% | 7% |
| 1905–12 | **347** | | **844** | | **26,433** | |
| | 304 | 43 | 762 | 82 | 23,668 | 2,765 |
| | 88% | 12% | 90% | 10% | 90% | 10% |

Annual numbers do not include pending cases. Other eastern ports include Boston, New Orleans, and Montreal (1912 only). Other western seaports include Portland, Oregon; Port Townsend, Washington; San Diego; Seattle; and Vancouver (1912 only). Northern land border ports include Buffalo, New York; Malone, New York; Portal, North Dakota; Richford, Vermont; and Sumas, Washington.

| Other western ports total applicants | | Honolulu total applicants | | Northern land border ports total applicants | | All ports total applicants | |
|---|---|---|---|---|---|---|---|
| Chinese admitted | Chinese rejected | Chinese admitted | Chinese rejected | Chinese admitted | Chinese rejected | Chinese admitted | Chinese rejected |
| % admitted | % admitted | % admitted | % admitted | % admitted | % admitted | % admitted | % admitted |
| **306** | | **249** | | **319** | | **3,086** | |
| 249 | 57 | 243 | 6 | 266 | 53 | 2,605 | 481 |
| 81% | 19% | 98% | 2% | 83% | 17% | 84% | 16% |
| **217** | | **199** | | **483** | | **2,922** | |
| 189 | 28 | 193 | 6 | 445 | 38 | 2,720 | 202 |
| 87% | 13% | 97% | 3% | 92% | 8% | 93% | 7% |
| **252** | | **208** | | **716** | | **3,506** | |
| 229 | 23 | 206 | 2 | 642 | 74 | 3,250 | 256 |
| 91% | 9% | 99% | 1% | 90% | 10% | 93% | 7% |
| **332** | | **252** | | **1,043** | | **4,984** | |
| 320 | 12 | 248 | 4 | 956 | 87 | 4,620 | 364 |
| 96% | 4% | 98% | 2% | 92% | 8% | 93% | 7% |
| **440** | | **440** | | **1,146** | | **7,007** | |
| 407 | 33 | 407 | 33 | 1,022 | 124 | 6,415 | 592 |
| 93% | 8% | 93% | 8% | 89% | 11% | 92% | 8% |
| **840** | | **548** | | **656** | | **7,004** | |
| 775 | 65 | 523 | 25 | 558 | 98 | 6,032 | 972 |
| 92% | 8% | 95% | 5% | 85% | 15% | 86% | 14% |
| **954** | | **690** | | **2** | | **5,798** | |
| 832 | 122 | 665 | 25 | 1 | 1 | 5,106 | 692 |
| 87% | 13% | 96% | 4% | 50% | 50% | 88% | 12% |
| **1,500** | | **665** | | **N/A*** | | **5,774** | |
| 1,377 | 123 | 635 | 30 | N/A | N/A | 5,374 | 400 |
| 92% | 8% | 95% | 5% | N/A | N/A | 93% | 7% |
| **4,841** | | **3,251** | | **4,365** | | **40,081** | |
| 4,378 | 463 | 3,120 | 131 | 3,890 | 475 | 36,122 | 3,959 |
| 90% | 10% | 96% | 4% | 89% | 11% | 90% | 10% |

Published data are not available before 1901. No land border ports are listed in the relevant table of the 1912 *Annual Report of the Commissioner-General of Immigration*. Source: *Annual Reports of the Commissioner-General of Immigration*, "Chinese Seeking Admission to the United States" (Table 1), 1905–1908; *Annual Reports of the Commissioner-General of Immigration*, "Chinese Seeking Admission to the United States" (Table 2), 1909–1912.

TABLE 2  Chinese Admitted and Rejected by Port of Arrival, 1913–32

| Year | New York total applicants | | | Northeastern ports total applicants | | | Southeastern, Florida, and Gulf ports total applicants | | | San Francisco total applicants | | |
|---|---|---|---|---|---|---|---|---|---|---|---|---|
| | Native-born admitted | Aliens admitted / Alien % admitted | Aliens debarred / Alien % debarred | Native-born admitted | Aliens admitted / Alien % admitted | Aliens debarred / Alien % debarred | Native-born admitted | Aliens admitted / Alien % admitted | Aliens debarred / Alien % debarred | Native-born admitted | Aliens admitted / Alien % admitted | Aliens debarred / Alien % debarred |
| 1913 | | 47 | | | 32 | | | 6 | | | 3,554 | |
| | 2 | 31 | 14 | 10 | 7 | 15 | 0 | 0 | 6 | 1,372 | 2,012 | 170 |
| | | 69% | 31% | | 32% | 68% | | 0% | 100% | | 92% | 8% |
| 1914 | | 124 | | | 34 | | | 11 | | | 3,851 | |
| | 1 | 106 | 17 | 1 | 7 | 26 | 0 | 7 | 4 | 1,485 | 2,125 | 241 |
| | | 86% | 14% | | 21% | 79% | | 64% | 36% | | 90% | 10% |
| 1915 | | 167 | | | 18 | | | 13 | | | 4,104 | |
| | 2 | 156 | 9 | 0 | 5 | 13 | 3 | 5 | 5 | 1,567 | 2,369 | 168 |
| | | 95% | 5% | | 28% | 72% | | 50% | 50% | | 93% | 7% |
| 1916 | | 157 | | | 11 | | | 4 | | | 3,858 | |
| | 5 | 137 | 15 | 0 | 8 | 3 | 0 | 3 | 1 | 1,470 | 2,047 | 341 |
| | | 90% | 10% | | 73% | 27% | | 75% | 25% | | 86% | 14% |
| 1917 | | 86 | | | 41 | | | 4 | | | 3,432 | |
| | 3 | 79 | 4 | 19 | 20 | 2 | 0 | 4 | 0 | 1,514 | 1,685 | 233 |
| | | 95% | 5% | | 91% | 9% | | 100% | 0% | | 88% | 12% |
| 1918 | | 97 | | | 59 | | | 17 | | | 2,156 | |
| | 0 | 94 | 3 | 15 | 16 | 28 | 0 | 16 | 1 | 620 | 1,285 | 251 |
| | | 97% | 3% | | 36% | 64% | | 94% | 6% | | 84% | 16% |
| 1919 | | 74 | | | 32 | | | 28 | | | 2,268 | |
| | 1 | 72 | 1 | 16 | 13 | 3 | 0 | 26 | 2 | 621 | 1,547 | 100 |
| | | 99% | 1% | | 81% | 19% | | 93% | 7% | | 94% | 6% |
| 1920 | | 238 | | | 322 | | | 99 | | | 2,857 | |
| | 3 | 228 | 7 | 149 | 163 | 10 | 0 | 93 | 6 | 1,118 | 1,658 | 81 |
| | | 97% | 3% | | 94% | 6% | | 94% | 6% | | 95% | 5% |
| Total 1913–20 | | 990 | | | 549 | | | 182 | | | 26,080 | |
| | 17 | 903 | 70 | 210 | 239 | 100 | 3 | 154 | 25 | 9,767 | 14,728 | 1,585 |
| | | 93% | 7% | | 71% | 29% | | 86% | 14% | | 90% | 10% |
| Avg 1913–20 | | 124 | | | 69 | | | 23 | | | 3,260 | |

|  | Other western ports total applicants | | | | Honolulu total applicants | | | | Land border port total applicants | | | | All ports total applicants | | | |
|---|---|---|---|---|---|---|---|---|---|---|---|---|---|---|---|---|
|  | Native-born admitted | Aliens admitted / Alien % admitted | Aliens debarred / Alien % debarred | | Native-born admitted | Aliens admitted / Alien % admitted | Aliens debarred / Alien % debarred | | Native-born admitted | Aliens admitted / Alien % admitted | Aliens debarred / Alien % debarred | | Native-born admitted | Aliens admitted / Alien % admitted | Aliens debarred / Alien % debarred | |
| **1,615** | | | | | **779** | | | | **14** | | | | **6,047** | | | |
| | 490 | 1,030 | 95 | | 296 | 402 | 81 | | 6 | 5 | 3 | | 2,176 | 3,487 | 384 | |
| | | 92% | 8% | | | 83% | 17% | | | 63% | 38% | | | 90% | 10% | |
| **1,450** | | | | | **705** | | | | **8** | | | | **6,183** | | | |
| | 481 | 882 | 87 | | 228 | 442 | 35 | | 5 | 3 | 0 | | 2,201 | 3,572 | 410 | |
| | | 91% | 9% | | | 93% | 7% | | | 100% | 0% | | | 90% | 10% | |
| **1,077** | | | | | **537** | | | | **13** | | | | **5,930** | | | |
| | 288 | 733 | 56 | | 150 | 370 | 17 | | 8 | 5 | 0 | | 2,018 | 3,643 | 269 | |
| | | 93% | 7% | | | 96% | 4% | | | 100% | 0% | | | 93% | 7% | |
| **997** | | | | | **588** | | | | **15** | | | | **5,630** | | | |
| | 255 | 684 | 58 | | 194 | 375 | 19 | | 8 | 7 | 0 | | 1,932 | 3,261 | 437 | |
| | | 92% | 8% | | | 95% | 5% | | | 100% | 0% | | | 88% | 12% | |
| **936** | | | | | **585** | | | | **11** | | | | **5,095** | | | |
| | 258 | 626 | 52 | | 222 | 334 | 29 | | 2 | 8 | 1 | | 2,018 | 2,756 | 321 | |
| | | 92% | 8% | | | 92% | 8% | | | 89% | 11% | | | 90% | 10% | |
| **688** | | | | | **419** | | | | **38** | | | | **3,474** | | | |
| | 179 | 494 | 15 | | 132 | 277 | 10 | | 0 | 38 | 0 | | 946 | 2,220 | 308 | |
| | | 97% | 3% | | | 97% | 3% | | | 100% | 0% | | | 88% | 12% | |
| **756** | | | | | **317** | | | | **16** | | | | **3,491** | | | |
| | 268 | 453 | 35 | | 48 | 259 | 10 | | 1 | 15 | 0 | | 955 | 2,385 | 151 | |
| | | 93% | 7% | | | 96% | 4% | | | 100% | 0% | | | 94% | 6% | |
| **856** | | | | | **432** | | | | **11** | | | | **4,815** | | | |
| | 340 | 503 | 13 | | 148 | 276 | 8 | | 3 | 8 | 0 | | 1,761 | 2,929 | 125 | |
| | | 97% | 3% | | | 97% | 3% | | | 100% | 0% | | | 96% | 4% | |
| **8,375** | | | | | **4,362** | | | | **126** | | | | **40,665** | | | |
| | 2,559 | 5,405 | 411 | | 1,418 | 2,735 | 209 | | 33 | 89 | 4 | | 14,007 | 24,253 | 2,405 | |
| | | 93% | 7% | | | 93% | 7% | | | 96% | 4% | | | 91% | 9% | |
| | 1,047 | | | | 545 | | | | 16 | | | | 5,083 | | | |

*(Continued)*

TABLE 2 Continued

| | New York total applicants | | | Northeastern ports total applicants | | | Southeastern, Florida, and Gulf ports total applicants | | | San Francisco total applicants | | |
|---|---|---|---|---|---|---|---|---|---|---|---|---|
| Year | Native-born admitted | Aliens admitted Alien % admitted | Aliens debarred Alien % debarred | Native-born admitted | Aliens admitted Alien % admitted | Aliens debarred Alien % debarred | Native-born admitted | Aliens admitted Alien % admitted | Aliens debarred Alien % debarred | Native-born admitted | Aliens admitted Alien % admitted | Aliens debarred Alien % debarred |
| 1921 | | 324 | | | 1,023 | | | 508 | | | 4,605 | |
| | 4 | 288 | 32 | 608 | 374 | 41 | 0 | 456 | 52 | 1,846 | 2,615 | 144 |
| | | 90% | 10% | | 90% | 10% | | 90% | 10% | | 95% | 5% |
| 1922 | | 603 | | | 258 | | | 83 | | | 4,798 | |
| | 194 | 309 | 100 | 130 | 109 | 19 | 2 | 77 | 4 | 1,873 | 2,626 | 299 |
| | | 76% | 24% | | 85% | 15% | | 95% | 5% | | 90% | 10% |
| 1923 | | 637 | | | 634 | | | 16 | | | 5,122 | |
| | 244 | 286 | 107 | 371 | 140 | 123 | 0 | 16 | 0 | 2,232 | 2,660 | 230 |
| | | 73% | 27% | | 53% | 47% | | 100% | 0% | | 92% | 8% |
| 1924 | | 391 | | | 450 | | | 26 | | | 5,192 | |
| | 137 | 207 | 47 | 276 | 91 | 83 | 0 | 25 | 1 | 2,438 | 2,455 | 299 |
| | | 81% | 19% | | 52% | 48% | | 96% | 4% | | 89% | 11% |
| 1925 | | 355 | | | 212 | | | 11 | | | 3,047 | |
| | 112 | 111 | 132 | 131 | 17 | 64 | 0 | 6 | 5 | 1,596 | 1,236 | 215 |
| | | 46% | 54% | | 21% | 79% | | 55% | 45% | | 85% | 15% |
| 1926 | | 241 | | | 129 | | | 13 | | | 2,438 | |
| | 77 | 113 | 51 | 93 | 18 | 18 | 1 | 9 | 3 | 1,155 | 1,106 | 177 |
| | | 69% | 31% | | 50% | 50% | | 75% | 25% | | 86% | 14% |
| 1927 | | 192 | | | 174 | | | 4 | | | 2,888 | |
| | 54 | 113 | 25 | 116 | 9 | 49 | 0 | 1 | 3 | 1,506 | 1,132 | 250 |
| | | 82% | 18% | | 16% | 84% | | 25% | 75% | | 82% | 18% |
| 1928 | | 326 | | | 242 | | | 13 | | | 3,149 | |
| | 128 | 135 | 63 | 168 | 39 | 35 | 0 | 5 | 8 | 1,581 | 1,430 | 138 |
| | | 68% | 32% | | 53% | 47% | | 38% | 62% | | 91% | 9% |
| 1929 | | 304 | | | 273 | | | 2 | | | 3,363 | |
| | 106 | 165 | 34 | 178 | 55 | 40 | 0 | 2 | 0 | 1,714 | 1,487 | 162 |
| | | 83% | 17% | | 58% | 42% | | 100% | 0% | | 90% | 10% |
| 1930 | | 331 | | | 203 | | | 12 | | | 2,716 | |
| | 139 | 125 | 67 | 128 | 47 | 28 | 0 | 4 | 8 | 1,398 | 1,208 | 110 |
| | | 65% | 35% | | 63% | 37% | | 33% | 67% | | 92% | 8% |

| Other western ports total applicants | | | Honolulu total applicants | | | Land border port total applicants | | | All ports total applicants | | |
|---|---|---|---|---|---|---|---|---|---|---|---|
| Native-born admitted | Aliens admitted / Alien % admitted | Aliens debarred / Alien % debarred | Native-born admitted | Aliens admitted / Alien % admitted | Aliens debarred / Alien % debarred | Native-born admitted | Aliens admitted / Alien % admitted | Aliens debarred / Alien % debarred | Native-born admitted | Aliens admitted / Alien % admitted | Aliens debarred / Alien % debarred |
| | **1,432** | | | **673** | | | **54** | | | **8,619** | |
| 484 | 928 | 20 | 269 | 397 | 7 | 28 | 26 | 0 | 3,239 | 5,084 | 296 |
| | 98% | 2% | | 98% | 2% | | 100% | 0% | | 94% | 6% |
| | **2,153** | | | **1,351** | | | **1,294** | | | **10,540** | |
| 636 | 1,475 | 42 | 585 | 750 | 16 | 624 | 635 | 35 | 4,044 | 5,981 | 515 |
| | 97% | 3% | | 98% | 2% | | 95% | 5% | | 92% | 8% |
| | **3,096** | | | **1,431** | | | **328** | | | **11,264** | |
| 931 | 1,970 | 195 | 737 | 666 | 28 | 175 | 130 | 23 | 4,690 | 5,868 | 706 |
| | 91% | 9% | | 96% | 4% | | 85% | 15% | | 89% | 11% |
| | **3,791** | | | **1,293** | | | **302** | | | **11,445** | |
| 1,030 | 2,555 | 206 | 703 | 484 | 106 | 170 | 123 | 9 | 4,754 | 5,940 | 751 |
| | 93% | 7% | | 82% | 18% | | 93% | 7% | | 89% | 11% |
| | **2,458** | | | **544** | | | **289** | | | **6,916** | |
| 806 | 1,513 | 139 | 235 | 291 | 18 | 143 | 46 | 100 | 3,023 | 3,220 | 673 |
| | 92% | 8% | | 94% | 6% | | 32% | 68% | | 83% | 17% |
| | **2,501** | | | **327** | | | **184** | | | **5,833** | |
| 793 | 1,610 | 98 | 135 | 173 | 19 | 142 | 34 | 8 | 2,396 | 3,063 | 374 |
| | 94% | 6% | | 90% | 10% | | 81% | 19% | | 89% | 11% |
| | **2,832** | | | **508** | | | **290** | | | **6,888** | |
| 1,127 | 1,545 | 160 | 227 | 255 | 26 | 146 | 62 | 82 | 3,176 | 3,117 | 595 |
| | 91% | 9% | | 91% | 9% | | 43% | 57% | | 84% | 16% |
| | **2,565** | | | **562** | | | **202** | | | **7,059** | |
| 1,041 | 1,401 | 123 | 244 | 294 | 24 | 114 | 43 | 45 | 3,276 | 3,347 | 436 |
| | 92% | 8% | | 92% | 8% | | 49% | 51% | | 88% | 12% |
| | **2,456** | | | **645** | | | **294** | | | **7,329** | |
| 1,065 | 1,301 | 90 | 307 | 333 | 5 | 164 | 85 | 45 | 3,534 | 3,428 | 367 |
| | 94% | 6% | | 99% | 1% | | 65% | 35% | | 90% | 10% |
| | **2,409** | | | **712** | | | **395** | | | **6,778** | |
| 997 | 1,348 | 64 | 347 | 362 | 3 | 211 | 181 | 3 | 3,220 | 3,275 | 283 |
| | 95% | 5% | | 99% | 1% | | 98% | 2% | | 92% | 8% |

(Continued)

TABLE 2 Continued

| Year | New York total applicants | | | Northeastern ports total applicants | | | Southeastern, Florida, and Gulf ports total applicants | | | San Francisco total applicants | | |
|---|---|---|---|---|---|---|---|---|---|---|---|---|
| | Native-born admitted | Aliens admitted / Alien % admitted | Aliens debarred / Alien % debarred | Native-born admitted | Aliens admitted / Alien % admitted | Aliens debarred / Alien % debarred | Native-born admitted | Aliens admitted / Alien % admitted | Aliens debarred / Alien % debarred | Native-born admitted | Aliens admitted / Alien % admitted | Aliens debarred / Alien % debarred |
| 1931 | 177 | 392 / 133 / 62% | 82 / 38% | 102 | 175 / 41 / 56% | 32 / 44% | 0 | 10 / 3 / 30% | 7 / 70% | 1,596 | 2,752 / 1,071 / 93% | 85 / 7% |
| 1932 | 107 | 211 / 87 / 84% | 17 / 16% | 129 | 162 / 21 / 64% | 12 / 36% | 0 | 108 / 108 / 100% | 0 / 0% | 1,444 | 2,523 / 951 / 88% | 128 / 12% |
| Total 1921–32 | 1,479 | 4,307 / 2,072 / 73% | 757 / 27% | 2,430 | 3,935 / 961 / 64% | 544 / 36% | 3 | 806 / 712 / 89% | 91 / 11% | 20,379 | 42,593 / 19,977 / 90% | 2,237 / 10% |
| Avg 1921–32 | | 359 | | | 328 | | | 67 | | | 3,549 | |

Northeastern ports include Baltimore, Boston, Philadelphia, and Montreal. Southeastern, Florida, and Gulf ports include Charleston, Galveston, Gulfport, Key West, New Orleans, Newport News, Norfolk, San Juan, P.R. (1915, 1918, 1919), Savannah, Tampa, and Wilmington, N.C. Other western ports include Portland, Oregon, Seattle, and Vancouver. Land border ports include Mexican border ports and Canadian border stations (in 1922 and 1923 when they are not listed separately as Montreal and Vancouver). Canadian border ports are included because they were operated by U.S. immigration officials and determined entry into the United States. Source: *Annual Reports of the Commissioner-General of Immigration*, "Miscellaneous Chinese Transactions by Ports" (Table 8), 1913–1922;

| | Other western ports total applicants | | | | Honolulu total applicants | | | | Land border port total applicants | | | | All ports total applicants | | |
|---|---|---|---|---|---|---|---|---|---|---|---|---|---|---|---|---|
| | | Aliens admitted | Aliens debarred | | | Aliens admitted | Aliens debarred | | | Aliens admitted | Aliens debarred | | | Aliens admitted | Aliens debarred |
| | Native-born admitted | Alien % admitted | Alien % debarred | | Native-born admitted | Alien % admitted | Alien % debarred | | Native-born admitted | Alien % admitted | Alien % debarred | | Native-born admitted | Alien % admitted | Alien % debarred |
| | **2,189** | | | | **785** | | | | **423** | | | | **6,726** | | |
| 1,075 | 1,074 | 40 | | 362 | 413 | 10 | | 272 | 147 | 4 | | 3,584 | 2,882 | 260 | |
| | 96% | 4% | | | 98% | 2% | | | 97% | 3% | | | 92% | 8% | |
| | **1,856** | | | | **718** | | | | **390** | | | | **5,968** | | |
| 898 | 940 | 18 | | 402 | 310 | 6 | | 272 | 109 | 9 | | 3,252 | 2,526 | 190 | |
| | 98% | 2% | | | 98% | 2% | | | 92% | 8% | | | 93% | 7% | |
| | **29,738** | | | | **9,549** | | | | **4,445** | | | | **95,365** | | |
| 10,883 | 17,660 | 1,195 | | 4,553 | 4,728 | 268 | | 2,461 | 1,621 | 363 | | 42,188 | 47,731 | 5,446 | |
| | 94% | 6% | | | 95% | 5% | | | 82% | 18% | | | 90% | 10% | |
| | **2,478** | | | | **796** | | | | **370** | | | | **7,947** | | |

*Annual Reports of the Commissioner-General of Immigration*, "Miscellaneous Chinese Transactions by Ports" (Table 6), 1923–1924; *Annual Report of the Commissioner-General of Immigration*, "Miscellaneous Chinese Transactions by Ports" (Table 64), 1926; *Annual Report of the Commissioner-General of Immigration*, "Miscellaneous Chinese Transactions by Ports" (Table 67), 1927; *Annual Reports of the Commissioner-General of Immigration*, "Miscellaneous Chinese Transactions by Ports" (Table 72), 1925, 1928–1931; *Annual Report of the Commissioner-General of Immigration*, "Miscellaneous Chinese Transactions by Ports" (Table 63), 1932.

TABLE 3  Japanese Admitted and Rejected by Port of Arrival, 1908–12

| Year | New York total applicants | | San Francisco total applicants | | Seattle total applicants | |
|---|---|---|---|---|---|---|
| | Japanese with proper passports (admitted) | Japanese without proper passports (rejected) | Japanese with proper passports (admitted) | Japanese without proper passports (rejected) | Japanese with proper passports (admitted) | Japanese without proper passports (rejected) |
| | % admitted | % rejected | % admitted | % rejected | % admitted | % rejected |
| 1908 | **N/A** | | **49** | | **363** | |
| | N/A | N/A | 45 | 4 | 362 | 1 |
| | | | 92% | 8% | 100% | 0% |
| 1909 | **N/A** | | **549** | | **1,549** | |
| | N/A | N/A | 510 | 39 | 1,540 | 9 |
| | | | 93% | 7% | 99% | 1% |
| 1910 | **222** | | **792** | | **1,363** | |
| | 176 | 46 | 760 | 32 | 1,341 | 22 |
| | 79% | 21% | 96% | 4% | 98% | 2% |
| 1911 | **287** | | **2,059** | | **1,833** | |
| | 247 | 40 | 2,037 | 22 | 1,824 | 9 |
| | 86% | 14% | 99% | 1% | 100% | 0% |
| 1912 | **270** | | **2,816** | | **2,213** | |
| | 239 | 31 | 2,783 | 33 | 2,182 | 31 |
| | 89% | 11% | 99% | 1% | 99% | 1% |
| 1908–12 | **779** | | **6,265** | | **7,321** | |
| | 662 | 117 | 6,135 | 130 | 7,249 | 72 |
| | 85% | 15% | 98% | 2% | 99% | 1% |

Published data are not available before 1908. Published data after 1912 are recorded by location of departure, not port of entry. In 1909, "other ports" may include New York; in 1912, "other ports" refers to Philadelphia. Source: *Annual Reports*

| Canada total applicants | | Mexico total applicants | | Other ports total applicants | | All ports total applicants | |
| --- | --- | --- | --- | --- | --- | --- | --- |
| Japanese with proper passports (admitted) % admitted | Japanese without proper passports (rejected) % rejected | Japanese with proper passports (admitted) % admitted | Japanese without proper passports (rejected) % rejected | Japanese with proper passports (admitted) % admitted | Japanese without proper passports (rejected) % rejected | Japanese with proper passports (admitted) % admitted | Japanese without proper passports (rejected) % rejected |
| 68 | | 5 | | N/A | | 485 | |
| 53 | 15 | 2 | 3 | N/A | N/A | 462 | 23 |
| 78% | 22% | 40% | 60% | | | 95% | 5% |
| 373 | | 62 | | 111 | | 2,644 | |
| 241 | 132 | 19 | 43 | 97 | 14 | 2,407 | 237 |
| 65% | 35% | 31% | 69% | 87% | 13% | 91% | 9% |
| 259 | | 51 | | N/A | | 2,687 | |
| 141 | 118 | 24 | 27 | N/A | N/A | 2,442 | 245 |
| 54% | 46% | 47% | 53% | | | 91% | 9% |
| 88 | | 61 | | N/A | | 4,328 | |
| 53 | 35 | 18 | 43 | N/A | N/A | 4,179 | 149 |
| 60% | 40% | 30% | 70% | | | 97% | 3% |
| 72 | | 87 | | 3 | | 5,461 | |
| 30 | 42 | 30 | 57 | 3 | 0 | 5,267 | 194 |
| 42% | 58% | 34% | 66% | 100% | 0% | 96% | 4% |
| 860 | | 266 | | 114 | | 15,605 | |
| 518 | 342 | 93 | 173 | 100 | 14 | 14,757 | 848 |
| 60% | 40% | 35% | 65% | 88% | 12% | 95% | 5% |

of the Commissioner-General of Immigration, "Japanese Arrivals in Continental United States, Showing Various Details Bearing on the Japanese Agreement" (Table E), 1908–1912.

TABLE 4  Japanese Admitted and Rejected by Country of Departure, 1908–23

| Fiscal year | Europe total applicants | | Japan total applicants | | Hawaii total applicants | |
|---|---|---|---|---|---|---|
| | Japanese admitted % admitted | Japanese rejected % rejected | Japanese admitted % admitted | Japanese rejected % rejected | Japanese admitted % admitted | Japanese rejected % rejected |
| 1908 | **N/A** N/A N/A | N/A | **480** 461 96% | 19 4% | **5** 1 20% | 4 80% |
| 1909 | **N/A** N/A N/A | N/A | **2,085** 2,062 99% | 23 1% | **48** 28 58% | 20 42% |
| 1910 | **N/A** N/A N/A | N/A | **2,124** 2,089 98% | 35 2% | **60** 38 63% | 22 37% |
| 1911 | **268** 239 89% | 29 11% | **3,868** 3,840 99% | 28 1% | **55** 48 87% | 7 13% |
| 1912 | **270** 239 89% | 31 11% | **4,951** 4,899 99% | 52 1% | **70** 66 94% | 4 6% |
| 1913 | **232** 212 91% | 20 9% | **6,381** 6,341 99% | 40 1% | **87** 78 90% | 9 10% |
| 1914 | **220** 196 89% | 24 11% | **8,115** 8,049 99% | 66 1% | **N/A** N/A | N/A |
| 1915 | **306** 292 95% | 14 5% | **8,572** 8,531 100% | 41 0% | **N/A** N/A | N/A |
| 1916 | **186** 184 99% | 2 1% | **8,686** 8,658 100% | 28 0% | **N/A** N/A | N/A |
| 1917 | **174** 165 95% | 9 5% | **8,807** 8,751 99% | 56 1% | **N/A** N/A | N/A |

| Canada total applicants | | Mexico total applicants | | Other locations total applicants | | All ports total applicants | |
|---|---|---|---|---|---|---|---|
| Japanese admitted % admitted | Japanese rejected % rejected | Japanese admitted % admitted | Japanese rejected % rejected | Japanese admitted % admitted | Japanese rejected % rejected | Japanese admitted % admitted | Japanese rejected % rejected |
| N/A | | N/A | | N/A | | 485 | |
| N/A | N/A | N/A | N/A | N/A | N/A | 462 | 23 |
| | | | | | | 95% | 5% |
| 321 | | 66 | | 124 | | 2,644 | |
| 194 | 127 | 20 | 46 | 103 | 21 | 2,407 | 237 |
| 60% | 40% | 30% | 70% | 83% | 17% | 91% | 9% |
| 227 | | 52 | | 224 | | 2,687 | |
| 111 | 116 | 25 | 27 | 179 | 45 | 2,442 | 245 |
| 49% | 51% | 48% | 52% | 80% | 20% | 91% | 9% |
| 59 | | 62 | | 16 | | 4,328 | |
| 28 | 31 | 15 | 47 | 9 | 7 | 4,179 | 149 |
| 47% | 53% | 24% | 76% | 56% | 44% | 97% | 3% |
| 67 | | 88 | | 3 | | 5,449 | |
| 26 | 41 | 30 | 58 | 3 | 0 | 5,263 | 186 |
| 39% | 61% | 34% | 66% | 100% | 0% | 97% | 3% |
| 46 | | 76 | | 37 | | 6,859 | |
| 26 | 20 | 28 | 48 | 30 | 7 | 6,715 | 144 |
| 57% | 43% | 37% | 63% | 81% | 19% | 98% | 2% |
| 64 | | 152 | | 53 | | 8,604 | |
| 17 | 47 | 42 | 110 | 46 | 7 | 8,350 | 254 |
| 27% | 73% | 28% | 72% | 87% | 13% | 97% | 3% |
| 121 | | 131 | | 57 | | 9,187 | |
| 22 | 99 | 42 | 89 | 50 | 7 | 8,937 | 250 |
| 18% | 82% | 32% | 68% | 88% | 12% | 97% | 3% |
| 173 | | 148 | | 73 | | 9,266 | |
| 24 | 149 | 51 | 97 | 68 | 5 | 8,985 | 281 |
| 14% | 86% | 34% | 66% | 93% | 7% | 97% | 3% |
| 138 | | 114 | | 67 | | 9,300 | |
| 42 | 96 | 64 | 50 | 59 | 8 | 9,081 | 219 |
| 30% | 70% | 56% | 44% | 88% | 12% | 98% | 2% |

*(Continued)*

TABLE 4 Continued

| Fiscal year | Europe total applicants | | Japan total applicants | | Hawaii total applicants | |
|---|---|---|---|---|---|---|
| | Japanese admitted % admitted | Japanese rejected % rejected | Japanese admitted % admitted | Japanese rejected % rejected | Japanese admitted % admitted | Japanese rejected % rejected |
| | **267** | | **10,695** | | **N/A** | |
| 1918 | 210 | 57 | 10,513 | 182 | N/A | N/A |
| | 79% | 21% | 98% | 2% | | |
| | **273** | | **10,923** | | **N/A** | |
| 1919 | 269 | 4 | 10,719 | 204 | N/A | N/A |
| | 99% | 1% | 98% | 2% | | |
| | **476** | | **12,261** | | **N/A** | |
| 1920 | 439 | 37 | 12,113 | 148 | N/A | N/A |
| | 92% | 8% | 99% | 1% | | |
| | **539** | | **9,982** | | **N/A** | |
| 1921 | 531 | 8 | 9,893 | 89 | N/A | N/A |
| | 99% | 1% | 99% | 1% | | |
| | **536** | | **8,163** | | **N/A** | |
| 1922 | 532 | 4 | 8,143 | 20 | N/A | N/A |
| | 99% | 1% | 100% | 0% | | |
| | **608** | | **7,228** | | **N/A** | |
| 1923 | 606 | 2 | 7,171 | 57 | N/A | N/A |
| | 100% | 0% | 99% | 1% | | |
| | **4,353** | | **108,575** | | **325** | |
| 1908–23 | 4,114 | 239 | 107,621 | 954 | 259 | 66 |
| | 95% | 5% | 99% | 1% | 80% | 20% |

In 1908, data are provided only for Japan and Hawaii. From 1914 to 1924, no data are provided for Hawaii. After fiscal year 1924, Japanese were formally barred from entering the United States and the Bureau of Immigration did not record

| Canada total applicants | | Mexico total applicants | | Other locations total applicants | | All ports total applicants | |
|---|---|---|---|---|---|---|---|
| Japanese admitted % admitted | Japanese rejected % rejected | Japanese admitted % admitted | Japanese rejected % rejected | Japanese admitted % admitted | Japanese rejected % rejected | Japanese admitted % admitted | Japanese rejected % rejected |
| **62** | | **120** | | **90** | | **11,234** | |
| 43 | 19 | 63 | 57 | 79 | 11 | 10,908 | 326 |
| 69% | 31% | 53% | 48% | 88% | 12% | 97% | 3% |
| **97** | | **109** | | **64** | | **11,466** | |
| 38 | 59 | 51 | 58 | 54 | 10 | 11,131 | 335 |
| 39% | 61% | 47% | 53% | 84% | 16% | 97% | 3% |
| **73** | | **103** | | **100** | | **13,013** | |
| 35 | 38 | 50 | 53 | 83 | 17 | 12,720 | 293 |
| 48% | 52% | 49% | 51% | 83% | 17% | 98% | 2% |
| **46** | | **113** | | **105** | | **10,785** | |
| 38 | 8 | 111 | 2 | 102 | 3 | 10,675 | 110 |
| 83% | 17% | 98% | 2% | 97% | 3% | 99% | 1% |
| **63** | | **168** | | **92** | | **9,022** | |
| 52 | 11 | 165 | 3 | 89 | 3 | 8,981 | 41 |
| 83% | 17% | 98% | 2% | 97% | 3% | 100% | 0% |
| **36** | | **163** | | **89** | | **8,124** | |
| 29 | 7 | 160 | 3 | 89 | 0 | 8,055 | 69 |
| 81% | 19% | 98% | 2% | N/A | N/A | 99% | 1% |
| **1,038** | | **1,544** | | **846** | | **116,568** | |
| 420 | 618 | 872 | 672 | 761 | 85 | 113,980 | 2,588 |
| 40% | 60% | 56% | 44% | 90% | 10% | 98% | 2% |

their entry. Source: *Annual Reports of the Commissioner-General of Immigration*, "Japanese Arrivals in Continental United States, Showing Various Details Bearing on the Japanese Agreement" (Table E), 1908–1923.

**TABLE 5** New York Asian Arrivals by Nationality, 1892–1916

| Year | Chinese | Japanese | Korean | South Asian | Filipino | Pacific Islander | Hawaiian | Total Asian and Pacific Islander |
|---|---|---|---|---|---|---|---|---|
| 1892 | 402 | 10 | 0 | 5 | 0 | 1 | 0 | 418 |
| 1893 | 602 | 30 | 0 | 11 | 0 | 1 | 1 | 645 |
| 1894 | 435 | 35 | 0 | 3 | 0 | 0 | 0 | 473 |
| 1895 | 901 | 51 | 0 | 3 | 0 | 0 | 0 | 955 |
| 1896 | 1,826 | 23 | 0 | 2 | 0 | 0 | 0 | 1,851 |
| 1897 | 301 | 37 | 0 | 17 | 0 | 0 | 0 | 355 |
| 1898 | 0 | 14 | 0 | 0 | 0 | 0 | 0 | 14 |
| 1899 | 4 | 9 | 0 | 1 | 0 | 0 | 1 | 15 |
| 1900 | 1 | 22 | 0 | 0 | 0 | 0 | 0 | 23 |
| 1901 | 0 | 10 | 0 | 0 | 1 | 0 | 0 | 11 |
| 1902 | 12 | 15 | 0 | 2 | 0 | 0 | 0 | 29 |
| 1903 | 128 | 161 | 4 | 47 | 0 | 0 | 1 | 341 |
| 1904 | 105 | 258 | 3 | 112 | 8 | 0 | 0 | 486 |
| 1905 | 156 | 228 | 8 | 53 | 2 | 1 | 0 | 448 |
| 1906 | 323 | 273 | 3 | 51 | 0 | 0 | 0 | 650 |
| 1907 | 292 | 261 | 2 | 50 | 1 | 1 | 0 | 607 |
| 1908 | 414 | 226 | 3 | 70 | 43 | 0 | 0 | 756 |
| 1909 | 398 | 278 | 9 | 104 | 112 | 1 | 0 | 902 |
| 1910 | 589 | 308 | 2 | 67 | 180 | 0 | 0 | 1,146 |
| 1911 | 479 | 275 | 4 | 99 | 31 | 0 | 0 | 888 |
| 1912 | 506 | 314 | 3 | 80 | 95 | 0 | 1 | 999 |
| 1913 | 668 | 258 | 6 | 112 | 37 | 1 | 0 | 1,082 |
| 1914 | 543 | 363 | 9 | 60 | 36 | 0 | 0 | 1,011 |
| 1915 | 620 | 201 | 0 | 38 | 10 | 2 | 1 | 872 |
| 1916 | 670 | 220 | 0 | 44 | 47 | 0 | 1 | 982 |
| **AVERAGE 1892–1916** | **415** | **155** | **2** | **41** | **24** | **0** | **0** | **639** |

These figures include all recorded arrivals, not only immigrants. Arrivals from Korea may have been recorded as Japanese subjects, as well as Chinese or other nationals. Arrivals from the Philippines were sometimes listed as Pacific Islanders and sometimes as Filipinos. In cases where individuals were misrecorded in the Ancestry database, digital images of the New York Passenger Lists were consulted for corrections. Source: New York, U.S., Arriving Passenger and Crew Lists, 1820–1957 (online database), Ancestry.com, 2010.

TABLE 6 New York Asian Arrivals by Nationality, 1917–54

| Year | Chinese | Japanese | Korean | South Asian | Filipino | Pacific Islander | Hawaiian | Total Asian and Pacific Islander |
|------|---------|----------|--------|-------------|----------|------------------|----------|----------------------------------|
| 1917 | 3,700 | 2,250 | 5 | 2,210 | 58 | 10 | 0 | 8,233 |
| 1918 | 11,694 | 4,005 | 11 | 6,726 | 102 | 22 | 1 | 22,561 |
| 1919 | 11,918 | 7,620 | 9 | 2,896 | 171 | 84 | 8 | 22,706 |
| 1920 | 10,068 | 4,977 | 18 | 1,286 | 437 | 239 | 35 | 17,060 |
| 1921 | 12,515 | 4,236 | 4 | 1,736 | 616 | 491 | 42 | 19,640 |
| 1922 | 6,618 | 3,135 | 3 | 1,552 | 636 | 637 | 19 | 12,600 |
| 1923 | 6,977 | 3,376 | 15 | 1,740 | 545 | 1,082 | 24 | 13,759 |
| 1924 | 8,821 | 2,845 | 20 | 1,393 | 606 | 1,099 | 11 | 14,795 |
| 1925 | 8,813 | 3,989 | 18 | 1,426 | 539 | 1,148 | 11 | 15,944 |
| 1926 | 9,034 | 3,438 | 1 | 2,161 | 1,111 | 924 | 14 | 16,683 |
| 1927 | 9,067 | 4,175 | 2 | 1,704 | 2,017 | 962 | 3 | 17,930 |
| 1928 | 12,341 | 3,964 | 10 | 2,580 | 809 | 2,580 | 30 | 22,314 |
| 1929 | 11,549 | 3,779 | 5 | 1,895 | 689 | 1,007 | 18 | 18,942 |
| 1930 | 10,703 | 3,846 | 7 | 1,822 | 681 | 1,510 | 25 | 18,594 |
| 1931 | 11,266 | 4,303 | 9 | 2,095 | 558 | 1,021 | 33 | 19,285 |
| 1932 | 10,499 | 4,508 | 13 | 1,582 | 496 | 992 | 77 | 18,167 |
| 1933 | 9,997 | 4,238 | 8 | 800 | 507 | 1,061 | 12 | 16,623 |
| 1934 | 8,661 | 5,039 | 4 | 856 | 866 | 1,312 | 17 | 16,755 |
| 1935 | 9,654 | 5,517 | 8 | 1,495 | 1,622 | 1,388 | 28 | 19,712 |
| 1936 | 8,270 | 5,171 | 3 | 1,073 | 1,553 | 2,348 | 18 | 18,436 |
| 1937 | 7,505 | 5,985 | 5 | 1,718 | 1,694 | 2,714 | 17 | 19,638 |
| 1938 | 5,667 | 6,124 | 6 | 1,467 | 1,985 | 2,078 | 22 | 17,349 |
| 1939 | 5,198 | 7,534 | 6 | 1,834 | 2,465 | 1,842 | 31 | 18,910 |
| 1940 | 4,599 | 5,724 | 11 | 1,920 | 2,955 | 1,384 | 53 | 16,646 |
| 1941 | 6,779 | 2,389 | 6 | 1,894 | 3,663 | 1,472 | 29 | 16,232 |
| 1942 | 6,343 | 29 | 3 | 3,597 | 1,638 | 1,157 | 20 | 12,787 |
| 1943 | 12,036 | 70 | 4 | 3,757 | 2,556 | 2,130 | 52 | 20,605 |
| 1944 | 12,068 | 74 | 4 | 4,436 | 2,946 | 1,783 | 70 | 21,381 |
| 1945 | 11,076 | 109 | 13 | 2,142 | 2,524 | 1,579 | 56 | 17,499 |
| 1946 | 7,377 | 78 | 20 | 2,396 | 2,787 | 1,798 | 91 | 14,547 |
| 1947 | 6,719 | 51 | 22 | 2,614 | 2,798 | 2,614 | 130 | 14,948 |
| 1948 | 7,223 | 77 | 15 | 1,121 | 4,343 | 1,235 | 95 | 14,109 |
| 1949 | 6,851 | 62 | 9 | 665 | 3,342 | 998 | 63 | 11,990 |
| 1950 | 5,804 | 276 | 2 | 1,030 | 3,403 | 945 | 42 | 11,502 |
| 1951 | 5,235 | 1,101 | 20 | 1,151 | 3,697 | 944 | 59 | 12,207 |
| 1952 | 4,437 | 4,489 | 16 | 1,649 | 2,493 | 1,247 | 57 | 14,388 |
| 1953 | 1,880 | 7,129 | 5 | 1,468 | 1,023 | 434 | 25 | 11,964 |
| 1954 | 1,608 | 8,492 | 4 | 315 | 619 | 127 | 7 | 11,172 |
| AVERAGE 1917–54 | 8,173 | 3,532 | 9 | 1,953 | 1,620 | 1,221 | 35 | 16,542 |

These figures include all recorded arrivals, not only immigrants. Starting in 1917, these arrivals included seamen. This table is based on both reviews of the Ancestry database and the digital images of the New York Passenger Lists. Source: New York, U.S., Arriving Passenger and Crew Lists, 1820–1957 (online database), Ancestry.com, 2010.

TABLE 7 Stowaways by Port and Race (1914–20 and 1928–32)

| | New York total stowaways | | |
| --- | --- | --- | --- |
| | Other stowaways | Chinese stowaways | Japanese stowaways |
| Year | Percentage of total stowaways | Percentage of total stowaways | Percentage of total stowaways |
| 1914 | 380 96% | 396 16 4% | |
| 1915 | 214 97% | 220 6 3% | |
| 1916 | 347 97% | 359 12* 3% | |
| 1917 | 435 100% | 436 1 0% | |
| 1918 | 301 100% | 302 1 0% | |
| 1919 | 399 100% | 400 1 0% | |
| 1920 | 1,246 99% | 1,264 11 1% | 7 1% |
| 1928 | | 660 | |
| 1929 | | 582 | |
| 1930 | | 638 | |
| 1931 | | 385 | |
| 1932 | | 222 | |

New York did not provide data on Japanese stowaways, except in 1920, or on stowaways by race in 1928–31. San Francisco did not provide data on stowaways by race in 1914 or 1928–31. Annual reports did not compile data on stowaways from all ports by race until 1928. *In addition to this number, the *ARCGI* (1916) also reported fourteen Chinese stowaways. Data on Chinese stowaways in New York are located in Report of the Chinese Inspector in Charge District No. 3, Comprising New York and New Jersey; *ARCGI* (1914), 231; *ARCGI* (1915), 224; *ARCGI* (1916), 179; *ARCGI* (1917), 180; *ARCGI* (1918), 273; *ARCGI* (1919), 309. Data on Chinese and Japanese stowaways for

| San Francisco total stowaways | | | All ports total stowaways | | |
|---|---|---|---|---|---|
| Other stowaways | Chinese stowaways | Japanese stowaways | Other stowaways | Chinese stowaways | Japanese stowaways |
| Percentage of total stowaways | Percentage of total stowaways | Percentage of total stowaways | Percentage of total stowaways | Percentage of total stowaways | Percentage of total stowaways |
|  |  |  |  | 787 |  |
|  | 44 |  |  |  |  |
| 26 | 2 | 16 |  |  |  |
| 59% | 5% | 36% |  |  |  |
|  | 250 |  |  |  |  |
| 146 | 104 | 0 |  |  |  |
| 58% | 42% | 0% |  |  |  |
|  | 52 |  |  |  |  |
| 32 | 18 | 2 |  |  |  |
| 62% | 35% | 4% |  |  |  |
|  | 37 |  |  |  |  |
| 25 | 1 | 11 |  |  |  |
| 68% | 3% | 30% |  |  |  |
|  | 43 |  |  |  |  |
| 15 | 6 | 22 |  |  |  |
| 35% | 14% | 51% |  |  |  |
|  | 37 |  |  |  |  |
| 22 | 1 | 14 |  |  |  |
| 59% | 3% | 38% |  |  |  |
|  | 3 |  |  | 1,383 |  |
|  |  |  | 1,287 | 80 | 16 |
|  |  |  | 93% | 6% | 1% |
|  | 8 |  |  | 1,073 |  |
|  |  |  | 1,007 | 36 | 30 |
|  |  |  | 94% | 3% | 3% |
|  | 6 |  |  | 1,048 |  |
|  |  |  | 960 | 80 | 8 |
|  |  |  | 92% | 8% | 1% |
|  | 12 |  |  | 741 |  |
|  |  |  | 653 | 76 | 12 |
|  |  |  | 88% | 10% | 2% |
|  | 3 |  |  | 441 |  |
|  |  |  | 430 | 8 | 3 |
|  |  |  | 98% | 2% | 1% |

1920 are located in the Report of the Commissioner of Immigration at New York, in Charge of District No. 3, Comprising New York and New Jersey and the Immigration Station at Ellis Island, New York Harbor; *ARCGI* (1920), 314. Data on stowaways in San Francisco are located in the Report of the Commissioner of Immigration, San Francisco, in charge of District No. 18, Comprising Northern California and Nevada and the Angel Island Immigration Station; *ARCGI* (1915), 243; *ARCGI* (1916), 200; *ARCGI* (1917), 200; *ARCGI* (1918), 294; *ARCGI* (1919) 349; *ARCGI* (1920), 365. All reports in Appendix III, Digest of Reports of Commissioners and Inspectors in Charge of Districts, Annual Reports 1914–1920. Data on total stowaways are located in table 68 (1928–1931) and in table 62 (1932). Data on Chinese and Japanese stowaways are located in the unnumbered table "Alien Stowaways Found on Board Vessels Arriving from Foreign Ports"; *ARCGI* (1928), 7; *ARCGI* (1929), 10; *ARCGI* (1930), 13; *ARCGI* (1931), 33; *ARCGI* (1932), 26. Source: *Annual Reports of the Commissioner-General of Immigration*, 1914–1920 and 1928–1932.

TABLE 8 Deserting Alien Seamen by Port and Race, 1907–32

| Year | Alien deserting seamen (all ports) | Alien deserting seamen (NY port) | Chinese deserting seamen (NY port) | Japanese deserting seamen (NY port) | Alien deserting seamen (SF port) | Chinese deserting seamen (SF port) | Japanese deserting seamen (SF port) |
|------|------|------|------|------|------|------|------|
| 1907 | 9,616 | 493 | | | 1,435 | | |
| 1908 | 13,235 | 6,942 | | | 586 | | |
| 1909 | 5,839 | 2,292 | | | 236 | | |
| 1910 | 9,816 | 5,116 | | | 403 | | |
| 1911 | 6,594 | 1,723 | | | 414 | | |
| 1912 | 6,384 | 967 | | | 606 | | |
| 1913 | 9,136 | 2,272 | 39 | | 879 | | |
| 1914 | 9,747 | 4,767 | 27 | | 227 | | |
| 1915 | 6,458 | 2,047 | 38 | | 229 | 8 | |
| 1916 | 6,584 | 1,965 | 67 | | 68 | 6 | 29 |
| 1917 | 8,572 | 1,953 | 145 | | | 1 | 14 |
| 1918 | 8,852 | 4,096 | 283 | | 63 | 4 | |
| 1919 | 9,277 | 5,889 | | | 58 | 18 | 64 |
| 1920 | 13,543 | 7,183 | 1,637 | | 44 | 135 | 85 |
| 1921 | 21,839 | 8,149 | | | 842 | | |
| 1922 | 5,879 | 3,292 | | | 402 | | |
| 1923 | 23,194 | 14,734 | | | 429 | | |
| 1924 | 35,013 | 22,252 | | | 438 | | |
| 1925 | 19,710 | 11,218 | | | 185 | | |
| 1926 | 18,456 | 11,465 | | | 458 | | |
| 1927 | 23,447 | 12,888 | 354 | 21 | 435 | 24 | 1 |
| 1928 | 12,357 | 8,186 | 143 | 28 | 227 | 24 | 8 |
| 1929 | 11,314 | 7,837 | 288 | 11 | 289 | 41 | 4 |
| 1930 | 9,117 | 6,244 | 245 | 8 | 229 | 53 | 2 |
| 1931 | 3,341 | 2,260 | 65 | 5 | 127 | 16 | 0 |
| 1932 | 1,344 | 835 | 40 | 3 | 73 | 7 | 1 |

Total numbers of alien deserting seamen in all ports, New York, and San Francisco are provided in table XVIA (1907–1908); table XX (1909–1920); table XIX (1921–1924); table 66 (1925); table 58 (1926); table 62 (1927); (1928), 12; (1929), 13; (1930), 19; (1931), 32; (1932), 25. In 1918 and 1919, when complete data are not provided for New York, additional data are drawn from *ARCGI* (1927), table 103. Chinese deserting seamen in New York and Chinese and Japanese deserting seamen in San Francisco are unevenly reported and compiled from Appendix III, Digest of Reports of Commissioners and Inspectors in Charge of Districts, Annual Reports 1913–1920. Chinese deserting seamen in New York: *ARCGI* (1913), 189; *ARCGI* (1914), 233; *ARCGI* (1915), 224; *ARCGI* (1916), 179; *ARCGI* (1917), 179; *ARCGI* (1918), 273; *ARCGI* (1920), 321. Chinese and Japanese deserting seamen in San Francisco: *ARCGI* (1915), 243; *ARCGI* (1916), 200; *ARCGI* (1917), 200; *ARCGI* (1918), 294; *ARCGI* (1919), 349; *ARCGI* (1920), 365. Figures are not provided for South Asian and Other Asians from 1907 to 1930. In 1920, San Francisco reported fifty-three deserting Javanese seamen, but Javanese are not mentioned in other years or by other ports. Alien and Chinese seamen are counted separately; therefore, Chinese seamen are not counted as aliens. Japanese deserting seamen are not reported separately for the port of New York but are included within alien seamen. Source: *Annual Reports of the Commissioner-General of Immigration, 1907–1932*.

# Notes

## Abbreviations

| | |
|---|---|
| (AE)LCF | (Alien Enemy) Litigation Case Files, 1941–1949, General Records of the Department of Justice, Record Group 60, NARA–College Park, Md. |
| ARCGI | *Annual Report of the Commissioner General of Immigration* |
| ARSOL | *Annual Report of the Secretary of Labor* |
| ARINS | *Annual Report of the Immigration and Naturalization Service* |
| EIOHP | Ellis Island Oral History Project |
| INSAIE | Records of the US Immigration and Naturalization Service, Record Group 85, Microfilm Records, Series A, Part 1, Asian Immigration and Exclusion, 1906–1913 (Bethesda, Md.: American University Publications, 1994) |
| NARA | National Archives and Records Administration |
| USCWRIC | Randolph Boehm and Robert Lester, *Papers of the US Commission on Wartime Relocation and Internment of Civilians, Part 1* microfilm (Frederick, Md., 1984) |
| WWIIJIC | World War II Japanese Internee Cards, UD-UP entry 4, Record Group 60, NARA—College Park, Md. |

## Introduction

1. "Thirty-Five Goanese Held at Ellis Island," *New York Times*, October 27, 1919; "Held at Ellis Island," *New York Times*, November 24, 1919. After November, there is no further reference to the sailors in the *New York Times*. There is no reference to the Goan sailors' release date in the manifest, Belgic Passenger Lists, October 4, 1919, New York, New York, U.S., Arriving Passenger and Crew Lists (including Castle Garden and Ellis Island), 1820–1957 (online database), Ancestry.com, 2010; Perea, "Statue of Liberty," 44–48.

2. Daniels, *Guarding the Golden Door*, 19; Salyer, *Laws Harsh as Tigers*; Daniels, "No Lamps Were Lit for Them"; Luibhéid, *Entry Denied*; Lee, *At America's Gates*.

3. The East of California division within the Association for Asian American Studies was founded in 1991. Publications "de-centering the field" include Okihiro, *Privileging Positions*; Brooks, "In the Twilight Zone between Black and White"; McKeown, *Chinese Migrant Networks and Cultural Change*; Dirlik and Yeung, *Chinese on the American Frontier*; Harden, *Double Cross*; Chan, *Remapping Asian American History*; Ling, *Chinese St. Louis*; Jung, *Coolies and Cane*; Bow, *Partly Colored*; Lan, *Diaspora and Class Consciousness*; Ling, *Chinese Chicago*; Desai and Joshi, *Asian Americans in Dixie*.

4. Ngai, "Asian American History," 97.

5. Young, *Alien Nation*; Kang, *INS on the Line*; Lim, *Porous Borders*; Lew-Williams, *Chinese Must Go*.

6. Chang, "China and the Pursuit of America's Destiny"; Lew-Williams, *Chinese Must Go*, 51–62.

7. Kurashige, *Two Faces of Exclusion*, 6.

8. Hsu, *Good Immigrants*, 8.

9. Coolidge, *Chinese Immigration*; Sandmeyer, *Anti-Chinese Movement in California*; Daniels, *Politics of Prejudice*; Saxton, *Indispensable Enemy*; McClain, *In Search of Equality*.

10. "New Way to Spell 'Chinese,'" *New York Tribune*, June 12, 1878, 4.

11. Kanazawa, "Immigration, Exclusion, and Taxation," 783–87; McClain, *In Search of Equality*, 9–36.

12. Lew-Williams, *Chinese Must Go*, 40–43; McClain, *In Search of Equality*, 79–83.

13. Tchen, *New York before Chinatown*, 79.

14. Tchen, *New York before Chinatown*, 70–91.

15. Inouye, *Distant Islands*, 24.

16. Bald, *Bengali Harlem*, 15.

17. Immigration Act of March 3, 1875 (19 Stat. 477); Act of May 6, 1882 (22 Stat. 58); Svejda, *Castle Garden as an Immigrant Depot*; Lew-Williams, *Chinese Must Go*, 8, 51–52.

18. Weber, *Autobiography of John B. Weber*, 89–90, 99–100.

19. Julian Ralph, "Landing the Immigrant," *Harper's Weekly*, October 24, 1891, 823; House of Representatives, *Investigation of Immigration at Ellis Island, with Minority Reports and Testimony*, Report 2090, July 28, 1892, 52nd Cong., 1st Sess., 462.

20. Desai, "Korla Pandit Plays America." See also Augustus Sherman, "Sikh," in Mesenholler, *Augustus F. Sherman*, 75.

21. Ralph, "Landing the Immigrant," 823. See also Pegler-Gordon, *In Sight of America*, 34–39, 124–26.

22. U.S. Census, Table V, "Population by Race and by Counties," in *Report on the Social Statistics of Cities*, 402–3.

23. U.S. Census, *Compendium of the Eleventh Census 1890*, 520.

24. W. H. Allen, Statement on Restriction of Immigration, in *Reports of the Industrial Commission on Immigration, and on Education* (Washington, D.C.: GPO, 1899), 15: 162.

25. Tchen, *New York before Chinatown*, 225.

26. U.S. Census, Table V, "Population, by Race, of Cities and Towns," in *Tenth Census 1880*, 422; U.S. Census, *Compendium of the Eleventh Census 1890*, 526; U.S. Census, *Twelfth Census 1900*, cxx; U.S. Census, Table 25, "Indians, Chinese and Japanese, by Sex, for Counties, and for Cities of 10,000 to 100,000," in *Sixteenth Census 1940, Population*, 66; U.S. Census, Table Series A 91–104, "Population, by Sex and Race: 1790–1970," *Historical Statistics of the United States*, 14.

27. "Crowds along the Shores," *New York Times*, October 12, 1892, 9.

28. Pegler-Gordon, *In Sight of America*, 2–6.

29. Although this book focuses on the fact that Asian immigrants arrived at Ellis Island from Europe and other locations outside Asia, Chinese and other Asian immigrants were separated in immigration records. Therefore, references to European immigrants follow this practice and do not include Asian immigrants from Europe. On settlement in New York, see Bogen, *Immigration in New York*, 11. On numbers and percentages of European immigrants, see Table I, *ARCGI* (1892–1924); Table 1, *ARCGI* (1925–1941); Table 82, *ARCGI* (1931); Table 2, *ARCGI* (1944); Table 1, *ARCGI* (1945); Table 1A, *ARCGI* (1946–1948); Table 5, *ARCGI* (1947–1954); Unrau, *Ellis Island Historic Resource Study*, Tables 1 and 2, 185–86.

30. Ralph, "Landing the Immigrant," 823; Birn, "Six Seconds per Eyelid," 290; Markel and Stern, "Which Face? Whose Nation?," 1317–20; Pegler-Gordon, *In Sight of America*, 112–20.

31. "Snatched from the Fire," *Los Angeles Times*, June 16, 1897, 2; "Caring for Immigrants," *New York Times*, June 16, 1897, 1; Cannato, *American Passage*, 16–20, 22, 107, 350–51, 402.

32. Twombly, "Architectural History," 122–37.

33. Salyer, *Laws Harsh as Tigers*; Lee, *At America's Gates*, 48–51; Pegler-Gordon, *In Sight of America*, 28.

34. Sung, *Mountain of Gold*, 100.

35. Commissioner-General of Immigration, Washington, D.C., to Commissioners and Inspectors in Charge, letter, June 12, 1907; Acting Commissioner-General of Immigration, Washington, D.C., to Commissioner of Immigration, Ellis Island, letter, November 22, 1907; F. Sargent, Commissioner-General of Immigration, Washington, D.C., to Commissioner of Immigration, Ellis Island, letter, December 23, 1907; Daniel Keefe, Commissioner-General of Immigration, Washington, D.C., to Robert Watchorn, Commissioner of Immigration, Ellis Island, letter, November 20, 1908; all in file 51930B, INSAIE.

36. "Chinese Should Stay Here; Brooklyn Ministers Denounce the Law with Vigor," *Brooklyn Daily Eagle*, May 28, 1893, 1.

37. See, for example, "Invading by Evasion," *New York Times*, August 6, 1893, 4; Francis Sterne Palmer, "The Chinaman and the Exclusion Laws," *Harpers Weekly*, December 3, 1898, 1177; and Weiss, *Sieve*, 90.

38. Palmer, "Chinaman and the Exclusion Laws," 1177.

39. Wong, *Patronage, Brokerage, Entrepreneurship*, 34.

40. U.S. Census, Table V, "Population, by Race, of Cities and Towns," in *Tenth Census 1880, Statistics of the Population of the United States*, 422; U.S. Census, *Compendium of the 11th Census 1890, Part I—Population*, 526; U.S. Census, *Twelfth Census 1900, Vol. 1, Part. 1—Population*, cxx; U.S. Census, Table 25, "Indians, Chinese and Japanese, by Sex, for Counties, and for Cities of 10,000 to 100,000," in *Sixteenth Census 1940, Vol. II Part 5, Population*, 66; U.S. Census, Table Series A 91–104, "Population, by Sex and Race: 1790–1970," in *Historical Statistics of the United States*, Part 1, 14.

41. Bald, *Bengali Harlem*, 117–18.

42. McKenzie, *Oriental Exclusion*, 168–69.

43. Lui, *Chinatown Trunk Mystery*, 143–74; Bald, *Bengali Harlem*, 97–98, 164–71; Gluck, "Ecological Study of the Japanese in New York," 49.

44. Kanstroom, *Deportation Nation*, 110–13; Pfaelzer, *Driven Out*, 68, 93, 263.

45. Lui, *Chinatown Trunk Mystery*, 59–62.

46. Ellis Island Committee, *Report of the Ellis Island Committee*, 74–75; Chan, *Entry Denied*, 132–37; Lee, *At America's Gates*, 224–37; Lau, *Paper Families*, 135–39.

47. "Chinese Deportees to Sail Tomorrow," *New York Times*, September 25, 1925; Gong and Grant, *Tong War!*, 268.

48. Clark, *Deportation of Aliens*; Kanstroom, *Deportation Nation*; Moloney, *National Insecurities*.

49. "Germans Ordered to Stay on Ships," *New York Times*, February 7, 1917, 4.

50. Curran, *Pillar to Post*, 293.

51. Unrau, *Ellis Island Historic Resource Study*, 1243; Yee, "EIOHP Interview of William Fook Yee."

52. Louis Adamic, "Aliens and Alien-Baiters," *Harper's Magazine*, November 1936, 561.

53. Subdivision 2, rule 3, Chinese Immigration Rules of October 1, 1926, cited in Edward Haff, Lecture No. 24, *Boards of Special Inquiry*, November 26, 1934 (Washington, D.C.: Government Printing Office, 1934), 13; Weiss, *Sieve*, 36.

54. *ARCGI* (1910), 133; Weiss, *Sieve*, 34.

55. Sánchez, *Becoming Mexican American*, 38–62; Lee, *At America's Gates*, 151–87; Pegler-Gordon, *In Sight of America*, 174–220; Ettinger, *Imaginary Lines*; Delgado, *Making the Chinese Mexican*, 73–103; Chang, *Pacific Connections*, 39–41, 149–57.

56. Exceptions include Griffith, "Border Crossings"; Ngai, *Lucky Ones*; Lee, "Hunting for Sailors."

57. Amy B. Wang, "Why You've Never Heard of the Six Chinese Men Who Survived the Titanic," *Washington Post*, April 19, 2018, https://www.washingtonpost.com/news/retropolis/wp/2018/04/19/why-youve-never-heard-of-the-six-chinese-men-who-survived-the-titanic/.

58. Appendix III, Digest of Reports of Commissioners and Inspectors in Charge of Districts, *ARCGI* (1913–1920); Table 62, *ARCGI* (1927–1932).

59. Weiss, *Sieve*, 109.

60. *ARCGI* (1919), 273; *ARCGI* (1930), 19.

61. Historians of the Asian diaspora have paid more attention to maritime workers than have other immigration historians: Tchen, *New York before Chinatown*; Kwong, *Chinatown, New York*; Ahuja, "Mobility and Containment," 120–26; Amenda, "'Chinese Quarters'"; Benton, *Chinese Migrants and Internationalism*; Ngai, *Lucky Ones*; Bald, *Bengali Harlem*, 94–159; Lee, "Hunting for Sailors."

62. *ARINS* (1947), 67.

63. See, for example, Daniels, *Concentration Camps USA*; Hayashi, *Democratizing the Enemy*; Inada, *Only What We Could Carry*; United States Commission on Wartime Relocation and Internment of Civilians, *Personal Justice Denied*; Weglyn, *Years of Infamy*.

64. Unrau, *Ellis Island Historic Resource Study*, 1004.

65. Cannato, *American Passage,* 396–99.

66. Riis, "In the Gateway of Nations," 675.

67. Cited in Cannato, *American Passage,* 396.

68. Spickard, *Almost All Aliens,* 6–17.

69. Reeves, *Gateway to the American Dream,* 9. See also Brownstone, Franck, and Brownstone, *Island of Hope, Island of Tears,* 15; Kotker and Jonas, *Echoes from a Nation's Past,* 42.

70. Fleegler, *Ellis Island Nation,* 189.

71. Unrau, *Ellis Island Historic Resource Study,* 9.

72. Works Progress Administration, Federal Writers' Project in New York City, *New York City Guide,* 416–17.

73. N. D. Collaer, Chief of Detention and Deportation Section, to W. F. Kelly, Assistant Commissioner for Alien Control, memorandum, December 21, 1944, 4, file 56125-3, entry 323, Subject and Policy Files, INS, NARA–Washington, D.C. See also *ARINS* (1944), 22; *ARINS* (1945), 28.

74. Photograph Caption, "Ellis Island Series," Rescues—Ellis Island, October, 1949, Rescue Operations-Floods, box 102 (of 157), Records of the U.S. Coast Guard, General Photographic File of Activities, Facilities, and Personalities, 1886–1967, RG 26-G, NARA–College Park, Md.

75. Ellis Island Committee, *Report of the Ellis Island Committee,* 12.

76. Kanstroom, *Deportation Nation,* 166.

77. Fairchild, *Science at the Borders.* See also Pegler-Gordon, *In Sight of America,* 104–73.

78. Rand, *Ellis Island Snow Globe.*

79. Conway, *Forgotten Ellis Island,* x; Conway, *Forgotten Ellis Island,* DVD.

80. "Young and Old Beg to Enter US; Men at Bridge Know Lots of Secrets about El Pasoans," *El Paso Herald,* March 10, 1921, 11; Stern, *Eugenic Nation.*

81. Unrau, *Ellis Island Historic Resource Study,* xix; Sánchez, *Becoming Mexican American,* 13.

82. Markel and Stern, "Which Face? Whose Nation?"; Bavery, *Bootlegged Aliens.*

83. Marinbach, *Galveston, Ellis Island of the West*; Stolarik, *Forgotten Doors*; Fairchild, *Science at the Borders*; Garland, *After They Closed the Gates.*

84. Preface, in Bamford, *Angel Island,* 5.

85. In addition to overlooking the centrality of racial exclusion, this model has also been critiqued for ignoring processes of colonization and transnational migration. See Omi and Winant, *Racial Formation in the United States*; Sánchez, "Race, Nation, and Culture"; Spickard, *Almost All Aliens*; Pegler-Gordon, "Debating the Racial Turn."

86. Lai, Lim, and Yung, *Island* (2014), 3, 17–18.

87. Lee, *At America's Gates,* 50–58, 68–74, 77–78, 90, 93–97.

88. Daniels, "No Lamps Were Lit for Them," 3. On the rejection of Angel Island as an Ellis Island of the West, see 9–10; Rand, *Ellis Island Snow Globe,* 27.

89. Lee, *At America's Gates,* 251.

90. See also Lowe, *Our Own Ellis Island.*

91. Lee and Yung, *Immigrant Gateway,* 23.

92. Sakovich, "Angel Island Immigration Station Reconsidered," 3, 230–36. See also Lee and Yung, *Immigrant Gateway*, 330–31.

93. Harriet Hyde, "San Francisco's New Ellis Island," *San Francisco Sunday Call*, January 19, 1908; Gee, "Sifting the Arrivals"; Sakovich, "Angel Island Immigration Station Reconsidered"; Lee and Yung, *Immigrant Gateway*.

94. Table X, *ARCGI* (1902), 33; Teague, "I, Too, Am American," 7–8; Bayor, *Encountering Ellis Island*, 77; "The Asiatic Situation," *ARCGI* (1920), 4; Weiss, *Sieve*, 235–36. Although immigration authorities questioned whether Syrian, Lebanese, and Armenian immigrants were Asian, these groups are not considered as part of this study.

95. Moreno, *Encyclopedia of Ellis Island*, 26, 34–35, 75–77, 85, 112. Two other encyclopedias mention Asians at Ellis Island: "Ellis Island (Detention Facility)," Densho Encyclopedia, last updated July 14, 2015, http://encyclopedia.densho.org/Ellis%20Island%20(detention%20facility)/; and Danico and Ocampo, *Asian American Society*, 307–10.

96. Lai, Lim, and Yung, *Island* (2014), 40–41, 180–83. This research builds on Him Mark Lai's news brief, "Chinese Detainees," 1; Lai, Lim, and Yung, *Island* (1991), 110.

97. Bald, *Bengali Harlem*, 11–14, 23, 113. See also Ahuja, "Mobility and Containment," 121.

98. Embry, "Asian Arrivals @ Ellis Island;" Embry, "Filipinos Arrivals @ Ellis Island"; Embry, "Filipinos in Ellis Island." See also Nadal and Filipino American National Historical Society Metropolitan New York Chapter, *Filipinos in New York City*, 12–15.

99. Bayor, *Encountering Ellis Island*, 75–76; Cannato, *American Passage*, 22, 107, 350–51, 402. See also Pegler-Gordon, *In Sight of America*, 134–37.

100. Email communication with the author, May 21, 2009.

101. The Immigration Bureau reported entries into the United States by port, starting with the first annual report in 1892, and by race, after 1899. *ARCGI* (1892), 3; and *ARCGI* (1899), 5–8. But the bureau did not consistently report entries by both race and port. Therefore, it is hard to determine the numbers of different Asian groups who arrived through Ellis Island.

102. Palmer, "Chinaman and the Exclusion Laws," 1177.

103. Keefe to Watchorn, letter, November 20, 1908, file 51930B, INSAIE.

104. "Japanese Arrivals in Continental United States Showing Various Details Bearing on the Japanese Agreement" (Table E), *ARCGI* (1908–1923). In 1910–12, comparisons between Japanese arriving from Europe and those arriving at Ellis Island show that these numbers were relatively similar. The Immigration Bureau stopped reporting detailed figures on Japanese immigrants in 1924.

105. Keefe to Watchorn, letter, November 20, 1908, file 51930B, INSAIE.

106. "Chinese Seeking Admission to the United States" (Table 1), *ARCGI* (1905–1908); "Chinese Seeking Admission to the United States" (Table 2), *ARCGI* (1909–1912); "Miscellaneous Chinese Transactions by Ports" (Table 8), *ARCGI* (1913–1922); "Miscellaneous Chinese Transactions by Ports" (Table 6), *ARCGI* (1923–1924); "Miscellaneous Chinese Transactions by Ports" (Table 64), *ARCGI* (1926); "Miscellaneous Chinese Transactions by Ports" (Table 67), *ARCGI* (1927); "Miscellaneous

Chinese Transactions by Ports" (Table 72), *ARCGI* (1925, 1928–1931); "Miscellaneous Chinese Transactions by Ports" (Table 63), *ARCGI* (1932).

107. Corsi, *In the Shadow of Liberty*, 165.

108. Amenda, "'Chinese Quarters'"; Bald, *Bengali Harlem*; Embry, "Asian Arrivals @ Ellis Island."

109. Embry, "Filipinos in Ellis Island."

110. The numbers do not match exactly as the total Chinese arrivals are listed by calendar year, whereas Chinese immigrants admitted and rejected are listed by fiscal year. Demographic data on immigration by race and port were not reported consistently by the Immigration Bureau, and different sources of data are sometimes inconsistent with one another. "Chinese Seeking Admission to the United States" (Table 1), U.S. Bureau of Immigration, *ARCGI* (1905–1908); "Chinese Seeking Admission to the United States" (Table 2), U.S. Bureau of Immigration, *ARCGI* (1909–1912); "Miscellaneous Chinese Transactions by Ports" (Table 8), *ARCGI* (1913–1922); New York, U.S., Arriving Passenger and Crew Lists, 1820–1957 (online database), Ancestry.com, 2010.

111. Bodnar, *History of Immigrants*; Handlin, *Epic Story*.

112. *ARCGI* (1920), 320; "Chinaman 149 Years Old," *New York Times*, June 30, 1913; Pedro Zulen, file 6/1931, Chinese Files, 1921–1944, INS, NARA–New York.

113. Hu-DeHart and López, "Asian Diasporas in Latin America and the Caribbean."

114. Look Lai, "Chinese Indenture System," 7; Munasinghe, "Redefining the Nation," 9.

115. Crowley, "Plural and Differential Acculturation in Trinidad"; Look Lai, "Chinese Indenture System," 4; Look Lai, *Essays on the Chinese Diaspora in the Caribbean*; Look Lai and Beng Tan, *Chinese in Latin America and the Caribbean*; López, *Chinese Cubans*; Hu-DeHart, "Voluntary Associations."

116. Chin and Chin, *Paper Son*, 9.

117. F. S. Pierce, Chinese Inspector in Charge, New York, to Commissioner-General of Immigration, Washington, D.C., February 21, 1922, file 6/1950, Chinese Files, 1921–1944, INS, NARA–New York.

118. F. S. Pierce, Chinese Inspector in Charge, New York, to Immigrant Inspector in Charge, Detroit, February 9, 1922; and Pierce to Commissioner-General of Immigration, Washington, D.C., February 21, 1922; Inspector in Charge, Detroit, Michigan, to US Commissioner of Immigration, Montreal, Canada, February 8, 1922; all in file 6/1950, Chinese Files, 1921–1944, INS, NARA–New York.

119. In the matter of Dang Ham, file 6/2028, Chinese Files, 1921–1944, INS, NARA–New York.

120. Yunkering Kinnen and Kinnie S. Kinnen, S.S. Morro Castle, November 10, 1903; Ge Hill Rome, S.S. Morro Castle, December 22, 1903; Hurn Seek Kim and Gung Seek Kim, S.S. Grenada, May 25, 1904; Gung Jee Kier and Chi Lucke Oke, S.S. Vigiliancia, March 11, 1905; all in New York, U.S., Arriving Passenger and Crew Lists, 1820–1957 (online database), Ancestry.com, 2010.

121. Lew, "EIOHP Interview of Harry Gem Hoy Lew"; "Order Hindu Deported," *New York Times*, January 23, 1915; "Havel Fast in the Sand," *New York Times*,

March 8, 1895. In the matter of Cesareo Chiu Fuksan, December 11, 1922, file 6/1418, Chinese Files, 1921–1944, INS, NARA–New York.

122. "Tried to Wed at Sea but Parson Refused," *New York Times*, June 21, 1915, 16; "Chinaman 149 Years Old," *New York Times*, June 30, 1913, 16.

123. "Havel Fast in the Sand."

124. In the Matter of Tcheng Ka Ling, May 12, 1915, file 6/1902, Chinese Files, 1921–1944, INS, NARA–New York.

125. Sani Sang Lee, James H. Song, and Pyong Kor Yoon, S.S. Majestic, February 27, 1908; Jack Sang Chang, S.S. St. Paul, December 16, 1914; Arung Kim, S.S. Berengaria, November 2, 1923; all in New York, U.S., Arriving Passenger and Crew Lists, 1820–1957 (online database), Ancestry.com, 2010.

126. "Aliens Must Appeal to Washington," *New York Times*, November 6, 1894.

127. Young, "EIOHP Interview of Joseph Eng Young."

128. *ARCGI* (1910), 138–39.

129. *ARCGI* (1910), 138; Smith, "Immigration and Naturalization Service at the U.S.-Canadian Border."

130. James Bronson, "Enforcement of the Chinese Exclusion Law," 143–44.

131. Saum Song Bo, "Chinese View of the Statue of Liberty."

132. Chew, "Life Story of a Chinaman," 287, 296–97, 299.

133. Cheung, "Afterword," 224.


## Chapter 1

1. Yee, "EIOHP Interview of William Fook Yee."

2. Record of Fook Yee, Lists of Chinese Passengers Arriving at Vancouver and Victoria, British Columbia, Canada, June 1929–January 1941, series A3446, roll 9; and Record of Fook Yee, New York, U.S., Arriving Passenger and Crew Lists, 1820–1957; both accessed via (online database) Ancestry.com; Yee, "EIOHP Interview of William Fook Yee."

3. Yee, "EIOHP Interview of William Fook Yee"; Lee and Yung, *Immigrant Gateway*, 84; Pegler-Gordon, *In Sight of America*, 27.

4. Yee, "EIOHP Interview of William Fook Yee."

5. Yee, "EIOHP Interview of William Fook Yee."

6. Yee, "EIOHP Interview of William Fook Yee."

7. Yee, "EIOHP Interview of William Yee," 13; Lew, "EIOHP Interview of Harry Gem Hoy Lew," 17, 21; Young, "EIOHP Interview of Joseph Eng Young," 14.

8. "Invading by Evasion," *New York Times*, August 6, 1893, 4.

9. "Scharf's Retort to Hendricks," *New York Times*, August 8, 1893, 5; Lee, *At America's Gates*, 51.

10. Lai, Lim, and Yung, *Island* (2014), 36, 40–41, 124.

11. Lai, Lim, and Yung, *Island* (2014), 180; Lai, "Chinese Detainees."

12. Lai, Lim, and Yung, *Island* (2014), 8.

13. Lai, Lim, and Yung, *Island* (2014).

14. Lee, *At America's Gates*, 48–64.

15. Lee, *At America's Gates*, 11, 63.

16. Immigration Act of March 3, 1875 (19 Stat. 477).

17. Act of May 6, 1882 (22 Stat. 58); Chinese Legation, memorandum, December 9, 1901, Notes from the Chinese Legation in the United States to the Department of State, 1868–1906 (Volume 4), National Archives, Nineteenth Century Collections Online.

18. On the limitations of the law and its early description as a restriction law, see Lew-Williams, *Chinese Must Go*, 51–62. On the centrality of exclusion, see Daniels, "No Lamps Were Lit for Them"; Lee, *At America's Gates*; McClain, *In Search of Equality*; Salyer, *Laws Harsh as Tigers*.

19. Act of March 4, 1884 (23 Stat. 115); Act of October 1, 1888 (25 Stat. 504); Daniels, *Guarding the Golden Door*, 20.

20. Immigration Act of August 3, 1882 (23 Stat. 214); Contract Labor Act of February 26, 1885 (23 Stat. 332); Immigration Act of March 3, 1891 (26 Stat. 1084).

21. *ARCGI* (1901), 46; Smith, "Immigration and Naturalization Service at the U.S.-Canadian Border."

22. *ARCGI* (1908), 220. At the beginning of the federalization of immigration policy, from 1891 until 1895, the highest official in charge of immigration was known as the superintendent of immigration. However, commissioner-general was the title most commonly used to describe the director of the national immigration service. In this book, "commissioner-general" is hyphenated throughout. However, in U.S. government usage, the title was hyphenated from 1895–1910 and not hyphenated from 1911–1933. Between 1934 and 1956, the end point of this study, the highest official in the newly integrated Immigration and Naturalization Service was called the "commissioner." U.S. Citizenship and Immigration Services, "Commissioners and Directors," https://www.uscis.gov/about-us/our-history/commissioners -and-directors (2019). Commissioner also referred to the director of Ellis Island. U.S. commissioners were individuals appointed by U.S. circuit courts to enforce federal laws.

23. Daniels, *Guarding the Golden Door*, 44–45; Geiger, *Subverting Exclusion*, 36–43.

24. Immigration Act of February 5, 1917 (39 Stat. 874); Daniels, *Guarding the Golden Door*, 46–47.

25. Immigration Act of 1924 (43 Stat. 153); Daniels, *Guarding the Golden Door*, 49–57. This shift is also signaled in U.S. government reports on and documents about U.S. citizens of Asian descent. Before the 1920s, the Immigration Bureau listed Chinese who applied for admission on the basis of U.S. citizenship, recording those who were admitted and those denied. However, starting with the 1923 annual report, the bureau lists only "US Citizens (Chinese)" who were admitted, creating the appearance that there were no applicants for admission as U.S. citizens who were denied. In addition, documents from this time period consistently emphasize that Chinese individuals "claimed" U.S. birth and held citizenship documents without accepting their claims. See, for example, J. L. Hughes, Commissioner, Philadelphia, to Chinese inspector in charge, New York, letter, February 12, 1924, file 55/58, Chinese Files, 1921–1944, INS, NARA–New York.

26. Letter cited in "Scharf's Retort to Hendricks," 5.

27. Lee, *At America's Gates*, 51.

28. Bonner, *Alas! What Brought Thee Hither?*, 138.

29. Kurashige, *Two Faces of Exclusion*, 35–55, 92–98.

30. Francis Sterne Palmer, "The Chinaman and the Exclusion Laws," *Harper's Weekly*, December 3, 1898, 1177.

31. *ARCGI* (1904), 137.

32. Weiss, *Sieve*, 90.

33. "Chinese Immigration—Its Sources and Stimulants," *New York Herald*, October 6, 1870, 6. See also Tchen, *New York before Chinatown*, 178–84; Kanstroom, *Deportation Nation*, 103–4.

34. "Absolute Exclusion of the Chinese," *New York Tribune*, March 9, 1888, 4.

35. "The Celts and the Celestials," *New York Times*, December 17, 1871, 4; "Capitalists in Disgrace," *New York Times*, January 25, 1878, 4; "American Boycotting," *New York Times*, May 7, 1882, 8; "A Chinese Immigrant," *New York Times*, June 9, 1883, 4; "The Registry of Chinamen," *New York Times*, September 29, 1892, 4; "The Smuggling of Chinamen," *New York Times*, July 27, 1893, 4.

36. Tchen, *New York before Chinatown*, 278; Gyory, *Closing the Gate*, 237–39.

37. W. H. Allen, "Statement on Restriction of Immigration," in *Reports of the Industrial Commission on Immigration, and on Education* (Washington, D.C.: GPO, 1899), 15:164. See also *ARCGI* (1904), 140.

38. "Scharf's Retort to Hendricks," 5; "Col. Scharf Transferred to Boston," *New York Times*, September 15, 1895, 15; Scharf, "Farce of the Chinese Exclusion Laws," 94.

39. "Scharf Protests in Vain," *New York Times*, July 28, 1893, 8; "His Authority under Review," *New York Times*, August 1, 1893, 8.

40. "Col. Scharf Gives It Up," *New York Times*, October 14, 1897, 1.

41. "Col. J.T. Scharf Dead," *New York Times*, March 3, 1898, 3; "His Authority under Review," 8.

42. "Scharf's Retort to Hendricks," 5.

43. "Colonel Scharf Lively as Ever," *New York Times*, July 27, 1893, 1; "Chinese Enter by Fraud," *New York Times*, July 25, 1893, 1; "Celestials Slept on Ship," July 26, 1893, 8; Lee, *At America's Gates*, 49–56.

44. "Inspector Scharf's Evidence," *New York Times*, November 29, 1896, 1.

45. "Colonel Scharf Lively as Ever," 1; "Col. Scharf Gives It Up," 1.

46. Act of May 6, 1882 (22 Stat. 58); "Col. Scharf Lively as Ever," 1.

47. Letter from Secretary Carlisle to Customs Collector Hendricks, July 29, 1893, published in "His Authority under Review," 8.

48. "New Collector for Port of New York," *Boston Daily Globe*, July 29, 1893, 1.

49. "Chinamen Allowed to Land," *New York Times*, September 3, 1893, 10; "Mr. Scharf Appeals to Mr. Carlisle," *New York Times*, December 7, 1894, 13.

50. "Case of J. Thomas Scharf," *New York Times*, October 19, 1897, 4. See also "Secretary Gage and Colonel Scharf," *New York Times*, October 16, 1897, 6; Bonner, *Alas! What Brought Thee Hither?*, 139.

51. "Secretary Gage and Colonel Scharf," 6.

52. Palmer, "Chinaman and the Exclusion Laws," 1177.

53. Marcus Braun, Immigrant Inspector, "First Detail to Mexico" (February 1907), file 52320/1, reel 2, in United States Immigration and Naturalization Service, *Records of the U.S. Immigration and Naturalization Service*, Record Group 85, Microfilm Records, Series A, Subject Correspondence Files, Part 2, Mexican Immigration, 1906–1930 (Bethesda, Md.: American University Publications, 1994); Braun, "How Can We Enforce Our Exclusion Laws?" 140–42; Department of Commerce and Labor, *Official Register: Persons in the Civil, Military and Naval Service of the United States* (Washington, D.C.: GPO, 1909), 1:76.

54. Yu, *To Save China, to Save Ourselves*, 15–19.

55. Although there was a Chinese Chamber of Commerce, Corsi seems to be describing the work of the CCBA. Corsi, *In the Shadow of Liberty*, 169.

56. *ARCGI* (1904), 137.

57. Markel and Stern, "Which Face? Whose Nation?"

58. Unrau, *Ellis Island Historic Resource Study*, 34–36, 45, 50, 57, 218–20, 230.

59. *ARCGI* (1920), 320; F. S. Pierce, Inspector in Charge, Chinese Division, Ellis Island, to Commissioner-General of Immigration, Washington, D.C., letter, May 18, 1922, file 6/1952, Chen Mao Gen, Chinese Files, 1921–1944, INS, NARA–New York; Wu Ting Fang, Chinese Legation, to John Hay, Secretary of State, letter, April 5, 1900, Notes from the Chinese Legation in the United States to the Department of State, 1868–1906 (Volume 4), National Archives, Nineteenth Century Collections Online.

60. *ARCGI* (1910), 134. Regarding Angel Island, see Lee and Yung, *Immigrant Gateway*, 14–15. Regarding Seattle, see *ARCGI* (1907), 80.

61. Robert Watchorn, Commissioner of Immigration, Ellis Island, to Frank Sargent, Commissioner-General of Immigration, Washington, D.C., letter, June 15, 1907, INSAIE.

62. For files showing the repeated movements of the New York Chinese Division, see Alexander Hamilton US Customs House, New York, N.Y., *Port of New York*, 18; Folder markings, file 47/619, Young Sing, Chinese Files, 1921–1944, INS, NARA–New York; *ARCGI* (1901), 46; F. W. Berkshire, Officer in Charge, to H. E. Owen, Assistant U.S. Attorney, Port Henry, New York, December 29, 1904, file 19/1355, Ah Hong and Jim Chong (Tom), Chinese Files, 1921–1944, INS, NARA–New York; F. Sargent, Commissioner-General, to Chinese Inspector in Charge, Custom House, New York, April 10, 1908, file 52102-17, entry 9, RG 85, NARA–Washington, D.C.; H. R. Sisson, Inspector in Charge, New York, to Commissioner-General of Immigration, April 18, 1908, file 52102-17, entry 9, RG 85, NARA–Washington, D.C.; Ansel W. Paine, Acting Inspector in Charge, New York, to Commissioner-General of Immigration, Washington, D.C., January 8, 1908, file 19/1148, Goey Wah, Chinese Files, 1921–1944, INS, NARA–New York; A. W. Brough, Inspector in Charge, New York, to US Commissioner of Immigration, Montreal, Canada, September 11, 1924, file 6/1421; and Thomas B. R. Mudd, Commissioner, Baltimore, to Chinese Inspector in Charge, US Barge Office, Battery Park, New York, September 10, 1925, file 6/1438, Chin Tung Jung, both in Chinese Files, 1921–1944, INS, NARA–New York.

63. A. W. Brough, Inspector in Charge, New York, to Commissioner of Immigration, Seattle, Wash., August 17, 1927, file 19/1158, Yee Bow and Yee Soon, Chinese

Files, 1921–1944, INS, NARA–New York. Ellis Island continued to be used as a Chinese "detention facility"; however, by 1954, administrative responsibilities had been moved to 70 Columbus Avenue, New York. Edward Shaugnessy, District Director, New York, to Walter Downey, Regional Director, General Services Administration, letter, June 18, 1954, file 56126-619, Subject and Policy Files, INS, NARA–Washington, D.C.

64. Wu Ting Fang, *Oriental Diplomat*, 87–88; Pegler-Gordon, *In Sight of America*, 113–21.

65. U.S. Treasury Department, *Operations of the United States Marine-Hospital Service* (Washington, D.C.: GPO, 1893, 1894); U.S. Treasury Department, *Annual Report of the Supervising Surgeon-General of the Marine-Hospital Service of the United States* (Washington, D.C.: GPO, 1895–1901); U.S. Treasury Department, *Annual Report of the Supervising Surgeon-General of the Public Health and Marine-Hospital Service of the United States* (Washington, D.C.: GPO, 1902–10); Shah, *Contagious Divides*, 179–203.

66. Pegler-Gordon, *In Sight of America*, 30–33.

67. Corsi, *In the Shadow of Liberty*, 164–65.

68. From at least 1910 until 1920, the New York district also included New Jersey. *ARCGI* (1910), 134; *ARCGI* (1920), 314. Previously, New Jersey was part of a three-state district with Pennsylvania and Delaware headquartered at Philadelphia. *ARCGI* (1906), 97.

69. *ARCGI* (1913), 188; *ARCGI* (1916), 181. For comparison, see *ARCGI* (1914), 231; *ARCGI* (1915), 225.

70. Ellis Island Committee, *Report of the Ellis Island Committee* (1934), 52.

71. Ngai, "'Slight Knowledge of the Barbarian Language,'" 14–15, 28–29.

72. V. H. Metcalf, Secretary of Commerce and Labor, and F. Sargent, Commissioner-General of Immigration, memorandum, to All Commissioners of Immigration and Inspectors in Charge, May 23, 1906, file 51831-23, entry 9, RG 85, INS, NARA–Washington, D.C.; Lawrence Murray, Assistant Secretary, Department of Commerce and Labor, to Commissioner-General of Immigration, January 2, 1908, file 51831-23, entry 9, RG 85, INS, NARA–Washington, D.C.; Lawrence Murray, Assistant Secretary, Department of Commerce and Labor, to Commissioner-General of Immigration, February 23, 1908, file 52149-1, entry 9, RG 85, INS, NARA–Washington, D.C.; *Government Officials and Employees Not under the Civil Service*, S. Doc. 173, January 10, 1933, 166. [Serial set ID 9658]

73. Ng Suey, BSI hearing transcript, October 13, 1923, file 55/86, Chinese Files, 1921–1944, NARA–New York; Sung, *Mountain of Gold*, 242; Lee and Yung, *Immigrant Gateway*; Wong, *Chinatown*, 37.

74. Ngai, "'Slight Knowledge of the Barbarian Language,'" 6–10.

75. Lee, *At America's Gates*, 58–63, 72–73.

76. "Col. Scharf Lively as Ever," 1.

77. Chin Kong Kwock, file 150/150, Chinese Files, 1921–1944, INS, NARA–New York.

78. "Highbinders as They Are: Worry Charles Says They Are Not Bad Fellows," *Washington Post*, August 12, 1895, 2.

79. "Chinatown Moguls: Harrison Avenues Celestial Moguls, for Whom the Geary Act Has No Terrors," *Boston Daily Globe*, May 7, 1893, 28.

80. Ngai, "'Slight Knowledge of the Barbarian Language,'" 15.

81. "Scharf Protests in Vain," 8.

82. "Inspector Scharf's Evidence," 1.

83. Ngai, "'Slight Knowledge of the Barbarian Language,'" 15.

84. Lee, *At America's Gates*, 61.

85. James Bronson, "Enforcement of the Chinese Exclusion Law," 146.

86. Commissioner-General to Chinese Inspector in Charge, New York, letter, October 19, 1914, file 53360-34, roll 2, INSAIE supplement microfilm. The other stations employing multiple interpreters were San Francisco, Seattle, El Paso, and Honolulu.

87. Lee, *At America's Gates*, 140; Wong, *Chinatown*, 37; Lee and Yung, *Immigrant Gateway*, 91–92.

88. *Official Register of the United States* (Washington, D.C.: GPO, 1905), 1:1094; "Smuggled in Wife and Child," *New York Times*, June 8, 1907; Application of Lawfully Domiciled Chinese Laborer for Return Certificate, October 20, 1911, Ong Gen, file 6/1416, Chinese Files, 1921–1944, INS, NARA–New York; Application of Alleged American Citizen of the Chinese Race for Preinvestigation of Status, Form 430, Wong Jam Hop, October 1, 1917, file 6/1421, Chinese Files, 1921–1944, INS, NARA–New York; *ARCGI* (1909), 140; *ARCGI* (1914), 234.

89. *ARCGI* (1919), 277–78.

90. A. W. Brough, Chinese Inspector in Charge, Ellis Island, to Commissioner of Immigration, Seattle (official copy to Messrs. Sisson and Booth for their information), September 13, 1926, file 6/1445; Statement by Witness, H. R. Sisson, In re: Tom Sun Hung, applicant for admission to the United States at Boston, Mass., as the minor son of a merchant, July 1, 1930, file 149/228; Byron H. Uhl to H. R. Sisson, May 25, 1931, file 6/1422; Byron Uhl, District Director, New York District, to Moy Cui, c/o H. R. Sisson, October 2, 1939, file 96/612; all in Chinese Files, 1921–1944, INS, NARA–New York.

91. Walter L. Brough, Alfred W. Brough Office, to Byron H. Uhl, District Director, New York District, letter, July 6, 1939, file 12/755, Chinese Files, 1921–1944, INS, NARA–New York.

92. "Smuggled in Wife and Child." The *Times* and New York City case files do not reveal the final outcome of this case. U.S. commissioners, appointed by circuit courts to enforce federal laws, were the first point of contact for most Chinese immigrants with the federal judiciary. Lindquist, "Origin and Development of the United States Commissioner System"; Hester, *Deportation*, 17, 22.

93. US ex rel. Moore v. Sisson, 206 Fed. 450 (1913).

94. *ARCGI* (1919), 277–78; Markel and Stern, "Which Face? Whose Nation?"

95. Statement by Witness, H. R. Sisson, In re: Tom Sun Hung, applicant for admission to the United States at Boston, Mass., as the minor son of a merchant, July 1, 1930, file 149/228, Tom Sun Hong, Chinese Files, 1921–1944, INS, NARA–New York.

96. Torok, "'Chinese Investigations,'" 192–212.

97. Torok, "'Chinese Investigations,'" 192–201.

98. "Cosmopolitan Heroes," *New York Times*, May 4, 1919, 49.

99. Torok, "'Chinese Investigations,'" 194–200.

100. Torok, "'Chinese Investigations,'" 202–3.

101. Torok, "'Chinese Investigations,'" 211–12.

102. *ARCGI* (1914), 231. See also *ARCGI* (1915), 223; *ARCGI* (1920), 320.

103. Daniel Keefe, Commissioner-General of Immigration, Washington, D.C., to Robert Watchorn, Commissioner of Immigration, Ellis Island, letters, January 16, 1909, and December 11, 1908; both in file 51930B, roll 2, INSAIE.

104. Mikayla Robinson, "Becoming Philip Jaisohn: 19th Century Korean Immigration and Soh Jae-pil" (unpublished paper in possession of the author, 2014); Yunkering Kinnen and Kinnie S. Kinnen, S.S. *Morro Castle*, November 10, 1903; Hurn Seek Kim and Gung Seek Kim, S.S. *Grenada*, May 25, 1904; Sol Sang, S.S. *Majestic*, July 24, 1907; all in New York, U.S., Arriving Passenger and Crew Lists, 1820–1957 (online database), Ancestry.com, 2010.

105. Lasker, *Filipino Immigration*, 7.

106. Embry, "Filipinos in Ellis Island."

107. "Lost a Crown," *St. Louis Post and Dispatch*, February 19, 1893, 1; "Princess Kaiulani's Visit: She Will Come to Washington To-Morrow to Visit the President," *Washington Post*, March 7, 1893, 8; Princess Victoria Kainlani [*sic*], S.S. *Teutonic*, March 2, 1893, New York, U.S., Arriving Passenger and Crew Lists, 1820–1957 (online database), Ancestry.com, 2010.

108. "Crown Prince of Siam Guest of the Nation," *New York Times*, October 11, 1902.

109. Lee, *At America's Gates*, 89.

110. Schedule A, Applicants for Admission to and the Privilege of Transit through the United States at the Port of New York; Schedule B, Table Showing Disposition of Case of Resident Chinese Applying for Return Certificates at the Port of New York, *ARCGI* (1913), 189; *ARCGI* (1914), 230–34; *ARCGI* (1915), 223–25; *ARCGI* (1916), 178–81; *ARCGI* (1917), 179–81; *ARCGI* (1918), 272–74; *ARCGI* (1919), 308–11; *ARCGI* (1920), 320–22.

111. Inspection Report Chinese Passenger (Holding Diplomatic Visa), U.S. Immigration Service, New York, March 2, 1934, file 164-391, Chick Yu Wat, Chinese Files, 1921–1944, INS, NARA–New York.

112. Embry, "Filipinos in Ellis Island."

113. "List or Manifest of Alien Passengers," S.S. *Philadelphia*, February 9, 1911, New York, U.S., Arriving Passenger and Crew Lists, 1820–1957 (online database), Ancestry.com, 2010; Sohi, *Echoes of Mutiny*, 49.

114. Li, "Wu Ting Fang," 321–22; Wu Ting Fang, memorandum, Chinese Legation, Washington, December 9, 1901, Notes from the Chinese Legation in the United States to the Department of State, 1868–1906 (Volume 4), National Archives, Nineteenth Century Collections Online.

115. Fang, *Oriental Diplomat*, 87–88.

116. Wu Ting Fang to Hay, letter, April 5, 1900, Notes from the Chinese Legation in the United States to the Department of State, 1868–1906 (Volume 4), National Archives, Nineteenth Century Collections Online.

117. *ARCGI* (1920), 320. See also Pierce to Commissioner-General of Immigration, Washington, D.C., letter, May 18, 1922, file 6/1952, Chen Mao Gen, Chinese Files, 1921–1944, INS, NARA–New York.

118. Hsu, *Good Immigrants*, 9, 48.

119. Arrivals were generally reported by port or status, but not both. Exceptions include *ARCGI* (1913), 189; *ARCGI* (1914), 231; *ARCGI* (1915), 223; *ARCGI* (1916), 178.

120. Hsu, *Good Immigrants*, 39–48, 52.

121. Baldoz, *Third Asiatic Invasion*, 45–46; Nadal and FANHS Chapter, *Filipinos in New York City*, 17, 22–23. See also Lasker, *Filipino Immigration*, 369–74.

122. E. C. A. Reed, American Consul, In the Matter of Andrew Chih Yi Cheng, December 21, 1920; Inspector in Charge to Commissioner-General of Immigration, January 25, 1921; both in file 25/577, Chinese Files, 1921–1944, INS, NARA–New York; "List or Manifest of Alien Passengers," S.S. *La Touraine*, January 14, 1921, New York, U.S., Arriving Passenger and Crew Lists, 1820–1957 (online database), Ancestry .com, 2010; *ARCGI* (1919), 310; Patrick Boehler, "The Forgotten Army of the First World War: How Chinese Labourers Helped Shape Europe," *South China Morning Post, SCMP Chronicles*, no date, accessed June 28, 2019, http://multimedia.scmp .com/ww1-china/. On missionary and YMCA educational sponsorship, see Hsu, *Good Immigrants*, 23–37.

123. "Order Hindu Deported," *New York Times*, January 23, 1915.

124. McKenzie, *Oriental Exclusion*, 147. On immigration policies concerning students, see also Hsu, *Good Immigrants*, 65–66.

125. Baldoz, *Third Asiatic Invasion*, 45–47.

126. Weiss, *Sieve*, 104–5.

127. "Chinese Author Gets Aid," *New York Times*, October 22, 1939, 42; "A Playwright on Union Square," *New York Times*, October 22, 1939, 2X; Leonard Lyons, "The New Yorker," *Washington Post*, November 21, 1940, 22.

128. Ferrand, *Question of Allegiance*, 74–75.

129. Wong, *Patronage, Brokerage, Entrepreneurship*, 79–80; McKenzie, *Oriental Exclusion*, 168–69; Bald, *Bengali Harlem*, 22–24.

130. Young Sing, Certificate of the Imperial Government of China, New York, New York, 1893; Young Sing to Hon. George Weed, US Collector, Plattsburg, N.Y., letter, January 4, 1898; Henry M. White, Commissioner, to Inspector in Charge, US Immigration Service, New York, letter, June 29, 1914; all in file 47/619, Chinese Files, 1921–1944, INS, NARA–New York.

131. Alfonso Jos, President, Cuban Asiatic Chamber of Commerce, to Carlos Manuel de Cespedes, Cuban Legation, January 2, 1922, file 6/1950, Chinese Files, 1921–1944, INS, NARA–New York.

132. *ARCGI* (1909), 128.

133. Lee, *At America's Gates*, 90–92; Pegler-Gordon, *In Sight of America*, 95–96.

134. *ARCGI* (1920), 320; W. W. Husband, Commissioner-General of Immigration, to All Commissioners of Immigration and Inspectors in Charge of Atlantic and Gulf Ports, August 9, 1922, file 55166/31, Subject and Policy Files, INS, NARA–Washington, D.C.; Henry Baker, US Consul, Trinidad, to US Secretary of State, letter concerning Chinese in Trinidad and attempts at unlawful entry into the United

States, October 12, 1922, file 55166/31a, Subject and Policy Files, INS, NARA–Washington, D.C.

135. "Scharf Protests in Vain," 8.

136. Baker to US Secretary of State, October 12, 1922, file 55166/31a, Subject and Policy Files, INS, NARA–Washington, D.C.

137. "Smuggling of Aliens and Narcotics through Cuba," 6–8, June 28, 1922, file 55166/31a, Subject and Policy Files, INS, NARA–Washington, D.C.

138. In the Matter of Tcheng Ka Ling, May 12, 1915, file 6-1902, Chinese Files, 1921–1944, INS, NARA–New York.

139. Bald, *Bengali Harlem*, 11–14.

140. In the Matter of Tcheng Ka Ling, May 12, 1915, file 6/1902, Chinese Files, 1921–1944, INS, NARA–New York.

141. In the matter of Dang Ham, July 3, 1922, file 6/2028, Chinese Files, 1921–1944, INS, NARA–New York.

142. Lee, *At America's Gates*, 72, 87, 133, 208–13.

143. H. Baker, American Consul, Trinidad, B.W.I., to the Chinese Inspector, New York, letter, August 17, 1920, file 25/196, Chinese Files, 1921–1944, INS, NARA–New York.

144. G. George, Export Manager, to the Chinese Inspector, New York, letter, August 11, 1922, file 12/236, Chinese Files, 1921–1944, INS, NARA–New York.

145. H. R. Sisson, Inspector in Charge, to Henry F. O'Brien, Senior Watchman, Barge Office, letter, January 15, 1920, file 34/501, Chinese Files, 1921–1944, INS, NARA–New York.

146. Chinese Legation, memorandum, December 9, 1901, Notes from the Chinese Legation in the United States to the Department of State, 1868–1906 (Volume 4), National Archives, Nineteenth Century Collections Online.

147. "Chinese Exclusion," *Outlook*, April 23, 1904, 963.

148. *ARCGI* (1906), 72. See also Scharf, "Farce of the Chinese Exclusion Laws," 93.

149. "Tried to Wed at Sea but Parson Refused," *New York Times*, June 21, 1915, 16.

150. "List or Manifest of Alien Passengers," S.S. *Rochambeaux*, June 6, 1915, NYNYPCL.

151. "Singhalese Woman on Board a Steamer in Brooklyn Waiting to Be Deported by U.S. Immigration Authorities after Their Expiration of Their Contract with Western Theatrical Troupe, NY," http://ark.cdlib.org/ark:/13030/ktop3012b0; and "Singhalese Dancers Waiting to Be Deported, NY City, NY," http://ark.cdlib.org/ark:/13030/kt6k4016ns; both in Keystone Mast Collection, UCR/California Museum of Photography, University of California at Riverside, accessed June 10, 2014; A. Morton Smith, "Circus Scout Finds New Thrills for the Big Top," *Popular Science Monthly*, March 1937, 108. In 1911, the Dreamland amusement park in Coney Island, Brooklyn, employed Filipinos to re-create an Igorot village, wearing traditional costumes and reenacting practices that were no longer common in the Philippines, for the entertainment of park attendees. Nadal and FANHS Chapter, *Filipinos in New York City*, 11.

152. Passenger manifest, S.S. *Vigiliancia*, March 11, 1905, NYNYPCL.

153. *ARCGI* (1914), 230–34; *ARCGI* (1915), 223–25. Chinese arrivals were reported by both profession and port in the annual reports in only these two years.

154. File 29/417, "Barnum & Bailey Circus," Chinese Files, 1921–1944, INS, NARA–New York; Rao, *Chinatown Opera Theater in North America*, 50–52. See also file 169/53, Chinese Files, 1921–1944, INS, NARA–New York; Marjorie Ing Kai, Lancastria, April 13, 1938, NYNYPCL.

155. Immigration Act of August 3, 1882 (23 Stat. 214); Immigration Act of February 20, 1907 (34 Stat. 898); Baynton, "American History," 45–51.

156. Pegler-Gordon, *In Sight of America*, 127–50.

157. "List or Manifest of Alien Passengers," S.S. *Adriatic*, April 8, 1911, NYNYPCL; Augustus Sherman Collection, Ellis Island Museum and Statue of Liberty National Monument, New York.

158. Weiss, *Sieve*, 245. See also "A Hindoo Freak," *San Francisco Chronicle*, September 8, 1891, 1.

159. "Chinese Seeking Admission to the United States" (Table 1), U.S. Bureau of Immigration, *ARCGI* (1905–1908); "Chinese Seeking Admission to the United States" (Table 2), U.S. Bureau of Immigration, *ARCGI* (1909–1912); "Miscellaneous Chinese Transactions by Ports" (Table 8), *ARCGI* (1913–1922); New York, U.S., Arriving Passenger and Crew Lists, 1820–1957 (online database), Ancestry.com, 2010.

160. Lai, "Chinese Detainees"; Lai, Lim, and Yung, *Island* (2014), 40–41, 76, 180.

161. Chang, *Chinese in America*, 148. On contrasting Ellis Island and Angel Island lengths of detention, see also Lee and Yung, *Immigrant Gateway*, 57.

162. Barde and Bobonis, "Detention at Angel Island," 104.

163. Barde and Bobonis, "Detention at Angel Island," 106.

164. Marian Smith, email communications with the author, June 30, 2009, and September 28, 2012; and Bonnie Sauer, email communication with the author, September 25, 2012.

165. Barde and Bobonis, "Detention at Angel Island," 113–14.

166. Pegler-Gordon, *In Sight of America*, 112–20; Lai, Lim, and Yung, *Island* (2014), 15, 341. These data are taken from *Lists of Chinese Applying for Admission to the United States through the Port of San Francisco, California, 1903–1947*, microfilm 1476, RG 85, National Archives, Washington, D.C. Unfortunately, there are no surviving comparable records from Ellis Island.

167. Sung, *Mountain of Gold*, 100.

168. "Chinese Salvationist," *New York Sun*, August 23, 1896, 7; Record of Yee Sing, roll 663, *Passenger Lists of Vessels Arriving at New York, New York, 1820–1897* (Microfilm Publication M237), Records of the U.S. Customs Service, Record Group 36, National Archives at Washington, D.C., accessed via Ancestry.com, 2010.

169. Report of Status of Entry-Seekers at Close of Business, October 31st, 1923, Office of Chinese Inspector in Charge, Chinese Branch, New York, November 1, 1923.

170. "Chinese Seeking Admission to the United States" (Table 1), *ARCGI* (1905–1908); "Chinese Seeking Admission to the United States" (Table 2), *ARCGI* (1909–1912); "Miscellaneous Chinese Transactions by Ports" (Table 8), *ARCGI* (1913–1922); "Miscellaneous Chinese Transactions by Ports" (Table 6), *ARCGI* (1923–1924); "Miscellaneous Chinese Transactions by Ports" (Table 72), *ARCGI* (1925); "Miscellaneous

Chinese Transactions by Ports" (Table 64), *ARCGI* (1926); "Miscellaneous Chinese Transactions by Ports" (Table 67), *ARCGI* (1927); "Miscellaneous Chinese Transactions by Ports" (Table 72), *ARCGI* (1928–1931); "Miscellaneous Chinese Transactions by Ports" (Table 63), *ARCGI* (1932).

171. *ARCGI* (1920), 320.

172. *ARDOL* (1933), 61. After the Immigration and Naturalization Bureaus were combined into the Immigration and Naturalization Service (INS) in 1933, it appears that there was no independent *Annual Report of the INS* (*ARINS*) until 1941. From 1933 until 1940, immigration statistics were released in the *Annual Report of the Secretary of Labor* (*ARSOL*).

173. *ARSOL* (1933), 61.

174. Record of Preinvestigation of the Status of Tom Lee, Alleged Native-Born Chinese, Applicant for Return Certificate, Examination of Witnesses at Watertown, New York, April 20, 1915, file 6/1900, Chinese Files, 1921–1944, INS, NARA–New York.

175. File 6/1900, Chinese Files, 1921–1944, INS, NARA–New York. See also In the Matter of Tom Guy, file 6/1904, Chinese Files, 1921–1944, INS, NARA–New York. See also coordination between Tampa and New York: file 55166/31, Subject and Policy Files, INS, NARA–Washington, D.C.

176. Tom Oy Ngan to Chief Officer in Charge, Immigration Service, Chinese Division, letter, July 12, 1929, file 6/1908, Chinese Files, 1921–1944, INS, NARA–New York.

177. *ARCGI* (1909), 121. On the numerical impacts of this law on Japanese immigration, see *ARCGI* (1908), 89, 213–14.

178. Commissioner-General of Immigration, Washington, D.C., to Commissioners and Inspectors in Charge, letter, June 12, 1907, file 51930B, INSAIE. See also Geiger, *Subverting Exclusion*, 36–43.

179. Acting Commissioner-General of Immigration, Washington, D.C., to Commissioner of Immigration, Ellis Island, letter, November 22, 1907; F. Sargent, Commissioner-General of Immigration, Washington, D.C., to Commissioner of Immigration, Ellis Island, letter, December 23, 1907; Robert Watchorn, Commissioner of Immigration, Ellis Island, to Daniel Keefe, Commissioner-General of Immigration, Washington, D.C., letter, January 25, 1909; all in file 51930B, INSAIE.

180. Robert Watchorn, Commissioner of Immigration, Ellis Island, to Daniel Keefe, Commissioner-General of Immigration, Washington, D.C., letter, November 20, 1908, file 51930B, INSAIE.

181. Daniel Keefe, Commissioner-General of Immigration, Washington, D.C., to Robert Watchorn, Commissioner of Immigration, Ellis Island, letter, November 20, 1908, file 51930B, INSAIE.

182. *ARCGI* (1909), 121; Geiger, *Subverting Exclusion*, 168–79.

183. *ARCGI* (1908), 127; U.S. Department of Commerce and Labor, Bureau of Immigration and Naturalization, *Immigration Laws and Regulations of July 1, 1907*, 5th ed. (Washington, D.C.: Government Printing Office, 1908), rule 21(d), 41; F. H. Larned, Assistant Commissioner-General, Washington, D.C., to Commissioner of Immigra-

tion, Ellis Island, letter, October 26, 1909, file 51930B, INSAIE. On the distinction between laborers and nonlaborers, see U.S. Department of Commerce and Labor, Bureau of Immigration and Naturalization, *Immigration Laws and Regulations*, rule 21(j).

184. Daniel Keefe, Commissioner-General of Immigration, Washington, D.C., to Commissioner of Immigration, Ellis Island, letter, April 15,1909; Robert Watchorn, Commissioner, Ellis Island, to Daniel Keefe, Commissioner-General of Immigration, Washington, D.C., letter, April 16, 1909; Daniel Keefe, Commissioner-General of Immigration, Washington, D.C., to Commissioner of Immigration, Ellis Island, letter, April 17,1909; Joseph Murray, Acting Commissioner, Ellis Island, to Daniel Keefe, Commissioner-General of Immigration, Washington, D.C., letter, April 28, 1909; F. H. Larned, Assistant Commissioner-General, Washington, D.C., to Commissioner of Immigration, New York, letter, May 4, 1909; Joseph Murray, Acting Commissioner, Ellis Island, to Commissioner-General of Immigration, Washington, D.C., letter, May 7, 1909; all in file 51930B, INSAIE.

185. F. H. Larned, Assistant Commissioner-General, Washington, D.C., to Commissioner of Immigration, Ellis Island, letter, July 21, 1909, file 51930B, INSAIE.

186. Gluck, "Ecological Study of the Japanese in New York," 38–41; Inouye, *Distant Islands*, 216.

187. "Scrapping the Gentlemen's Agreement," *New York Times*, February 7, 1923, 14. On the Japanese Association in the western United States, see Hayashi, *Democratizing the Enemy*, 41–55.

188. McKenzie, *Oriental Exclusion*, 172.

189. Gluck, "Ecological Study of the Japanese in New York," 38–41.

190. Lee and Yung, *Immigrant Gateway*, 113.

191. "Japanese Arrivals in Continental United States, Showing Various Details Bearing on the Japanese Agreement" (Table E), *ARCGI* (1910–1924). Published data are not available before 1908. Published data after 1912 are recorded by location of departure, not port of entry. After fiscal year 1924, Japanese were formally barred from entry to the United States, and the Bureau of Immigration did not record their entry. Table 6 shows substantially higher numbers of Japanese rejected when arriving from Hawaii, Canada, Mexico, and other locations compared with arrivals from Europe or Japan.

192. "Smuggling of Chinamen," 4.

193. Y. Y. Tang to Roderick McKenzie, letter, April 28, 1927, cited in McKenzie, *Oriental Exclusion*, 44.

## Chapter 2

1. "450 Chinese Seized; Tong Peace Signed," *New York Times*, September 15, 1925, 1; "Theatres and Places of Amusement," in *Brooklyn Daily Eagle Almanac* (New York: Brooklyn Daily Eagle, 1905), 12; Rao, *Chinatown Opera Theater*, 88–95, 269–81; Chiang, "Chinese Operas," 259–64; "Weather," *New York Times*, September 14, 1925, 1; Wong, *Patronage, Brokerage, Entrepreneurship*, 34.

2. *ARCGI* (1908), 147.

3. Francis Sterne Palmer, "The Chinaman and the Exclusion Laws," *Harper's Weekly*, December 3, 1898, 1177. The term "deportation" was, at different times, used by immigration authorities to refer to both those individuals who were returned to their countries of origin immediately upon being refused entry to the United States and those immigrants who were removed after entering and residing in the United States. In this chapter and throughout this book, I use "exclusion" to refer to those who were prevented from entering upon arrival and "deportation" to refer to those who were removed after their entry and residence in the United States. Clark, *Deportation of Aliens*, 27–28.

4. Ellis Island Committee, *Report of the Ellis Island Committee*, 74–75.

5. "Using the Law to Enforce Personal Prejudices," *New York Amsterdam News*, October 31, 1923, 12.

6. Fong Yue Ting v. United States 149 U.S. 698 (1893); *In re* Ny Look, C.C. New York (1893), 56 Fed. 81; United States v. Wong You, 223 U.S. 67 (1912).

7. Wong, *Chinatown*, 7.

8. U.S. Census, *Report on the Social Statistics of Cities, Part 1*, 402; U.S. Census, *Compendium of the Eleventh Census 1890, Part 1—Population*, 520; U.S. Census, *Twelfth Census 1900, Vol. 1, Part 1, Population*, cxx; Wong, *Patronage, Brokerage, Entrepreneurship*, 34.

9. Wong, *Patronage, Brokerage, Entrepreneurship*, 34; McKenzie, *Oriental Exclusion*, 168–69.

10. Lew-Williams, *Chinese Must Go*, 214–24; Tom, "Colonia Incognita," 45; Wang, *Surviving the City*, 10–11, 19; Lui, *Chinatown Trunk Mystery*, 59–61, 157–58.

11. Wong, *Chinatown*, 7.

12. Wong, *Patronage, Brokerage, Entrepreneurship*, 34, 79–80; Rao, *Chinatown Opera Theater*, 269–96.

13. Gong and Grant, *Tong War!*, 237.

14. Louis Adamic, "Aliens and Alien-Baiters," *Harper's Magazine*, November 1936, 561.

15. *ARCGI* (1909), 128. See also *ARCGI* (1914), 21.

16. New York Police Department, *Annual Report* (New York: Martin Brown, 1909), 108. The police report does not mention other Asians besides Chinese in relation to deportation.

17. Kanstroom, *Deportation Nation*, 4–6, 124–27.

18. *ARCGI* (1905), 94. Similar reports are also found in *ARCGI* (1903), 110–11; and *ARCGI* (1904), 148.

19. Ellis Island Committee, *Report of the Ellis Island Committee*, 74.

20. Act of May 6, 1882 (22 Stat. 58); Act of March 3, 1891 (26 Stat. 1084). On the time period during which immigrants were subject to deportation and the length of their deportation period, see Immigration Act of February 20, 1907 (34 Stat. 898), secs. 20–21; Immigration Act of February 5, 1917 (39 Stat. 874), sec. 19; Act of March 4, 1929 (45 Stat. 1551); Clark, *Deportation of Aliens*, 51–69; Kanstroom, *Deportation Nation*, 133–36.

21. The 1798 Alien and Sedition Acts were the first and only deportation laws prior to Chinese exclusion, although they did not provide a continuous basis for

current deportation policy. Kanstroom, *Deportation Nation*, 6–7, 91, 95; Hester, *Origins of U.S. Policy*, 9; Clark, *Deportation of Aliens*, 37–43, 51–54, 275–77, 465; Act of May 6, 1882 (22 Stat. 58); Act of March 3, 1891 (26 Stat. 1084), sec. 8; Act of May 5, 1892 (27 Stat. 25); Act of November 3, 1893 (28 Stat. 7); Pegler-Gordon, *In Sight of America*, 32–41.

22. Yu, *To Save China, to Save Ourselves*, 15–19. Translation of CCBA notice cited in McClain, *In Search of Equality*, 204.

23. Salyer, *Laws Harsh as Tigers*, 46–47. "The Chinese Exclusion Act," *New York Times*, July 22, 1892, 2.

24. *ARCGI* (1907), 90.

25. "Chinese Must Go: Supreme Court Sustains the Geary Act," *Boston Daily Globe*, May 16, 1893, 4.

26. "The Chinese Exclusion Bill," *New York Times*, April 15, 1892, 4; "China and the Geary Act," *New York Times*, April 18, 1893, 4; "Testing the Geary Act," *New York Times*, May 4, 1894, 4; "Congress Alone Responsible," *New York Times*, May 16, 1893, 4; "Chinese and the Geary Act," *Brooklyn Daily Eagle*, May 5, 1893, 4. The *New York Tribune* was less strongly opposed: "The Geary Act," *New York Tribune*, May 16, 1893, 16.

27. Notes on *New York Tribune*, September 23, 1892, in folder 1891–1900, Arthur Bonner Papers, Manuscripts and Archives Division, New York Public Library; "To Americanize Chinamen: An Equal Rights League Formed in Chicago," *New York Times*, April 4, 1897, 1; "Chinamen as Volunteers," *New York Times*, January 15, 1898, 3. See also "Chinese Should Stay Here; Brooklyn Ministers Denounce the Law with Vigor," *Brooklyn Daily Eagle*, May 28, 1893, 1.

28. Salyer, *Laws Harsh as Tigers*, 46.

29. Hernández, *City of Inmates*, 73.

30. Salyer, *Laws Harsh as Tigers*, 48.

31. "Chinese Must Go: Supreme Court Sustains the Geary Act," 4.

32. "Backward in Coming Forward," *New York Times*, April 20, 1893, 9.

33. "Chinese Must Go: Supreme Court Sustains the Geary Act," 4; "Chinatown Moguls," *Boston Daily Globe*, May 7, 1893, 28.

34. "Brooklyn Political Talk," *New York Times*, August 21, 1892, 16.

35. "Test Cases in New York," *Brooklyn Daily Eagle*, May 6, 1893, 1; Salyer, *Laws Harsh as Tigers*, 47–48.

36. Fong Yue Ting v. United States, 149 U.S. 698 (1893).

37. Kanstroom, *Deportation Nation*, 118–20.

38. Dred Scott v. Sandford, 60 U.S. 393 (1857); "Chinese Must Go: Supreme Court Sustains the Geary Act," 4. See also O. O. Howard, letter to the editor, "Chinese Exclusion Strongly Condemned," *Brooklyn Daily Eagle*, February 5, 1902, 7.

39. Kanstroom, *Deportation Nation*, 118.

40. Salyer, *Laws Harsh as Tigers*, 54.

41. Salyer, *Laws Harsh as Tigers*; Lew-Williams, *Chinese Must Go*, 204–5; "Notes on Recent Decisions," *Minnesota Law Journal* 1, no. 4 (August 1893): 86.

42. "The Ny Look Case," *Washington Post*, May 28, 1893, 4; "The Ny Look Test Case," *New York Times*, May 26, 1893, 4; *In re* Ny Look, C.C. New York (1893), 56 Fed.

81; "Notes on Recent Decisions," 86. See also "Attempts to Enforce the Geary Law," *Brooklyn Daily Eagle*, September 6, 1893, 5; Kanstroom, *Deportation Nation*, 120.

43. Act of November 3, 1893 (28 Stat. 7); Salyer, *Laws Harsh as Tigers*, 88.

44. "Chinese Enter by Fraud," *New York Times*, July 25, 1893, 1.

45. "Scharf's Raid on Chinese," *New York Times*, August 21, 1897, 12; "Case of J. Thomas Scharf," *New York Times*, October 19, 1897, 4.

46. On the Portland raids, see Letter and enclosures from Minister Wu Ting Fang to John Hay, Secretary of State, January 23, 1899, Notes from the Chinese Legation in the United States to the Department of State, 1868–1906, RG 59, microfilm M98, roll 3, NARA–College Park, Md.

47. Letter from Minister Wu Ting Fang, Chinese Legation, to John Sherman, Secretary of State, November 10, 1897, 2; Notes from the Chinese Legation in the United States to the Department of State, 1868–1906, RG 59, microfilm M98, roll 3, NARA–College Park, Md.

48. On New York and Boston in 1902, see Letter and enclosures from Minister Wu Ting Fang to Alvey Adee, Acting Secretary of State, August 30, 1902. On Boston in 1903, see Letter and enclosures from Minister Wu Ting Fang to John Hay, Secretary of State, November 10, 1903, both in Notes from the Chinese Legation in the United States to the Department of State, 1868–1906, RG 59, microfilm M98, NARA–College Park, Md.

49. *ARCGI* (1907), 90–91.

50. *ARCGI* (1907), 91.

51. *ARCGI* (1905), 11; *ARCGI* (1907), 130; *ARCGI* (1910), 131–32. On the alignment of deportation under general immigration and Chinese exclusion laws, see also Hester, *Origins of U.S. Policy*, 16–34.

52. United States v. Wong You, 223 U.S. 67 (1912); McKenzie, *Oriental Exclusion*, 163–64; Hester, *Origins of U.S. Policy*, 30–32.

53. *ARCGI* (1913), 25. On the reduction in Chinese deported under exclusion rules after this decision, see "Chinese Arrested and Deported by Judicial District" (Table 7), *ARCGI* (1910–1922); *ARCGI* (1912), 19; Chinese Inspector in Charge, District No. 3, Comprising New York and New Jersey, *ARCGI* (1920), 321.

54. Wong Ju, Deportation Card, November 12, 1923, file 55/20, Chinese Files, 1921–1944, NARA–New York.

55. *ARCGI* (1902), 57.

56. "Asks Ellis Island Inquiry," *New York Times*, June 13, 1913, 1; Lee, *At America's Gates*, 182; Pegler-Gordon, *In Sight of America*, 177–78.

57. Post, *Deportations Delirium of Nineteen-Twenty*, 5.

58. See chapter 4, "Asian Sailors: Shanghaied in Hoboken."

59. "Williams Accused of Terrorizing Men," *New York Times*, July 16, 1909, 14. See also H. Hansen, Mate, Receipt of three Chinese aboard S.S. *Cananova*, March 20, 1924, file 55/58, Chinese Files, 1921–1944, INS, NARA–New York.

60. Act of May 10, 1920 (41 Stat. 593); Act of May 26, 1922 (42 Stat. 596); Kanstroom, *Deportation Nation*, 134.

61. *ARCGI* (1920), 309.

62. *ARCGI* (1924), 12. See also *ARCGI* (1925), 9; *ARCGI* (1926), 18; *ARCGI* (1927), 10.

63. On concerns about costs, see *ARCGI* (1922), 17; *ARCGI* (1926), 21.

64. *ARCGI* (1925), 9. See, for example, Henry Brien, Guard, New York, to Inspector in Charge, New York, letter, August 14, 1922, file 6/1999; Chinese Inspector in Charge, District of New York and New Jersey, to Commissioner-General of Immigration, letter, July 7, 1924, In re: Chong Gon Yook, file 55-143; A. W. Brough, Inspector in Charge, New York, to May Chan, Port of Spain, Trinidad, letter, May 1, 1925, file 60/121; all in Chinese Files, 1921–1944, INS, NARA–New York.

65. McKenzie, *Oriental Exclusion*, 147; Byron Uhl, Assistant Commissioner of Immigration, New York District, to Hon. Howard Ameli, US Attorney, Post Office Building, Brooklyn, NY, letter, February 17, 1931; Byron Uhl, Assistant Commissioner of Immigration, New York District, to Commissioner-General of Immigration, Washington, D.C., December 18, 1930; both in file 125/386, Chinese Files, 1921–1944, INS, NARA–New York.

66. Alien Registration Act of 1940 (54 Stat. 672), sec. 20.

67. Kanstroom, *Deportation Nation*, 121, 33–36; Salyer, *Laws Harsh as Tigers*, 131.

68. Chin, *Chinese Subculture and Criminality*, 53–58; Ma, "Chinatown Organizations," 153–57; Heyer, "Pattern of Social Organization," 112–13. See also Leong, *Chinatown Inside Out*, 26–52.

69. San Francisco's Chinese population dipped from 10,582 in 1910 to a low point of 7,744 in 1920 and then rose to 16,303 by 1930. *U.S. Census, Fourteenth Census 1920, Population*, 3: 109. For contemporary and highly biased descriptions of tongs in San Francisco, see *Reports of the Industrial Commission on Immigration, and on Education* (Washington, D.C.: GPO, 1899), 15: 762–65, 767, 769–71, 775–82, 791, 793–94; Gong and Grant, *Tong War!*.

70. Chin, *Chinese Subculture and Criminality*, 55.

71. Chin, *Chinese Subculture and Criminality*, 49; Wong, *Patronage, Brokerage, Entrepreneurship*, 108; Harry Hites, "Averting a Chinese 'Tong' War," *Washington Post*, September 27, 1925, SM4.

72. Gong and Grant, *Tong War!*, 153; "Sze Moves to Aid Cleveland Chinese," *New York Times*, September 26, 1925, 8.

73. Leong, *Chinatown Inside Out*, 68–74; "Sze Moves to Aid Cleveland Chinese," 8.

74. Chen, "Cultural Crossroads at the 'Bloody Angle,'" 371–72.

75. Lui, *Chinatown Trunk Mystery*, 27, 55–56.

76. In New York, the On Leong tong controlled the three-block area bounded by Mulberry Street in the west, Bowery in the east, Bayard in the south, and Canal Street in the north. The Hip Sing tong was dominant in the area immediately south of this, also defined by Mulberry Street and Bowery, but with Worth Street in the south, Bayard Street as its northern boundary, and Pell Street as its central artery. Chin, *Chinese Subculture and Criminality*, 56; Leong, *Chinatown Inside Out*, 72–73.

77. Dillon, *Hatchet Men*, 52–53.

78. "Smuggled Pistols and Chinese Seized," *New York Times*, July 17, 1923, 20.

79. Chin, *Chinese Subculture and Criminality*, 63; Yu, *To Save China, to Save Ourselves*, 44, 55–56; Leong, *Chinatown Inside Out*, 78–79.

80. Gong and Grant, *Tong War!*, 158–60, 81–83; "Tong Heads Warned," *New York Times*, November 20, 1924, 2; "Hunt 11 Tong Chiefs as War Instigators," *New York Times*, November 30, 1924, 1.

81. Leong, *Chinatown Inside Out*, 74–77.

82. Ma, "Chinatown Organizations," 154, 64–65.

83. Kanstroom, *Deportation Nation*, 4–6, 124–27.

84. Leong, *Chinatown Inside Out*, 66–68.

85. Reynolds, "Chinese Tongs," 613–17.

86. Chin Ming, New York, letter, November 13, 1926, in file 55374-876, roll 14, INSAIE supplement microfilm. See also J.M. [indistinct], Los Angeles, Calif., to Secretary of Labor, Washington, D.C., letter, September 1, 1926; Frank Yeo Leo, Minneapolis, Minn., to Harry E. Hull, Bureau of Immigration, Washington, D.C., July 27, 1926; both in file 55374-876, roll 14, INSAIE supplement microfilm.

87. Reynolds, "Chinese Tongs," 613, 23.

88. Salyer, *Laws Harsh as Tigers*, 58, 89–90.

89. Brooks, *Between Mao and McCarthy*, 21; Gong and Grant, *Tong War!*, 164–66; "Highbinders as They Are: Worry Charles Says They Are Not Bad Fellows," *Washington Post*, August 12, 1895, 2; "Tong Dinner Peaceful; On Leongs Stayed Away," *New York Times*, February 12, 1906, 5.

90. Clark, *Deportation of Aliens*, 324.

91. Fong Yee Ying, file 75-339, cited in Torok, "'Chinese Investigations,'" 31. See also Clark, *Deportation of Aliens*, 31–34, 59–64.

92. Timothy J. Molloy, Chinese and Immigrant Inspector, memorandum, April 15, 1931; Chin Yee and Jin Ben, letter, translated by Chinese Interpreter Louis Fong, Ellis Island, February 18, 1930; both in Chin Yee, file 151-50, Chinese Case Files, NARA–New York.

93. "Highbinders as They Are," 2.

94. Warrant Hearing, Chinese Division, New York, Immigration Service, June 3, 1924, file 55/110, Chinese Files, 1921–1944, INS, NARA–New York; "Chinese Leader Is Indicted Here," *New York Times*, May 4, 1956, 1; Torok, "'Chinese Investigations,'" 194.

95. Frances G. DeNanny, Immigration Restriction League, to Secretary of Labor, Immigration Department, letter, March 28, 1925; and R. J. Henning, Assistant Secretary, to Frances DeNanny, letter, April 6, 1925, both in 55374/876 roll 14, INSAIE supplement microfilm.

96. *Reports of the Industrial Commission on Immigration, and on Education* (Washington, D.C.: Government Printing Office, 1901), 15: 764–65, 770, 771, 780, 791–92.

97. The bill's language stated, "the employment by or on behalf of any such alien of a bodyguard or guard to protect him, or ward off, or warn him of any danger to his person in any building, or other place, or in or upon any street, or other public place, shall be and is hereby made prima facie proof of his membership in such

tong." HR 15535, December 21, 1926, 69th Cong., 2d Sess. 55374-876 roll 14, INSAIE supplement microfilm.

98. "Tong Heads Warned Agree to Stop War," 2; "Hunt 11 Tong Chiefs as War Instigators," 1; "72 More Chinese Ordered Deported," *New York Times*, September 25, 1925, 1; Gong and Grant, *Tong War!*, 239, 46.

99. "Hunt 11 Tong Chiefs as War Instigators," 1.

100. Gong and Grant, *Tong War!*, 265.

101. On concerns about "crime waves" being linked to pressure for deportation, see Clark, *Deportation of Aliens*, 162–64; Kanstroom, *Deportation Nation*, 162–66.

102. "Tongs Agree to Sign Peace Treaty Today," *New York Times*, August 19, 1930, 20; "Asks Deportations to End Tong Wars," *New York Times*, August 27, 1930, 24.

103. "Federal Drive on to End War on Tongs," *New York Times*, September 13, 1925, 29; "New Tong Murders: 500 Chinese Seized," *New York Times*, September 19, 1925, 1.

104. "Federal Drive on to End War on Tongs," 29.

105. "Chinatown Cowers as Raids Continue," *New York Times*, September 16, 1925, 27.

106. "New Tong Murders: 500 Chinese Seized," 1.

107. "Chinese Deportees to Sail Tomorrow," *New York Times*, September 25, 1925.

108. "Chinese Deportees to Sail Tomorrow."

109. "Chinatown Cowers as Raids Continue," 27.

110. "New Tong Murders: 500 Chinese Seized," 1.

111. "Chinatown Cowers as Raids Continue," 27; "New Tong Murders: 500 Chinese Seized," 1; "72 More Chinese Ordered Deported," 1; Gong and Grant, *Tong War!*, 268.

112. "Tong Fighting Ends: Leaders Are Obeyed," *New York Times*, March 7, 1927, 3; "Federal Aid Asked to Halt Tong War," *New York Times*, July 30, 1933, 18.

113. Leong, *Chinatown Inside Out*, 74–75. Him Mark Lai has suggested that Gor Yun Leong is a pseudonym for Chinese American journalist Zhu Xia and a white journalist, as this name sounds like the Cantonese pronunciation of Liang Ge Ren (two persons). Cited in Chen, *Being Chinese*, 185.

114. Hites, "Averting a Chinese 'Tong War,'" SM 4.

115. "Chinatown Cowers as Raids Continue," 27.

116. "New Tong Murders: 500 Chinese Seized," 1.

117. James Romano, "Survey of Chinese Activities in the Newark Field Division," July 8, 1943, file 291.2—Chinese, box 381, Army Intelligence Vertical File, 1941–1948, Record Group 319, entry 47, NARA–College Park, Md.

118. Corsi, *In the Shadow of Liberty*, 174–75.

119. Corsi, *In the Shadow of Liberty*, 174–76.

120. Corsi, *In the Shadow of Liberty*, 174–76.

121. Clark, *Deportation of Aliens*, 325–26; "18 Aliens Seized at Finnish Dance," *New York Times*, February 16, 1931, 17.

122. Pegler-Gordon, *In Sight of America*, 221.

123. E. A. Loughran, Assistant Commissioner, Administrative Division, to H. J. Walls, Supervising Engineer, Summary of New York memoranda, June 30, 1954, file 56126-619, Subject and Policy Files, INS, NARA–Washington, D.C.

124. William C. White, "Illegal Residents Leave Lives of Fear," *New York Times*, November 11, 1934, XX2. MacCormack oversaw the reunification of the Bureaus of Immigration and Naturalization into the Immigration and Naturalization Service in 1933.

125. Blue, "Strange Passages"; Ngai, *Impossible Subjects*, 56–90.

126. Leo B. Russell, Immigrant Inspector in Charge of Transportation, to Commissioner-General of Immigration, Washington, D.C., letter re: eastbound deportation train, June 23, 1919; Leo B. Russell, Immigrant Inspector in Charge of Transportation, to Commissioner-General of Immigration, Washington, D.C., letter re: westbound deportation train, June 23, 1919; Commissioner-General of Immigration, Washington, D.C., to Leo B. Russell, Inspector in Charge of Transportation, Baltimore, Maryland, letter, May 23, 1919; all in 54519-3, INSAIE supplement.

127. Clark, *Deportation of Aliens*, 454–58. See also "16 Chinese to Head Alien Felon Exodus," *New York Times*, July 28, 1935, 22.

128. "16 Chinese to Head Alien Felon Exodus," 22. The article does not give a date or year during which this train was used.

129. "16 Chinese to Head Alien Felon Exodus," 22.

130. "Kline's Deportation Party Is Grim Affair for Immigrants," *Milwaukee Journal*, January 11, 1940.

131. Ed Kline, Deportation Officer, to Immigration and Naturalization Service, Washington, D.C., telegram, May 9, 1941, Historical Museum at Fort Missoula, Montana Memory Project, https://mtmemory.org/digital/collection/p16013coll22/id/440/rec/1. By 1948, the regular deportation trains were decommissioned, replaced largely by airplanes.

132. Clark, *Deportation of Aliens*, 454–58.

133. Commissioner-General of Immigration, Washington, D.C., to Leo B. Russell, Inspector in Charge of Transportation, Baltimore, Maryland, letter, May 23, 1919; Russell to Commissioner-General of Immigration, Washington, D.C., letter re: westbound deportation train, June 23, 1919; both in 54519-3, INSAIE supplement.

134. Clark, *Deportation of Aliens*, 454–58.

135. Russell to Commissioner-General of Immigration, Washington, D.C., letter re: eastbound deportation train, June 23, 1919, 54519-3, INSAIE supplement. An additional thirteen individuals were picked up and delivered for deportation at various points along the route.

136. "16 Chinese to Head Alien Felon Exodus," 22.

137. Russell to Commissioner-General of Immigration, Washington, D.C., letter re: westbound deportation train, June 23, 1919, 54519-3, INSAIE supplement. See also Blue, "Strange Passages," 180–84.

138. Corsi, *In the Shadow of Liberty*, 173.

139. Moreno, *Encyclopedia of Ellis Island*, 35.

140. Yee, "EIOHP Interview of William Fook Yee," 13.

141. Curran, *Pillar to Post*, 293. See also "Germans Ordered to Stay on Ships," *New York Times*, February 7, 1917, 4. As noted in chapter 1, Ellis Island detention data are unreliable because, unlike other immigration stations, Ellis Island officials were not required to forward monthly detention reports to the national office. As a result, these reports appear to have been lost or were destroyed. However, information on detention is available through government memoranda, newspaper reports, and the recollections of both immigrants and inspectors. Marian Smith, email communications with the author, June 30, 2009, and September 28, 2012; and Bonnie Sauer, email communication with the author, September 25, 2012. See also Clark, *Deportation of Aliens*, 389.

142. E. A. Loughran, Assistant Commissioner, memorandum, June 30, 1954, file 56126-619, Subject and Policy Files, INS, NARA–Washington, D.C.; Works Progress Administration, Federal Writers' Project in New York City, *New York City Guide*, 416.

143. Gardner Jackson, "Doak the Deportation Chief," *Nation* (March 18, 1931), 295–96.

144. Ellis Island Committee, *Report of the Ellis Island Committee*, 47; Loughran, memorandum, June 30, 1954, file 56126-619; Philip Forman, Acting Chief, Detention, Deportation and Parole Branch, Ellis Island, to Edward Shaugnessy, District Director, New York, memorandum re: Population at Ellis Island, June 22, 1954; both in Subject and Policy Files, INS, NARA–Washington, D.C. See also Jackson, "Doak the Deportation Chief."

145. Yee, "EIOHP Interview of William Fook Yee."

146. "Refugees Make Literary Haven of Ellis Island," *New York Herald Tribune*, July 13, 1940, 9.

147. Forman to Shaugnessy, memorandum re: Population at Ellis Island, June 22, 1954; Loughran, memorandum, June 30, 1954, file 56126-619; both in Subject and Policy Files, INS, NARA–Washington, D.C. Other documents provide lower estimates of between 600 and 800 detainees during the 1940s. See, for example, J. Zucker, District Operations Officer, to Loyd Jensen, Chief, District Alien Control Division, memorandum, December 4, 1944, file 56125-3, entry 323, Subject and Policy Files, INS, NARA–Washington, D.C.; Zucker to Commissioner, December 3, 1947, INS Records, 56233/740, cited in Unrau, *Ellis Island Historic Resource Study*, 834.

148. Ellis Island Committee, *Report of the Ellis Island Committee*, 12–13, 55.

149. Hsu, *Good Immigrants*, 91–103.

150. Louie, "EIOHP Interview of Thomas Louie"; Lew, "EIOHP Interview of Harry Gem Hoy Lew."

151. Wang, *Surviving the City*, 53–54.

152. Report of Status of Entry-Seekers at Close of Business, October 31st, 1923, Office of Chinese Inspector in Charge, Chinese Branch, New York, November 1, 1923. On the variation in lengths of detention, see Lew, "EIOHP Interview of Harry Gem Hoy Lew"; *Christian Science Monitor*, September 1, 1954, cited in Unrau, *Ellis Island Historic Resource Study*, 1002. On non-Chinese detention, see *ARINS* (1949), 24; Bayor, *Encountering Ellis Island*, 39–40, 66, 90–91.

153. "Chinatown Cowers as Raids Continue," 27; "72 More Chinese Ordered Deported," 1. For additional information, see chapter 4.

154. C. M. Oberoutcheff in Unrau, *Ellis Island Historic Resource Study*, 1120–21.

155. Lew, "EIOHP Interview of Harry Gem Hoy Lew," 21–22; Ferrand, "EIOHP Interview of Pierre Ferrand," 14–15; Yee, "EIOHP Interview of William Fook Yee," 13. See also Oberoutcheff in Unrau, *Ellis Island Historic Resource Study*, 1120–21.

156. Lew, "EIOHP Interview of Harry Gem Hoy Lew," 21–22; Yee, "EIOHP Interview of William Fook Yee," 13.

157. "Scharf's Raid on Chinese," 12.

158. Lew, "EIOHP Interview of Harry Gem Hoy Lew," 22.

159. Lew, "EIOHP Interview of Harry Gem Hoy Lew," 17–18.

160. Lew, "EIOHP Interview of Harry Gem Hoy Lew," 17, 20.

161. Lew, "EIOHP Interview of Harry Gem Hoy Lew," 19.

162. Louie, "EIOHP Interview of Thomas Louie," 26.

163. Libby Lackman, "Aid Immigrants at Ellis Island," *New York Times*, March 2, 1941, D4; "DAR Tutors Chinese," *New York Herald Tribune*, March 20, 1936, 3.

164. "Immigrants Get a Christmas Party," *New York Times*, December 25, 1925.

165. "Santa Appears at Ellis Island and Scares Sam," *New York Herald Tribune*, December 25, 1931, 2; "Artists from Many Lands Entertain Ellis Islanders," *New York Herald Tribune*, December 25, 1932, 3.

166. Margaret Jones, American Friends Service Committee, to Evelyn Hersey, Immigration and Naturalization Service, letter, January 5, 1945, file 56125-3, entry 323, Subject and Policy Files, INS, NARA–Washington, D.C.

167. Groups were segregated from one another on the basis of race, gender, legal, and enemy alien status. The nine segregated groups were Italian seamen (deportation or "warrant" cases); Italian seamen (not warrant cases); alien enemies, German; alien enemies, German, female; minority groups, Germans, Czechs, Australians, and others; "Miscellaneous seamen, white and black"; non seamen (warrant cases); Chinese (which appears to have included other Asians); and detainees in Ellis Island Hospital. Zucker to Jensen, memorandum, December 4, 1944, file 56125-3, entry 323, Subject and Policy Files, INS, NARA–Washington, D.C. See also Kraut, *Silent Travelers*, 65.

168. Cited in Unrau, *Ellis Island Historic Resource Study*, 1117.

169. Campbell Auckland Geddes, "Despatch from H.M. Ambassador at Washington Reporting on Conditions at Ellis Island Immigration Station" (1923), in Unrau, *Ellis Island Historic Resource Study*, 563–66.

170. Unrau, *Ellis Island Historic Resource Study*, 1218, 43.

171. Lee and Yung, *Immigrant Gateway*, 34.

172. E. W. Hersey, Assistant to the Commissioner, to W. F. Kelly, Commissioner for Alien Control, memorandum, November 27, 1944, file 56125-3, entry 323, Subject and Policy Files, INS, NARA–Washington, D.C.

173. Edward Shaugnessy, District Director, New York, to E. A. Loughran, Assistant Commissioner, memorandum, June 8, 1954, 3, file 56126-619, Subject and Policy Files, INS, NARA–Washington, D.C.

174. Yee, "EIOHP Interview of William Fook Yee."

175. See, for example, photograph in Chermayeff, Wasserman, and Shapiro, *Illustrated History*, 252.

176. Lew, "EIOHP Interview of Harry Gem Hoy Lew," 19–20.

177. Ferrand, "EIOHP Interview of Pierre Ferrand."

178. Zichlinsky, "EIOHP Interview of Luisa Zichlinsky."

179. Geddes, "Despatch from H.M. Ambassador at Washington Reporting on Conditions at Ellis Island Immigration Station" (1923), in Unrau, *Ellis Island Historic Resource Study*, 563–66.

180. Lew, "EIOHP Interview of Harry Gem Hoy Lew," 21–22; Ferrand, "EIOHP Interview of Pierre Ferrand," 14–15; Yee, "EIOHP Interview of William Fook Yee," 13. See also Oberoutcheff in Unrau, *Ellis Island Historic Resource Study*, 1120–21.

181. *ARCGI* (1926), 15.

182. Buff, "Deportation Terror," 527.

183. Ngai, *Impossible Subjects*; Kanstroom, *Deportation Nation*; Hernández, *Migra!*; Moloney, *National Insecurities*; Hester, *Origins of U.S. Policy*.

184. Irwin, *Strange Passage*, 12.

## Chapter 3

1. "Nine Killed on Ship in Night Fight with Smuggled Chinese," *New York Times*, June 15, 1923, 1.

2. "Nine Killed on Ship in Night Fight with Smuggled Chinese," 3.

3. "Nine Killed on Ship in Night Fight with Smuggled Chinese," 1, 3.

4. Scharf, "Farce of the Chinese Exclusion Laws," 94.

5. "Col. Scharf Gives It Up," *New York Times*, October 14, 1897, 1.

6. Lai, Lim, and Yung, *Island* (2014); Lee, *At America's Gates*; Ngai, *Impossible Subjects*; Lee and Yung, *Immigrant Gateway*, 84; Pegler-Gordon, *In Sight of America*, 27.

7. Sánchez, *Becoming Mexican American*, 50; Lee, *At America's Gates*, 151–87; Pegler-Gordon, *In Sight of America*, 174–220; Young, *Alien Nation*, 153–96; Kang, *INS on the Line*, 27–28; Lim, *Porous Borders*, 95–123.

8. Exceptions include Griffith, "Border Crossings," 473–92; Ngai, *Lucky Ones*, 142; Bald, *Bengali Harlem*.

9. "Smuggling of Aliens and Narcotics through Cuba," 15, June 28, 1922, file 55166/31a, Subject and Policy Files, INS, NARA–Washington, D.C.

10. On Trinidad, see W. W. Husband, Commissioner-General of Immigration, to All Commissioners of Immigration and Inspectors in Charge at Atlantic and Gulf Ports, August 9, 1922, file 55166/31, Subject and Policy Files, INS, NARA–Washington, D.C. On Mexico, see H. R. Sisson, Inspector in Charge, to Commissioner of Immigration, Ellis Island, New York, letter, June 11, 1915, file 27/528, Charlie Low and Charlie Sing, Chinese Case Files, NARA–New York. On Colombia, see "Stowaways at Ellis Island," *New York Times*, January 25, 1935, 7.

11. Lue Guay to Dock Fook, letter, June 1925, English translation; Lee New, letter to unidentified individual, Chinese year C.R. 13-3-11; both in file 55466/659, INSAIE. Smugglers also used letter codes. See "Smuggling of Aliens and Narcotics through

Cuba," 10–11, June 28, 1922, file 55166/31a, Subject and Policy Files, INS, NARA–Washington, D.C.

12. Confidential memorandum to Commissioner-General of Immigration, Washington, D.C., June 16, 1924, file 55166/31a, Subject and Policy Files, INS, NARA–Washington, D.C.

13. Griffith, "Border Crossings," 482–83.

14. "Smuggling of Aliens and Narcotics through Cuba," 9, June 28, 1922, file 55166/31a, Subject and Policy Files, INS, NARA–Washington, D.C. See also Leong, *Chinatown Inside Out*, 131.

15. Confidential memorandum to Commissioner-General of Immigration, Washington, D.C., June 16, 1924, file 55166/31a, Subject and Policy Files, INS, NARA–Washington, D.C.

16. "Nine Killed on Ship in Night Fight with Smuggled Chinese," 1, 3.

17. Erika Lee discusses the dehumanizing use of terms such as "smuggled Chinese" and "contraband" in Lee, *At America's Gates*, 149, 72. On the use of "contraband" to describe African Americans during the Civil War, see Masur, "'Rare Phenomenon of Philological Vegetation.'" See also *ARCGI* (1914), 21; Assistant Secretary of State to US Secretary of State, letter, August 3, 1922, file 55166/31; and W. W. Sibray, Assistant Commissioner-General, to Commissioner of Immigration, Ellis Island, letter, June 29, 1923, file 55166/31a; both in Subject and Policy Files, INS, NARA–Washington, D.C.; J. L. Hughes, Commissioner of Immigration, Philadelphia, to Chinese Inspector in Charge, New York, letter, November 28, 1923, file 55/39, SS *Bowes Castle*, Chinese Files, 1921–1944, INS, NARA–New York.

18. Cited in Coolidge, *Chinese Immigration*, 41.

19. Coolidge, *Chinese Immigration*, 41–54. See also Young, *Alien Nation*.

20. United States Department of Commerce and Labor, Bureau of Immigration and Naturalization, *Treaties, Laws, and Regulations*, 1910, 11; Act of February 5, 1917 (39 Stat. 874), secs. 3 and 39.

21. Weiss, *Sieve*, 34.

22. "Smuggled the Baby In," *New York Times*, December 14, 1905, 18. See also Weiss, *Sieve*, 33–57; Corsi, *In the Shadow of Liberty*, 129–30.

23. American Consul General to US Secretary of State, "Alleged Practice of Smuggling Aliens in United States from Chile," September 12, 1922, file 55166/31, Subject and Policy Files, INS, NARA–Washington, D.C.

24. Assistant Secretary of State to US Secretary of State, letter, August 3, 1922, 1, file 55166/31, Subject and Policy Files, INS, NARA–Washington, D.C.

25. Marcus Braun, "Report, First Detail to Mexico," February 1907, file 42320/1; and "Report, Second Detail to Mexico," June 1907, file 42320/1A, both on reel 2, in United States Immigration and Naturalization Service, *Records of the Immigration and Naturalization Service*. See also Braun, "How Can We Enforce Our Exclusion Laws?" On the Immigration Bureau's attention to Mexican and Canadian land borders with the United States, see *ARCGI* (1909), 130–31.

26. Confidential memorandum to Commissioner-General of Immigration, Washington, D.C., June 16, 1924, file 55166/31a, Subject and Policy Files, INS, NARA–

Washington, D.C.; "Nab 8 Chinese in Smuggling Plot," *Brooklyn Daily Eagle*, August 26, 1923, 1; Okrent, *Last Call*; Lescarboura, "Battle of Rum Row."

27. Griffith, "Border Crossings," 479. See also Lee Fook Sing to Bureau of Immigration, letter, August 20, 1919, file 55166/31a, Subject and Policy Files, INS, NARA–Washington, D.C.; and A. W. Brough, Acting Inspector in Charge, New York, to Commissioner-General of Immigration, Washington, D.C., letter, October 31, 1923, file 55/47, "Chinese, Narcotics, and Liquor," Chinese Files, 1921–1944, INS, NARA–New York. Drug smuggling through Caribbean locations to New York may have been helped by the fact that importation of opium was not outlawed by British authorities in Trinidad until 1921. Henry Baker, US Consul, Trinidad, to US Secretary of State, letter concerning Chinese in Trinidad and attempts at unlawful entry into the United States, October 12, 1922, file 55166/31a, Subject and Policy Files, INS, NARA–Washington, D.C.

28. "Smuggling of Aliens and Narcotics through Cuba," 8–9, June 28, 1922, file 55166/31a, Subject and Policy Files, INS, NARA–Washington, D.C.

29. "Smuggling of Aliens and Narcotics through Cuba," 15, June 28, 1922, file 55166/31a, Subject and Policy Files, INS, NARA–Washington, D.C.

30. *ARCGI* (1927), 15.

31. David Vergun, "Cries of Wonder: A Short Waterside Tour of New York Harbor," in Works Progress Administration, Federal Writers' Project in New York City, *Maritime History of New York* (2004), 5.

32. Information about stowaways was recorded from 1908 to 1932. *ARCGI*, Table XVIB (1908); Table XXI (1909–1921); Table XX (1922–1924); Table 67 (1925); Table 59 (1926); Table 104 (1927); Table 68 (1928–1931); Table 62 (1932).

33. On smuggling from Jamaica, see H. R. Sisson, Chinese Inspector in Charge, New York, to Commissioner-General of Immigration, Washington, D.C., letter, June 8, 1908, file 13/356, Norwich Stowaways, Chinese Files, 1921–1944, INS, NARA–New York. On smuggling from Bermuda to New Orleans, see "Smuggling of Aliens and Narcotics through Cuba," 4, June 28, 1922, file 55166/31a, Subject and Policy Files, INS, NARA–Washington, D.C.

34. Data calculated by research assistant Daniel Davis based on randomized departure dates (Cuba, Trinidad, Jamaica, and Tampico, Mexico) and arrival dates (New York, New York) between 1906 and 1930. New York, U.S., Arriving Passenger and Crew Lists, 1820–1957 (online database), Ancestry.com, 2010. See also Baker to US Secretary of State, letter concerning Chinese in Trinidad and attempts at unlawful entry into the United States, October 12, 1922, file 55166/31a, Subject and Policy Files, INS, NARA–Washington, D.C.

35. Leong Ah Tong, BSI hearing transcript, October 18, 1921, file 6/1980, MS *Dollar* Stowaways, Chinese Files, 1921–1944, INS, NARA–New York; "Eleven Chinese Stowaways Seized on Ship Here," *New York Times*, March 27, 1938, 29 (the journey from Shanghai took seventy-six days); James Bronson, "Enforcement of the Chinese Exclusion Law," 149–50.

36. C. F. Deichman, American Consul General, to Secretary of State, Washington, D.C., letter re: alleged practice of smuggling aliens into the United States from Chile,

September 12, 1922, file 55166/31, Subject and Policy Files, INS, NARA–Washington, D.C. On France, see Stowaways ex. SS *Canada*, Fabre Line, Brooklyn, memorandum, November 31, 1921, file 6/1990; Acting Inspector in Charge, New York, to US District Attorney, Brooklyn, New York, letter, December 8, 1921, file 6/1996; Albert Wiley, Acting Inspector in Charge, New York, to Commissioner-General of Immigration, Washington, D.C., letter, December 13, 1921, file 6/1996; Fook Sim to Song Long Gim, letter translated from Chinese, no date, file 6/1996; all in Chinese Files, 1921–1944, INS, NARA–New York. See also, on Marseilles: Mallee and Pieke, *Internal and International Migration*, 166. See also Amenda, "'Chinese Quarters,'" 51.

37. *ARCGI* (1909), 128.

38. Chinese Inspector in Charge, District No. 3, Comprising New York and New Jersey, *ARCGI* (1917), 181.

39. *ARCGI*, Table XXI (1909–1921); *ARCGI*, Table XX (1922–1924); *ARCGI*, Table 67 (1925); *ARCGI*, Table 59 (1926); *ARCGI*, Table 104 (1927); *ARCGI*, Table 68 (1928–1931).

40. Immigration Act of 1924 (43 Stat. 153).

41. Garland, *After They Closed the Gates*, 97.

42. *ARCGI* (1919), 322, 330.

43. Data on Chinese stowaways in New York are located in Report of the Chinese Inspector in Charge District No. 3, Comprising New York and New Jersey; *ARCGI* (1914), 225, 231; *ARCGI* (1915), 224; *ARCGI* (1916), 177–79; *ARCGI* (1917), 175, 180, 200; *ARCGI* (1918), 268, 273, 294; *ARCGI* (1919), 303, 309, 322, 330, 349. Data on Chinese and Japanese stowaways for 1920 are located in the Report of the Commissioner of Immigration at New York, in Charge of District No. 3, Comprising New York and New Jersey and the Immigration Station at Ellis Island, New York Harbor; *ARCGI* (1920), 314. In many years, there are small discrepancies between New York stowaways recorded in Table XXI and those reported by the commissioner of immigration at New York. In these cases, I have followed the numbers listed in Table XXI. However, in 1920, the difference is sixty-seven. In this case, I have used the higher number provided by the commissioner of immigration at New York as these figures also include details of Chinese and Japanese stowaways. For discussions of race and stowaways, see *ARCGI* (1914), 250; *ARCGI* (1919), 323, 332.

44. Data on stowaways in San Francisco are located in the Report of the Commissioner of Immigration, San Francisco, in charge of District No. 18, Comprising Northern California and Nevada and the Angel Island Immigration Station; *ARCGI* (1915), 243; *ARCGI* (1916), 200; *ARCGI* (1917), 200; *ARCGI* (1918), 294; *ARCGI* (1919), 349; *ARCGI* (1920), 365. All reports in Appendix III, Digest of Reports of Commissioners and Inspectors in Charge of Districts, Annual Reports 1914–1920. Data on total stowaways are located in Table 68 (1928–1931) and in Table 62 (1932). Data on Chinese and Japanese stowaways are located in the unnumbered table. "Alien Stowaways Found on Board Vessels Arriving from Foreign Ports"; *ARCGI* (1928), 7; *ARCGI* (1929), 10; *ARCGI* (1930), 13; *ARCGI* (1931), 33; *ARCGI* (1932), 26. See also McKenzie, *Oriental Exclusion*, 160–61; Foote, *Outcasts!*.

45. See Wong Kin Dock, BSI hearing transcript, December 8, 1921, file 6/1996, Chinese Files, 1921–1944, INS, NARA–New York.

46. *ARCGI* (1930), 13; *ARCGI* (1931), 33.

47. The regulation of sailors is explored in chapter 4, "Asian Sailors: Shanghaied in Hoboken."

48. Chin Ngaw and Chin Sue, BSI hearing transcripts, June 8, 1908, both in file 13/356, Norwich Stowaways, Chinese Files, 1921–1944, INS, NARA–New York; Low Sing, BSI hearing transcript, June 11, 1915, file 27/528, Charlie Low and Charlie Sing, Chinese Files, 1921–1944, INS, NARA–New York. See also "Smuggling of Aliens and Narcotics through Cuba," June 28, 1922, 2; and W. Henry Robertson, US Consul General, Buenos Aires, Argentina, to Secretary of State, Washington, D.C., letter, June 9, 1923; both in file 55166/31a, Subject and Policy Files, INS, NARA–Washington, D.C.

49. Low Sing, BSI hearing transcript, June 11, 1915, file 27/528, Charlie Low and Charlie Sing, Chinese Files, 1921–1944, INS, NARA–New York.

50. Chin Sue, BSI hearing transcript, June 8, 1908, file 13/356, Norwich Stowaways, Chinese Files, 1921–1944, INS, NARA–New York.

51. "Three Chinese Caught in Bay While Swimming Ashore," *New York Herald Tribune*, August 27, 1929, 12.

52. Griffith, "Border Crossings," 478–79. On smuggling rings in Kansas City, see Lee Fook Sing to Bureau of Immigration, letter, August 20, 1919, file 55166/31a, Subject and Policy Files, INS, NARA–Washington, D.C.

53. *ARCGI* (1921), 9.

54. "Smuggling of Aliens and Narcotics through Cuba," 5–9, June 28, 1922, file 55166/31a, Subject and Policy Files, INS, NARA–Washington, D.C.

55. "Find Smuggling Plot," *New York Daily Tribune*, March 2, 1909, 3.

56. William A. Whalen, Inspector in Charge, District 7, to Commissioner of Immigration, Philadelphia, July 26, 1922, file 55166/31, Subject and Policy Files, INS, NARA–Washington, D.C.; "Nine Killed on Ship in Night Fight with Smuggled Chinese," 1, 3.

57. On Baltimore, see file 13/356, Norwich Stowaways, Chinese Files, 1921–1944, INS, NARA–New York.

58. "Smuggling of Aliens and Narcotics through Cuba," 8, June 28, 1922, file 55166/31a, Subject and Policy Files, INS, NARA–Washington, D.C.

59. "Smuggling of Aliens and Narcotics through Cuba," 8, June 28, 1922, file 55166/31a, Subject and Policy Files, INS, NARA–Washington, D.C.

60. Whalen to Commissioner of Immigration, Philadelphia, July 26, 1922, file 55166/31, Subject and Policy Files, INS, NARA–Washington, D.C.

61. Whalen to Commissioner of Immigration, Philadelphia, July 26, 1922, file 55166/31, Subject and Policy Files, INS, NARA–Washington, D.C.

62. Thomas A. Riordan, Inspector in Charge, Jacksonville, Florida, to Commissioner-General of Immigration, Washington, D.C., letter, July 30, 1921, file 55166/31, Subject and Policy Files, INS, NARA–Washington, D.C.

63. William A. Whalen, Inspector in Charge, Tampa, Florida, to Inspector in Charge, Jacksonville, Florida, letter, July 29, 1921, file 55166/31, Subject and Policy Files, INS, NARA–Washington, D.C.

64. *ARCGI* (1909), 127.

65. *ARCGI* (1909), 127.

66. Choy Lum, BSI hearing transcript, November 3, 1921, file 6/1965, Chinese Files, 1921–1944, INS, NARA–New York.

67. Leong Ching, BSI hearing transcript, December 3, 1921, file 6/1992, Chinese Files, 1921–1944, INS, NARA–New York; Leong Ah Tong, BSI hearing transcript, November 3, 1921, file 6/1980, MS *Dollar* Stowaways, Chinese Files, 1921–1944, INS, NARA–New York.

68. Chin and Chin, *Paper Son*, 1; Lau, *Paper Families*, 66.

69. Low Yuen, letter number 2, no date; and Charlie Low, BSI hearing transcript, June 11, 1915; both in file 27/528, Charlie Low and Charlie Sing, Chinese Files, 1921–1944, INS, NARA–New York. Coatzacoalcos was known at this time as Puerto Mexico.

70. On costs from Cuba to Key West, see "Smuggling of Aliens and Narcotics through Cuba," 1, June 28, 1922, file 55166/31a, Subject and Policy Files, INS, NARA–Washington, D.C. On costs from Cuba to New York, see Eng Dow, BSI hearing transcript, May 1, 1922, file 6/2026, Chinese Files, 1921–1944, INS, NARA–New York.

71. "Smuggling of Aliens and Narcotics through Cuba," 10, June 28, 1922, file 55166/31a, Subject and Policy Files, INS, NARA–Washington, D.C.; "30,000 Chinese Seek to Beat Exclusion," *New York Times*, June 17, 1923, E1; "12 Chinese Stowaways Found on Cuban Liner," *New York Herald Tribune*, July 27, 1930, 3.

72. "Smuggling of Aliens and Narcotics through Cuba," 9, June 28, 1922, file 55166/31a, Subject and Policy Files, INS, NARA–Washington, D.C. See also Whalen to Inspector in Charge, Jacksonville, Florida, letter, July 29, 1921, file 55166/31, Subject and Policy Files, INS, NARA–Washington, D.C.

73. Lee Ting to Chin Nom, letter, May 2, 1908, file 13/356, Norwich Stowaways, Chinese Files, 1921–1944, INS, NARA–New York. Lee Ting was not associated with the East Asia Company.

74. *ARCGI* (1909), 128.

75. *ARCGI* (1910), 133.

76. Corsi, *In the Shadow of Liberty*, 173.

77. Wang, *Surviving the City*, 96.

78. Chin Sue, BSI hearing transcript, June 8, 1908, file 13/356, Norwich Stowaways; Leong Ching, BSI hearing transcript, December 3, 1921, file 6/1992; both in Chinese Files, 1921–1944, INS, NARA–New York.

79. Low Sing, BSI hearing transcript, June 11, 1915, file 27/528, Charlie Low and Charlie Sing, Chinese Files, 1921–1944, INS, NARA–New York.

80. Carleton Bailey Hurst, American Consul General, to US Secretary of State, letter, September 19, 1922, file 55166/31, Subject and Policy Files, INS, NARA–Washington, D.C.

81. Sibray to Commissioner of Immigration, Ellis Island, New York, letter, June 29, 1923, file 55166/31; American Consul, Havana, to Secretary of State, Washington, D.C., June 14, 1924, telegram, file 55166/31a; Acting Commissioner-General of Immigration to Chinese Inspector in Charge, New York, letter, June 18, 1924, file 55166/31a; all in Subject and Policy Files, INS, NARA–Washington, D.C.

82. Alva Hernandez, BSI interview transcript, January 28, 1914, file 47/424, Chin Sai Wong et al., Chinese Files, 1921–1944, INS, NARA–New York.

83. Deichman to Secretary of State, Washington, D.C., letter re: alleged practice of smuggling aliens into the United States from Chile, September 12, 1922, file 55166/31, Subject and Policy Files, INS, NARA–Washington, D.C.

84. On storekeepers, see Bulmara Rendon, BSI hearing transcript, June 11, 1915, file 27/528, Charlie Low and Charlie Sing, Chinese Files, 1921–1944, INS, NARA–New York. On boatswains, see F. S. Pierce, Inspector in Charge, New York, to Sherriff, Essex County Jail, New Jersey, letter, February 24, 1922, file 6/1980, MS *Dollar Stowaways*, Chinese Files, 1921–1944, INS, NARA–New York. On stewards, see H. R. Sisson, Chinese Inspector in Charge, to Commissioner-General of Immigration, Washington, D.C., letter, February 11, 1916, file 29/433, Jung Kie Ging and Jung Ching; Chu You, statement, November 15, 1923, file 55/58; both in Chinese Files, 1921–1944, INS, NARA–New York.

85. Low Sing, BSI hearing transcript, June 11, 1915, file 27/528, Charlie Low and Charlie Sing; Chan Goon (Aldwin Chan), BSI hearing transcript, February 5, 1925, file 60/121; both in Chinese Files, 1921–1944, INS, NARA–New York.

86. "Eleven Chinese Stowaways Seized on Ship Here," 29.

87. Sisson to Commissioner-General of Immigration, Washington, D.C., letter, June 8, 1908, file 13/356, Norwich Stowaways; SS *Canada* Arrived 11/30/21, memorandum, November 30, 1921, file 6/1990; SS *Britannia* Arrived 12/6/21, memorandum, December 6, 1921, file 6/1996; file 27/528; Jung Ching, BSI hearing transcript, February 9, 1916, file 29/433, Jung Kie Ging and Jung Ching; all in Chinese Files, 1921–1944, INS, NARA–New York. On Puerto Rican and Hawaiian firemen working together, see Corsi, *In the Shadow of Liberty*, 136. On Italian smugglers, see "Find Smuggling Plot," 3. On Chinese perspectives on non-Chinese smugglers, see Lee Ting to Chin Nom, letter, May 2, 1908; Fritz Bush, BSI hearing transcript, June 8, 1908; and Chin Sue, BSI hearing transcript, June 8, 1908; all in file 13/356, Norwich Stowaways, Chinese Files, 1921–1944, INS, NARA–New York.

88. Low Sing and Charlie Low, BSI hearing transcripts, June 11, 1915; both in file 27/528, Charlie Low and Charlie Sing, Chinese Files, 1921–1944, INS, NARA–New York.

89. Chan Goon (Aldwin Chan), BSI hearing transcript, February 5, 1925, file 60/121, Chinese Files, 1921–1944, INS, NARA–New York.

90. Eng Dow, BSI hearing transcript, May 1, 1922, file 6/2026, Chinese Files, 1921–1944, INS, NARA–New York.

91. Eng Ah Sing, BSI hearing transcript, May 1, 1922, file 6/2026, Chinese Files, 1921–1944, INS, NARA–New York.

92. Gee Kwong, BSI hearing transcript, May 1, 1922, file 6/2026, Chinese Files, 1921–1944, INS, NARA–New York.

93. Sisson to Commissioner-General of Immigration, Washington, D.C., letter, June 8, 1908; and Chin Sue, BSI hearing transcript, June 8, 1908; both in file 13/356, Norwich Stowaways, Chinese Files, 1921–1944, INS, NARA–New York.

94. File 47/424, Chin Sai Wong et al., Chinese Files, 1921–1944, INS, NARA–New York.

95. *ARCGI* (1914), 217.

96. Sisson to Commissioner-General of Immigration, Washington, D.C., letter, February 11, 1916, file 29/433, Jung Kie Ging and Jung Ching, Chinese Files, 1921–1944, INS, NARA–New York.

97. Leong Ching, BSI hearing transcript, December 3, 1921, file 6/1992, Chinese Files, 1921–1944, INS, NARA–New York.

98. Leong Ah Tong, BSI hearing transcript, October 18, 1921, file 6/1980, MS *Dollar* Stowaways, Chinese Files, 1921–1944, INS, NARA–New York.

99. Lue Guay to Dock Fook, letter, June 1925 [no exact date], English translation, file 55466/659, INSAIE.

100. Weiss, *Sieve*, 35.

101. Assistant Secretary of State to US Secretary of State, letter, August 3, 1922, file 55166/31, Subject and Policy Files, INS, NARA–Washington, D.C.; James Bronson, "Enforcement of the Chinese Exclusion Law," 151–52.

102. "Nine Killed on Ship in Night Fight with Smuggled Chinese," 1, 3.

103. López, *Chinese Cubans*, 1; Look Lai and Tan, *Chinese in Latin America*.

104. López, "Chinese in Cuban History"; Wong, *Patronage, Brokerage, Entrepreneurship*, 34.

105. "Nine Killed on Ship in Night Fight with Smuggled Chinese," 1.

106. Assistant Secretary of State to US Secretary of State, letter, August 3, 1922, file 55166/31; "Smuggling of Aliens and Narcotics through Cuba," 5–7, June 28, 1922, file 55166/31a; both in Subject and Policy Files, INS, NARA–Washington, D.C.

107. Assistant Secretary of State to US Secretary of State, letter, August 3, 1922, 1, file 55166/31, Subject and Policy Files, INS, NARA–Washington, D.C. See also C. F. Kirschley and C. B. Stringham to Representative Hamilton Fish, letter, August 28, 1922, file 55166/31, Subject and Policy Files, INS, NARA–Washington, D.C.

108. "Smuggling of Aliens and Narcotics through Cuba," June 28, 1922, file 55166/31a, Subject and Policy Files, INS, NARA–Washington, D.C.

109. See also Assistant Secretary of State to US Secretary of State, letter, August 3, 1922, file 55166/31, Subject and Policy Files, INS, NARA–Washington, D.C.

110. "30,000 Chinese Seek to Beat Exclusion," *New York Times*, June 17, 1923, E1.

111. Minot S. Morgan, Detroit, Michigan, to US Commissioner-General of Immigration, Washington, D.C., letter, September 22, 1922, file 55166/31, Subject and Policy Files, INS, NARA–Washington, D.C.

112. Baker to US Secretary of State, letter concerning Chinese in Trinidad and attempts at unlawful entry into the United States, October 12, 1922, file 55166/31a, Subject and Policy Files, INS, NARA–Washington, D.C. See also Husband to All Commissioners of Immigration and Inspectors in Charge of Atlantic and Gulf Ports, August 9, 1922, file 55166/31, Subject and Policy Files, INS, NARA–Washington, D.C.

113. Corsi, *In the Shadow of Liberty*, 167–69.

114. Ho Chi Gong (pseudonym), BSI hearing transcript, February 5, 1942, file 173/727, Chinese Files, 1921–1944, INS, NARA–New York. Pseudonyms are used to preserve the privacy of this individual and others whose files contain incidents of hospitalization. Thanks to Cecilia Tang for her assistance with selecting these pseudonyms.

115. Corsi, *In the Shadow of Liberty*, 167–69.

116. "30,000 Chinese Seek to Beat Exclusion," E1; "Smuggling of Aliens and Narcotics through Cuba," June 28, 1922, file 55166/31a, Subject and Policy Files, INS, NARA–Washington, D.C.

117. Corsi, *In the Shadow of Liberty*, 166.

118. Leong, *Chinatown Inside Out*, 131.

119. Corsi, *In the Shadow of Liberty*, 166. A cutter is a small ship used by the Coast Guard and customs authorities in their enforcement of maritime laws.

120. Corsi, *In the Shadow of Liberty*, 137.

121. *ARCGI* (1927), 15.

122. Weiss, *Sieve*, 35–36.

123. Alva Hernandez, BSI interview transcript, January 28, 1914, file 47/424, Chin Sai Wong et al., Chinese Files, 1921–1944, INS, NARA–New York.

124. Fritz Bush, BSI hearing transcript, June 8, 1908, file 13/356, Norwich Stowaways, Chinese Files, 1921–1944, INS, NARA–New York.

125. Regarding regular inspections, see Edgar Morrison, BSI interview transcript, January 28, 1914, file 47/424, Chin Sai Wong et al., Chinese Files, 1921–1944, INS, NARA–New York. Regarding inspections in port, see F. S. Pierce, Inspector in Charge, to Commissioner-General, Washington, D.C., letter, October 18, 1921, file 6/1964, SS *Helenus* Stowaways, Chinese Files, 1921–1944, INS, NARA–New York; "Eleven Chinese Stowaways Seized on Ship Here," 29.

126. "Eleven Chinese Stowaways Seized on Ship Here," 29.

127. Captain Smith to Customs Department, New York, letter, September 29, 1923, file 55/40, Chinese Files, 1921–1944, INS, NARA–New York.

128. Edgar Morrison, BSI interview transcript, January 28, 1914, file 47/424, Chin Sai Wong et al., Chinese Files, 1921–1944, INS, NARA–New York.

129. Robert Smith, BSI hearing transcript, June 8, 1908, file 13/356, Norwich Stowaways, Chinese Files, 1921–1944, INS, NARA–New York.

130. Ng Suey, BSI hearing transcript, October 13, 1923, file 55/86; Lee Mok, BSI hearing transcript, December 4, 1923, file 55/58; both in Chinese Files, 1921–1944, INS, NARA–New York.

131. Alva Hernandez, BSI interview transcript, January 28, 1914, file 47/424, Chin Sai Wong et al., Chinese Files, 1921–1944, INS, NARA–New York.

132. Sisson to Commissioner-General of Immigration, Washington, D.C., letter, February 11, 1916, file 29/433, Jung Kie Ging and Jung Ching, Chinese Files, 1921–1944, INS, NARA–New York.

133. Wong Kin Dock, BSI hearing transcript, December 8, 1921, file 6/1996, Chinese Files, 1921–1944, INS, NARA–New York; Low Sing, BSI hearing transcript, June 11, 1915; Charlie Sing, BSI hearing transcript, June 11, 1915; George Cerf, BSI hearing transcript, June 12, 1915; and H. R. Sisson, Chinese Inspector in Charge, New York, to Collector of Customs, New York, June 22, 1915; all in file 27/528, Charlie Low and Charlie Sing, Chinese Files, 1921–1944, INS, NARA–New York. See also Sisson to Commissioner-General of Immigration, Washington, D.C., letter, February 11, 1916, file 29/433, Jung Kie Ging and Jung Ching, Chinese Files, 1921–1944, INS, NARA–New York.

134. Weiss, *Sieve*, 106–7.

135. "Stowaways at Ellis Island," 7.

136. "Nine Killed on Ship in Night Fight with Smuggled Chinese," 3.

137. American Consul in Charge, Havana, to Secretary of State, Washington, D.C., paraphrase of a telegram, June 4, 1924, file 55166/31a, Subject and Policy Files, INS, NARA–Washington, D.C.

138. Acting Commissioner-General to Chinese Inspector in Charge, New York, letter, June 18, 1924, file 55166/31a, Subject and Policy Files, INS, NARA–Washington, D.C.

139. Confidential memorandum to Commissioner-General of Immigration, Washington, D.C., June 16, 1924, file 55166/31a, Subject and Policy Files, INS, NARA–Washington, D.C.

140. Pierce to Commissioner-General, Washington, D.C., letter, October 18, 1921, file 6/1964, SS *Helenus* Stowaways, Chinese Files, 1921–1944, INS, NARA–New York; "Seek Drugs and Find Chinese Stow Aways," *New York Times*, October 15, 1921, 25. See also "Held for Smuggling Chinese," *New York Herald*, August 17, 1921, 6; Corsi, *In the Shadow of Liberty*, 136.

141. "Ten Chinese Stowaways Found in Sizzling Hold," *New York Herald Tribune*, July 8, 1926, 12.

142. Corsi, *In the Shadow of Liberty*, 173–74.

143. "Saves Three in Bay," *New York Times*, August 27, 1929, 55.

144. "Nine Killed on Ship in Night Fight with Smuggled Chinese," 1.

145. Pierce to Commissioner-General, Washington, D.C., letter, October 18, 1921, file 6/1964, SS *Helenus* Stowaways, Chinese Files, 1921–1944, INS, NARA–New York. See also "26 Starving Chinese Hidden in Ship's Hold," *New York Times*, August 14, 1921, 8; "Stowaways at Ellis Island," 7.

146. Corsi, *In the Shadow of Liberty*, 130.

147. Corsi, *In the Shadow of Liberty*, 166.

148. Fook Sim to Song Long Gim, letter translated from Chinese, no date, file 6/1996, Chinese Files, 1921–1944, INS, NARA–New York.

149. Storey and Sisson to Chinese Inspector in Charge, New York, letter, December 20, 1921, file 6/1996, Chinese Files, 1921–1944, INS, NARA–New York.

150. *ARCGI* (1909), 128.

151. "Smuggling of Aliens and Narcotics through Cuba," 6, June 28, 1922, file 55166/31a, Subject and Policy Files, INS, NARA–Washington, D.C.

152. Confidential memorandum to Commissioner-General of Immigration, Washington, D.C., June 16, 1924, file 55166/31a, Subject and Policy Files, INS, NARA–Washington, D.C.

153. Lee, *At America's Gates*, 195–96, 98–200.

154. "Jap Adrift in the Narrows," *New York Times*, June 8, 1913, C5.

155. "To Deport Young Hindus," *New York Times*, March 9, 1924, 6.

156. Weiss, *Sieve*, 36.

157. *ARCGI* (1906), 57.

158. Weiss, *Sieve*, 36.

159. Weiss, *Sieve*, 36, 52.

160. Subdivision 2, rule 3, Chinese Immigration Rules of October 1, 1926, cited in Edward Haff, *Boards of Special Inquiry*, Lecture No. 24 (Washington, D.C.: Government Printing Office, 1934), 13.

161. See, for example, BSI interview transcripts for ten stowaways on board the SS *Glendoyle*, March 8, 1922, all in file 6/2008, Chinese Files, 1921–1944, INS, NARA–New York.

162. Leong Ah Tong, BSI hearing transcript, November 3, 1921; and Albert B. Wiley, Assistant Inspector in Charge, New York, to Commissioner of Immigration, San Francisco, letter, November 4, 1921; both in file 6/1980, MS *Dollar* Stowaways, Chinese Files, 1921–1944, INS, NARA–New York.

163. Stowaways ex. SS *Canada*, Fabre Line, Brooklyn, memorandum, November 31, 1921; and A. W. Brough, Inspector in Charge, New York, to Commissioner-General of Immigration, Washington, D.C., letter, June 13, 1924; both in file 6/1990, Chinese Files, 1921–1944, INS, NARA–New York.

164. Honolulu Immigration Office to New York Immigration Office, telegram, July 23, 1948; Ng Yuie Seung (Ng Yue Thung), Statement by Applicant, October 19, 1938; both in file 171/33, Ng Yue Thung, Chinese Files, 1921–1944, INS, NARA–New York. See also A. W. Brough, Acting Inspector in Charge, New York, to Sinclair Navigation Company, New York, letter, September 25, 1923, file 55/56, Chinese Files, 1921–1944, INS, NARA–New York. U.S. stowaways do not appear in the alien stowaway data provided in the *Annual Reports of the Commissioner-General of Immigration*.

165. "Loopholes in Law Let Undesirables In," *New York Times*, May 28, 1911, 7. See also *ARCGI* (1914), 225.

166. Act of February 5, 1917 (39 Stat. 874, secs. 3 and 39). On New York immigration commissioner support for laws excluding stowaways, see US Congress House Committee on Immigration and Naturalization, *Alien Seamen and Stowaways: Hearings before the Committee on Immigration and Nationalization*, 61st Cong., 3d Sess., 1911, 40.

167. *ARCGI* (1917), 175.

168. *ARCGI* (1917), 224.

169. *ARCGI* (1920), 9.

170. *ARCGI* (1928), 7; *ARCGI* (1929), 10; *ARCGI* (1930), 13; *ARCGI* (1931), 33. In addition, not one alien Chinese or Japanese stowaway was admitted in the following years. *ARCGI* (1914), 225, 231; *ARCGI* (1915), 224; *ARCGI* (1916), 177–79; *ARCGI* (1917), 175, 180, 200; *ARCGI* (1918), 268, 273, 294; *ARCGI* (1919), 303, 309, 322, 330, 349; *ARCGI* (1920), 314, 365. On the disparate treatment between white and Black stowaways at Angel Island, see also Lee and Yung, *Immigrant Gateway*, 50.

171. Chin Wah, photograph, file 55/58, Chinese Files, 1921–1944, INS, NARA–New York.

172. Pegler-Gordon, *In Sight of America*, 181–82.

173. H. R. Sisson, Inspector in Charge, New York, to Albert B. Wiley, c/o United States Attorney, Albany, New York, letter, March 3, 1915, file 23/141, Lew King, Soo Hing, Soo Foo, King Cho, Chinese Files, 1921–1944, INS, NARA–New York.

174. Robert Smith, BSI hearing transcript, June 8, 1908, file 13/356, Norwich Stowaways, Chinese Files, 1921–1944, INS, NARA–New York.

175. To Commissioner-General of Immigration, Washington, D.C., letter, December 13, 1921, file 6/1990, Chinese Files, 1921–1944, INS, NARA–New York.

176. Immigration Commissioner, Boston, Mass., to H. R. Sisson, Chinese Inspector in Charge, New York, letter, June 30, 1915; Walter Kilton, Postmaster, to Henry Skeffington, Immigration Commissioner, Boston, Mass., letter, July 1, 1915; both in file 27/528, Charlie Low and Charlie Sing, Chinese Files, 1921–1944, INS, NARA–New York.

177. Acting Commissioner, Boston, Mass., to Chinese Inspector in Charge, New York, letter, November 18, 1921, file 6/1892, SS *Java* Stowaways, Chinese Files, 1921–1944, INS, NARA–New York.

178. Sisson to Commissioner-General of Immigration, Washington, D.C., letter, June 8, 1908, file 13/356, Norwich Stowaways, Chinese Files, 1921–1944, INS, NARA–New York.

179. H. R. Sisson, Chinese Inspector in Charge, New York, to Melville France, US Attorney, Brooklyn, New York, letter, June 17, 1915, file 27/528, Charlie Low and Charlie Sing, Chinese Files, 1921–1944, INS, NARA–New York.

180. H. R. Sisson, Chinese Inspector in Charge, New York, to US Attorney, Brooklyn, New York, June 15, 1915, file 27/528, Charlie Low and Charlie Sing, Chinese Files, 1921–1944, INS, NARA–New York.

181. Sisson to France, letter, June 17, 1915; A. Caminetti, Commissioner-General of Immigration, to H. R. Sisson, Chinese Inspector in Charge, New York, letter, July 3, 1915; US District Court Order, Eastern District of New York, July 21, 1915; all in file 27/528, Charlie Low and Charlie Sing, Chinese Files, 1921–1944, INS, NARA–New York. On witness fees as a deterrent to prosecution, see Acting Commissioner, Boston, Mass., to Chinese Inspector in Charge, New York, letter, November 18, 1921, SS *Java* Stowaways, Chinese Files, 1921–1944, INS, NARA–New York.

182. On earlier detention, see Charlie Low and Charlie Sing, 1915, file 27/528. On practices in the 1920s, see A. W. Brough, Acting Inspector in Charge, to Commissioner-General of Immigration, Washington, D.C., letter, October 27, 1923, file 55/86; both in Chinese Files, 1921–1944, INS, NARA–New York.

183. File 27/528, Charlie Low and Charlie Sing, Chinese Files, 1921–1944, INS, NARA–New York.

184. Acting Commissioner, Boston, Mass., to Chinese Inspector in Charge, New York, letter, November 18, 1921, SS *Java* Stowaways, Chinese Files, 1921–1944, INS, NARA–New York.

185. *ARCGI* (1920), 314.

186. A. W. Brough, Inspector in Charge, New York, to Messrs. Sanderson and Son, Agents, Lamport and Holt, New York, letter, April 1, 1925, file 60/121, Chinese Files, 1921–1944, INS, NARA–New York.

187. F. S. Pierce, Inspector in Charge, New York, to Warden, US Penitentiary, Atlanta, Georgia, letter, February 24, 1922, file 6/1694, SS *Helenus* Stowaways, Chinese Files, 1921–1944, INS, NARA–New York.

188. Pierce to Warden, US Penitentiary, Atlanta, Georgia, February 24, 1922, file 6/1694, SS *Helenus* Stowaways, Chinese Files, 1921–1944, INS, NARA–New York.

189. Chinese Inspector in Charge, New York, to Immigrant Inspector in Charge, Honolulu, letter, April 11, 1922, file 6-1954, Quay Choy, Chinese Files, 1921–1944, INS, NARA–New York.

190. See also Inspector in Charge, New York, to Commissioner-General of Immigration, Washington, D.C., Resume of status of Chinese stowaways, March 23, 1922, file 6/1954, Quay Choy, Chinese Files, 1921–1944, INS, NARA–New York; F. S. Pierce, Inspector in Charge, New York, to Commissioner-General of Immigration, Washington, D.C., letter, January 5, 1922, file 6/1980, MS *Dollar* Stowaways, Chinese Files, 1921–1944, INS, NARA–New York.

191. F. S. Pierce, Inspector in Charge, New York, to Commissioner-General of Immigration, Washington, D.C., letter, October 31, 1921, file 6/1980, MS *Dollar* Stowaways, Chinese Files, 1921–1944, INS, NARA–New York. See also Pierce to Commissioner-General of Immigration, Washington, D.C., letter, January 5, 1922, file 6/1980, MS *Dollar* Stowaways, Chinese Files, 1921–1944, INS, NARA–New York.

192. Storey and Sisson to Secretary of Labor, Washington, D.C., letter, December 23, 1921; Albert Wiley, Acting Inspector in Charge, New York, to Commissioner-General of Immigration, Washington, D.C., letter, December 23, 1921; both in file 6/1999, Chinese Files, 1921–1944, INS, NARA–New York.

193. F. S. Pierce, Inspector in Charge, New York, to Inspector in Charge, Norfolk, Va., letter, February 27, 1922, file 6/1978, Lum Ling, Chinese Files, 1921–1944, INS, NARA–New York. See also *Knight Templar* Stowaways, file 6/1999, Chinese Files, 1921–1944, INS, NARA–New York.

194. J. F. Dunton, Inspector in Charge, to Mr. Flynn, Inspector in Charge, Record Division, Ellis Island, letter, March 6, 1923, file 6/1694, SS *Helenus* Stowaways, Chinese Files, 1921–1944, INS, NARA–New York.

195. Inspector in Charge, New York, to Commissioner-General of Immigration, Washington, D.C., Resume of status of Chinese stowaways, March 23, 1922, file 6/1954, Quay Choy, Chinese Files, 1921–1944, INS, NARA–New York.

196. Brough to Commissioner-General of Immigration, Washington, D.C., letter, October 27, 1923, file 55/86, Chinese Files, 1921–1944, INS, NARA–New York.

197. Inspector in Charge, New York, to National Surety Company, New York, letter, April 5, 1922, file 6/1983, Suey Lung Leung, Chinese Files, 1921–1944, INS, NARA–New York. See also file 6/1960, Hong King, Chinese Files, 1921–1944, INS, NARA–New York.

198. Lew Koon, BSI hearing transcript, March 31, 1922, file 6/1983, Suey Lung Leung, Chinese Files, 1921–1944, INS, NARA–New York; Lee, *At America's Gates*, 199.

199. File 29/380, Ah Bow, Chinese Files, 1921–1944, INS, NARA–New York.

200. See, for example, Henry Brien, Guard, New York, to Inspector in Charge, New York, letter, August 14, 1922, file 6/1999; A. W. Brough, Inspector in Charge, New York, to May Chan, Port of Spain, Trinidad, letter, May 1, 1925, file 60/121; both in Chinese Files, 1921–1944, INS, NARA–New York.

201. May Chan, letter, April 15, 1925; Brough to May Chan, Port of Spain, Trinidad, letter, May 1, 1925; and Chan Goon (Alduin Chan), BSI hearing transcript, February 5, 1925; all in file 60/121, Chinese Files, 1921–1944, INS, NARA–New York.

202. Corsi, *In the Shadow of Liberty*, 173.

203. *ARINS* (1950), 6.

204. "Find Smuggling Plot," 3.

205. Statement by Witness, H. R. Sisson, In re: Tom Sun Hung, applicant for admission to the United States at Boston, Mass., as the minor son of a merchant, July 1, 1930, file 149/228; Byron H. Uhl to H. R. Sisson, May 25, 1931, file 6/1422; file 6/1445; Byron Uhl, District Director, New York District, to Moy Cui, c/o H. R. Sisson, October 2, 1939, file 96/612; all in Chinese Files, 1921–1944, INS, NARA–New York.

206. "Col. Scharf Gives It Up," 1.

## Chapter 4

1. "Police Hold Chinese Crew," *New York Times*, June 30, 1927, 29; "Acts on Arrest of Coolies," *New York Times*, July 1, 1927, 8; "Dutch Ship's Chinese Mutineers Transferred to Ellis Island," *New York Herald Tribune*, July 3, 1927, C12; "Davis to Investigate Mutiny of Chinese," *New York Times*, July 16, 1927, 12; "Chinese Mutineers Deported Secretly," *New York Times*, July 17, 1927; "Chinese Makes Complaint," *New York Times*, July 24, 1927, 7; "The Weather," *New York Herald Tribune*, June 28, 1927, 20.

2. "Police Hold Chinese Crew," 29; "Wants Inquiry for Chinese," *New York Times*, July 14, 1927; "Acts on Arrest of Coolies," 8; "Aids 54 Chinese Seamen," *New York Times*, July 9, 1927, 30.

3. "Acts on Arrest of Coolies," 8; "Chinese Makes Complaint," 7.

4. "Acts on Arrest of Coolies," 8; "US Ignores Rights of Chinese Sailors; Helps Dutch Owners," *Labor's News: The News Magazine of the Labor Movement (The Federated Press Labor Letter)*, July 21, 1927, 4.

5. "Aids 54 Chinese Seamen," 30. A similar concern was raised in a Department of Labor investigation into Asian Indian sailors who had illegally entered the United States and were detained by immigration authorities, but were subsequently released to work on a British ship rather than being deported. The investigation explored the possibility of "collusion between immigration officers and British interests to Shanghai Hindu seamen into the British merchant marine service." "Probe of Hindu's Arrests," *Washington Post*, August 17, 1920. In 1914, Andrew Furuseth, president of the International Seamen's Union, claimed that "New York was the most notorious 'Shanghai port' in the world." "Shanghai System at Its Worst Here," *New York Times*, January 6, 1914, 5.

6. Sixteen of the men had been transported back to Holland earlier in the week, with the remaining thirty-eight men continuing to be detained at Ellis Island. "Chinese Mutineers Deported Secretly."

7. McKeown, *Melancholy Order*; Pegler-Gordon, *In Sight of America*; Torpey, *Invention of the Passport*.

8. *ARCGI* (1932), 23; *ARCGI* (1928), 11.

9. Act of March 4, 1915 (28 Stat. 1164); Act of February 5, 1917 (39 Stat. 874); *ARCGI* (1921), 8; *ARCGI* (1922), 11.

10. Kwong, *Chinatown, New York*. See also Frykman et al., "Mutiny and Maritime Radicalism."

11. Alfred W. McCann, "Starved at Sea, Hindoos Assert," *New York Globe*, May 16, 1921, cited in Ahuja, "Mobility and Containment," 121. Vivek Bald has noted that mostly Bengali Muslim seamen did not think of or refer to themselves as lascars, a term that was imposed by the British and other Western authorities. Bald, *Bengali Harlem*, 95, 100–102.

12. Although limited, Asian American and Asian historians have paid more attention to maritime workers than have other immigration historians: Tchen, *New York before Chinatown*; Kwong, *Chinatown, New York*; Benton, *Chinese Migrants and Internationalism*; Ngai, *Lucky Ones*; Amenda, "'Chinese Quarters'"; Bald, *Bengali Harlem*; Lee, "Hunting for Sailors." Among maritime historians, Ravi Ahuja has considered the intersection of immigration and maritime law in Ahuja, "Mobility and Containment," 120–26.

13. Frykman et al., "Mutiny and Maritime Radicalism," 6.

14. Kwong, *Chinatown, New York*, 116.

15. Amenda, "'Chinese Quarters,'" 46.

16. Tchen, *New York before Chinatown*. See also Bald, *Bengali Harlem*; Amenda, "'Chinese Quarters,'" 48–51.

17. *ARINS* (1947), 67.

18. *ARCGI* (1906), 57.

19. "Making a Law Unpopular," *New York Times*, September 29, 1882, 4; Li, *Congressional Policy of Chinese Immigration*, 44–45.

20. "Chinese Exclusion Bill," *New York Times*, April 15, 1902, 3; "Proceedings in Detail," *New York Times*, April 17, 1902, 1. See also "Employment of Chinese on Vessels Flying the American Flag," S. Doc. 281, 57th Cong., 1st Sess., April 3, 1902. Additional restrictions, including seamen under the definition of laborers, were also proposed in 1898. Li, *Congressional Policy of Chinese Immigration*, 92–93.

21. *ARCGI* (1912), 21. See also *ARCGI* (1903), 86–96; *ARCGI* (1904), 103; *ARCGI* (1907), 131; *ARCGI* (1909), 13.

22. Special Representative (Seamen's Work), Department of Labor, to Assistant Secretary, memorandum, September 8, 1922, file 54490-7, INSAIE supplement.

23. *ARCGI* (1930), 1. See also Clark, *Deportation of Aliens*, 273.

24. Daniels and Graham, *Debating American Immigration*, 7.

25. *ARCGI* (1903), 86–96; *ARCGI* (1904), 103; *ARCGI* (1907), 131.

26. *ARCGI* (1907), 182.

27. *ARCGI* (1907), 182.

28. *ARCGI* (1908), 159.

29. Weiss, *Sieve*, 114–16; *ARCGI* (1908), 10–11.

30. "30,000 Chinese Seek to Beat Exclusion," *New York Times*, June 17, 1923, E1.

31. Corsi, *In the Shadow of Liberty*, 165.

32. *ARCGI* (1921), 8. See also Lew-Williams, *Chinese Must Go*, 194–95.

33. *ARCGI* (1928), 11.

34. *ARCGI* (1903), 69.

35. Mr. Walker, Testimony, US Congress House Committee on Immigration and Naturalization, *Alien Seamen and Stowaways: Hearings before the Committee on Immigration and Nationalization*, 61st Cong., 3d Sess. (1911), 23.

36. *ARCGI* (1931), 31; "30,000 Chinese Seek to Beat Exclusion," E1.

37. "Chinese Swarm In," *New York Times*, February 6, 1910, 4.

38. *ARCGI* (1918), 273; Appendix III, Report on Seamen's Work, in *ARCGI* (1919), 273; *ARCGI* (1920), 297; *ARCGI* (1921), 165; *ARCGI* (1922), 153; *ARCGI* (1923), 30; *ARCGI* (1925), 22; *ARCGI* (1926), 4; Table 62, *ARCGI* (1927), 179; Unnumbered table, "Vessels boarded and alien seamen examined," *ARCGI* (1928), 12; *ARCGI* (1929), 13; *ARCGI* (1930), 19; *ARCGI* (1931), 33; *ARCGI* (1932), 25. The higher number of examinations in New York may in part be due to the larger crews of the ships arriving in port. It may also be that New York was a busier port with more traffic: the numbers are for individual examinations rather than individual seamen. If a sailor made multiple trips to the same port, he would be examined multiple times. *ARCGI* (1919), 9.

39. Weiss, *Sieve*, 109.

40. *ARCGI* (1909), 13; *ARCGI* (1910), 12.

41. *ARCGI* (1913), 26, 189.

42. *ARCGI* (1914), 233; *ARCGI* (1915), 224; *ARCGI* (1916), 179; *ARCGI* (1918), 273; *ARCGI* (1920), 321.

43. Bald, *Bengali Harlem*, 114.

44. *ARCGI* (1922), 12.

45. Other estimates appear to be lower: in 1922, the assistant secretary of labor claimed that a "formidable" number of Chinese sailors deserted their ships at U.S. ports, citing a figure of at least 125 sailors each month. Assistant Secretary of Labor to Attorney General, letter, September 29, 1922, file 54490-7, INSAIE supplement microfilm.

46. *ARCGI* (1921), 10.

47. *ARCGI* (1930), 18.

48. "On Board a Tea Ship," *Harper's Weekly*, April 9, 1892, 352–53; Tchen, *New York before Chinatown*, 75–85.

49. Wong Chin Foo, "Chinese in the United States," 217.

50. Lee, "Hunting for Sailors," 112–13.

51. V. L. Jensen, Port Steward, Atlantic Fruit Company, New York, Statement, November 15, 1923; Chow Kai, Statement, November 15, 1923; both in file 55/58, Chinese Files, 1921–1944, INS, NARA–New York; Works Progress Administration, Federal Writers' Project in New York City, *New York City Guide*, 450; Amenda, "'Chinese Quarters," 48.

52. "On Board a Tea Ship," 352–53. The *New York Times* also described a series of boardinghouses in this area in the 1870s: "Chinese in New York: How They Live, and Where," *New York Times*, December 26, 1873, 3.

53. Bald, *Bengali Harlem*, 117–35.

54. Works Progress Administration, Federal Writers' Project in New York City, *New York City Guide*, 450.

55. Of eleven addresses given in a sample of 227 Filipino arrivals, five of these were on Sands Street (sometimes listed as Sand Street). Analysis of data collected by Maria del Valle Embry, Filipino Arrivals @ Ellis Island, 2011, https:// filipinosgone2ellis-island.tripod.com/.

56. Lasker, *Filipino Immigration*, 62–63. In New York, Bernardo A. Bunuan worked at the New York post office. Data collected by Maria del Valle Embry, Filipino Arrival Names A-B, Filipino Arrivals @ Ellis Island, 2011, https://filipinosgone2ellis -island.tripod.com/id10.html. On post office work, see also Buaken, *I Have Lived*, 238–40.

57. Lasker, *Filipino Immigration*, 62.

58. Manzon, *Strange Case*, 12.

59. Of eleven addresses given in a sample of 227 Filipino arrivals, two arrivals gave the address of 25 South Street in Manhattan. Analysis of data collected by Maria del Valle Embry, Filipino Arrivals @ Ellis Island, 2011, https://filipinos gone2ellis-island.tripod.com/.

60. "On Board a Tea Ship," 352–53.

61. Tabili, *We Ask for British Justice*, 47; Balachandran, "Crossing the Last Frontier," 97–98. See also Bald, "Hands across the Water," 99–109.

62. On the merchant marine, see Works Progress Administration, Federal Writers' Project in New York City, *Maritime History of New York* (1941), 233. Military naval service is beyond the scope of this study, although it has been a conduit to merchant marine service. On military service, see Lasker, *Filipino Immigration*, 25, 58–63; Buaken, *I Have Lived*, 38–43; Schwendinger, *Ocean of Bitter Dreams*, 185–86; Oades, *Beyond the Mask*; Miller, *Messman Chronicles*, 6, 51–52, 326; Salyer, "Baptism by Fire,"; Baldoz, *Third Asiatic Invasion*, 46.

63. Tchen, *New York before Chinatown*, 81.

64. Fajardo, *Filipino Crosscurrents*, 41–76; Tchen, *New York before Chinatown*, 79.

65. Ahuja, "Mobility and Containment," 115–20; Tabili, *We Ask for British Justice*, 44–47; Lahiri, "Contested Relations," 169–81.

66. Tabili, *We Ask for British Justice*, 49–50.

67. Lasker, *Filipino Immigration*, 59.

68. Tabili, *We Ask for British Justice*, 49.

69. "Thirty-Five Goanese Held at Ellis Island," *New York Times*, October 27, 1919.

70. Weiss, *Sieve*, 48. See also Tabili, *We Ask for British Justice*, 48. Although the Immigration Bureau defined all ship workers as seamen, "sailors" referred to workers on sailing ships and in the U.S. Navy, whereas "seamen" generally referred to workers in the merchant marine, especially those who were not employed on deck. The U.S. Immigration Bureau regulated only private, commercial merchant marine ships.

71. Wong Wah Ling, BSI hearing transcript, November 4, 1921, file 6/1981; Chow Kai, Statement, November 15, 1923, file 55/58; both in Chinese Files, 1921–1944, INS, NARA–New York.

72. "Chinese Crew Happy Though Held in Jail," *New York Times*, July 13, 1908, 14.

73. "Chinese Go on Lusitania," *New York Sun,* July 14, 1908, 5; "Oust a Passenger from the Lusitania," *New York Times,* July 16, 1908, 3; "Asks Strathyre Captain's Arrest," *New York Daily Tribune,* July 17, 1908, 5.

74. "Chinese in Chains Resist Deportation," *New York Times,* May 24, 1909, 5.

75. Ahuja, "Mobility and Containment," 120–21; "List or Manifest of Aliens Employed on the Vessel as Members of Crew," City of Norwich, February 1921, New York, New York, U.S., Arriving Passenger and Crew Lists, 1820–1957 (online database), Ancestry.com, 2010. On such abuses, see also Khan, *Chains to Lose.*

76. At the same time, the British National Union of Seamen was also engaged in campaigns against Black, Chinese, and other Asian sailors. Tabili, *We Ask for British Justice,* 81–134.

77. Saxton, *Indispensable Enemy*; Roediger, *Wages of Whiteness.*

78. "Transfer of Chinese Crews," *New York Times,* January 4, 1903, 15; "Urges Washington to Bar Chinese Crew," *New York Times,* January 20, 1933, 37; "Inquiry on Coolies to Be Opened Today," *New York Times,* January 31, 1933, 32.

79. Bald, *Bengali Harlem,* 111–12.

80. US Congress House Committee on Immigration and Naturalization, *Alien Seamen and Stowaways: Hearings before the Committee on Immigration and Naturalization,* 61st Cong., 3d Sess. (1911); US Congress House Committee on Immigration and Naturalization, *Alien Seamen and Stowaways: Hearings before the Committee on Immigration and Naturalization,* 62nd Cong., 1st Sess. (1912); US Congress House Committee on Immigration and Naturalization, *Deportation of Alien Seamen: Hearings before the Committee on Immigration and Naturalization,* 71st Cong., 3d Sess. (1931). See also "Unions and the Chinese," *New York Times,* February 13, 1902, 6; Andrew Furuseth, "The Decay of Seamanship in Europe and America," S. Doc. 216, 63d Cong., 1st Sess. (1913).

81. The resolution was passed at the 1928 American Federation of Labor convention but was not acted on in Congress. Baldoz, *Third Asiatic Invasion,* 161.

82. Senator Gallinger, *Congressional Record,* 63d Cong., 2d Sess., 1915, vol. 52, 2563.

83. Tabili, *We Ask for British Justice*; Ahuja, "Mobility and Containment."

84. "Chinese Is Freed," *New York Times,* February 20, 1937.

85. Song, *Shaping and Reshaping Chinese American Identity,* 42–43. Filipinos also formed alliances with radical unions in agricultural labor. Baldoz, *Third Asiatic Invasion,* 152–55.

86. Tchen, *New York before Chinatown,* 68–69; Young, *Alien Nation,* 21–96.

87. "Loopholes in Law," *New York Times,* May 28, 1911.

88. 23 Op. Atty. Gen. 521, September 10, 1901.

89. A. R. Archibald, "Alien Seamen," Lecture No. 26, December 10, 1934, 2, file 55875/26, Subject and Policy Files, INS, NARA–Washington, D.C.

90. See reference to Act of Sept. 13, 1888, in F. Sargent, Commissioner-General of Immigration, to F. W. Berkshire, Inspector in Charge, New York, letter, December 23, 1904; and F. W. Berkshire, Officer in Charge, New York, to Commissioner-General of Immigration, Washington, D.C., letter, December 21, 1904; both in file 52157-19, INS, NARA–Washington, D.C.

91. On similar laws in Australia and connections to U.S. shipping, see Blue, "Finding Margins on Borders."

92. Commissioner of Immigration, San Francisco, District Report, in *ARCGI* (1916), 200.

93. In December 1904, F. W. Berkshire, the officer in charge of Chinese exclusion, reported "several" recent escapes. In 1908, there were "fourteen escapes from eight vessels"; in the first half of 1909, there were "six escapes from four vessels." Berkshire to Commissioner-General of Immigration, Washington, D.C., letter, December 21, 1904, file 52157-19, Subject and Policy Files, INS, NARA–Washington, D.C.; H. R. Sisson, Chinese Inspector in Charge, New York, to Commissioner-General of Immigration, letter, August 27, 1909, file 52157-19, Subject and Policy Files, INS, NARA–Washington, D.C.

94. F. W. Berkshire, Chinese Inspector in Charge, New York, to Commissioner-General of Immigration, letter, May 15, 1907; F. W. Berkshire, Chinese Inspector in Charge, New York, to Commissioner-General of Immigration, letter, January 9, 1905; both in file 52157-19, Subject and Policy Files, INS, NARA–Washington, D.C.

95. Sisson to Commissioner-General of Immigration, letter, August 27, 1909, file 52157-19, Subject and Policy Files, INS, NARA–Washington, D.C.

96. Sisson to Commissioner-General of Immigration, letter, August 27, 1909, file 52157-19, Subject and Policy Files, INS, NARA–Washington, D.C. See also "Loopholes in Law."

97. Commissioner-General of Immigration to Chinese Inspector in Charge, New York, letter, December 13, 1904, file 52157-19, Subject and Policy Files, INS, NARA–Washington, D.C.; Commissioner-General of Immigration to Secretary of Commerce and Labor, letter, December 27, 1904, file 52157-19, Subject and Policy Files, INS, NARA–Washington, D.C.

98. Commissioner-General of Immigration to Chinese Inspector in Charge, New York, letter, December 13, 1904, file 52157-19, Subject and Policy Files, INS, NARA–Washington, D.C.

99. Pegler-Gordon, *In Sight of America*. Photos were also used for identification purposes for seamen departing in lieu of deportation. Edwin B. Schmucker, District Director, Norfolk, Va., to Chinese Inspector in Charge, New York, letter, April 9, 1924, file 55/60, Chinese Files, 1921–1944, INS, NARA–New York.

100. Rule 32, United States Department of Commerce and Labor, *Treaty, Laws, and Regulations Governing the Admission of Chinese 1907*, 47–48. A statutory requirement is written into legislation passed by Congress or another legislative body. Regulations or rules are promulgated to flesh out the enforcement of these statutes. But in some cases the executive interpretation of how to enforce the law exceeded the original requirements. In the case of Chinese exclusion, the Immigration Bureau regularly overreached its authority with little opposition. Rule 32 governing the bonding of sailors was similar to the $500 bond required of Chinese passengers in transit through the United States (rule 33); however, at this time, seamen were subject only to the bond, whereas passengers in transit also had to produce their ticket, satisfy the immigration official that they were genuinely in transit, and provide photographs for documents that would be carried with them as well

as forwarded to their final U.S. destination to ensure their departure. The $500 bond on seamen was renewed in the 1910 *Regulations Governing the Admission of Chinese*.

101. United States Department of Commerce and Labor, *Immigration Laws and Regulations of 1907*.

102. "Chinese Sailors Desert," *New York Times*, January 2, 1907, 12. The *New York Times* describes a $1,000 fine. However, according to the 1907 *Treaty, Laws and Regulations Governing the Admission of Chinese*, the bond required to ensure the departure of Chinese seamen was $500. No fines are mentioned. In 1910, the *New York Times* reported that the fine had been reduced to $500. "Chinese Mutineers Drown," *New York Times*, June 18, 1910, 5. A $1,000 fine was introduced in the 68th Congress, held from 1923 to 1925.

103. "Chinese Seamen Halted in Dash for the Shore," *New York Times*, June 21, 1941, 31.

104. "Chinese Sailors Desert," 12.

105. "Chinese Mutineers Drown," 5.

106. "Customs Men Fight Japanese," *New York Times*, April 30, 1909, 1.

107. "40 Rioting Lascars Fell Ship Officers," *New York Times*, November 9, 1930, 28. See also Khan, *Chains to Lose* 1:114–16, 37–40.

108. "Two Killed in Fire at Liner on Pier," *New York Times*, February 1, 1929, 28.

109. "Fire Rages in Liner 6 Hours at Pier Here," *New York Times*, August 1, 1930, 5.

110. Mundane references to mutiny are found in the following sources: "Chinese Mutineers Drown"; "Skipper Feared Chinese," *New York Times*, January 25, 1914; "Crewman Is Killed in a Mutiny Here," *New York Times*, April 12, 1942, 1, 15. See also the inclusion of the *Rotterdam* incident at Hoboken in Haine, *Mutiny on the High Seas*, 116.

111. "Skipper Feared Chinese," 14.

112. Act of March 4, 1915 (28 Stat. 1164). The law's formal title was "An Act to Promote the Welfare of American Seamen in the Merchant Marine of the United States," but it was commonly known as the Seamen's Act.

113. Act of February 5, 1917 (39 Stat. 874). On the contemporaneous debate, see Archibald, "Alien Seamen," December 10, 1934, 3, file 55875/26, Subject and Policy Files, INS, NARA–Washington, D.C. On later tensions between the laws, see US Congress House Committee on Immigration and Naturalization, "Strengthening of Alien Seamen's Deportation Procedures," April 5, 1920 (unpublished hearings), accessed via Proquest Congressional database.

114. Act of March 4, 1915 (28 Stat. 1164), sec. 13. See also "The Seamen's Act Fiasco," *New York Times*, March 16, 1916, 12.

115. On challenges to the law, see "Defends Seamen's Act," *New York Times*, August 15, 1915, 4; "Seamen's Act Hits Lumber," *New York Times*, September 26, 1915, 4; "Seamen's Act Attacked," *New York Times*, October 23, 1915, 20; "May Work Revenge with Seamen's Act," *New York Times*, November 14, 1915, 13; "Seamen's Act Fiasco," 12. On the defense of the act, see "Seamen's Act a Model," *New York Times*, September 13, 1915, 14.

116. "Manila Sees Peril in Seamen's Bill," *New York Times*, October 11, 1915, 12.

117. Act of February 5, 1917 (39 Stat. 874). On the contemporaneous debate, see Archibald, "Alien Seamen," December 10, 1934, 3, file 55875/26, Subject and Policy Files, INS, NARA–Washington, D.C.

118. *ARCGI* (1919), 20.

119. Act of February 5, 1917 (39 Stat. 874), secs. 34 and 36.

120. Act of February 5, 1917 (39 Stat. 874), sec. 35.

121. Act of February 5, 1917 (39 Stat. 874), sec. 31.

122. Archibald, "Alien Seamen," December 10, 1934, 3, file 55875/26, Subject and Policy Files, INS, NARA–Washington, D.C.

122. *ARCGI* (1919).

123. Archibald, "Alien Seamen," December 10, 1934, 3, file 55875/26, Subject and Policy Files, INS, NARA–Washington, D.C.

124. US Congress House Committee on Immigration and Naturalization, "Strengthening of Alien Seamen's Deportation Procedures."

125. Treasury Decision 37753, September 3, 1918, in United States Department of the Treasury, *Treasury Decisions under Customs and Other Laws*, 35:86–87. Similar requirements also existed in British ports in 1918. Khan, *Chains to Lose*, 134–35.

126. United States Department of Labor, Bureau of Immigration, *Treaty, Laws and Rules Governing the Admission of Chinese 1917*, 6.

127. Statement of Andrew Furuseth, US Congress House Committee on Immigration and Naturalization, "Strengthening of Alien Seamen's Deportation Procedures."

128. American Consul General to US Secretary of State, "Alleged Practice of Smuggling Aliens in United States from Chile," September 12, 1922, file 55166/31, Subject and Policy Files, INS, NARA–Washington, D.C. On Chinese practices of using immigration identity documentation to enter the United States in spite of exclusion laws, see Pegler-Gordon, *In Sight of America*, 22–103.

129. *ARCGI* (1920), 321.

130. *ARCGI* (1920), 273. See also Masanz, *History of the Immigration and Naturalization Service*, 24.

131. *ARCGI* (1919), 21. The numbers of inspections represent individual inspections rather than individual sailors, as one sailor could be inspected multiple times if he entered port multiple times during one year.

132. *ARCGI* (1919), 20; *ARCGI* (1920), 20.

133. *ARCGI* (1919), 273–74.

134. On sailor inspections, see ARCGI (1930), 8. On immigrants admitted, see United States Department of Homeland Security, *Yearbook of Immigration Statistics*, 5. The peak immigration years in the early twentieth century were 1907 (1,285,349) and 1914 (1,218,480). On comparisons, see *ARCGI* (1921), 6.

135. Act of February 5, 1917 (39 Stat. 874), sec. 3; Special Representative (Seamen's Work), Department of Labor, to Assistant Secretary, memorandum, September 8, 1922, file 54490-7, INSAIE supplement.

136. US Congress House Committee on Immigration and Naturalization, *Alien Seamen and Stowaways* 62nd Cong., 1st Sess. (1912), 11.

137. Assistant Secretary of Labor to Attorney General, letter, September 29, 1922, file 54490-7, INSAIE supplement.

138. *ARCGI* (1921), 8; *ARCGI* (1922), 11. Assistant Secretary of Labor to Attorney General, letter, September 29, 1922; Assistant Commissioner-General of Immigration, Washington, D.C., to S. Wen King-Sing, Boston, Mass., letter, September 18, 1922; William F. Christy, New Orleans, La., to Commissioner-General of Immigration, Washington, D.C., memorandum, September 9, 1922; all in file 54490-7, INSAIE supplement.

139. Alexander Wedell, American Consul-General, Calcutta, India, memorandum, January 3, 1923; Robe Carl White, Second Assistant Secretary, Department of State, to Secretary of State, letter, February 26, 1923; both in file 54490-7, INSAIE supplement.

140. Suzuki and Co., New York agents of Kokusai Kisen Kabushiki Kaisha, to E. J. Henning, Department of Labor, February 5, 1923, file 54490-7, INSAIE supplement.

141. Chinese Rule 7, subdivision 4(a), cited in Assistant Secretary of Labor to Attorney General, September 29, 1922, file 54490-7, INSAIE supplement.

142. King Jay Association, Brooklyn, New York, to President Harding, letter, September 14, 1922, file 54490-7, INSAIE.

143. L. Weedin, Seattle, Washington, to Commissioner-General of Immigration, Washington, D.C., memorandum, August 29, 1922, file 54490-7, INSAIE.

144. Weedin to Commissioner-General of Immigration, Washington, D.C., memorandum, August 29, 1922, file 54490-7, INSAIE supplement.

145. J. G. Johnson, Sinclair Navigation Company, New York, to Mr. Brough, Acting Chinese Inspector in Charge, New York, letter, September 25, 1923, file 55/56, Chinese Files, 1921–1944, INS, NARA–New York.

146. *ARCGI* (1918), 273.

147. "30,000 Chinese Seek to Beat Exclusion," E1. On Chinese seamen as deportees, see also "Chinese Deportees to Sail Tomorrow," *New York Times*, September 25, 1925.

148. *ARCGI* (1931), 31.

149. David Provinse, "FBI Survey of Chinese Activities in the New York Field Division," 12, January 11, 1944, file 291.2—Chinese, box 382, Army Intelligence Vertical File, 1941–1948, Record Group 319, entry 47, NARA–College Park, Md.

150. Tsang, *Modern History of Hong Kong*, 87–90. See also Benton, *Chinese Migrants and Internationalism*, 54–60.

151. Chinese Seamen's Institute, "Chinese Seamen Appeal to American Labor," *China Review* 2, no. 3 (March 1922): 162.

152. Visram, *Asians in Britain*, 225–53.

153. "Smuggled Pistols and Chinese Seized," *New York Times*, July 17, 1923, 20.

154. Julius Mayer, Ruling, August 10, 1922, file 54490-7, INSAIE.

155. Assistant Secretary to James V. Storey, memorandum, September 11, 1922, file 54490-7, INSAIE.

156. Admiral Oriental Line, Bond Issued for the Temporary Landing of Chinese Seamen and Seamen Who Are Natives of the Asiatic Barred Zone, Seattle, Washington, December 13, 1922; Wixom, Acting Commissioner-General of Immigration, memorandum, November 1, 1922; both in file 54490-7, INSAIE supplement.

157. Inspector in Charge, New York, to Commissioner-General of Immigration, Washington, D.C., letter, September 22, 1923, file 54490-7, INSAIE supplement.

158. A. W. Brough, Acting Inspector in Charge, New York, to Commissioner-General of Immigration, letter, October 27, 1923, file 54490-7, INSAIE supplement.

159. Immigration Act of 1924 (43 Stat. 153).

160. Archibald, "Alien Seamen," December 10, 1934, 15–16, file 55875/26, Subject and Policy Files, INS, NARA–Washington, D.C.

161. Archibald, "Alien Seamen."

162. *ARCGI* (1903), 69.

163. Archibald, "Alien Seamen," December 10, 1934, 19, file 55875/26, Subject and Policy Files, INS, NARA–Washington, D.C.

164. *ARCGI* (1925), 22.

165. "Huge Grant Charged in Bootlegging Aliens," *New York Times*, February 19, 1927, 2.

166. *ARCGI* (1931), 30, 50.

167. "Urges Washington to Bar Chinese Crew," 37; "Inquiry on Coolies to Be Opened Today," 32; "206 Chinese Coolies Ordered Deported," *New York Times*, February 2, 1933, 37; "Chinese Crew Plea Fails," *New York Times*, February 4, 1933, 31; "Chinese Is Freed," 7.

168. The CSU was also known as the Lien Yi (or Lung Yee) Society. It was active as a seamen's branch of the Kuomintang Party from 1913 until 1927, then re-formed as an independent seamen's union in 1936. Kwong, *Chinatown, New York*, 116–30. See also Song, *Shaping and Reshaping Chinese American Identity*, 42–44; Provinse, "FBI Survey of Chinese Activities in the New York Field Division," 12, January 11, 1944, file 291.2—Chinese, box 382, Army Intelligence Vertical File, 1941–1948, Record Group 319, entry 47, NARA–College Park, Md.

169. Baldoz, *Third Asiatic Invasion*, 274–75; McWilliams, *Brothers under the Skin*, 237.

170. Kwong, *Chinatown, New York*, 122.

171. Kwong, *Chinatown, New York*, 116–30; Hsiao, "100 Years of Hell-Raising."

172. *ARINS* (1942), 19.

173. *ARINS* (1947), 29.

174. Benton, *Chinese Migrants and Internationalism*, 56.

175. Wong, *Americans First*; Oyen, "Allies, Enemies and Aliens"; "Chinese Seamen Feted," *New York Times*, July 22, 1942, 9.

176. Hong, *Opening the Gates to Asia*, 48–62.

177. "18 Chinese Seamen Like Jail," *New York Herald Tribune*, July 7, 1941, 1A; "Chinese Refuses to Sail," *New York Herald Tribune*, July 10, 1941, 10; "Crewman Is Killed in a Mutiny Here," 1, 15.

178. In addition to the events described here, see also "Chinese Seamen Win Agreement with British Merchant Marine," *New York Times*, May 10, 1942, F10; "Events of Interest in Shipping World," *New York Times*, June 7, 1942, F7.

179. "Crewman Is Killed in a Mutiny Here," 1; "British Captain Held in Mutiny Slaying," *New York Times*, April 14, 1942, 8.

180. "Crewman Is Killed in a Mutiny Here," 1; "British Captain Held in Mutiny Slaying," 8; "Freed in Mutiny Death," *New York Times*, April 16, 1942, 8.

181. "Two Chinese Seamen Shot," *New York Times*, June 5, 1942, 10.

182. Lee, "Hunting for Sailors," 114–18.

183. Takaki, *Double Victory*, 22–57; Phillips, *War! What Is It Good For?*, 20–63.

184. "Chinese Seamen Win Agreement with British Merchant Marine," F10. See also "Chinese Held Mistreated," *New York Times*, April 15, 1942, 2.

185. "Chinese Seamen Win Agreement with British Merchant Marine," F10; "Events of Interest in Shipping World," F7; Benton, *Chinese Migrants and Internationalism*, 57–58; Lee, "Hunting for Sailors," 110–11.

186. "62 Chinese Seamen Get Shore Leave," *New York Times*, August 5, 1942, 12; "China Comes Ashore," *New York Times*, August 6, 1942, 18.

187. "62 Chinese Seamen Get Shore Leave," 12.

188. Although the photographs are marked as "created/published in September 1942," the presence of the Chinese consul confirms that they were taken as the first Chinese seamen were granted shore leave in August. Edward Gruber, photographer, LC-USE6-D-006000, LC-USE6-D-006001, LC-USE6-D-006002, LC-USE6-D-006003, LC-USE6-D-006004, LC-USE6- D-006005, LC-USE6- D-006006, all in Farm Security Administration-Office of War Information (FSA-OWI) Photograph Collection, Library of Congress Prints and Photographs Division.

189. La Guardia summarized in "Club Is Dedicated to Chinese Seamen," *New York Times*, September 11, 1943, 15. See also "Events of Interest in Shipping World," S3. The club provided recreation facilities, including a library and game room. "Chinatown Struck by Mythical Bomb," *New York Times*, August 13, 1943. On the Manhattan Chinatown club, "a social organization for Chinese seamen" with several hundred members, see Provinse, "FBI Survey of Chinese Activities in the New York Field Division," 12, January 11, 1944, file 291.2—Chinese, box 382, Army Intelligence Vertical File, 1941–1948, Record Group 319, Entry 47, NARA–College Park, Md.

190. An Act to Repeal the Chinese Exclusion Acts, December 17, 1943 (57 Stat. 600); "In Fairness to an Ally," *New York Herald Tribune*, May 31, 1943, 10; "President Urges Congress Repeal Chinese Exclusion Act as War Aid," *New York Times*, October 12, 1943, 10; Hong, *Opening the Gates to Asia*, 21–47.

191. Cited in Lee, "Hunting for Sailors," 114.

192. "Two Soldiers Cleared of Robbery Charge," *New York Times*, February 3, 1944, 12. Villanova's address is given as 240 High Street, just off Sand Street and part of the Filipino community in Brooklyn.

193. American Merchant Marine at War, "U.S. Merchant Marine Casualties during World War II," http://www.usmm.org/casualty.html, February 12, 2007; "Events of Interest in Shipping World," S3.

194. "Foreign Sailors on Our Ships," *New York Times*, July 22, 1945, 70; "Alien Round-Up Traps 46," *New York Times*, July 19, 1949, 45; "Pakistanis Seek Deportation Bail," *New York Times*, August 24, 1949, 15; *ARINS* (1950), 5–6; Buff, "Deportation Terror," 532; Wong, *Chinatown*, 34.

195. *ARINS* (1947), 15; *ARINS* (1950–1956), Tables 22 and 23.

196. US Congress House Committee on Immigration and Naturalization, "Strengthening of Alien Seamen's Deportation Procedures," April 5, 1920.

## Chapter 5

1. "Entire City Put on War Footing," *New York Times*, December 8, 1941, 1, 3; "FBI Rounding Up Germans," *New York Times*, December 9, 1941, 40; Larry Tajiri, "Over 200 Japanese Held as Dangerous Aliens in New York's Ellis Island," *Nichi Bei*, December 31, 1941, in Robinson, *Pacific Citizens*, 34–35. On the Nippon Club, see Gluck, "Ecological Study of the Japanese in New York," 41.

2. This description of Iwamoto's experience is compiled from his own testimony before the Commission on Wartime Relocation and Civilian Internment and *New York Times* coverage of raids on Japanese aliens. "Entire City Put on War Footing"; U. J. Gerdes, FBI report on Kinichi Iwamoto, January 10, 1942, file 146-13-2-51-645, (AE)LCF; Hohri, *Repairing America*, 179. See also Kashima, *Judgment without Trial*, 5, 24–29; Kumamoto, "Search for Spies."

3. "Entire City Put on War Footing," 3; "FBI Rounding Up Germans," 40; "367 Are Arrested Here," *New York Times*, December 10, 1941, 30; "Seizure of Aliens about Completed," *New York Times*, December 12, 1941, 21. The captioned photograph does not appear in the *New York Times*; it was located in the Bettman Archives via Getty Images.

4. On immigration raids against Chinese and Mexican communities, see Lee, *At America's Gates*, 230–32; Ngai, *Impossible Subjects*, 73. On immigration inspectors, see Norman Gangloff, Immigrant Inspector, New York, Parolee Investigation re: Kinichi Iwamoto, September 11, 1943, file 466-F, entry A1, Records of the Office of the Provost Marshal General, 1920–1975, RG 389, NARA–College Park, Md.

5. Harrison, "Civilian Internment," 233.

6. *ARINS* (1942), 4–5; Unrau, *Ellis Island Historic Resource Study*, 834.

7. See, for example, Alien Enemy Questionnaire, Osam Uyeno, no date, file 146-13-2-51-47; Alien Enemy Questionnaire, Shiro Abe, no date, file 146-3-2-52-11; both in (AE)LCF.

8. Gangloff, Parolee Investigation re: Kinichi Iwamoto, September 11, 1943, file 466-F, entry A1, Records of the Office of the Provost Marshal General, 1920–1975, Record Group 389, NARA–College Park, Md.

9. *ARINS* (1920), 310; "Kline's Deportation Party Is Grim Affair for Immigrants," *Milwaukee Journal*, January 11, 1940; Memorandum for Enemy Alien Information Bureau, February 26, 1942, Ensuke Fukuba, file 146-13-2-11-713, (AE)LCF; Ed Kline, Deportation Officer, to Immigration and Naturalization Service, Washington, DC, telegram, May 9, 1941, Historical Museum at Fort Missoula, Montana Memory Project, http://cdm15018.contentdm.oclc.org/cdm/compoundobject/collection/p16013coll22/id/440/rec/4.

10. *ARINS* (1942), 22–23.

11. On discussions of the term "concentration camp" to describe U.S. sites of confinement, see Daniels, "Words Do Matter."

12. Clair Price, "Harbor Camp for Enemy Aliens," *New York Times Sunday Magazine*, January 25, 1942, 29. On discussions of the term "concentration camp" to describe U.S. sites of confinement, see Daniels, "Words Do Matter." In other examples of the routine early use of "concentration camp," *Newsweek* reported that "the Department of Justice rushed plans to open an American version of the European concentration camp in the mountainous wilds of New Mexico and to transfer there as its first 'guests' 410 distressed seamen." "A Camp for Aliens," *Newsweek*, January 27, 1941, 17. Another magazine noted that "the American-model camps are de luxe jobs that bear about as much resemblance to their Nazi prototypes as an easy chair does to an electric chair." "Our Three Concentration Camps," *American Magazine*, January 8, 1942, 46.

13. Exceptions include Cannato, *American Passage*; Moreno, *Encyclopedia of Ellis Island*.

14. Daniels, *Concentration Camps USA*; Hayashi, *Democratizing the Enemy*; Inada, *Only What We Could Carry*; Lyon, *Prisons and Patriots*; Okihiro, "Japanese Resistance in America's Concentration Camps"; Weglyn, *Years of Infamy*.

15. It is difficult to determine exact numbers of interned Japanese enemy aliens because INS annual reports and other records do not provide a final total of individuals arrested, detained, interned, paroled, released, or repatriated under the auspices of the Alien Enemy Control Unit. Instead, INS officials provided a general statement of "approximately 20,000 aliens detained in the custody of the Service during the War." *ARINS* (1946), 6. Annual reports also provide the numbers of individuals at the end of each fiscal year while the program was in operation. The figure of up to 15,000 Japanese internees is based on the following reports: Annual Report of Lemuel Scofield, Special Assistant to the Attorney General in Charge of the INS Year Ended June 30, 1942; *ARINS* (1943); *ARINS* (1944); *ARINS* (1945); *ARINS* (1946); *ARINS* (1947); *ARINS* (1948). The INS was created in 1933 through the consolidation of the Bureau of Immigration and the Bureau of Naturalization.

16. Fiset, *Imprisoned Apart*, 30–31; Houston and Houston, *Farewell to Manzanar*, 6–7; Ngai, *Impossible Subjects*, 175–76; Spickard, *Japanese Americans*, 94–95.

17. Histories that address the ways in which Japanese alien enemy internment has been overlooked include Clark, "Those Other Camps"; Kumamoto, "Search for Spies," 45–46; Roxworthy, *Spectacle of Japanese American Trauma*, 59.

18. See, for example, Azuma, *Between Two Empires*; Lon Kurashige, *Japanese American Celebration and Conflict*; Scott Kurashige, *Shifting Grounds of Race*.

19. The number of Japanese civilian detainees in INS internment (15,000) as a percentage of the total number of incarcerated people of Japanese descent (including 110,000 Japanese and Japanese Americans relocated from the western United States in WRA camps and 15,000 INS internees) is 12 percent. However, it is difficult to know the exact proportions of these two overlapping populations. The percentage of INS detainees may have been lower.

20. On the legal basis for enemy alien internment, see Kashima, *Judgment without Trial*, 23–27; Daniels, "Internment of Japanese Nationals"; Culley, "Santa Fe Internment Camp," 57. See also Lyle E. Cook, Captain, Office of the Judge Advo-

cate, memorandum re: Regulation of Enemy Aliens, December 21, 1941, reel 3, in Boehm and Lester, *Papers of the US Commission on Wartime Relocation and Internment of Civilians*.

21. *ARINS* (1942), 3.

22. United States Commission on Wartime Relocation and Internment of Civilians, *Personal Justice Denied*, 18.

23. Daniels, "Words Do Matter," 190–214.

24. Christgau, *"Enemies"*; Connell, *America's Japanese Hostages*; Daniels, "Internment of Japanese Nationals"; DiStasi, *Una Storia Segreta*; Elleman, *Japanese-American Civilian Prisoner Exchanges*; Fox, *America's Invisible Gulag*; Fox, "General John Dewitt"; Gardiner, *Pawns in a Triangle of Hate*; Kashima, *Judgment without Trial*; Krammer, *Undue Process*; Sheridan, *Internment of German and Italian Aliens*.

25. The comprehensive Densho map is located at http://encyclopedia.densho .org/map/. Maps of the western United States include Burton et al., *Confinement and Ethnicity*, 2; Daniels et al., *Japanese Americans*, xvii; Weglyn, *Years of Infamy*, 7. Maps that include varied facilities across the United States without including Ellis Island are found in Fukuda, *My Six Years of Internment*, xi; Kashima, *Judgment without Trial*, 12–13.

26. Burton et al., *Confinement and Ethnicity*, 380; Kashima, *Judgment without Trial*, 49, 107, 109–10, 123; Clark, "Those Other Camps," 18. Exceptions to the oversight of internment at Ellis Island include Cannato, *American Passage*; Moreno, *Encyclopedia of Ellis Island*.

27. *ARINS* (1944), 22.

28. Ishizuka, *Lost and Found*, 154–72; Murray, *Historical Memories*, 406–30.

29. Sallie Han, "The 'Enemy' Camp Japanese-Americans Recall Their World War II Imprisonment on Ellis Island," *New York Daily News*, April 12, 1998, 22. Thanks to Roger Daniels for sharing this and other articles related to the exhibition.

30. See, for example, Bayor, *Encountering Ellis Island*; Fairchild, *Science at the Borders*, 271; Kraut, *Silent Travelers*, 31–49; Pegler-Gordon, *In Sight of America*, 104–73.

31. Robinson, "Nisei in Gotham," 581–82; Table 25, "New York: Indians, Chinese and Japanese, by Sex, for Counties and for Cities of 10,000 to 100,000," U.S. Census, *Sixteenth Census 1940, Vol. II, Part 5, Population*, 66–67.

32. Robinson, *After Camp*, 53–56; Inouye, *Distant Islands*, 138–88.

33. Gluck, "Ecological Study of the Japanese in New York," 49.

34. Table 33, "Japanese Population by Age, Nativity, and Sex, for Selected States, Urban and Rural, and for Selected Cities," in U.S. Census, *Sixteenth Census 1940, Population: Characteristics of the Nonwhite Population by Race*, 99; Table 25, "Indians, Chinese and Japanese, by Sex, for Counties, and for Cities of 10,000 to 100,000," in U.S. Census, *Sixteenth Census 1940, Vol. II, Part 5, Population*, 66; Conroy and Miyakawa, *East across the Pacific*, 153; Daniels, *Decision to Relocate the Japanese Americans*, 4; Kashima, *Judgment without Trial*, 9.

35. Gluck, "Ecological Study of the Japanese in New York," 24–26, 50; Inouye, *Distant Islands*, 34, 149–88.

36. Mr. Kawamura cited in Daniel J. Griffin, FBI Report on Shinji Fujishiro, May 3, 1943, file 146-13-2-36-381, (AE)LCF.

37. Yeita Sokei-An Sasaki, "Conclusion to Anti-Japanese Sentiment," New York *Japanese American*, July 27, 1940, translated by George Furiya, file 146-13-2-51-1537, (AE)LCF.

38. "Planes Guard City from Air Attack," *New York Times*, December 9, 1941, 26; Taido Ogihara, a.k.a. Teddy Hara, FBI report, December 1, 1942, 1; Taido Ogihara, a.k.a. Teddy Hara, FBI report, July 16, 1942, 2; both in file 146-13-2-51-1972, (AE)LCF.

39. Wegars, *As Rugged as the Terrain*, 127.

40. "Planes Guard City from Air Attack," 26; "Entire City Put on War Footing," 3; "45 Japanese Homes in New Jersey Raided," *New York Times*, April 29, 1942, 9; Hohri, *Repairing America*, 177.

41. "367 Are Arrested Here," *New York Times*, December 10, 1941, 30; "Seize 2,303 Aliens of Axis Nations," *New York Times*, December 11, 1941, 24; *ARINS* (1942), 3; Lemuel B. Schofield to Mr. Ennis, memorandum, December 10, 1941; and W. F. Kelly, Chief Supervisor, Border Patrol, memorandum for the file, December 10, 1941; both in file 56125-29, reel 9, *USCWRIC*.

42. Figures based on author's review of World War II Japanese Internee Cards, UD-UP entry 4, Record Group 60, NARA–College Park, Md. Despite widescale arrests, a review of World War II Japanese internee cards suggests that some Issei, particularly those who lived in suburbs farther from New York City, were investigated but not arrested.

43. Lemuel B. Schofield, Special Assistant to the Attorney General, to J. Edgar Hoover, Director, FBI, memorandum, January 14, 1942, file 56125-29, reel 9, *USCWRIC*.

44. "Entire City Put on War Footing," 3.

45. Schofield to Ennis, memorandum, December 10, 1941, file 56125-29, reel 9, *USCWRIC*.

46. Ichiro Isaac Shirato, Card, WWIIJIC; Clement A. O'Brien, FBI Report on James Kiyozane Furukawa, September 23, 1942, file 146-13-2-51-2672, (AE)LCF.

47. Nori Sato is a pseudonym. On Nori Sato, see "Case Files," BANC MSS 67/14 c, folder T1.9945, Japanese American Evacuation and Resettlement Study, University of California, Berkeley, Digital Archive, accessed August 13, 2015, http://digital assets.lib.berkeley.edu/jarda/ucb/text/cubanc6714_b284t01_9945.pdf. On Naoye Suzuki, see Han, "'Enemy' Camp Japanese-Americans Recall Their World War II Imprisonment on Ellis Island," 22; Naoye Suzuki, Card, WWIIJIC; Naoye Suzuki, file 146-13-2-51-822, (AE)LCF. There are numerous discrepancies between the news article and different case files.

48. Tajiri, "Over 200 Japanese Held as Dangerous Aliens in New York's Ellis Island," in Robinson, *Pacific Citizens*, 34–35.

49. "Planes Guard City from Air Attack," *New York Times*, December 9, 1941, 26.

50. Ngai, *Impossible Subjects*, 186–87; Culley, "Santa Fe Internment Camp," 63–65.

51. See, for example, Sadakichi Miki and Tsunesue Miyagawa, Cards; both in WWIIJIC. See also Yuji Ichioka, "Japanese Immigrant Nationalism."

52. Yuki Kijima, Card, WWIIJIC.

53. Kyuzaburo Saito, Card, WWIIJIC.

54. During the war, some naturalization restrictions were placed on citizens of Axis nations. "Alien Curbs Aimed Only at Disloyal," *New York Times*, December 14, 1941, 9; Haney López, *White by Law*.

55. Norman Gangloff, Immigrant Inspector, to District Director, INS, New York, letter re: Kinichi Iwamoto, September 4, 1943; Memorandum to Chief of Review Section, Enemy Alien Unit, no date; and Gerdes, FBI report on Kinichi Iwamoto, January 10, 1942; all in file 146-13-2-51-645, (AE)LCF.

56. J. Procknau, Pastor, Peapack Reformed Church, Gladstone, N.J., to Mathias Correa, US Attorney, Foley Square, New York City, January 9, 1942, file 146-13-2-48-140, (AE)LCF. See also Mary Outland Katsuki to George Schoonmaker, US Attorney, letter, December 28, 1942, file 146-13-2-51-31; "We Are Glad, Mr Uyeno," Copy of Editorial from Port Chester Daily Item, Monday, April 13, 1942, file 146-13-2-51-47; Kikuno Fukuba to Edward Ennis, Director of Enemy Alien Control, July 23, 1943, file 146-13-2-11-713; all in (AE)LCF.

57. Gangloff to District Director, INS, New York, letter re: Kinichi Iwamoto, September 4, 1943; H. W. Ramsey, Special Inspector, Interview with Kinichi Iwamoto, June 23, 1943, Ellis Island; and Memorandum to Chief of Review Section, Enemy Alien Unit, no date; all in file 146-13-2-51-645, (AE)LCF.

58. There were 272 Issei women and 1,085 Issei men in New York City in 1940. Table 34, "Japanese Population 15 Years Old and Over by Marital Status, Age, Nativity, and Sex, for Selected States, Urban and Rural, and for Selected Cities," in U.S. Census, *Sixteenth Census 1940, Population: Characteristics of the Nonwhite Population by* Race, 101; Fumi Aoyama, Tatsugoro Okajima, Hatsiji Yatsui, Florence May Tsukamoto, Cards; all in WWIIJIC.

59. Hohri, *Repairing America*, 180.

60. Matsumoto and Lerrigo, *Brother Is a Stranger*, 218; Toru Matsumoto and Matsuhei Matsuo, Cards; both in WWIIJIC; Statement of Dr. Frederick Newall, no date, file 146-13-2-51-104, (AE)LCF; *ARINS* (1943), 15. There is no further information about Matsuhei Matsuo's unnamed wife in these records.

61. Gangloff, Parolee Investigation re: Kinichi Iwamoto, September 11, 1943, file 466-F, entry A1, RG 389, Records of the Office of the Provost Marshal General, NARA–College Park, Md.

62. Josephine Emy to Attorney General Francis Biddle, letter, January 1, 1942, file 146-13-2-51-80; Memorandum to Chief of the Review Section re: Dr. Saburo Emy, Enemy Alien Unit, September 1, 1942, file 146-13-2-51-80; both in (AE)LCF.

63. Wegars, *As Rugged as the Terrain*, 131–35, 54–57.

64. Matsumoto and Lerrigo, *Brother Is a Stranger*, 218.

65. "Entire City Put on War Footing," 3. John Christgau notes that "complaints about alien espionage were coming into the Justice Department at the rate of three thousand a day." Christgau, *"Enemies,"* 10.

66. Hartzell and New York State War Council, *Empire State at War*, 92.

67. These camps were located in Baltimore, Maryland; Boston, Massachusetts; Camp Kenedy, Texas; Chicago, Illinois; Cincinnati, Ohio; Crystal City, Texas; Detroit, Michigan; El Paso, Texas; Ellis Island, New York; Fort Lincoln, North Dakota;

Fort Missoula, Montana; Fort Stanton, New Mexico; Gloucester City, New Jersey; Kansas City; Kooskia, Idaho; Miami, Florida; New Orleans, Louisiana; Niagara Falls, New York; Old Raton Ranch, New Mexico; Sharp Park/San Francisco, California; San Pedro/Los Angeles, California; Santa Fe, New Mexico; Seagoville, Texas; Seattle, Washington; and Tuna Canyon/Los Angeles, California. *ARINS* (1942), 4–5; Burton et al., *Confinement and Ethnicity*; Christgau, *"Enemies"*; Kashima, *Judgment without Trial*; Weglyn, *Years of Infamy*. In addition to these facilities, other immigration stations and police stations were used to briefly detain enemy aliens when they were initially arrested.

68. Camps with facilities for women included Gloucester City (New Jersey), Sharp Park (California), and Seagoville (Texas). Crystal City (Texas) had more extensive facilities to accommodate the internment of families. *ARINS* (1942), 5; *ARINS* (1944), 23–24; Burton et al., *Confinement and Ethnicity*, 381–82; Howard, *Concentration Camps on the Home Front*, 99–107; Matsumoto, "Japanese American Women," 8; Kashima, *Judgment without Trial*, 119–21.

69. *ARINS* (1942), 23; *ARINS* (1945), 25–26; *ARINS* (1946), 31. See also Siyokiti Mogami, Kame Muraoka, Yukio Suetugu, Syuzi Taguchi; all in Cards, WWIIJIC.

70. *ARINS* (1942), 22–23; "Jap Internees Work Hard, Well Treated, at Kooskia Road Camp," *Lewiston (Idaho) Morning Tribune*, September 26, 1943, section 2, 1; Burton et al., *Confinement and Ethnicity*, 388–90; Christgau, *"Enemies"* 10–19.

71. Daniels, "Forced Migrations of West Coast Japanese Americans," 74.

72. Burton et al., *Confinement and Ethnicity*, 381, 386. Loyd Jensen, Chief, District Alien Control Division, to W. F. Kelly, Assistant Commissioner for Alien Control, memorandum, June 11, 1945, file 56125-3, entry 323, Subject and Policy Files, INS, National Archives, Washington, D.C. On various types of enemy aliens, see *ARINS* (1942), 25. On immigration detainees, see Ugo Carusi, Commissioner, to W. F. Kelly, Assistant Commissioner for Alien Control, memorandum, July 16, 1945, file 56125-3, entry 323, Subject and Policy Files, INS, NARA–Washington, D.C. On unauthorized immigrants, including sailors, see Price, "Harbor Camp for Enemy Aliens," 29. Most of the Axis crews were held at Staten Island.

73. List of Civilian Aliens in the Custody of the Immigration and Naturalization Service at the Close of Business, June 30, 1943, Ellis Island Detention Station; Records of World War II Internment Camps: Kenedy, Texas, 1942–1945; Records of the Immigration and Naturalization Service, Record Group 85; NARA–Washington, D.C. My thanks to Lynn Goodsell for sharing this research with me.

74. Of the 528 aliens in detention at Ellis Island, there were 178 enemy aliens, 325 deportees, 19 arrivals awaiting review of their cases, and 2 "safekeeping cases." There were also 80 aliens in the hospital. Jensen to Kelly, memorandum, June 11, 1945, file 56125-3, entry 323, Subject and Policy Files, INS, NARA–Washington, D.C.

75. Price, "Harbor Camp for Enemy Aliens," 29; "Protest Unequal Wages, Indonesian Seamen Held," *Chicago Defender* (national edition), October 23, 1943, 2; "Indonesian Seamen Freed by US, Return to Harlem," *Chicago Defender* (national edition), January 26, 1946, 8.

76. Markel and Stern, "Which Face? Whose Nation?"; *ARINS* (1943) and Reports of Enemy Aliens Paroled, Ellis Island (NY District), 1942–1944, 56293/380, INS, NARA, both cited in Unrau, *Ellis Island Historic Resource Study*, 835.

77. Kumamoto, "Search for Spies," 51–54, 58–67; Muller, *American Inquisition*; Ngai, *Impossible Subjects*, 177–201.

78. Muller, *American Inquisition*, 3–4.

79. Hohri, *Repairing America*, 179–80.

80. Reports of Enemy Aliens Paroled, Ellis Island (NY District), 1942–1944, 56293/380, INS, National Archives, Washington, D.C., cited in Unrau, *Ellis Island Historic Resource Study*, 835. Figures based on author's review of cards for Japanese detained at Ellis Island, WWIIJIC.

81. Daniels, "Internment of Japanese Nationals," 69; Hohri, *Repairing America*, 180.

82. Memorandum, In the Matter of the Detention of Tomito Hirano, August 2, 1942, file 146-13-2-48-87; Edward J. Ennis, Director, Enemy Alien Control Unit, to Matthias F. Correa, US Attorney, letter, May 7, 1943, file 146-13-2-51-2171; both in (AE)LCF. See also index card records for Yoshitsugus Fujimoto, Kinnosuke Fujisake, Hisako Gallo, Sampey Iseda, Toyaji Ina, Masatsugu Ito, William Kajita, Cecilia Yohann Nomi, Kunsung Rie, Kenjiro Taguchi, and Naoki Yamanaka; all in WWIIJIC.

83. Clark, "Those Other Camps," 9–11. Naoye Suzuki, Card; Ichiro Isaac Shirato, Card; both in WWIIJIC; O'Brien, FBI Report on James Kiyozane Furukawa, September 23, 1942, file 146-13-2-51-2672, (AE)LCF.

84. Memorandum to Chief of the Review Section re: Dr. Saburo Emy, Enemy Alien Unit, September 1, 1942, file 146-13-2-51-80, (AE)LCF.

85. Report and Recommendation re: Takashi Katsuki, January 17, 1942, file 146-13-2-51-31, (AE)LCF.

86. Kayao Kawano, Card, WWIIJIC.

87. Memorandum for Chief of Review Section, Alien Enemy Control Unit, re: Iwajiro Noda, no date; both in file 146-13-2-51-287, (AE)LCF.

88. Nobuji Ashikaga, Kayo Hukuhara, Toshio Kono, Otansuke Maki, Cards; all in WWIIJIC.

89. In the Matter of the Detention of Takeji Kusanobu, February 18, 1942, file 146-13-2-48-251; Reconsideration Memorandum for Chief of Review Section, Re: Yeita Sokei-An Sasaki, April 7, 1945, file 146-13-2-51-1537; both in (AE)LCF; Lee, *At America's Gates*, 91–92, 106, 37–38.

90. About 6 percent of all Issei internees at Ellis Island were not released until 1946 because of problems with their cases. Seiki Naito to Lane Novack, May 3, 1943; Reconsideration of Closed Case: memorandum, July 30, 1942; both in file 146-13-2-51-104, (AE)LCF; Fred (Seiki) Naito, Card, WWIIJIC.

91. Kumamoto, "Search for Spies," 59; Muller, *American Inquisition*, 44–53.

92. Toyaji Ina, Card, WWIIJIC; and Gangloff to District Director, INS, New York, letter re: Kinichi Iwamoto, September 4, 1943, file 146-13-2-51-645, (AE)LCF; Robinson, "Nisei in Gotham."

93. Takeji Kusanobu, Card, WWIIJIC; Hohri, *Repairing America*, 180.

94. Francis Biddle, Attorney General, to Matthias Correa, US Attorney, memorandum, October 15, 1942; J. Atkinson, FBI Report on Kuro Murasi, July 1, 1942; both in file 146-13-2-51-1662, (AE)LCF.

95. Gerdes, FBI report on Kinichi Iwamoto, January 10, 1942; Gangloff to District Director, INS, New York, letter re: Kinichi Iwamoto, September 4, 1943; Attorney General, memorandum, In the Matter of Kinichi Iwamoto, December 9, 1943; all in file 146-13-2-51-645, (AE)LCF.

96. Byron Uhl, District Director, New York, Confirmation of Telegram, March 27, 1942; Gangloff to District Director, INS, New York, letter re: Kinichi Iwamoto, September 4, 1943; Attorney General, memorandum, In the Matter of Kinichi Iwamoto, December 9, 1943; all in file 146-13-2-51-645, (AE)LCF. By 1945, Iwamoto was no longer registered on the INS's list of civilian alien enemies in New York City. Loyd Jensen, Chief, District Alien Control Division, to W. F. Kelly, Assistant Commissioner for Alien Control, memorandum, June 11, 1945, file 56125/3d, entry 323, Subject and Policy Files, INS, NARA–Washington, D.C.

97. Han, "'Enemy' Camp Japanese-Americans Recall Their World War II Imprisonment on Ellis Island," 22.

98. Earl G. Harrison, Commissioner, INS, memorandum for Alien Enemy Information Bureau, January 5, 1944; Attorney General, memorandum, In the Matter of Kinichi Iwamoto, December 9, 1943; both in file 146-13-2-51-645, (AE)LCF. By 1945, Iwamoto was no longer registered on the INS's list of civilian alien enemies in New York City. Jensen to Kelly, memorandum, June 11, 1945, file 56125/3d, entry 323, Subject and Policy Files, INS, NARA–Washington, D.C.

99. Togo Tanaka to Morton Grodzins, memorandum re: Exclusion from the Eastern Defense Command Area, April 8, 1943, "Case files," BANC MSS 67/14 c, folder T1.9945, Japanese American Evacuation and Resettlement Study, University of California, Berkeley, Digital Archive, http://digitalassets.lib.berkeley.edu/jarda/ucb/text/cubanc6714_b284to1_9945.pdf; Han, "'Enemy' Camp Japanese-Americans Recall Their World War II Imprisonment on Ellis Island," 22; Naoye Suzuki, Card, WWIIJIC.

100. "Case files," BANC MSS 67/14 c, folder T1.9945, Japanese American Evacuation and Resettlement Study, University of California, Berkeley, Digital Archive, accessed August 13, 2015, http://digitalassets.lib.berkeley.edu/jarda/ucb/text/cubanc6714_b284to1_9945.pdf.

101. Han, "'Enemy' Camp Japanese-Americans Recall Their World War II Imprisonment on Ellis Island," 22.

102. Burton et al., *Confinement and Ethnicity*, 381, 86.

103. Price, "Harbor Camp for Enemy Aliens," 29.

104. Iwamoto in Hohri, *Repairing America*, 179.

105. Yae Aihara, Interview Segments 11 and 12, "Reuniting with Her Father at Ellis Island," interviewed by Megan Asaka, July 4, 2008, Densho Visual History Collection, Densho ID: denshovh-ayae-01-0012, Densho Digital Archive.

106. Han, "'Enemy' Camp Japanese-Americans Recall Their World War II Imprisonment on Ellis Island," 22.

107. Iwamato in Hohri, *Repairing America*, 179. Price, "Harbor Camp for Enemy Aliens," 29; Han, "'Enemy' Camp Japanese-Americans Recall Their World War II Imprisonment on Ellis Island," 22; Margaret Jones, American Friends Service Committee, to Evelyn Hersey, Immigration and Naturalization Service, letter, January 5, 1945, file 56125-3, entry 323, Subject and Policy Files, INS, NARA–Washington, D.C.

108. Iwamoto in Hohri, *Repairing America*, 179.

109. Adjutant General to Commanding General, First Corps Area, Boston, Mass., Radio Message, January 6, 1942, reel 3, [scan 0530], *USCWRIC* microfilm (Frederick, Md.: University Publications of America, 1984).

110. Iwamoto in Hohri, *Repairing America*, 179. See also Gloria Noda to Harold M. Kennedy, US Attorney, letter, January 5, 1942, file 146-13-2-51-287, (AE)LCF; Katsusaburo Shibata, Interview with Joseph LaGiudice, Immigrant Inspector, July 26, 1943, file 146-13-2-51-1622, (AE)LCF; Price, "Harbor Camp for Enemy Aliens," 29.

111. Ferrand, "EIOHP Interview of Pierre Ferrand."

112. W. J. Zucker, District Operations Officer, to Loyd Jensen, Chief, District Alien Control Division, memorandum, December 4, 1944, file 56125-3, entry 323, Subject and Policy Files, INS, NARA–Washington, D.C.

113. Zucker to Jensen, memorandum, December 4, 1944, file 56125-3, entry 323, Subject and Policy Files, INS, NARA–Washington, D.C.

114. Ichio Kushihashi, WWIIJIC.

115. Iwamoto in Hohri, *Repairing America*, 179.

116. Price, "Harbor Camp for Enemy Aliens," 29. Price reports that detainees were allowed out to the exercise yard freely, although many chose to stay inside because of the cold weather. Given the difference between Iwamato's recollections and Price's reporting, it seems likely that exercise rules changed after the period of Iwamoto's detention.

117. Price, "Harbor Camp for Enemy Aliens," 29.

118. Iwamoto in Hohri, *Repairing America*, 179.

119. Price, "Harbor Camp for Enemy Aliens," 29.

120. Joint Agreement of the Secretary of War and Attorney General Respecting the Internment of Alien Enemies, July 18, 1941, 3, reel 3, *USCWRIC*.

121. N. D. Collaer, Chief, Detention and Deportation Service, to W. F. Kelly, Assistant Commissioner for Alien Control, memorandum, December 21, 1944, file 56125-3, entry 323, Subject and Policy Files, INS, NARA–Washington, D.C.

122. Zucker to Jensen, December 4, 1944, file 56125-3, entry 323, Subject and Policy Files, INS, NARA–Washington, D.C.

123. Clark, "Those Other Camps," 31–38; Kashima, "American Mistreatment of Internees," 52–56.

124. R. F. Smith to Inspector in Charge, Detention Division, August 13, 1942, file 146-13-2-51-1369; Frederick Walter D'Esquiva to Byron H. Uhl, District Director, no date, file 146-13-2-51-1369; Memorandum, September 1, 1942, file 146-13-2-51-1622; Byron Uhl, District Director, and S. A. Diana, Inspector in Charge, New York, to Edward Ennis, Director, Enemy Alien Control Unit, letter, September 23, 1942, file 146-13-2-51-1369; Memorandum re: Adolf Gustav Preuss, no date, file 146-13-2-51-1369; William L. Caraway, Attorney, to Chief of Review Section, memorandum,

October 30, 1942, file 146-13-2-51-1622; Memorandum, August 27, 1942, file 146-13-2-51-1369; all in (AE)LCF.

125. Jack Midzuno, Card, WWIIJIC; Memorandum re: Kenjiro Sugimoto, October 1, 1942, file 146-13-2-48-712, (AE)LCF. On hunger strikes, see also Curran, *Pillar to Post*, 292–93.

126. Clark, "Those Other Camps," 97–98.

127. Kelly to Carusi, memorandum, July 16, 1945, file 56125-3d, entry 323, Subject and Policy Files, INS, NARA–Washington, D.C.

128. "A More Modern Ellis Island Set-Up Favored for Detention of Aliens," *New York Times*, March 19, 1948, 25.

129. Figures based on author's review of cards for Japanese detained at Ellis Island under the Enemy Alien program. WWIIJIC.

130. "Barriers Set Up for Diplomatic Ship," *New York Times*, August 22, 1942, 3; United States Commission on Wartime Relocation and Internment of Civilians, *Personal Justice Denied*, 310, note 31; Elleman, *Japanese-American Civilian Prisoner Exchanges*, 131–38.

131. "Barriers Set Up for Diplomatic Ship," 3; "US Refugees Due from Orient Today," *New York Times*, August 25, 1942, 21; "Gripsholm Brings 1500 from Orient," *New York Times*, August 26, 1942, 7; "30 from Gripsholm Are under Inquiry," *New York Times*, December 3, 1943, 25.

132. New York, U.S., Arriving Passenger and Crew Lists, 1820–1957 (online database), Ancestry.com, 2010.

133. Yuji Kawamoto, Card, WWIIJIC.

134. Gangloff to District Director, INS, New York, letter re: Kinichi Iwamoto, September 4, 1943, file 146-13-2-51-645, (AE)LCF; Iwamoto in Hohri, *Repairing America*, 180.

135. Hohri, *Repairing America*, 180.

136. Aizo Hayasaka, Toyaji Ina, Tatsuo Ando, Yuki Kijima, Misao Kahwasa; all in WWIIJIC; Memorandum to the Chief of the Review Section re: Shigero Mori, June 14, 1944, file 146-13-2-51-1844, (AE)LCF.

137. Memorandum, August 20, 1942, file 146-13-2-48-87, (AE)LCF. See also records of Tokuzo Hosai and Kasanu Kodaka, both in WWIIJIC.

138. Iwamoto in Hohri, *Repairing America*, 179.

139. On espionage, see Takashi Ikeuchi, WWIIJIC.

140. The following individuals detained at Ellis Island were repatriated to Japan despite their recorded desire not to be repatriated: Sakae Hirata, Ishizaki Ichimatsu, Riichi Kinugawa, Shigeo Matsumoto, Shinachi Otani; all in WWIIJIC. See also Elleman, *Japanese-American Civilian Prisoner Exchanges*, 76–77.

141. Aihara, Interview Segments 11 and 12, "Leaving Camp for New York," and "Reuniting with Father at Ellis Island," July 4, 2008, Densho Visual History Collection, Densho ID: denshovh-ayae-01-0011 and denshovh-ayae-01-0012, Densho Digital Archive.

142. Aihara, Interview Segments 11 and 12, "Leaving Camp for New York," and "Reuniting with Father at Ellis Island," July 4, 2008, Densho Visual History Collec-

tion, Densho ID: denshovh-ayae-01-0011 and denshovh-ayae-01-0012, Densho Digital Archive.

143. Aihara, Interview Segment 12, "Reuniting with Father at Ellis Island," July 4, 2008, Densho Visual History Collection, Densho ID: denshovh-ayae-01-0012, Densho Digital Archive.

144. On the spectacle of raids on Japanese communities during World War II, see Roxworthy, *Spectacle of Japanese American Trauma*.

145. W. F. Kelly, memorandum for the file, December 19, 1941, file 56125-29, reel 9, *USCWRIC*.

146. Aihara, Interview Segments 16 and 17, "Moving to Los Angeles After Leaving Camp," "Father's Postwar Work," July 4, 2008, Densho Visual History Collection, Densho ID: denshovh-ayae-01-0016 and denshovh-ayae-01-0017, Densho Digital Archive.

147. US Department of Agriculture, "Relocated Persons of Japanese Ancestry," September 1, 1944, map, reel 3, *USCWRIC*; Robinson, "Nisei in Gotham," 584.

148. Memorandum to the Chief of the Review Section re: Takashi Katsuki, February 17, 1942, file 146-13-2-51-31; Mathias Corea, US Attorney, to Director, Enemy Alien Control Unit, April 28, 1942, file 146-13-2-51-104; both in (AE)LCF.

149. William B. Howes, FBI report on Naoye Suzuki, May 19, 1945, file 146-13-2-51-822, (AE)LCF.

150. Yasuo Matsui, Card, WWIIJIC; Arthur Meyer, Immigrant Inspector, to District Director, INS, New York, Parolee Report Re: Osam Uyeno, November 11, 1943, file 146-13-2-51-47, (AE)LCF.

151. Gangloff to District Director, INS, New York, letter re: Kinichi Iwamoto, September 4, 1943; K. S. Brechler, Immigrant Inspector, to Inspector in Charge, Chief District Parole Officer, Ellis Island, May 18, 1942; and Gerdes, FBI report on Kinichi Iwamoto, January 10, 1942; all in file 146-13-2-51-645, (AE)LCF.

152. *ARINS* (1946), 6, 21–23, 34–35.

## Conclusion

1. Chan Fo was also known as Chen Ke. Chen Ke, "Fangwen lu Mei Huaqiao Chen Ke xiansheng" [An interview with Mr. Chen Ke, a Chinese returned from America], in *Huaqiao shi lunwen ji* [Essays on overseas Chinese history] (Guangzhou: Ji'nan Daxue Huaqiao Yanjiusuo, 1981), 2:341–49, cited in Yu, *To Save China, to Save Ourselves*, 191–92.

2. An Act to Repeal the Chinese Exclusion Acts, December 17, 1943 (57 Stat. 600).

3. Louie, "EIOHP Interview of Thomas Louie"; Lew, "EIOHP Interview of Harry Gem Hoy Lew."

4. Brooks, *Between Mao and McCarthy*, 1–5.

5. Indian and Filipino Immigration and Naturalization Act, July 2, 1946 (60 Stat. 416); An Act to Revise the Laws Related to Immigration, Naturalization and Nationality, July 27, 1952 (66 Stat. 163); Hong, *Opening the Gates to Asia*, 2–3, 48–81, 123–43, 48–49.

6. Yu, *To Save China, to Save Ourselves*, 36–39, 43–56, 131–47. See also "Chinese Meet Peacefully," *Los Angeles Times*, February 27, 1928, A9.

7. Yu, *To Save China, to Save Ourselves*, 184–86; Chin and Chin, *Paper Son*.

8. Heyer, "Pattern of Social Organization," 42, 49–50.

9. Hsu, *Good Immigrants*, 130–65.

10. Chin and Chin, *Paper Son*, 49–56, 68–71, 85–88, 91–99, 106. On FBI surveillance of CHLA and the *China Daily News*, see also Yu, *To Save China, to Save Ourselves*, 186–91; Cheng, *Citizens of Asian America*, 160–72.

11. Chin and Chin, *Paper Son*, 106, 94–96, 88.

12. Chin and Chin, *Paper Son*, 83–84.

13. "83 Chinese Aliens in Raids," *New York Times*, February 1, 1951, 4; "83 Chinese Aliens Rounded Up in Brooklyn Raids," *New York Herald Tribune*, February 1, 1951, 11.

14. Lai, *Becoming Chinese American*, 257; Schrecker, "Immigration and Internal Security," 408; Zhao, *Remaking Chinese America*, 166.

15. Schrecker, "Immigration and Internal Security," 407–9; Kwong, *Chinatown, New York*, 144. Kwong Hai Chew v. Colding, 344 U.S. 590 (1953).

16. Schrecker, "Immigration and Internal Security," 414.

17. *ARINS* (1951), 40.

18. DeVera, "Without Parallel."

19. *ARINS* (1947), 28.

20. *ARINS* (1946), 6, 21–23; *ARINS* (1954), 41; Hernández, *Migra!*, 169–94; Ngai, *Impossible Subjects*, 152–66.

21. *ARINS* (1948), 23; *ARINS* (1954), 41.

22. *ARINS* (1950), 52; *ARINS* (1954), 41. There are no separate numbers reported in 1948 or 1949; Schrecker, "Immigration and Internal Security," 401–3.

23. Schrecker, "Immigration and Internal Security," 416.

24. *ARCGI* (1922), 17; *ARCGI* (1925), 9; *ARCGI* (1926), 21.

25. Alien Registration Act of 1940 (54 Stat. 670), secs. 2, 20, 31.

26. *ARINS* (1948), 23; *ARINS* (1954), 41.

27. *ARINS* (1948), 19.

28. *ARINS* (1947), 32; *ARINS* (1952), 45, 50. Before 1947, the number of deportable aliens under parole is difficult to distinguish from paroled enemy aliens.

29. *ARINS* (1948), 19–20; *ARINS* (1954), 36–37.

30. *ARINS* (1954), 36. See also *ARINS* (1950), 41–43.

31. *ARINS* (1947), 34; *ARINS* (1948), 10.

32. *ARINS* (1947), 29, 34; *ARINS* (1948), 10, 21.

33. Clair Price, "Harbor Camp for Enemy Aliens," *New York Times Sunday Magazine*, January 25, 1942, 29.

34. *ARINS* (1951), 53; "Proposes Closing of Ellis Island," *New York Times*, May 6, 1947, 55; Unrau, *Ellis Island Historic Resource Study*, 842; Edward Shaugnessy, District Director, New York, to Walter Downey, Regional Director, General Services Administration, letter, June 18, 1954, file 56126-619, Subject and Policy Files, INS, NARA–Washington, D.C. Although most administrative staff moved to Manhattan,

Ellis Island continued to house those who processed deportation warrants and the special inquiry officers who interviewed deportees.

35. "Proposes Closing of Ellis Island," 55.

36. Edward Shaugnessy, District Director, New York, to E. A. Loughran, Assistant Commissioner, memorandum, June 8, 1954, 3, file 56126-619, Subject and Policy Files, INS, NARA–Washington, D.C.

37. Philip Forman, Acting Chief, Detention, Deportation and Parole Branch, Ellis Island, to Edward Shaugnessy, District Director, New York, memorandum re: Population at Ellis Island, June 22, 1954, Subject and Policy Files, INS, NARA–Washington, D.C.

38. Ngai, *Impossible Subjects*, 206–7; Hsu, *Good Immigrants*, 153–57.

39. Forman to Shaugnessy, memorandum re: Population at Ellis Island, June 22, 1954, Subject and Policy Files, INS, NARA–Washington, D.C.; E. A. Loughran, Assistant Commissioner, memorandum, June 30, 1954, file 56126-619, Subject and Policy Files, INS, NARA–Washington, D.C.; Knauff, *Ellen Knauff Story*, 161–63.

40. Lew, "EIOHP Interview of Harry Gem Hoy Lew," 17–18.

41. *ARINS* (1951), 54.

42. Unrau, *Ellis Island History Resource Study*, 999; *Christian Science Monitor*, September 1, 1954, cited in Unrau, *Ellis Island Historic Resource Study*, 1002; Loughran, memorandum, June 30, 1954, file 56126-619, Subject and Policy Files, INS, NARA–Washington, D.C.

43. *Christian Science Monitor*, September 1, 1954, cited in Unrau, *Ellis Island Historic Resource Study*, 1002; Loughran, memorandum, June 30, 1954, file 56126-619, Subject and Policy Files, INS, NARA–Washington, D.C.

44. *ARINS* (1954), 36.

45. *ARINS* (1952), 48–49.

46. *ARINS* (1949), 24; *ARINS* (1952), 45; *ARINS* (1953), 47; *ARINS* (1954), 37.

47. *ARINS* (1954), 37; *ARINS* (1952), 45.

48. *Christian Science Monitor*, September 1, 1954, cited in Unrau, *Ellis Island Historic Resource Study*, 1002.

49. *ARINS* (1952), 45.

50. *Christian Science Monitor*, September 1, 1954, cited in Unrau, *Ellis Island Historic Resource Study*, 1002. For most immigrants, however, detention upon arrival typically did not lead to rejection. Out of 38,000 individuals of all races detained upon arrival in 1953, only 1,600 were eventually excluded. "Aliens Entry," *New York Times*, November 18, 1954, 32.

51. *ARINS* (1951), 46–47; "Thousands of Chinese Aliens Entering US," *Baltimore Sun*, March 24, 1956, 1; Ngai, *Impossible Subjects*, 206–12; Cheng, *Citizens of Asian America*, 178–89; Brooks, *Between Mao and McCarthy: Chinese American Politics in the Cold War Years*, 157–59.

52. Sung, *Mountain of Gold*, 104–7.

53. Chin and Chin, *Paper Son*, 111–12, 21–25; Ngai, *Impossible Subjects*, 212–24. For a sample confession, see file 170-892, Lew King Moon, Chinese Files, 1921–1944, INS, NARA–New York.

54. *ARINS* (1951), 54.

55. Ferrand, "EIOHP Interview of Pierre Ferrand."

56. *ARINS* (1952), 48; *ARINS* (1953), 49.

57. *ARINS* (1952), 48; *ARINS* (1953), 49.

58. Edward Shaugnessy, District Director, New York, to E. A. Loughran, Assistant Commissioner, memorandum re: Possible Evacuation of Ellis Island, June 7, 1954, file 56126-619, Subject and Policy Files, INS, NARA–Washington, D.C.

59. *ARINS* (1954), 37. See also *ARINS* (1951), 54–55.

60. Edward Shaugnessy, District Director, New York, to E. A. Loughran, Assistant Commissioner, memorandum re: Space for Detention Facility, June 10, 1954, 4, file 56126-619, Subject and Policy Files, INS, NARA–Washington, D.C.

61. Shaugnessy to Loughran, memorandum, June 8, 1954, 2, file 56126-619, Subject and Policy Files, INS, NARA–Washington, D.C.; Edward Shaugnessy, District Director, New York, to Walter Downey, Regional Director, General Services Administration, June 30, 1954, file 56126-619, Subject and Policy Files, INS, NARA–Washington, D.C.; Edward Shaugnessy, District Director, New York, to H. L. Booth, Chief, Maintenance Division, memorandum re: possible move of functions from Ellis Island, June 28, 1954, 4, file 56126-619, Subject and Policy Files, INS, NARA–Washington, D.C.; Memorandum of Telephone Call, June 21, 1954, 56126-619, Subject and Policy Files, INS, NARA–Washington, D.C.

62. Shaugnessy to Downey, letter, June 30, 1954, file 56126-619, Subject and Policy Files, INS, NARA–Washington, D.C.

63. File 56126-619, Subject and Policy Files, INS, NARA–Washington, D.C.

64. Joseph Swing, Commissioner, to Lieutenant General Withers (Pinkey) Burress, Commanding General, First Army, Governor's Island, New York, letter, June 4, 1954, file 56126-619, Subject and Policy Files, INS, NARA–Washington, D.C. See also Shaugnessy to Downey, letter, June 30, 1954, file 56126-619, Subject and Policy Files, INS, NARA–Washington, D.C.

65. Milton Bracker, "16,000 Take Oaths as Citizens," *New York Times*, November 12, 1954, 1; *ARINS* (1946), 34–35.

66. Mr. Montgomery, Testimony, US Congress House Committee on Immigration and Naturalization, *Alien Seamen and Stowaways: Hearings before the Committee on Immigration and Nationalization*, 61st Cong., 3d Sess., 1911, 35.

67. Senator Hayakawa, speaking on Angel Island, *Congressional Record*, 97th Cong., 1st Sess. (December 2, 1981), 29321; Chow cited in Sakovich, "Angel Island Immigration Station Reconsidered," 10; Bamford, *Angel Island*. See also Marinbach, *Galveston, Ellis Island of the West*.

68. See, for example, Curtis Hartman, "The New Ellis Islands," *Inc. Magazine*, July 1, 1986; Ed Hicks, "The New Ellis Island," *Memphis Business Journal*, December 9, 2001; "Old and New 'Ellis Islands,'" a chapter section in Zhou, "Contemporary Immigration and the Dynamics of Race and Ethnicity," 214–15; Barkan, "Immigration through Los Angeles," 81, 174.

69. "Boat People Reach Los Angeles After Three Months," *New York Times*, January 23, 1979, A14. See also Kurt Anderson, "Los Angeles: The New Ellis Island,"

*Time Magazine,* June 13, 1983; Scott Armstrong, "Los Angeles a New Ellis Island," *Sunday Telegraph* (Nashua), August 6, 1989, 43.

70. As noted in the introduction, academic histories that focus on the 1892–1924 period include Bayor, *Encountering Ellis Island;* Fairchild, *Science at the Borders;* Fleegler, *Ellis Island Nation;* Pegler-Gordon, *In Sight of America.* Popular histories that follow this approach include Benton, *Pictorial History;* Brownstone, Franck, and Brownstone, *Island of Hope, Island of Tears;* Reeves, *Gateway to the American Dream.*

71. *ARCGI* (1910), 132.

72. Unrau, *Ellis Island Historic Resource Study,* 1165–69; Presidential Proclamation 3656, "Adding Ellis Island to the Statue of Liberty National Monument," May 11, 1965, in Unrau, *Ellis Island Historic Resource Study,* appendix A, 1206–7.

# Bibliography

## Archives

Columbia University Rare Book and Manuscript Library, New York, N.Y.
Library of Congress, Washington, D.C.
    Asian and Pacific Islander Collection. Asian Division.
    Prints and Photographs Division.
Museum of the Chinese in America, New York, N.Y.
National Archives Records Administration–Northeast Region, New York, N.Y.
    Records of the US Immigration and Naturalization Service. Record Group 85.
National Archives Records Administration, Washington, D.C.
    Records of the US Immigration and Naturalization Service. Record Group 85.
        Microfilm Records, Series A, Part 1, Asian Immigration and Exclusion,
            1906–1913. Bethesda, Md.: American University Publications, 1994.
        Microfilm Records, Series A, Part 1, Asian Immigration and Exclusion,
            1906–1913. Supplement. Bethesda, Md.: American University
            Publications, 1994.
        Microfilm T-458. Subject Index to Correspondence and Case Files of the
            Immigration and Naturalization Service, 1903–52.
National Archives Records Administration, College Park, Md.
    Notes from the Chinese Legation in the United States to the Department of
        State, 1868–1906. Record Group 59. Microfilm M98.
    Records of the Office of the Provost Marshal General, 1920–1975. Record
        Group 389. Records of the Alien Enemy Information Bureau, consisting of
        Records Relating to Japanese, German, Italian, and other Alien Civilian
        Internees during World War II, 1941–46.
    Records of the Office of the Provost Marshal General, 1920–1975. Record
        Group 389. Entry 434: Administrative Division, Mail and Records Branch,
        Unclassified Decimal File, Project Technical Services, 1941–1945
    Records of the Office of the Provost Marshal General, 1920–1975. Record
        Group 389. Photographs and other Graphic Materials and Textual Records
        from the War Department. Office of the Provost Marshal General. American
        Prisoner of War Information Bureau. Enemy Alien Branch. (c.1941–c.1947)
    Records of the US Army Staff. Record Group 319.
    Records of the US Coast Guard. Record Group 26-G. General Photographic File
        of Activities, Facilities, and Personalities, 1886–1967.
    Records of the US Department of Justice. Record Group 60. Japanese Internee
        or "Alien Enemy" Cards from World War II, 1941–1947.

Records of the US Department of Justice. Record Group 60. World War II Alien
Enemy Internment Case Files, 1941–1951.
Records of the US Department of Justice. Record Group 60-G. Prints: Photographs
of Agency Officials and Activities, 1928–c.1981.
United States, Randolph Boehm, and Robert Lester, *Papers of the US
Commission on Wartime Relocation and Internment of Civilians, Part 1,
Numerical File Archive*, microfilm (Frederick, Md.: University Publications
of America, 1984).
New York Public Library, New York, N.Y.
Arthur Bonner Papers, 1980–1996. Manuscripts and Archives Division.
William Williams Papers, 1902–1943. Manuscripts and Archives Division.
Statue of Liberty National Monument, National Park Service, New York, N.Y.
Augustus Sherman Photograph Collection.
Colonel Weber Photograph Collection.
Ellis Island Oral History Project.

## Electronic Collections

Ancestry.com. Provo, Utah: Ancestry.com Operations, 2010.
Lists of Chinese Passengers Arriving at Vancouver and Victoria, British
Columbia, Canada, June 1929–January 1941
New York, U.S., Arriving Passenger and Crew Lists (including Castle Garden
and Ellis Island), 1820–1957
Passenger and Crew Lists of Vessels Arriving at New York, New York, 1897–1957
(National Archives Microfilm Publication T715), Records of the Immigration
and Naturalization Service, National Archives, Washington, D.C.
Subject Index to Correspondence and Case Files of the Immigration and
Naturalization Service, 1903–52 (National Archives Microfilm Publication
T458), Records of the Immigration and Naturalization Service, National
Archives, Washington, D.C.
Densho Digital Archive, Densho Visual History Collection.
Ellis Island Oral History Project. *North American Immigrant Letters, Diaries, and
Oral Histories*. Alexandria, Va.: Alexander Street Press, 1985.
Montana Memory Project, Historical Museum at Fort Missoula.
Notes from the Chinese Legation in the United States to the Department of State,
1868–1906 (Volume 4), National Archives, Nineteenth Century Collections
Online.
University of California, Berkeley, Digital Archive, Japanese American
Evacuation and Resettlement Study.
US Congressional Serial Set.

## Newspapers and Periodicals

*Brooklyn Daily Eagle*           *New York Times*
*Harper's Weekly*                *New York Times Magazine*

New York Amsterdam News    New York Tribune
New York Herald            Washington Post
New York Herald-Tribune


## Books and Articles

Ahuja, Ravi. "Mobility and Containment: The Voyages of South Asian Seamen,
c. 1900–1960." *International Review of Social History Supplement S14* 51 (2006):
111–41.

Alexander Hamilton US Customs House, New York, N.Y. *The Port of New York:
A Souvenir of the US Custom House*. No publisher, 1894.

Amenda, Lars. "'Chinese Quarters': Maritime Labor, Chinese Migration, and
Location Imagination in Rotterdam and Hamburg, 1900–1950." In *Chinatowns
in a Transnational World: Myths and Realities of an Urban Phenomenon*,
edited by Vanessa Kunnemann and Ruth Mayer, 45–61. New York: Routledge,
2011.

Azuma, Eiichiro. *Between Two Empires: Race, History, and Transnationalism in
Japanese America*. Oxford: Oxford University Press, 2005.

Balachandran, G. "Crossing the Last Frontier: Transatlantic Movements of Asian
Maritime Workers, c. 1900–1945." *Maritime Transport and Migration: The
Connections Between Maritime and Migration Networks*, edited by Torsten Feys,
Lewis R. Fischer, Stephane Hoste and Stephan Vanfraechem, 97–111. St. John's,
Newfoundland: Liverpool University Press, 2007.

Bald, Vivek. *Bengali Harlem and the Lost Histories of South Asian America*.
Cambridge, Mass.: Harvard University Press, 2013.

———. "Hands across the Water: Indian Sailors, Peddlers, and Radicals in the U.S.,
1890–1965." PhD diss., New York University, 2009.

Baldoz, Rick. *The Third Asiatic Invasion: Migration and Empire in Filipino
America, 1898–1946*. New York: New York University Press, 2011.

Bamford, Mary E. *Angel Island: The Ellis Island of the West*. Chicago: Woman's
American Baptist Home Mission Society, 1917.

Barde, Robert, and Gustavo Bobonis. "Detention at Angel Island: First Empirical
Evidence." *Social Science History* 30, no. 1 (Spring 2006): 103–36.

Barkan, Elliott Robert. "Immigration through Los Angeles." In *Forgotten Doors:
The Other Ports of Entry to the United States*, edited by M. Mark Stolarik,
161–91. Philadelphia: Balch Institute Press, 1988.

Bavery, Ashley Johnson. *Bootlegged Aliens: Immigration Politics on America's
Northern Border*. Philadelphia: University of Pennsylvania Press, 2020.

Baynton, Douglas C. "Disability and the Justification of Inequality in American
History." In *The New Disability History: American Perspectives*, edited by
Paul K. Longmore and Lauri Umanski, 33–57. New York: New York University
Press, 2001.

Bayor, Ronald H. *Encountering Ellis Island: How European Immigrants Entered
America*. Baltimore: Johns Hopkins University Press, 2014.

Benton, Barbara. *Ellis Island: A Pictorial History*. New York: Facts on File, 1985.

Benton, Gregor. *Chinese Migrants and Internationalism: Forgotten Histories, 1917–1945*. London: Routledge, 2007.

Birn, Anne-Emmanuelle. "Six Seconds per Eyelid: The Medical Inspection of Immigrants at Ellis Island, 1892–1914." *Dynamis* 17 (1997): 281–316.

Blue, Ethan. "Finding Margins on Borders: Shipping Firms and Immigration Control across Settler Space." *Occasion: Interdisciplinary Studies in the Humanities* 5 (March 1, 2013): 1–20.

———. "Strange Passages: Carceral Mobility and the Liminal in the Catastrophic History of American Deportation." *National Identities* 17, no. 2 (2015): 175–94.

Bodnar, John E. *The Transplanted: A History of Immigrants in Urban America*. Bloomington: Indiana University Press, 1985.

Bogen, Elizabeth. *Immigration in New York*. New York: Praeger, 1987.

Bonner, Arthur. *Alas! What Brought Thee Hither? The Chinese in New York, 1800–1950*. Teaneck, N.J.: Fairleigh Dickinson University Press, 1997.

Bow, Leslie. *Partly Colored: Asian Americans and Racial Anomaly in the Segregated South*. New York: New York University Press, 2010.

Braun, Marcus. "How Can We Enforce Our Exclusion Laws?" *Annals of the American Academy of Political and Social Science* 34, no. 2 (1909): 140–42.

Brooks, Charlotte. *Between Mao and McCarthy: Chinese American Politics in the Cold War Years*. Chicago: University of Chicago Press, 2015.

———. "In the Twilight Zone between Black and White: Japanese American Resettlement and Community in Chicago, 1942–1945." *Journal of American History* 86, no. 4 (2000): 1655–87.

Brownstone, David M., Irene M. Franck, and Douglass L. Brownstone. *Island of Hope, Island of Tears*. New York: Penguin Books, 1986.

Buaken, Manuel. *I Have Lived with the American People*. Caldwell, Idaho: Caxton Printers, 1948.

Buff, Rachel. "The Deportation Terror." *American Quarterly* 60, no. 3 (2008): 523–51.

Burton, Jeffery F., Mary M. Farrell, Florence B. Lord, and Richard W. Lord. *Confinement and Ethnicity: An Overview of World War Two Japanese American Relocation Sites*. Seattle: University of Washington Press, 2002.

Cannato, Vincent J. *American Passage: The History of Ellis Island*. New York: Harper, 2009.

Chan, Sucheng. *Entry Denied: Exclusion and the Chinese Community in America, 1882–1943*. Philadelphia: Temple University Press, 1991.

———, ed. *Remapping Asian American History*. Vol. 11. Walnut Creek, Calif.: AltaMira Press, 2003.

Chang, Gordon H. "China and the Pursuit of America's Destiny: Nineteenth-Century Imagining and Why Immigration Restriction Took So Long." *Journal of Asian American Studies* 15, no. 2 (2012): 145–69.

Chang, Iris. *The Chinese in America: A Narrative History*. New York: Viking, 2003.

Chang, Kornel S. *Pacific Connections: The Making of the U.S.-Canadian Borderlands*. Berkeley: University of California Press, 2012.

Chen, Michelle. "A Cultural Crossroads at the 'Bloody Angle': The Chinatown Tongs and the Development of New York City's Chinese American History." *Journal of Urban History* 40, no. 2 (2014): 357–79.

Chen, Shehong. *Being Chinese, Becoming Chinese American.* Urbana: University of Illinois Press, 2002.

Cheng, Cindy I-Fen. *Citizens of Asian America: Democracy and Race during the Cold War.* New York: New York University Press, 2013.

Chermayeff, Ivan, Fred Wasserman, and Mary J. Shapiro. *Ellis Island: An Illustrated History of the Immigrant Experience.* New York: Macmillan, 1991.

Cheung, Floyd. Afterword to *The Hanging on Union Square*, by H. T. Tsiang, 223–37. 1935. Reprint, Los Angeles: Kaya Press, 2013.

Chew, Lee. "The Life Story of a Chinaman." In *The Life Stories of Undistinguished Americans as told by Themselves*, edited by Hamilton Holt, 281–99. New York: James Pott, 1906.

Chiang, May May. "Chinese Operas." In *Chinese Americans: The History and Culture of a People*, edited by Jonathan H. X. Lee, 259–65. Santa Barbara, Calif.: ABC Clio, 2016.

Chin, Ko-lin. *Chinese Subculture and Criminality: Non-traditional Crime Groups in America.* New York: Greenwood Press, 1990.

Chin, Tung Pok, and Winifred C. Chin. *Paper Son: One Man's Story.* Philadelphia: Temple University Press, 2000.

Christgau, John. *"Enemies": World War Two Alien Internment.* Ames: Iowa State University Press, 1985.

Clark, Jane Perry. *Deportation of Aliens from the United States to Europe.* 1931. Reprint, New York: Arno Press, 1969.

Clark, Paul Frederick. "Those Other Camps: An Oral History Analysis of Japanese Alien Enemy Internment during World War Two." Master's thesis, California State University, Fullerton, 1980.

Cloud, Frederick D. *A Digest of the Treaty, Laws, and Regulations Governing the Admission of Chinese, Their Residence in and Transit Through the United States and its Insular Possessions, Approved May 5, 1908.* Washington, D.C.: GPO, 1908.

Connell, Thomas. *America's Japanese Hostages: The World War Two Plan for a Japanese-Free Latin America.* Westport, Conn.: Praeger, 2002.

Conroy, Hilary, and Tetsuo Scott Miyakawa, eds. *East across the Pacific: Historical and Sociological Studies of Japanese Immigration and Assimilation.* Santa Barbara, Calif.: American Bibliographical Center-Clio Press, 1972.

Conway, Lorie. *Forgotten Ellis Island: The Extraordinary Story of America's Immigrant Hospital.* New York: Smithsonian Books, 2007.

———. *Forgotten Ellis Island: The Extraordinary Story of America's Immigrant Hospital.* 56 min. Boston Film & Video Productions, 2007.

Coolidge, Mary Roberts. *Chinese Immigration.* New York: Henry Holt, 1909.

Corsi, Edward. *In the Shadow of Liberty.* 1935. Reprint, New York: Arno Press, 1969.

Crowley, Daniel T. "Plural and Differential Acculturation in Trinidad." *American Anthropologist* 59, no. 5 (1957): 817–24.

Culley, John J. "The Santa Fe Internment Camp and the Justice Department Program for Enemy Aliens." In *Japanese Americans: From Relocation to Redress*, edited by Roger Daniels, Sandra C. Taylor, and Harry H. L. Kitano, 57–71. Rev. ed. Seattle: University of Washington Press, 1991.

Curran, Henry. *Pillar to Post*. New York: Charles Scribner's Sons, 1941.

Danico, Mary Yu, and Anthony Christian Ocampo, eds. *Asian American Society: An Encyclopedia*. Los Angeles: SAGE Publications, 2014.

Daniels, Roger. *Concentration Camps USA: Japanese Americans and World War Two*. New York: Holt, 1971.

——. *The Decision to Relocate the Japanese Americans*. Philadelphia: Lippincott, 1975.

——. "The Forced Migrations of West Coast Japanese Americans, 1942–1946: A Quantitative Note." In *Japanese Americans: From Relocation to Redress*, edited by Roger Daniels, Sandra C. Taylor, and Harry H. L. Kitano, 72–74. Rev. ed. Seattle: University of Washington Press, 1991.

——. *Guarding the Golden Door: American Immigration Policy and Immigrants since 1882*. New York: Hill and Wang, 2004.

——. "The Internment of Japanese Nationals in the United States during World War Two." *Halcyon* 17 (1995): 65–75.

——. "No Lamps Were Lit for Them: Angel Island and the Historiography of Asian American Immigration." *Journal of American Ethnic History* 17, no. 1 (1997): 3–18.

——. *The Politics of Prejudice: The Anti-Japanese Movement in California and the Struggle for Japanese Exclusion*. Berkeley: University of California Press, 1962.

——. "Words Do Matter: A Note on Inappropriate Terminology and the Incarceration of the Japanese Americans." In *Nikkei in the Pacific Northwest: Japanese Americans and Japanese Canadians in the Twentieth Century*, edited by Louis Fiset and Gail Nomura, 183–207. Seattle: University of Washington Press, 2005.

Daniels, Roger, and Otis L. Graham. *Debating American Immigration, 1882–Present*. Lanham, Md.: Rowman & Littlefield Publishers, 2001.

Daniels, Roger, Sandra C. Taylor, and Harry H. L. Kitano, eds. *Japanese Americans: From Relocation to Redress*. Rev. ed. Seattle: University of Washington Press, 1991.

Delgado, Grace. *Making the Chinese Mexican: Global Migration, Localism, and Exclusion in the U.S.-Mexico Borderlands*. Stanford, Calif.: Stanford University Press, 2012.

Desai, Jigna, and Khyati Y. Joshi. *Asian Americans in Dixie: Race and Migration in the South*. Urbana: University of Illinois Press, 2013.

Desai, Manan. "Korla Pandit Plays America: Exotica, Racial Performance, and Fantasies of Containment in Cold War Culture." *Journal of Popular Culture* 48, no. 4 (2015): 714–30.

DeVera, Arleen. "Without Parallel: The Local 7 Deportation Cases, 1949–1955." *Amerasia Journal* 20, no. 2 (1994): 1–25.

Dillon, Richard H. *The Hatchet Men: The Story of the Tong Wars in San Francisco's Chinatown.* New York: Coward-McCann, 1962.

Dirlik, Arif, and Malcolm Yeung. *Chinese on the American Frontier.* Lanham, Md.: Rowman & Littlefield, 2001.

DiStasi, Lawrence. *Una Storia Segreta: The Secret History of Italian American Evacuation and Internment during World War Two.* Berkeley, Calif.: Heyday Books, 2001.

Elleman, Bruce. *Japanese-American Civilian Prisoner Exchanges and Detention Camps, 1941–45.* London: Routledge, 2006.

Ellis Island Committee. *Report of the Ellis Island Committee.* 1934. Reprint, New York: J. S. Ozer, 1971.

Embry, Maria Elizabeth del Valle. "Asian Arrivals @ Ellis Island." https://asian2ellis-island.tripod.com/. 2011.

———. "Filipino Arrivals @ Ellis Island." http://filipinosgone2ellis-island.tripod.com/. 2011.

———. "Filipinos in Ellis Island." *Heritage Matters,* Spring 2009. http://digitalcommons.unl.edu/cgi/viewcontent.cgi?article=1064&context=natlpark.

Ettinger, Patrick W. *Imaginary Lines: Border Enforcement and the Origins of Undocumented Immigration, 1882–1930.* Austin: University of Texas Press, 2009.

Fairchild, Amy L. *Science at the Borders: Immigrant Medical Inspection and the Shaping of the Modern Industrial Labor Force.* Baltimore: Johns Hopkins University Press, 2003.

Fajardo, Kale Bantigue. *Filipino Crosscurrents: Oceanographies of Seafaring, Masculinities, and Globalization.* Minneapolis: University of Minnesota Press, 2011.

Ferrand, Pierre. "EIOHP Interview of Pierre Ferrand." In *North American Immigrant Letters, Diaries, and Oral Histories.* Alexandria, Va.: Alexander Street Press, 1985. https://search.alexanderstreet.com/imld.

———. *A Question of Allegiance.* Tampa, Fla.: American Studies Press, 1990.

Fiset, Louis. *Imprisoned Apart: The World War Two Correspondence of an Issei Couple.* Seattle: University of Washington Press, 1997.

Fleegler, Robert L. *Ellis Island Nation: Immigration Policy and American Identity in the Twentieth Century.* Philadelphia: University of Pennsylvania Press, 2013.

Foote, Caleb. *Outcasts! The Story of America's Treatment of Her Japanese-American Minority.* New York: Fellowship of Reconciliation, 1943.

Fox, Stephen. *America's Invisible Gulag: A Biography of German American Internment and Exclusion in World War Two.* New York: Peter Lang, 2000.

Fox, Stephen C. "General John Dewitt and the Proposed Internment of German and Italian Aliens during World War Two." *Pacific Historical Review* 57, no. 4 (1988): 407–38.

Frykman, Niklas, Clare Anderson, Lex Heerma van Voss, and Marcus Rediker. "Mutiny and Maritime Radicalism: An Introduction." *International Review of Social History Supplement S21* 58 (2013): 1–14.

Fukuda, Yoshiaki. *My Six Years of Internment: An Issei's Struggle for Justice.* San Francisco: Konko Church of San Francisco, 1990.

Gardiner, C. Harvey. *Pawns in a Triangle of Hate: The Peruvian Japanese and the United States.* Seattle: University of Washington Press, 1981.

Garland, Libby. *After They Closed the Gates: Jewish Illegal Immigration to the United States, 1921–1965.* Chicago: University of Chicago Press, 2014.

Gee, Jennifer Gayle. "Sifting the Arrivals: Asian Immigrants and the Angel Island Immigration Station, San Francisco, 1910–1940." PhD diss., Stanford University, 1999.

Geiger, Andrea. *Subverting Exclusion: Transpacific Encounters with Race, Caste, and Borders, 1885–1928.* New Haven, Ct.: Yale University Press, 2011.

Gluck, Eleanor. "An Ecological Study of the Japanese in New York." Master's thesis, Columbia University, 1940.

Gong, Eng Ying, and Bruce Grant. *Tong War! The First Complete History of the Tongs in America.* New York: N. L. Brown, 1930.

Griffith, Sarah M. "Border Crossings: Race, Class, and Smuggling in Pacific Coast Chinese Immigrant Society." *Western Historical Quarterly* 35, no. 4 (2004): 473–92.

Gyory, Andrew. *Closing the Gate: Race, Politics, and the Chinese Exclusion Act.* Chapel Hill: University of North Carolina Press, 1998.

Haine, Edgar. *Mutiny on the High Seas.* Cranbury, N.J.:Cornwall Books, 1992.

Handlin, Oscar. *The Uprooted: The Epic Story of the Great Migrations That Made the American People.* Boston: Little, Brown, 1951.

Haney López, Ian. *White by Law: The Legal Construction of Race.* Rev. ed. New York: New York University Press, 2006.

Harden, Jacalyn D. *Double Cross: Japanese Americans in Black and White Chicago.* Minneapolis: University of Minnesota Press, 2003.

Harrison, Earl. "Civilian Internment—American Way." *Survey Graphic* 33 (May 1944): 229–30.

Hartzell, Karl Drew, and New York State War Council. *The Empire State at War: World War Two.* Albany: State of New York, 1949.

Hayashi, Brian Masaru. *Democratizing the Enemy: The Japanese American Internment.* Princeton, N.J.: Princeton University Press, 2004.

Hernández, Kelly Lytle. *City of Inmates: Conquest, Rebellion, and the Rise of Human Caging in Los Angeles, 1771–1965.* Chapel Hill: University of North Carolina Press, 2017.

———. *Migra! A History of the U.S. Border Patrol.* Berkeley: University of California Press, 2010.

Hester, Torrie. *Deportation: The Origins of U.S. Policy.* Philadelphia: University of Pennsylvania Press, 2017.

Heyer, Virginia. "Pattern of Social Organization in New York City's Chinatown." PhD diss., Columbia University 1953.

Hohri, William Minoru. *Repairing America: An Account of the Movement for Japanese-American Redress.* Pullman: Washington State University Press, 1988.

Hong, Jane H. *Opening the Gates to Asia: A Transpacific History of How America Repealed Asian Exclusion.* Chapel Hill: University of North Carolina Press, 2019.

Houston, Jeanne Wakatsuki, and James D. Houston. *Farewell to Manzanar: A True Story of Japanese American Experience during and after the World War II Internment.* Boston: Houghton Mifflin, 1973.

Howard, John. *Concentration Camps on the Home Front: Japanese Americans in the House of Jim Crow.* Chicago: University of Chicago Press, 2008.

Hsiao, Andrew. "100 Years of Hell-Raising: The Hidden History of Asian American Activism in New York City." *Village Voice*, June 23, 1998.

Hsu, Madeline Yuan-yin. *The Good Immigrants: How the Yellow Peril Became the Model Minority.* Princeton, N.J.: Princeton University Press, 2015.

Hu-DeHart, Evelyn. "Voluntary Associations in a Predominantly Male Immigrant Community: The Chinese on the Northern Mexican Frontier, 1880–1930." In *Voluntary Organizations in the Chinese Diaspora*, edited by Khun Eng Kuah and Evelyn Hu-DeHart, 141–68. Hong Kong: Hong Kong University Press, 2006.

Hu-DeHart, Evelyn, and Kathleen López. "Asian Diasporas in Latin America and the Caribbean: An Historical Overview." *Afro-Hispanic Review* 27, no. 1 (2008): 9–22.

Ichioka, Yuji. "Japanese Immigrant Nationalism: The Issei and the Sino-Japanese War, 1937–1941." In Yuji Ichioka, *Before Internment: Essays in Prewar Japanese American History*, edited by Gordon H. Chang and Eiichiro Azuma, 180–203. Stanford, Calif.: Stanford University Press, 2006.

Inada, Lawson Fusao. *Only What We Could Carry: The Japanese American Internment Experience.* Berkeley, Calif.: Heyday Books, 2000.

Inouye, Daniel H. *Distant Islands: The Japanese American Community in New York City, 1876–1930s.* Boulder: University of Colorado Press, 2018.

Irwin, Theodore. *Strange Passage.* New York: Harrison Smith and Robert Haas, 1935.

Ishizuka, Karen L. *Lost and Found: Reclaiming the Japanese American Incarceration.* Urbana: University of Illinois Press, 2006.

Jackson, Gardner. "Doak the Deportation Chief." *Nation*, March 18, 1931, 295–96.

James Bronson, Reynolds. "Enforcement of the Chinese Exclusion Law." *Annals of the American Academy of Political and Social Science* 34, no. 2 (1909): 143–54.

Jung, Moon-Ho. *Coolies and Cane: Race, Labor, and Sugar in the Age of Emancipation.* Baltimore: Johns Hopkins University Press, 2006.

Kanazawa, Mark. "Immigration, Exclusion, and Taxation: Anti-Chinese Legislation in Gold Rush California." *Journal of Economic History* 65, no. 3 (2005): 779–805.

Kang, S. Deborah. *The INS on the Line: Making Immigration Law on the US-Mexico Border, 1917–1954.* New York: Oxford University Press, 2017.

Kanstroom, Daniel. *Deportation Nation: Outsiders in American History.* Cambridge, Mass.: Harvard University Press, 2007.

Kashima, Tetsuden. "American Mistreatment of Internees during World War Two: Enemy Alien Japanese." In *Japanese Americans: From Relocation to Redress,*

edited by Roger Daniels, Sandra C. Taylor, Harry H. L. Kitano, 52–56. Rev. ed.
Seattle: University of Washington Press, 1991.

———. *Judgment without Trial: Japanese American Imprisonment during World War Two.* Seattle: University of Washington Press, 2003.

Khan, Dada Amir Haider. *Chains to Lose: Life and Struggles of a Revolutionary.* Vol. 1. Karachi: Pakistan Study Center, University of Karachi, 2007.

Knauff, Ellen Raphael. *The Ellen Knauff Story.* New York: W. W. Norton, 1952.

Kotker, Norman, and Susan Jonas. *Ellis Island: Echoes from a Nation's Past.* New York: Aperture Foundation, 1989.

Krammer, Arnold. *Undue Process: The Untold Story of America's German Alien Internees.* London: Rowman & Littlefield, 1997.

Kraut, Alan M. *Silent Travelers: Germs, Genes, and the "Immigrant Menace."* New York: BasicBooks, 1994.

Kumamoto, Bob. "The Search for Spies: American Counterintelligence and the Japanese American Community 1931–1942." *Amerasia Journal* 6, no. 2 (1979): 45–75.

Kurashige, Lon. *Japanese American Celebration and Conflict: A History of Ethnic Identity and Festival, 1934–1990.* Berkeley: University of California Press, 2002.

———. *Two Faces of Exclusion: The Untold History of Anti-Asian Racism in the United States.* Chapel Hill: University of North Carolina Press, 2016.

Kurashige, Scott. *The Shifting Grounds of Race: Black and Japanese Americans in the Making of Multiethnic Los Angeles.* Princeton, N.J.: Princeton University Press, 2008.

Kwong, Peter. *Chinatown, New York: Labor and Politics, 1930–1950.* Rev. ed. New York: New Press, 2001.

Lahiri, Shompa. "Contested Relations: The East India Company and Lascars in London." In *The Worlds of the East India Company,* edited by H. V. Bowen, Margarette Lincoln, and Nigel Rigby, 169–81. Rochester, N.Y.: D. S. Brewer, 2002.

Lai, H. Mark. *Becoming Chinese American: A History of Communities and Institutions.* Walnut Creek, Calif.: AltaMira, 2004.

———. "Chinese Detainees at N.Y.'s Ellis Island Also Wrote Poems on Barrack Walls." *East West: The Chinese American Journal,* November 6, 1985.

Lai, H. Mark, Genny Lim, and Judy Yung. *Island: Poetry and History of Chinese Immigrants on Angel Island, 1910–1940.* Seattle: University of Washington Press, 1991.

———. *Island: Poetry and History of Chinese Immigrants on Angel Island, 1910–1940.* Rev. ed. Seattle: University of Washington Press, 2014.

Lan, Shanshan. *Diaspora and Class Consciousness: Chinese Immigrant Workers in Multiracial Chicago.* New York: Routledge, 2012.

Lasker, Bruno. *Filipino Immigration to Continental United States and Hawaii.* Edited by American Council Institute of Pacific Relations. Chicago: University of Chicago Press, 1931.

Lau, Estelle T. *Paper Families: Identity, Immigration Administration, and Chinese Exclusion.* Durham, N.C.: Duke University Press, 2006.

Lee, Erika. *At America's Gates: Chinese Immigration during the Exclusion Era, 1882–1943*. Chapel Hill: University of North Carolina Press, 2003.

Lee, Erika, and Judy Yung. *Angel Island: Immigrant Gateway to America*. Oxford: Oxford University Press, 2010.

Lee, Heather. "Hunting for Sailors: Restaurant Raids and Conscription of Laborers during World War Two." In *A Nation of Immigrants Reconsidered: U.S. Society in an Age of Restriction, 1924–1965*, edited by Maddalena Marinari, Madeline Hsu, and Maria Cristina Garcia, 107–22. Urbana: University of Illinois Press, 2019.

Leong, Gor Yun. *Chinatown Inside Out*. New York: B. Mussey, 1936.

Lescarboura, Austin. "The Battle of Rum Row." *Popular Mechanics* 45, no. 6 (1926): 955–59.

Lew, Harry Gem Hoy. "EIOHP Interview of Harry Gem Hoy Lew." In *North American Immigrant Letters, Diaries, and Oral Histories*. Alexandria, Va.: Alexander Street Press, 2003. https://search.alexanderstreet.com/imld.

Lew-Williams, Beth. *The Chinese Must Go: Violence, Exclusion, and the Making of the Alien in America*. Cambridge, Mass.: Harvard University Press, 2018.

Li, Hongshan. "Wu Tingfang." In *Encyclopedia of Chinese-American Relations*, edited by Yuwu Song, 321–22. Jefferson, N.C.: McFarland, 2006.

Li, Tien Lu. *Congressional Policy of Chinese Immigration; or, Legislation Relating to Chinese Immigration to the United States*. Nashville, Tenn.: Publishing House of the Methodist Episcopal Church, South, 1916.

Lim, Julian. *Porous Borders: Multiracial Migrations and the Law in the U.S.-Mexico Borderlands*. Chapel Hill: University of North Carolina Press, 2017.

Lindquist, Charles. "The Origin and Development of the United States Commissioner System." *American Journal of Legal History* 14, no. 1 (1970): 1–16.

Ling, Huping. *Chinese Chicago: Race, Transnational Migration, and Community since 1870*. Stanford, Calif.: Stanford University Press, 2012.

———. *Chinese St. Louis: From Enclave to Cultural Community*. Philadelphia, Pa.: Temple University Press, 2004.

Look Lai, Walton. "The Chinese Indenture System in the British West Indies and Its Aftermath." In *The Chinese in the Caribbean*, edited by Andrew R. Wilson, 3–24. Princeton, N.J.: M. Wiener Publishers, 2004.

———, ed. *Essays on the Chinese Diaspora in the Caribbean*. Trinidad and Tobago: n.p., 2006.

Look Lai, Walton, and Chee Beng Tan. *The Chinese in Latin America and the Caribbean*. Leiden, The Netherlands: Brill, 2010.

López, Kathleen. *Chinese Cubans: A Transnational History*. Chapel Hill: University of North Carolina Press, 2013.

———. "The Chinese in Cuban History." In *Essays on the Chinese Diaspora in the Caribbean*, edited by Walton Look Lai, 105–29. Trinidad and Tobago: n.p., 2006.

Louie, Thomas. "EIOHP Interview of Thomas Louie." In *North American Immigrant Letters, Diaries and Oral Histories*. Alexandria, Va.: Alexander Street Press, 2003. https://search.alexanderstreet.com/imld.

Lowe, Felicia. *Our Own Ellis Island: Carved in Silence.* 45 mins. San Francisco: CrossCurrent Media, 1998.

Lui, Mary Ting Li. *The Chinatown Trunk Mystery: Murder, Miscegenation, and Other Dangerous Encounters in Turn-of-the-Century New York City.* Princeton, N.J.: Princeton University Press, 2005.

Luibhéid, Eithne. *Entry Denied: Controlling Sexuality at the Border.* Minneapolis: University of Minnesota Press, 2002.

Lyon, Cherstin. *Prisons and Patriots: Japanese American Wartime Citizenship, Civil Disobedience, and Historical Memory.* Philadelphia: Temple University Press, 2012.

Ma, L. Eve Armentrout. "Chinatown Organizations and the Anti-Chinese Movement, 1882–1914." In *Entry Denied: Exclusion and the Chinese Community in America, 1882–1943,* edited by Sucheng Chan, 147–69. Philadelphia: Temple University Press, 1991.

Mallee, Hein, and Frank N. Pieke. *Internal and International Migration: Chinese Perspectives.* Richmond, Surrey: Curzon, 1999.

Manzon, Maximo C. *The Strange Case of the Filipinos in the United States.* New York: American Committee for Protection of Foreign Born, 1938.

Marinbach, Bernard. *Galveston, Ellis Island of the West.* Albany: State University of New York Press, 1983.

Markel, Howard, and Alexandra Minna Stern. "Which Face? Whose Nation? Immigration, Public Health, and the Construction of Disease at America's Ports and Borders, 1891–1928." *American Behavioral Scientist* 42, no. 9 (June/July 1999): 1313–30.

Masanz, Sharon D. *History of the Immigration and Naturalization Service: A Congressional Research Service Report.* Washington: GPO, 1980.

Masur, Kate. "'A Rare Phenomenon of Philological Vegetation': The Word 'Contraband' and the Meanings of Emancipation in the United States." *Journal of American History* 93, no. 4 (March 2007): 1050–84.

Matsumoto, Toru and Marion O. Lerrigo. *A Brother is a Stranger.* New York: John Day Company, 1946.

Matsumoto, Valerie. "Japanese American Women during World War Two." *Frontiers* 8, no. 1 (1984): 6–14.

McClain, Charles J. *In Search of Equality: The Chinese Struggle against Discrimination in Nineteenth-Century America.* Berkeley: University of California Press, 1996.

McKenzie, Roderick Duncan. *Oriental Exclusion: The Effect of American Immigration Laws, Regulations, and Judicial Decisions upon the Chinese and Japanese on the American Pacific Coast.* New York: American Group Institute of Pacific Relations, 1927.

McKeown, Adam. *Chinese Migrant Networks and Cultural Change: Peru, Chicago, Hawaii, 1900–1936.* Chicago: University of Chicago Press, 2001.

———. *Melancholy Order: Asian Migration and the Globalization of Borders.* New York: Columbia University Press, 2008.

McWilliams, Carey. *Brothers under the Skin.* 1943. Rev., Boston: Little, Brown, 1964.

Mesenholler, Peter. *Augustus F. Sherman: Ellis Island Portraits, 1905–1920*. New York: Aperture, 2005.

Miller, Richard E. *The Messman Chronicles: African Americans in the U.S. Navy, 1932–1943*. Annapolis, Md.: Naval Institute Press, 2004.

Moloney, Deirdre M. *National Insecurities: Immigrants and U.S. Deportation Policy since 1882*. Chapel Hill: University of North Carolina Press, 2012.

Moreno, Barry. *Encyclopedia of Ellis Island*. Westport, Conn.: Greenwood Press, 2004.

Muller, Eric L. *American Inquisition: The Hunt for Japanese American Disloyalty in World War Two*. Chapel Hill: University of North Carolina Press, 2007.

Munasinghe, Viranjini. "Redefining the Nation: The East Indian Struggle for Inclusion in Trinidad." *Journal of Asian American Studies* 4, no. 1 (February 2001): 1–34.

Murray, Alice Yang. *Historical Memories of the Japanese American Internment and the Struggle for Redress*. Stanford, Calif.: Stanford University Press, 2008.

Nadal, Kevin L., and Filipino American National Historical Society Metropolitan New York Chapter. *Filipinos in New York City*. Charleston, S.C.: Arcadia Publishing, 2015.

Ngai, Mae. "Asian American History: Reflections on the De-centering of the Field." *Journal of American Ethnic History* 25, no. 4 (2006): 97–108.

———. *Impossible Subjects: Illegal Aliens and the Making of Modern America*. Princeton, N.J.: Princeton University Press, 2004.

———. *The Lucky Ones: One Family and the Extraordinary Invention of Chinese America*. Princeton, N.J.: Princeton University Press, 2010.

———. "'A Slight Knowledge of the Barbarian Language': Chinese Interpreters in Late-Nineteenth and Early-Twentieth-Century America." *Journal of American Ethnic History* 30, no. 2 (2011): 05–32.

Oades, Riz A. *Beyond the Mask: Untold Stories of U.S. Navy Filipinos*. National City, Calif.: KCS Publishing, 2004.

Odo, Franklin, ed. *Columbia Documentary History of the Asian American Experience*. New York: Columbia University Press, 2002.

Okihiro, Gary Y. "Japanese Resistance in America's Concentration Camps: A Re-evaluation." *Amerasia Journal* 2 (Fall 1973): 20–34.

———. *Privileging Positions: The Sites of Asian American Studies*. Pullman: Washington State University Press, 1995.

Okrent, Daniel. *Last Call: The Rise and Fall of Prohibition*. New York: Scribner, 2010.

Omi, Michael, and Howard Winant. *Racial Formation in the United States: From the 1960s to the 1980s*. New York: Routledge, 1986.

Oyen, Meredith Leigh. "Allies, Enemies and Aliens: Migration and U.S.-Chinese Relations, 1940–1965." PhD diss., Georgetown University, 2007.

Pegler-Gordon, Anna. "Debating the Racial Turn in U.S. Ethnic and Immigration History." *Journal of American Ethnic History* 36, no. 2 (2017): 40–53.

———. *In Sight of America: Photography and the Development of U.S. Immigration Policy*. Berkeley: University of California Press, 2009.

Perea, Juan F. "The Statue of Liberty: Notes from behind the Gilded Door." In *Immigrants Out! The New Nativism and the Anti-immigrant Impulse in the United States*, edited by Juan F. Perea, 44–58. New York: New York University Press, 1997.

Pfaelzer, Jean. *Driven Out: The Forgotten War against Chinese Americans*. New York: Random House, 2007.

Phillips, Kimberley L. *War! What Is It Good For? Black Freedom Struggles and the U.S. Military from World War Two to Iraq*. Chapel Hill: University of North Carolina Press, 2012.

Post, Louis F. *The Deportations Delirium of Nineteen-Twenty: A Personal Narrative of an Historic Official Experience*. Chicago: C. H. Kerr, 1923.

Rand, Erica. *The Ellis Island Snow Globe*. Durham, N.C.: Duke University Press, 2005.

Rao, Nancy Yunhwa. *Chinatown Opera Theater in North America*. Urbana: University of Illinois Press, 2017.

Reeves, Pamela. *Ellis Island: Gateway to the American Dream*. New York: Dorset Press, 1991.

Reynolds, C. N. "The Chinese Tongs." *American Journal of Sociology* 40, no. 5 (1935): 612–23.

Riis, Jacob A. "In the Gateway of Nations." *Century* 65, no. 5 (1903): 674–82.

Robinson, Greg. *After Camp: Portraits in Midcentury Japanese American Life and Politics*. Berkeley: University of California Press, 2012.

——. "Nisei in Gotham: The JACD and Japanese Americans in 1940s New York." *Prospects: An Annual of American Cultural Studies* 30 (2005): 1–16.

——, ed. *Pacific Citizens: Larry and Guyo Tajiri and Japanese American Journalism in the World War Two Era*. Urbana: University of Illinois Press, 2012.

Roediger, David. *The Wages of Whiteness: Race and the Making of the American Working Class*. London: Verso, 1999.

Roxworthy, Emily. *The Spectacle of Japanese American Trauma: Racial Performativity and World War Two*. Honolulu: University of Hawaii Press, 2008.

Sakovich, Maria. "Angel Island Immigration Station Reconsidered: Non-Asian Encounters with the Immigration Laws, 1910–1940." Master's thesis, Sonoma State University, 2002.

Salyer, Lucy E. "Baptism by Fire: Race, Military Service, and U.S. Citizenship Policy, 1918–1935." *Journal of American History* 91, no. 3 (2004): 847–76.

——. *Laws Harsh as Tigers: Chinese Immigrants and the Shaping of Modern Immigration Law*. Chapel Hill: University of North Carolina Press, 1995.

Sánchez, George J. *Becoming Mexican American: Ethnicity, Culture, and Identity in Chicano Los Angeles, 1900–1945*. New York: Oxford University Press, 1993.

——. "Race, Nation, and Culture in Recent Immigration Studies." *Journal of American Ethnic History* 18, no. 4 (1999): 66–84.

Sandmeyer, Elmer Clarence. *The Anti-Chinese Movement in California*. Urbana: University of Illinois Press, 1939.

Saum Song Bo. "A Chinese View of the Statue of Liberty." *American Missionary* 39, no. 10 (October 1885). Reprinted in Franklin Odo, ed. *Columbia Documentary History of the Asian American Experience* (New York: Columbia University Press, 2002), 74–75.

Saxton, Alexander. *The Indispensable Enemy: Labor and the Anti-Chinese Movement in California.* Berkeley: University of California Press, 1971.

Scharf, J. Thomas. "The Farce of the Chinese Exclusion Laws." *North American Review* 166, no. 494 (1898): 85–97.

Schrecker, Ellen. "Immigration and Internal Security: Political Deportation during the McCarthy Era." *Science and Society* 60, no. 4 (1996–1997): 393–426.

Schwendinger, Robert J. *Ocean of Bitter Dreams: Maritime Relations between China and the United States, 1850–1915.* Tucson, Ariz.: Westernlore Press, 1988.

Shah, Nayan. *Contagious Divides: Epidemics and Race in San Francisco's Chinatown.* Berkeley: University of California Press, 2001.

Sheridan, Peter B. *The Internment of German and Italian Aliens Compared with the Internment of Japanese Aliens in the United States during World War Two: A Brief History and Analysis.* Congressional Research Service. Washington, D.C.: GPO, 1980.

Smith, Marian L. "The Immigration and Naturalization Service at the U.S.-Canadian Border, 1893–1993: An Overview of Issues and Topics." *Michigan Historical Review* 26, no. 2 (2000): 127–47.

Sohi, Seema. *Echoes of Mutiny: Race, Surveillance, and Indian Anticolonialism in North America.* Oxford: Oxford University Press, 2014.

Song, Jingyi. *Shaping and Reshaping Chinese American Identity: New York's Chinese during the Depression and World War Two.* Lanham, Md.: Lexington Books, 2010.

Spickard, Paul R. *Almost All Aliens: Immigration, Race, and Colonialism in American History and Identity.* New York: Routledge, 2007.

———. *Japanese Americans: The Formation and Transformations of an Ethnic Group.* New York: Twayne Publishers, 1996.

Stern, Alexandra Minna. *Eugenic Nation: Faults and Frontiers of Better Breeding in Modern America.* Berkeley: University of California Press, 2005.

Stolarik, M. Mark, ed. *Forgotten Doors: The Other Ports of Entry to the United States.* Philadelphia: Balch Institute Press, 1988.

Sung, Betty Lee. *Mountain of Gold: The Story of the Chinese in America.* New York: MacMillan, 1967.

Svejda, George. *Castle Garden as an Immigrant Depot, 1855–1890.* Washington, D.C.: Division of History, Office of Archeology and Historic Preservation, National Park Service, U.S. Department of the Interior, 1968.

Tabili, Laura. *We Ask for British Justice: Workers and Racial Difference in Late Imperial Britain.* Ithaca, N.Y.: Cornell University Press, 1994.

Takaki, Ronald T. *Double Victory: A Multicultural History of America in World War Two.* Boston: Little, Brown, 2000.

Tchen, John Kuo Wei. *New York before Chinatown: Orientalism and the Shaping of American Culture, 1776–1882*. Baltimore, Md.: Johns Hopkins University Press, 1999.

Teague, Janira Phedre. "I, too, am America: African-American and Afro-Caribbean Identity, Citizenship and Migrations to New York City, 1830s to 1930s." PhD diss., University of California, Los Angeles, 2015.

Tom, Henry. "Colonia Incognita: The Formation of Chinatown, New York City, 1850–1890." Master's thesis, University of Maryland, 1975.

Torok, John. "'Chinese Investigations': Immigration Policy Enforcement in Cold War New York Chinatown, 1946–1965." PhD diss., University of California, Berkeley, 2008.

Torpey, John. *The Invention of the Passport: Surveillance, Citizenship and the State*. Cambridge: Cambridge University Press, 2000.

Tsang, Steve. *A Modern History of Hong Kong*. London: I.B. Tauris, 2004.

Twombly, Robert. "Ellis Island: An Architectural History." In *Ellis Island: Echoes from a Nation's Past*, edited by Norman Kotker and Susan Jonas, 122–37. New York: Aperture Foundation, 1989.

Udell, Gilman G. *Seamen's Act as Amended and Other Laws Relating to Seamen*. Washington, D.C.: Government Printing Office, 1971.

United States Census. *Compendium of the Eleventh Census 1890, Part 1—Population*. Washington, D.C.: GPO, 1892.

——. *Historical Statistics of the United States Colonial Times to 1970, Part 1*. Washington, D.C.: GPO, 1975.

——. *Report on the Social Statistics of Cities, Part 1: The New England and the Middle States*. Washington, D.C.: GPO, 1886.

——. *Sixteenth Census 1940, Population: Characteristics of the Nonwhite Population by Race*. Washington, D.C.: GPO, 1943.

——. *Sixteenth Census 1940, Vol. II, Part 5, Population: New York-Oregon*. Washington, D.C.: GPO, 1943.

——. *Tenth Census 1880, Statistics of the Population of the United States*. Washington, D.C.: GPO, 1883.

——. *Twelfth Census 1900, Vol. I, Part 1, Population*. Washington, D.C.: GPO, 1901.

——. Vital Statistics of New York City and Brooklyn, covering a period of six years ending May 31, 1890. Washington, D.C.: GPO, 1894.

United States Commission on Wartime Relocation and Internment of Civilians. *Personal Justice Denied: Report of the Commission on Wartime Relocation and Internment of Civilians*. Washington, D.C.: GPO, 1982.

United States Department of Commerce and Labor, Bureau of Immigration and Naturalization. *Immigration Laws and Regulations of July 1, 1907*. 5th ed. Washington, D.C.: GPO, 1908.

——. *Immigration Laws and Regulations of July 1, 1907*. 6th ed. Washington, D.C.: GPO, 1909.

——. *Immigration Laws, Rules of November 15, 1911*. Edition of February 12, 1916. Washington, D.C.: GPO, 1916.

——. *Immigration Laws, Rules of May 1, 1917.* 6th ed. Washington, D.C.: GPO, 1921.

——. *Treaty, Laws, and Regulations Governing the Admission of Chinese, Regulations Approved February 26, 1907.* Washington, D.C.: GPO, 1907.

——. *Treaties, Laws, and Regulations Governing the Admission of Chinese Approved April 18, 1910.* Washington, D.C.: GPO, 1911.

United States Department of Homeland Security. *Yearbook of Immigration Statistics.* Washington, D.C.: U.S. Department of Homeland Security, 2011.

United States Department of Labor, Bureau of Immigration. *Treaty, Laws and Rules Governing the Admission of Chinese,* Rules of May 1, 1917, 3rd ed. Washington, D.C.: GPO, 1920.

United States Department of the Treasury. *Treasury Decisions under Customs and Other Laws.* Vol. 35, *July-December, 1918.* Washington, D.C.: GPO, 1919.

United States Immigration and Naturalization Service. *Records of the Immigration and Naturalization Service, Record Group 85, Series a, Subject Correspondence Files, pt. 2. Mexican Immigration, 1906–1930.* Bethesda, Md.: University Publications of America, 1992.

Unrau, Harlan D. *Ellis Island Historic Resource Study.* Denver: U.S. National Park Service, 1984.

Visram, Rozina. *Asians in Britain: 400 Years of History.* London: Pluto Press, 2002.

Wang, Xinyang. *Surviving the City: The Chinese Immigrant Experience in New York City, 1890–1970.* Lanham, Md.: Rowman & Littlefield, 2001.

Weber, John B. *Autobiography of John B. Weber.* Buffalo, N.Y.: J. W. Clement, 1924.

Wegars, Priscilla. *As Rugged as the Terrain: CCC "Boys," Federal Convicts, and World War II Alien Internees Wrestle with a Mountain Wilderness.* Caldwell, Idaho: Caxton Press, 2013.

Weglyn, Michi. *Years of Infamy: The Untold Story of America's Concentration Camps.* New York: Morrow, 1976.

Weiss, Feri Felix. *The Sieve; or, Revelations of the Man Mill, Being the Truth about American Immigration.* Boston: Page, 1921.

Wong, Bernard P. *Chinatown: Economic Adaptation and Ethnic Identity of the Chinese.* New York: Holt, Rinehart and Winston, 1982.

——. *Patronage, Brokerage, Entrepreneurship, and the Chinese Community of New York.* New York: AMS Press, 1988.

Wong, Kevin Scott. *Americans First: Chinese Americans and the Second World War.* Cambridge, Mass.: Harvard University Press, 2005.

Wong Chin Foo. "The Chinese in the United States." *Chautauquan* 9, no. 4 (January 1889): 215–17.

Works Progress Administration. Federal Writers' Project in New York City. *A Maritime History of New York.* Garden City, N.Y.: Doubleday, Doran, 1941.

——. *A Maritime History of New York.* 1941. Reprint, Going Coastal, 2004.

——. *New York City Guide.* New York: Random House, 1939.

Wu Ting Fang. *America, through the Spectacles of an Oriental Diplomat.* New York: Frederick A. Stokes, 1914.

Yee, William Fook. "EIOHP Interview of William Fook Yee." In *North American Immigrant Letters, Diaries, and Oral Histories*. Alexandria, Va.: Alexander Street Press, 1994. https://search.alexanderstreet.com/imld.

Young, Elliott. *Alien Nation: Chinese Migration in the Americas from the Coolie Era through World War Two*. Chapel Hill: University of North Carolina Press, 2014.

Young, Joseph Eng. "EIOHP Interview of Joseph Eng Young." In *North American Immigrant Letters, Diaries, and Oral Histories*. Alexandria, Va.: Alexander Street Press, 2001. https://search.alexanderstreet.com/imld.

Yu, Renqiu. *To Save China, to Save Ourselves: The Chinese Hand Laundry Alliance of New York*. Philadelphia: Temple University Press, 1992.

Yung, Judy, Gordon H. Chang, and H. Mark Lai. *Chinese American Voices: From the Gold Rush to the Present*. Berkeley: University of California Press, 2006.

Zhao, Xiaojian. *Remaking Chinese America: Immigration, Family, and Community, 1940–1965*. New Brunswick, N.J.: Rutgers University Press, 2002.

Zhou, Min. "Contemporary Immigration and the Dynamics of Race and Ethnicity." In *America Becoming: Racial Trends and Their Consequences*. Vol. 1. Edited by William Julius Wilson Neil Smelser, Faith Mitchell, 200–42. Washington, D.C.: National Academy Press, 2001.

Zichlinsky, Luisa. "EIOHP Interview of Luisa Zichlinsky." In *North American Immigrant Letters, Diaries and Oral Histories*. Alexandria, Va.: Alexander Street Press, 1996. https://search.alexanderstreet.com/imld.

# Index

Note: Page numbers in italics refer to illustrations. Page numbers followed by "t" refer to tables.